THE INDIGENOUS WORLD 2004

IWGIA
Copenhagen   2004

THE INDIGENOUS WORLD 2004

Compilation and editing: Diana Vinding
Regional editors:
 The Circumpolar North & North America: Kathrin Wessendorf
 Mexico, Central America & the Circumcaribbean: Diana Vinding
 South America: Alejandro Parellada
 Australia & New Zealand: Diana Vinding
 Asia: Christian Erni and Sille Stidsen
 Middle East: Diana Vinding
 Africa: Marianne Wiben Jensen and Diana Vinding
 International Processes: Lola García-Alix

Cover, typesetting and maps: Jorge Monrás
English translation: Elaine Bolton
English proofreading: Elaine Bolton, Leslie Cole and Zachary Whyte

Prepress and Print: Eks-Skolens Trykkeri, Copenhagen, Denmark
ISSN 0105-4503 - ISBN 87-90730-83-6

The Indigenous World is published annually in English and Spanish by IWGIA.
Director: Jens Dahl
Deputy Director: Lola García Alix
Administrator: Karen Bundgaard Andersen

This book has been produced with financial support from the Norwegian Agency for Development Cooperation and the Danish Ministry of Foreign Affairs.

INTERNATIONAL WORK GROUP FOR INDIGENOUS AFFAIRS
Classensgade 11 E, DK 2100 - Copenhagen, Denmark
Tel: (+45) 35 27 05 00 - Fax: (+45) 35 27 05 07
E-mail: iwgia@iwgia.org - www.iwgia.org

CONTENTS

Southern Africa

PART II - International Proceses

IWGIA general information

EDITORIAL

T he impression one has on reading this year's contributions to *The Indigenous World* is that, despite notable advances, the situation of indigenous peoples still remains extremely precarious and even, in many cases, alarming. As the article on the Amazigh people of Algeria notes, it is clear that "achievements are still the result of bitter struggles and are never irreversible".

Political developments in 2003 have negatively affected many indigenous peoples. The serious crisis in Bolivia, the military repression in Burma, the conflict in the Great Lakes region of Africa, to name but a few examples, have cost the lives of many indigenous people, undermined the livelihoods of entire communities and endangered their survival. In other countries, where the political situation has been unstable (Venezuela) or where elections are imminent (the Philippines), indigenous organisations live in constant fear of finding recently acquired rights abolished overnight. On a more positive note, the peace process in Angola made it possible for a team of consultants to visit San communities for the first time in more than 20 years in order to assess their situation with a view to providing future development support.

2003 witnessed two interesting political experiments. For the first time in the country's modern history, Ecuador's indigenous people participated in government. The alliance between the political arm of CONAIE - the Pachakutik party - and President Gutiérrez was short-lived, however, once CONAIE realized that Gutiérrez's political project was totally alien to their own ideals. The costs were high and both CONAIE and the other indigenous organisations have been weakened. In Chiapas, Mexico, the Zapatistas launched a new political strategy to make the autonomous municipalities less dependent on the Liberation Army (EZLN), strengthen civil society and ensure good governance principles. Welcomed by indigenous communities throughout the country, it constitutes an exemplary response to the Mexican government's blatant failure to solve the Chiapas conflict.

For indigenous peoples worldwide, land rights continued to be the major issue. Some real progress was made: in Nicaragua, with the adoption of Law No. 445 recognizing the communal property of the indigenous peoples and ethnic communities of the Autonomous Regions of the Atlantic Coast of Nicaragua; in Canada, with the signing of a comprehensive land claim agreement which, after almost 20 years of negotiations, will provide the Labrador Inuit with a form of explicit self-government; in Iraq, with the fall of the former regime making it possible for the Arab marsh dwellers to rehabilitate some of their traditional wetlands and go back to live there.

But in Bolivia and in the Philippines - two of the few countries in the world to have officially recognized indigenous peoples' land rights - the land titling process continued to drag on: in Bolivia, less than 10% of the area originally set aside 7 years ago has so far been titled. In the Philippines, implementation is being delayed by administrative and technical discussions. Elsewhere, indigenous communities continued to see their land appropriated or encroached upon.

Among the many cases documented in this issue are the Garo of Bangladesh (national parks), the Ogiek of Kenya and the "uncontacted" Nahua in Peru (logging interests), the Barbaig of Tanzania (large-scale development projects) and the Nenets in Russia (oil exploration). In India, more than ten million forest-dependent indigenous people are facing eviction from their habitat; in Israel, the government is destroying the houses and crops of the Arab Bedouins in order to force them to move into government built settlements.

In a few cases, the indigenous peoples in question have reacted by taking their case to court. Such is the case, for instance, of the Anak Negeri and the Penan of Malaysia, the San and the Bakgalagadi of Botswana, and the Richtersveld Nama of South Africa. So far, only the Nama have won a court victory that recognizes their aboriginal title rights. In other cases (Argentina, Chile, Ecuador), indigenous organisations have petitioned the Inter-American Court of Human Rights for legal support.

Throughout 2003, indigenous representatives played an active role in the many activities within the UN system, at international and regional levels in general (e.g. in the Arctic Council and the African Commission on Human and Peoples' Rights), and in events such as the World Parks Congress, the World Summit on the Information Society or in relation to the Convention on Biological Diversity.

The Permanent Forum's second session was attended by increasing numbers of UN agencies and bodies. This clearly indicates a growing interest within the UN system for the Forum's work, and for the possibility the Forum provides states, indigenous peoples and UN agencies in terms of engaging in constructive dialogue.

Less positive was the lack of political will and commitment on the part of a small number of governments during the 9th session of the Working Group on the Draft Declaration on the Rights of Indigenous Peoples, which seriously jeopardized the future of the whole process.

However, a number of indigenous organizations with consultative status with ECOSOC have reacted constructively, recommending in their Joint Submission to ECOSOC that the UN and Member States renew the mandate of the inter-sessional Working Group and that the operations and procedures of the UN CHR Working Group be significantly improved, in a manner consistent with the unique status and essential role of indigenous peoples.

At regional level, a major breakthrough was the adoption by the African Commission on Human and Peoples' Rights of the comprehensive *"Report of the African Commission's Working Group on Indigenous Populations/Communities"*. Furthermore, recognizing not only the existence of indigenous peoples in Africa but also that they suffer from a range of human rights violations that need to be addressed, the Commission decided to establish a Working Group of Experts with the mandate to gather information on violations of the human rights and fundamental freedoms of indigenous populations/communities in Africa.

While indigenous participation in all these events is of vital importance, both to their own peoples and to the international community in general, these people are increasingly confronted with excessive demands in terms of workload and specialisation. And yet the real challenge lies in creating a link between international and regional processes and the local level. Good progress is being made at international and regional level in terms of recognising indigenous peoples' rights but the situation at local level continues to be a cause for real concern. This is where racist attitudes continue to thrive. This is where land appropriations, repression and massacres continue to occur. Hence the need to (1) ensure that international progress is widely disseminated and discussed at grassroots level so that people are aware of their rights; and (2) ensure constant monitoring of the situation in indigenous communities. This work should be done by local and national indigenous organisations in close collaboration with international bodies such as the Permanent Forum, the African Working Group, etc. and particularly the mechanism of the Special Rapporteur, which is tremendously important in terms of taking indigenous human rights issues from local up to international level. Such collaboration would make it possible to engage in sustained dialogue with governments and local authorities and put pressure on them to ensure that lasting improvements in the lives of indigenous peoples can be achieved. ❑

Diana Vinding
Coordinating editor

ABOUT OUR CONTRIBUTORS

IWGIA would like to extend warm thanks to the following people and organizations for having contributed to *The Indigenous World 2004*. We would also like to thank those contributors who wished to remain anonymous and are therefore not mentioned below. Without the help of these people, this book would not have been published.

PART I

THE CIRCUMPOLAR NORTH AND NORTH AMERICA

This section has been compiled and edited by *Kathrin Wessendorf*, Programme Coordinator for the Circumpolar North Program.

Gunn-Britt Retter is a Saami from Norway. She has been working at the Arctic Council Indigenous Peoples' Secretariat in Copenhagen, Denmark since 2001. (*Arctic Council*)

Mette Uldall Jensen is an eskimologist from the University of Copenhagen. She has been an active member of the IWGIA national group in Denmark for many years. (*Greenland*)

Rune Fjellheim is an economist and works for the Saami Council as head of the Arctic and environmental unit. He is also co-owner of and senior advisor to Jaruma AS, a company working on Saami and Indigenous Peoples' issues. (*Sápmi, Norway*)

Mattias Åhren is a Saami lawyer from Sweden. He is head of the Human Rights Unit of the Saami Council. (*Sápmi, Sweden*)

Thomas Køhler has an MA in Russian and Political Science from the University of Copenhagen, Denmark, and works as a consultant on indigenous issues in Russia. (*Russia*)

Gordon L. Pullar, a Kodiak Island Sugpiaq (Alutiiq), is the Director of the Department of Alaska Native and Rural Development (DANRD) at the University of Alaska Fairbanks and President of the Leisnoi Village Tribal Council. *Dixie Masak Dayo*, an Inupiaq, is an Assistant Professor at DANRD at the University of Alaska Fairbanks. She is a former president of the Bean Ridge Corporation, the indigenous corporation for her home village of Manley Hot Springs. *Richard A. Caulfield* is an Associate Dean of the College of Rural Alaska and a Professor of Rural Development at the University of Alaska Fairbanks. He has conducted extensive research among the indigenous peoples of both Alaska and Greenland. *Ralph Gabrielli* is an Associate Professor of Rural Development at the University of Alaska Fairbanks and has been involved in providing higher education to the indigenous people of rural Alaska for more than 25 years. *Miranda Wright*, an Athabascan, is an Assistant Professor and the Academic Program Head for the DANRD at the University of Alaska Fairbanks. She also serves on the Board of Directors of Doyon, Ltd., the Native regional corporation for interior Alaska. (*Alaska*)

David Roddick is Senior Advisor to the Arctic Athabaskan Council and an independent consultant based in Whitehorse. (*Yukon*)

C.D. James Paci is an Advisor to the Arctic Athabaskan Council, and Manager of Lands and Environment, Dene Nation. Dr Paci holds an interdisciplinary doctorate, University of Manitoba (2000), and is a member of the Roving Faculty, University of the Arctic. He has published articles on First Nations issues. (*Northwest Territories*)

Jack Hicks lives in Iqaluit, Nunavut, where he works for the Government of Nunavut. (*Nunavut, Nunavik, Nunatsiavut and First Nations GA, Canada*)

Sarah Chandler works as an independent facilitator/trainer. She has worked for the Canadian Human Rights Foundation, Montreal, Quebec and for local communities and First Nations in BC. Sarah holds an MA in Understanding and Securing Human Rights from the Institute of Commonwealth Studies, University of London (UK). She lives in Lillooet, British Columbia. (*British Columbia*)

Martha McCollough works as an Assistant Professor in Cultural Anthropology at the Anthropology and Ethnic Studies Department of the University of Nebraska. Her research interests include the relationship between states and non-state societies. She is currently working on a book that explores terrorism prior to the reservation era in the United States. (*USA*)

MEXICO, CENTRAL AMERICA AND THE CIRCUMCARIBBEAN

This section has been compiled and edited by *Diana Vinding*, Programme Coordinator for Mexico, Central America & the Pacific.

Gabriel Baeza Espejel is an ethnohistorian. He is a Professor at the Mexican National School of Anthropology and History (ENAH) and an Assistant Researcher at the Colegio de Mexico. *Abel Barrera Hernández* is an anthropologist and the Director of the Centre for Human Rights of the Montaña region -Tlachinollan, an NGO based in Tlapa, Guerrero, Mexico. Web page: www.tlachinollan.org *(Mexico)*

Romeo Tiu is a Mayan and works as a lawyer in Totonicapán. He formerly worked as a judge in a rural zone, and for a number of years in MINUGUA. He was also advisor to COPMAGUA in the negotiations on indigenous issues with the Government. *(Guatemala)*

Dennis Williamson Cuthbert is an economist and the Director of the Research and Investigation Centre of the Atlantic Coast of Nicaragua, CIDCA. williamson@ns.uca.edu.ni. *(Nicaragua)*

Atencio López is a Kuna lawyer. He works with development issues and is a former President of the NGO "Napguana". *(Panama)*

Maximilian Forte is an Assistant Professor in Anthropology at the University College of Cape Breton, Canada. He has spent four years engaged in research and support for the Santa Rosa Carib Community of Arima, Trinidad & Tobago. His book, *Ruins of Absence, Presence of Caribs* is soon to be published by the University Press of Florida. *(Trinidad)*

SOUTH AMERICA

This section has been compiled and edited by *Alejandro Parellada*, Programme Coordinator for South America.

Efraím Jaramillo is an anthropologist and collaborates with various indigenous organizations. *(Colombia)*

Carlos Botto, David Ibarrola, Martha Espejo, María Teresa Quispe, and *Nelson Mavio* are members of the advisory team to the Regional Organization of Indigenous Peoples of the Amazonas (ORPIA). *(Venezuela)*

Jorge Agurto is a social communicator who has for years been supporting indigenous communities and peoples in Peru in the defence of their fundamental rights. He is Technical Secretary of the Permanent Conference of the Indigenous Peoples of Peru, COPPIP (coppip@amauta.rcp.net.pe), and in charge of the Indigenous Information Service, SERVINDI, which pub-

lishes an electronic bulletin specialising in indigenous and environmental issues.
jorgeagurto@hotmail.com; servindi@yahoo.com (*Peru*)

Carlos Romero Bonifaz is a lawyer and the Executive Director of the Centre for Legal Studies and Social Research (CEJIS). He also works as a consultant to indigenous organizations in Bolivia. (*Bolivia*)

Paulo Celso de Oliveira belongs to the Pankararu people and works as a lawyer for the indigenous movement in Brazil. He is currently preparing his master degree in law at the Catholic University of Paraná. (*Brazil*)

Andrés Ramírez is a member of Tierraviva's legal department. He is a fellow at the Inter-American Court of Human Rights. (*Paraguay*)

Morita Carrasco is an anthropologist, lecturer and researcher at the University of Buenos Aires. In recent years, she has worked at the Centre for Legal and Social Studies (CELS), forming part of the team of technical/legal advisors supporting the Lhaka Honhat organization in its lawsuit before the Inter-American Commission on Human Rights. (*Argentina*)

Luis Llanquilef R. is a sociologist. He is a Lafkenche leader and the legal coordinator of the University of Arcis. (*Chile*)

AUSTRALIA AND NEW ZEALAND

This section has been compiled and edited by *Diana Vinding*, Programme Coordinator for Mexico, Central America and the Pacific.

Peter Jull is Adjunct Associate Professor, School of Political Science & International Studies, University of Queensland, Brisbane, Australia, and a member of IWGIA's Advisory Board. He has worked with Torres Strait Islander and Aboriginal peoples in Northern Australia, and for decades with Inuit and other Arctic and Sub-Arctic peoples. (*Australia*)

Evan Poata-Smith belongs to the Ngāti Kahu *iwi* and is a lecturer in sociology at the School of Sociology and Anthropology, University of Canterbury, Christchurch, New Zealand. Prior to his arrival at Canterbury, he was employed as a policy analyst in the Māori unit at the Ministry of Education in Wellington. His published work focuses on the political economy of inequality between Māori and Pākehā (non-Māori), Māori educational inequality, the Treaty of Waitangi settlement process and Māori protest politics. (*Aotearoa*)

ASIA

This section has been compiled and edited by *Christian Erni*, Programme Coordinator for Asia, and *Sille Stidsen*, Assistant Desk Officer for Asia.

East and Southeast Asia

Osamu Hasegawa is an Ainu but lives near Tokyo. He is a member of the Rera Association in Tokyo. *Kanako Uzawa*, who is a member of the Ainu Resource Centre in Tokyo, translated the article into English (kanakouzawa@yahoo.com). (*Japan*)

Charlotte Mathiassen is a social anthropologist and a consultant on development projects. She has worked with Tibetan communities in the Himalayas and on Tibetan issues generally for many years. She is a long-term active member of the Danish Tibet Support Committee and a member of the Network for Indigenous Peoples in Denmark. (*Tibet*)

The Association for Taiwan Indigenous People's Policies (ATIPP) is an NGO established and administered by Taiwan indigenous activists. As a research and advocacy group, ATIPP works for the empowerment of the indigenous peoples of Taiwan and the promotion of their rights. atipp.taiwan@msa.hinet.net (*Taiwan*)

Perla Espiel (p_espiel@anthrowatch.org) and *Maria Teresa Guia-Padilla* (miksgp@anthrowatch.org) are anthropologists working for AnthroWatch, a non-governmental organization supporting indigenous communities in ancestral domain titling and in policy advocacy work (www.geocities.com/abepad74d/org.htm). *Joan Carling* is the Chairperson of the Cordillera Peoples Alliance (CPA), a regional alliance of indigenous peoples' organizations in the Cordillera. *Christian Erni*, IWGIA's Asia Coordinator, compiled and assisted in writing the article. (*Philippines*)

Ulrik Norup Jørgensen has recently qualified as a journalist. He visited Timor Lorosa'e in October 2003 as part of his training with the Danish High School of Journalism. The purpose of his visit was to look into the democratisation process in Timor Lorosa'e. Ulriknorup@hotmail.com (*Timor Lorosa'e*)

Emilianus Ola Kleden, is the Executive Secretary of AMAN (Alyansi Masyarakat Adat Nusantara / The Indigenous Peoples' Alliance of the Archipelago), the Indonesian national indigenous peoples' umbrella organization. *Rikardo Simarmata* is Program Development Coordinator and co-founder of HuMa (the Association for Community and Ecologically-based Law Reform). As a public interest lawyer, he facilitates participatory law making processes, and critical legal analysis mainly on the issues of land and other natural wealth. (*Indonesia*)

Jannie Lasimbang is a Kadazan from Sabah, Malaysia. She is the Vice-Chairperson of PACOS Trust, Sabah and has been involved in the Indigenous Peoples Network of Malaysia (IPNM / JOAS) since its inception in 1992. She is currently the Secretary General of the Asia Indigenous Peoples Pact (AIPP) Foundation based in Chiang Mai, Thailand. (*Malaysia*)

Helen Leake works for the Secretariat of the International Alliance of Indigenous and Tribal Peoples of the Tropical Forests, currently based in Chiang Mai, Thailand (www.international-alliance.org). She previously worked for a number of years with indigenous highland peoples in Thailand, and the Inter Mountain Peoples Education and Culture in Thailand Association (IMPECT). helen@international-alliance.org (*Thailand*)

Graeme Brown is the Ratanakiri Coordinator of Community Forestry International, which works in partnership with the Ratanakiri Natural Resource Management Network, a network of indigenous community people. He has worked in Ratanakiri for the past 5 years. graemeb@camintel.com (*Cambodia*)

Koos Neefjes works in the broad field of sustainable development, and is a consultant for various development agencies. He is currently based in Vietnam and draws on experience from around 30 developing countries. He has written a wide range of articles and reports, including a paper on ethnic minority development in Vietnam (*Localizing International Development Targets (IDT) for poverty reduction in Vietnam: Promoting ethnic minority development.* Paper for the UNDP Poverty Task Force, 2001). *Luong Thi Truong* works for the Centre for Sustainable Development in Mountainous Areas (CSDMA), an NGO working with poor and vulnerable peoples, especially ethnic minorities in mountainous areas. CSDMA's mission is to preserve ethnic identity, indigenous knowledge and natural resource management as well as assist peoples in poverty reduction. *Sheelagh O'Reilly* currently works as a team leader in a Community Based Conservation Project in the Hoang Lien Son. She has been working with community natural resource management and local capacity building in the mountains of north Vietnam for the past 4 ½   years.(*Vietnam*)

Ian Baird, originally from Canada, has been working on natural resource management and indigenous issues in mainland South-east Asia for 17 years, and has been living in Laos for most of the last 12 years. He is President of the Global Association for People and the Environment, a Canadian NGO active in Laos. He is also active in natural resource management and indigenous issues in the north-eastern Cambodian provinces of Ratanakiri and Stung Treng. (*Laos*)

Natalie Drolet, a Canadian, is a Research Officer with Altsean-Burma (The Alternative ASEAN Network on Burma) - a network of organizations from ASEAN member states supporting human rights and democratic development in Burma. natalie@altsean.org   http://www.altsean.org/ (*Burma*)

M. Kikon is currently Convenor of the Naga Peoples Movement for Human Rights, Delhi Sector and has been involved in human rights work for around five years. *Nepuni Piku* is a human rights activist with the Naga Peoples Movement for Human Rights and is Convenor in its office in South Nagalim. *Aküm Longchari* is pursuing studies on implementation of self-determination as a source of conflict transformation. (*Nagalim*)

South Asia

The Jumma Peoples Network (JUPNET) is an organization established and administered by indigenous Jummas based in various countries of Europe and elsewhere. JUPNET seeks to promote the rights of the indigenous Jummas through dialogue, negotiation and other peaceful means. *Sanjeeb Drong*, a Garo from north Bangladesh, is the Secretary General of the Bangladesh Indigenous Peoples Forum, a national forum representing 45 different indigenous communities in Bangladesh. He has published extensively on indigenous issues. sdrong@mail.bangla.net. (*Bangladesh*)

Balkrishna Mabuhang is a lecturer at the Central Department of Population Studies at Tribhuvan University, Kathmandu (mabuhang@infoclub.com.np). He has been active in the Nepal Federation of Indigenous Nationalities – NEFIN (formerly NEFEN) for a number of years, and is currently advisor to the organization. (*Nepal*)

Samar Bosu Mullick (also known as Sanjay) is a political activist, teacher and researcher who has been working in solidarity

17

with the indigenous peoples of Jharkhand for the last quarter of a century. He was one of the frontline persons of the Jharkhand separate state movement. He compiled and wrote the section on Jharkhand (and the forest eviction issue) in cooperation with *Tony Herbert* and *Souparna Lahiri*, Co-ordinator of the Delhi Forum. *C. R. Bijoy* is a human rights activist based in Tamil Nadu, South India. For the last sixteen years he has been involved in and associated with indigenous issues and organization in India and written about these and associated matters. He compiled and wrote the sections on Kerala and Orissa. *Walter Fernandes* has been working on tribal issues in India for two decades. He is the former Director of the Indian Social Institute, New Delhi and the editor of *Social Action*. He is currently Director of the North Eastern Social Research Centre. He wrote the section on the Northeast in collaboration with *Xonxoi Barboa,* an activist and researcher working at the North Eastern Social Research Centre. Barboa is currently conducting PhD research into indigenous peoples and migrant settlers in North Cachar and Kharbi Anglong in Assam. (*India*)

THE MIDDLE EAST

This section has been compiled and edited by *Diana Vinding*, IWGIA.

> *Dr. Suzie Alwash* is Senior Technical Advisor to the Iraq Foundation's "Eden Again" Project, dedicated to promoting the restoration of the Mesopotamian Marshlands. (*Iraq*)
> *Diana Vinding,* IWGIA, compiled and wrote the article on the Bedouins of Israel based on information material provided by *Adam Keller* and **Bustan L'Shalom**. *Adam Keller* is an Israeli peace activist and spokesperson for Gush Shalom (Peace Bloc) - a grassroots peace movement founded in 1992, advocating Israeli-Palestinian peace. He is the editor of *The Other Israel,* a newsletter published by the Israeli Council for Israeli-Palestinian Peace (founded in 1975). www.gush-shalom.org **Bustan L'Shalom** is a grassroots social/environmental justice organization that works with indigenous and marginalized sectors in Israel/Palestine, raising public awareness around issues of systemic discrimination through actions of resistance. bustanlshalom@yahoogroups.com (*Israel*)

AFRICA

This section has been compiled and edited by *Marianne Wiben Jensen,* Africa Programme Coordinator and *Diana Vinding,* IWGIA.

Hassan Idbalkassm is an Amazigh (Berber) from Morocco. He is a lawyer and President of the Amazigh association "Tamaynut", which he founded in 1978. He is also the Vice-President of the "Congrès Mondial Amazigh", which has a membership of more than 70 Amazigh associations in North Africa and Europe. (*Morocco*)

Mouloud Lounaouci is an Amazigh from Kabylia, Algeria. He holds a doctorate in linguistics, and is a long time activist for the rights of the Imazighen. He is spokesperson for the Berber Cultural Movement (Mouvement Culturel Berbère). (*Algeria*)

Melakou Tegegn is Ethiopian and director of Panos Ethiopia. He is currently chairman of the board of the Pastoralist Forum Ethiopia. He has worked in the Middle East, North Africa, South East Asia and Europe as coordinator for various NGO capacity-building and advocacy projects. He is a PhD candidate at the University of South Africa and conducts research into the link between democratization/civil society and poverty in Ethiopia. He also teaches political science at Addis Ababa University. *Marianne Jensen* compiled and partly wrote the section on the Gambella region. (*Ethiopia*)

Naomi Kipuri is a Maasai from the Kajiado district of Kenya. She is an anthropologist by training and has taught at the University of Nairobi. She now works as a development consultant, conducts research and is especially interested in development concerns and issues relating to human rights and the rights of indigenous peoples. (*Kenya*)

Benedict Ole Nangoro, is a Maasai from Kiteto, in Tanzania. He currently works with CORDS, a local NGO working with the Maasai people in collective land demarcation, mapping, registration and titling. (*Tanzania*)

Dorothy Jackson is the Africa Programme Coordinator for the Forest Peoples Programme (FPP), an NGO working to promote rights of forest peoples worldwide, and its charitable wing, the Forest Peoples Project. She has worked with Twa people and organizations since 1992. *John Nelson* is a Policy Advisor to the UK-based Forest Peoples Programme and has been coordinating FPP's project work in Cameroon and Uganda since 2001. www.forestpeoples.org (*Central Africa and Cameroon*)

Diana Vinding, IWGIA, compiled the article on Angola on the basis of a report produced by *Americo Kwononoka* and *Richard Pakleppa* for WIMSA Namibia and Trócaire Angola. *Americo Kwononoka* holds a PhD in history and is currently the director of Angola's National Institute of Anthropology. He has undertaken anthropological studies into numerous ethnic groups in Angola. *Richard Pakleppa* is a Namibian filmmaker and organizational consultant. Richard has undertaken consultancies around issues of the land rights and human rights of San communities in Namibia and Angola. (*Angola*)

Robert K. Hitchcock is a Professor of Anthropology and Geography at the University of Nebraska-Lincoln, USA. He has for many years researched and written on San issues. (*Namibia and Botswana*)

Nigel Crawhall is an activist for indigenous peoples' rights. He has worked with the Indigenous Peoples of Africa Co-ordinating Committee (IPACC) and is project manager on an indigenous knowledge and cultural resources management and training project with the South African San Institute (SASI). (*South Africa*)

PART II

INTERNATIONAL PROCESSES

This section has been compiled and edited by *Lola García-Alix*, Coordinator of Human Rights Activities.

Pablo Espinella works in the Office of the High Commissioner for Human Rights as Legal Assistant for the mandate of the Special Rapporteur on the Human Rights and Fundamental Freedoms of Indigenous Peoples. pespiniella@ohchr.org . (*The Special Rapporteur: 2003 Overview*).

Diana Vinding and *Lola García Alix* wrote the section *Facilitating the Dialogue.*

Lola García Alix has compiled and partly written the following chapters:: *The UN Permanent Forum on Indigenous issues;* and *The UN Draft Declaration: 2003 Developments.*

Marianne Wiben Jensen is the Coordinator of IWGIA's Africa

Pro-gramme. (*Breakthrough at the African Commission on Human and Peoples' Rights*)

Pascal Richard is a cultural anthropologist specialized in indigenous media. He has worked with indigenous filmmakers in Australia and was one of the coordinators of the Indigenous Film Forum organized by the IWGIA local group in Switzerland. pascal.richard@gmx.net (*The process of the World Summit on the Information Society*)

Paul Oldham is an anthropologist and works at the ESRC Centre for Economic and Social Aspects of Genomics (CESAGen) at Lancaster University in the UK. (*Indigenous Peoples and the CBD in 2003*)

Dorothy Jackson is the Africa Programme Coordinator for the Forest Peoples Programme (FPP) and its charitable wing, the Forest Peoples Project. (*The World Congress on Parks*)   ❏

PART I

REGION AND COUNTRY REPORTS

THE CIRCUMPOLAR NORTH

ARCTIC COUNCIL

The Arctic Council (AC) is an intergovernmental organisation comprising 8 member states with territories in the Arctic realm. These are: Canada, the USA, the Russian Federation, Finland, Sweden, Norway, Denmark/Greenland/Faeroe Islands and Iceland.

Six indigenous organisations have the status of Permanent Participants to the AC. These are: the Aleut International Association (AIA), the Arctic Athabaskan Council (AAC), the Gwich'in Council International (GCI), the Inuit Circumpolar Conference (ICC), the Russian Association of Indigenous Peoples of the North (RAIPON) and the Saami Council.

The AC has a number of observers, including states (France, Poland, Germany, the Netherlands and the United Kingdom), international organisations and NGOs. IWGIA received observer status in 2002. The more technical and scientific work is carried out by working groups: the Arctic Monitoring and Assessment Programme (AMAP); Conservation of Arctic Flora and Fauna (CAFF); Emergency Prevention, Preparedness and Response (EPPR); Protection of Arctic Marine Environment (PAME); and the Sustainable Development Working Group (SDWG). The SDWG, for example, is involved in projects on sustainable reindeer husbandry, co-management of marine resources and a Survey of Living Conditions in the Arctic.

Iceland took over the chairmanship of the AC in 2003 for two years. During its chairmanship, Iceland will emphasise the human aspect of sustainable development and information and communication technology (ICT). In these regards, Iceland is at the forefront of developing an Arctic Human Development Report and organised a Conference on Information and Communication Technology (ICT) in 2003. The AC Ministerial meeting in Finland in 2002 welcomed capacity building, sustainable development, traditional knowledge and gender as cross-cutting themes in the AC activities.

Arctic Climate Impact Assessment

The Arctic Climate Impact Assessment (ACIA) is soon coming to an end. The aim of the ACIA has been to assess the impact of climate change across the ecosystems, communities and socio-economic activities of the Arctic region. Three documents are in progress: a scientific report, an overview document and political recommendations. The Permanent Participants have been heavily involved at different levels

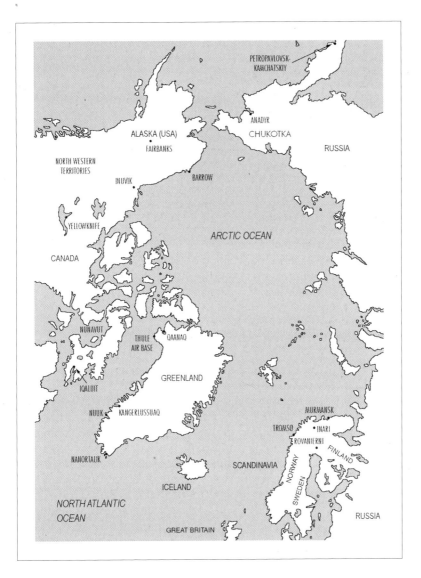

of the work with the assessment, in which the integration of traditional knowledge and science has been of great importance. In 2003, one of the main discussions evolved around the political recommendations. There have been efforts on the part of some member states, particularly the USA, to try to delay the process of drafting recommendations, arguing that it would be difficult to make recommendations before the scientific document was ready. The indigenous organisations have strongly supported the development of political recommendations for the Ministerial meeting in 2004, as scheduled and without any delay.

Arctic Human Development Report

Alongside the far more technical and scientific ACIA report, the Icelandic chairmanship has initiated work on an Arctic Human Development Report to focus on the human aspects of sustainable development. The objectives are to identify common challenges and opportunities in the Arctic region, and to identify gaps where future research is needed. The indigenous organisations are represented on the report steering committee and have therefore been involved in the whole process of selecting lead authors and suggesting contributing authors, and in the review process of individual chapters. Many indigenous researchers are lead authors for chapters such as those on legal systems, political systems and human health, and many are contributing authors.

Information and communication technology

One of the Icelandic Chairmanship's priorities is information and communications technology (ICT). In October, an ICT Conference was held in Akureyri, Iceland, to discuss the challenges, needs and opportunities of ICT in the north, in particular in the fields of distance education and health. Due to the remote location of many communities, information technology, and particularly telehealth / telemedicine (the use of telecommunications for medical diagnosis and patient care), are important topics for the local people. However, it must also not be forgotten that many regions, particularly in Russia, do not yet have the capacity to be involved in these technologically high level projects. Unfortunately, no indigenous representative from Russia had the opportunity of making a presentation at the conference.

Sustainable Development Action Plan

The Arctic Council Ministerial meeting in 2002 requested that a Sustainable Development Action Plan (SDAP) be developed for the Arctic. Russia is lead country for this AC activity and responsible for the draft document. The aim of this project is to identify gaps in the work towards achieving sustainable development in the north. Whereas the Arctic Council has been discussing environmental issues and development issues in general, it has thus far been the Sustainable Development Working Group that has focused on the human dimension and the sustainability of development. ❑

GREENLAND

Greenland is a self-governing unit within the Danish realm. The first Danish colonial settlement was established in 1721 close to the current capital, Nuuk, on the west coast. In 1953, Greenland became an integrated part of Denmark by law and, in 1979 when Home Rule was established, some kind of real autonomy was introduced.

Greenland has its own Home Rule Parliament and Government responsible for most internal matters. The population of Greenland numbers 56,000 inhabitants, 87 per cent of whom are ethnic Greenlanders (Inuit).

The Commission on Self-government

In 1999, the Home Rule Government established a Commission on Self-government to investigate the possibilities for taking over more responsibilities from the Danish state, thereby developing a more independent Greenland. Core issues are foreign affairs, security matters, economic development and language policy. The report from the commission was delivered in spring 2003.

Every year, Greenland receives around 3 thousand million Danish crowns (DKK) - approximately 486 million US$ - in grants from the Danish state. This has made it possible to develop a modern society but has also resulted in dependency and apathy. The self-government commission therefore concluded that self-government had to rest upon a self-sufficient economy, with a considerable reduction in the yearly grant. There is thus a need to strengthen the Greenlandic development of trade and industry. In order to do so, the educational level of the population must be increased and the education system adapted to future needs. Among other problems to be overcome are the infrastructure, the widespread settlement pattern and a public sector that is much bigger than in most other countries.

In August, the Danish and Greenlandic governments decided to appoint a Danish-Greenlandic self-government commission with parity between Danish and Greenlandic participants to work on a plan for increased Greenlandic self-government. One key Greenlandic demand is the establishment of a partnership agreement that recognises Greenland and Denmark as equal partners within the realm.

The process of preparing the Greenlandic platform with the Commission on Self-government and the ensuing debate in the Home Rule Parliament were remarkable in at least one respect. Although there were diverging viewpoints on the scale and speed of the quest for self-governance, it was unanimously agreed that Greenland should be as independent as is possible for a country with little more than 50,000 inhabitants.

Politics

Elections for the Home Rule Parliament were held in December 2002, resulting in a coalition between Siumut (the Social Democratic Party) and the left-wing IA (Inuit Ataqatigiit) party, with the Siumut party leader, Hans Enoksen, as Premier. A few weeks after the elections, however, the Home Rule Government faced severe problems because Siumut had replaced a number of civil servants in the Home Rule administration with party colleagues and because of a healing ceremony within the Home Rule Government's offices. The healing and the camaraderie made IA demand that Hans Enoksen step down. Hans Enoksen consequently rescinded the coalition agreement with IA and began negotiations with the conservative Atassut. In January 2003, Siumut and Atassut formed a new coalition.

The new coalition, however, was to survive less than one year before severe problems again arose when a miscalculation of 100 million DKK (approximately 16 million US$) was discovered. Responsibility was placed with the Minister of Finances, who was from Atassut. This was the culmination of several months of poor co-operation and, in September, the Siumut / Atassut government coalition broke down. A new coalition was formed between Siumut and IA. A new ministry also saw the light, the Ministry of Self-governance, Justice and Resources. This ministry is to prepare a referendum on self-government in 2006.

Thule

In early 2003, the United States gave back the old hunting area, Dundas, close to the U.S.airbase in Thule (Northern Greenland) to its

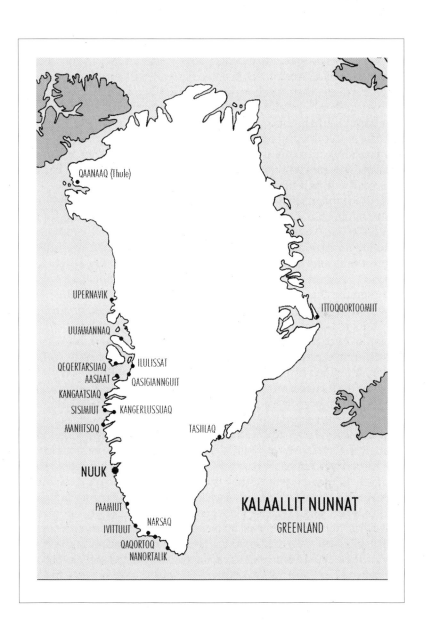

QAANAAQ (Thule)

UPERNAVIK

ITTOQQORTOOMIIT

UUMMANNAQ

QEQERTARSUAQ ILULISSAT
AASIAAT QASIGIANNGUIT
KANGAATSIAQ
SISIMIUT KANGERLUSSUAQ
MANIITSOQ TASIILAQ

NUUK

PAAMIUT
NARSAQ
IVITTUUT
QAQORTOQ
NANORTALIK

KALAALLIT NUNNAT

GREENLAND

original occupants. The Thule population, Inughuit, were forced to
move in 1953 due to a military agreement between the United States
and Denmark. In recent years, they and their descendants have intensified their struggle to regain the title to the whole Thule airbase and

not just Dundas. After the restitution of Dundas, it was revealed that the United States had used the site as a military waste dump and, during 2003, a great deal of discussion has been going on regarding whose responsibility it is to clean up and how severe the pollution of the area is.

Denmark/Greenland signed a contract with the US concerning Dundas at the beginning of 2003, by which Denmark/Greenland has to take responsibility for cleaning the site. According to the agreement, Inughuit are not allowed to move back for the next 3 years and for the 3 following years will not be allowed to renovate old houses or build new ones without first consulting the American authorities.

In November 2003, the Supreme Court in Denmark heard the case of the Thule area. It was the Inughuit organisation, Hingitaq 53, that had taken legal action against the Danish State on behalf of Inughuit, claiming compensation of 235 million DKK and the right to re-settle and hunt in their old hunting area. The lawyer representing Hingitaq 53 argued that Inughuit make up a special indigenous group in Greenland and therefore have special rights. According to the Home Rule Law, however, the population in Greenland is one people and no group or individual has special ownership to any area of Greenland.

In the end, the Supreme Court rejected the claims, as the Danish constitution's protection of ownership to land was not in force in Greenland when Inughuit were moved. As a result, Inughuit will try to bring the case before the European Court of Human Rights.

Another major problem concerning the Thule area was a request from the United States concerning an upgrading of the Thule radar as part of their plans for national missile defence. Defence is not under Home Rule authority but the Home Rule Government has asked to be directly involved in decisions relating to the future of the military base in Thule. The Danish Government reacted positively to the upgrading. They hoped to find a common ground with Greenland on the issue but were not willing to give them a right of veto. In May 2003, the Greenlandic premier, Hans Enoksen, signed a Danish/Greenlandic declaration of principle concerning increased Greenlandic authority to deal with foreign affairs. According to this declaration, Greenland has a say and needs to be involved in questions concerning foreign and security policy of relevance to Greenland. This declaration, however, was seen as a first step towards allowing the United States to upgrade the Thule radar.

Living resources

On 1 January 2003, new and more restrictive regulations concerning bird hunting came into force, prolonging the closed season for seabird hunting. This caused discussions and disagreement among hunters, biologists and managers and, because of the criticism from the fishermen's and hunters' organisation (KNAPK), the Home Rule Government gave dispensation concerning the spring hunt, in the breeding season. This caused indignation not only in Greenland but also internationally as it set a very poor example of nature management in Greenland. In November, a report from the World Wide Fund for Nature (WWF) was released, claiming that Greenland did not live up to international conventions and agreements concerning nature and wildlife. In response, the Home Rule Government said that they were already working on implementing the international conventions and agreements, for example, througha new law on nature protection. They are also working on by-laws regarding some endangered species, such as beluga and walrus. The question is what the end result will be, as 2003 has already seen a dispensation and a suggestion for a new by-law on bird hunting that is less restrictive than the old one.

Mineral and oil resources

The Greenland Home Rule places great expectations on both oil and minerals as a means of improving the economy and thereby making the country more self-reliant and independent from Denmark.

With regard to gold, prospecting has been going on in the area of Nanortalik, in southern Greenland, since the 1980s and, in 2003, mining was initiated by the production company, Nalunaq Goldmine A/S, which is owned by the Greenlandic company NunaMinerals and the Canadian Crew Development Corporation. At the end of December 2003, the first cargo of ore was shipped to Spain for processing. NunaMinerals A/S is also prospecting close to the capital, Nuuk, and promising finds were made at the end of December.

The income from the gold has to be split between Greenland and Denmark, as Greenland does not hold the property rights to the subsoil.

The hope for oil and minerals also has an international dimension as recent years have brought renewed interest in the North Pole and the resources of the Polar Sea. Russia has already submitted a rights claim to the UN Sea Rights Commission while Denmark did not sign the Convention until spring 2003. Nonetheless, the Danish Government has already set several million DKK aside to investigate the Greenlandic continental shelf over the coming years. The fight for the North Pole and its potential resources has begun. ❑

SAPMI - NORWAY

N orway presented a new land management act for Finnmark County on April 4, 2003. The Act was supposed to close a process that started in the 1970s and 80s following controversies over the Saami land rights question in relation to the establishment of a hydroelectric power plant in Alta.

The so-called Finnmark Act has been heavily criticised by the Saami Parliament in Norway due to several breaches of political promises and also failure to comply with international law. During the spring and fall of 2003, several observations were made both domestically and internationally, all pointing in the same direction of non-compliance with international law on indigenous issues (for more details please see *The Indigenous World 2002-2003*).

The Saami Parliament's view

During the second Permanent Forum meeting in New York (May 2003), the Saami Parliament presented its view on the proposed Finnmark Act during a side-event. MP and member of the Executive Council of the Saami Parliament, Johan Mikkel Sara, presented the Parliament's initial concerns and stated that:

> *This leads us to the conclusion that the Norwegian government totally disregards 23 years of hard work in the Saami Rights Committee, and also breaches the agreement with the Saami organisations made in 1981.*

Just days after the presentation was made to the UN representatives in New York, the Saami Parliament, in its plenary session, issued a statement that:

> *The Bill does not give the Sámi people any special legal protection for their culture and their economic activities in competition with other interests. It is in conformity with neither the internal or international rules by which the state is bound, nor the state's moral and political obligations vis-à-vis its indigenous people. Nor does the Bill provide a sufficient legal protection against future statutory regulations that weaken the population's control over its resources, as prescribed by international law.*

This view has, since May 2003, been advocated by the Saami Parliament, and has been the main argument in seeking to persuade the Norwegian Parliament (*Storting*) to either reject the proposed act and send it back to the government or embark on a process of direct negotiations between the two parliaments, the latter being a new constitutional procedure never before invoked in Norway.

A concrete result of the Saami Parliament's criticism was that the Legal committee of the Norwegian Parliament asked the government to come up with an expert review of the Finnmark Act and its compliance with international law by October 2003.

International attention

International attention was also drawn to the new Finnmark Act. In August 2003, CERD (the Committee on the Elimination of Racial Discrimination) commented on Norway's report on the Convention on the Elimination of all forms of Racial Discrimination with reference to the proposed Finnmark Act. In its observations, the Committee states that:

> 19. *The Committee is concerned that the recently proposed Finnmark Act will significantly restrict the control and decision-making powers of the Saami population over the right to own and use land and natural resources in the Finnmark County. The Committee draws the attention of the State Party to its General Recommendation XXIII on the rights of indigenous peoples which, inter alia, calls upon the State Party to recognize and protect the right of indigenous peoples to own, develop, control and use their communal lands, territories and resources.*
>
> *The Committee recommends that the State Party find an adequate solution concerning the control and decision-making powers over the right to land and natural resources in the Finnmark County in agreement with the Saami people.*

The comments from CERD raised awareness among the domestic media that Norway was in breach of international law , and all the major newspapers, including *Aftenposten, VG (Verdens Gang)* and *Dagbladet*, took strong positions criticising the government for its failure in the Saami land rights issue. The biggest newspaper, VG, even called the so-called "state owned" property in Saami areas the "biggest robbery in Norwegian history".

In compliance with ILO 169?

Norway's report to the ILO on Convention No. 169, was due on August 31, 2003. In accordance with the agreement with the Saami Parliament on reporting procedures, the Saami Parliament produced its own report, focusing on the proposed Finnmark Act. The Saami Parliament report was submitted directly to the ILO and commented on the following main points:

- The Government's failure to comply with ILO 169 by neglecting to gain consent from the Saami Parliament prior to the final proposal. The Government thereby failed to adhere to Articles 2, 6 and 7.
- No recognition of Saami rights to ownership, and no identification of the lands in question. The Finnmark Act thereby failed to comply with Articles 14 and 15.
- Wrong use of reference to Article 34 in that it is an argument for not complying with Articles 14 and 15.

The ILO Committee of Experts will present its concluding observations in early March 2004.

The report of the Norwegian government's appointed legal experts was presented in October 2003, and the conclusions were strickingly similar to those previously drawn by the Saami Parliament. The experts concluded that without proper identification and recognition of the Saami rights to their land both on an individual, community and collective level, Norway would be failing to adhere to contemporary international law protecting indigenous peoples.

There was, during the second half of 2003, an initial dialogue between the Norwegian Parliament and its Judicial Committee and the Saami Parliament in order to find a procedure that would move the issue forward. One possible path to follow would be the establishment of a negotiating team from the Saami Parliament as well as the Norwegian Parliament with a mandate to produce a legal text that is agreeable to both parties and in conformity with international law on indigenous issues. There is currently no established procedure, and the government seems to be upholding its proposal as tabled to the Norwegian parliament.

The only thing that is certain at the moment is that there is a strong desire on the part of Norwegian Parliament members to make sure that any final legislation must be in compliance with international law. In any case, we will hopefully see positive developments on the Saami land rights issue during 2004. ❑

SAPMI – SWEDEN

Sápmi - the Swedish side

This report aims to review developments of importance to the part of the indigenous Saami people residing on the Swedish side of Sápmi during the previous year. The Saami population inhabit an area known as Sápmi divided by the borders of what are today four countries Finland, Norway, the Russian Federation and Sweden. Even though the report only covers the Swedish side of Sápmi, most of the issues dealt with are also relevant to the Saami population residing outside present-day Sweden.

Constant investigations

Nothing happened in regard to Saami people's right to land during 2003. Sweden is simply still not ready to return any rights to the land it once colonized. As a consequence, the following problems continue to exist.

Since the mid 1900s, Sweden has appointed investigation after investigation to review the Saami people's rights. During 2003, three committees appointed by the Swedish government to look into the rights of the Saami people continued their work - the Reindeer Breeding Policy Committee, the Boundary Commission and the governmental committee with the task of investigating the Saami people's right to hunting and fishing on its traditional land. These are governmental investigations no. 18, 19 and 20 during the 20th and 21st century. Many of the recent investigations have concluded that Sweden does violate the Saami people's right to land, waters and natural resources. During 2003, Sweden took no steps towards recognizing the rights of the Saami people.

The Boundary Commission's task is to identify what constitutes traditional Saami land, as called for by ILO Convention No. 169 on Indigenous and Tribal Peoples in Independent Countries, Art. 14.2. The committee constitutes a commendable effort to start dealing with Saami land issues. However, it has pointed out repeatedly during 2003 that only limited resources have been allocated for the project. This raises concern, since the committee has declared that under such circumstances, it will, to a substantial degree, have to depend on material furnished by interested parties. The Swedish farmers, their associations, the Swedish forest industries, organizations of Swedish leisure hunters, the power plant industries etc. have almost unlimited

36

resources available to prove that particular lands *do not* constitute traditional Saami land. The Saami people on the other hand, already deprived of most of its resources, have few resources available for providing the Committee with documentation.

Sweden did not take any steps towards ratifying ILO Convention No. 169 during 2003, even though in 1999, the government's own investigator recommended Sweden should do so, a recommendation that UN bodies have echoed.

The right to self-determination

The Human Rights Committee - with direct reference to Article 1.2 of the International Covenant on Civil and Political Rights (CCPR) - has called on Sweden to award the Saami people greater influence in decision-making affecting their natural environment and their means of subsistence.[1] Still, Sweden retains control over the Saami people's traditional land and resources. The lack of political willingness to provide the Saami people with necessary authority to administer its own society constitutes perhaps the greatest threat to the sustainability of the Saami culture.

The right to land

As indicated above, Sweden's policy towards legal rights to Saami traditional land, waters and natural resources remains essentially the same as during the era when Sweden viewed the Saami culture as inferior to the Swedish culture. The Saami people were the first settlers in the Saami traditional territories and Swedish law recognizes occupation as a way to acquire legal title to land.[2] Still, non-Saami courts have constantly found in favour of non-Saami parties in conflicts over Saami traditional land. Even though no authority today would claim that the Saami culture is inferior to the non-Saami cultures, Swedish courts' and administrative authorities' assumption continues to be that the Saami people has no legal right to its traditional land. This trend continued during 2003, with detrimental effects on the Saami population.

Resources

The Saami people is entitled to pursue reindeer husbandry on land it has traditionally utilized together with the non-Saami population.

Swedish legislation formally requires that forestry companies do not pursue activities that seriously hamper the possibility of pursuing reindeer husbandry in such areas. In case of a conflict, Swedish authorities should seek a balance between the Saami people's interests and competing interests. In reality, however, as acknowledged by the Swedish government's own survey, when Swedish authorities in concrete cases are supposed to examine whether logging activities seriously hamper the possibilities for pursuing reindeer husbandry in an area, they have never refused forestry companies the right to deforest Saami pasture areas.[3] There was no shift during 2003.

Further, forestry companies are supposed to consult with affected Saami communities before entering into major logging projects. In reality, however, these consultations in most instances simply meant that forest companies informed the Saami communities about their intention to cut trees in certain areas, with no intention of taking the Saami communities' concerns into account. And why should they, knowing that Swedish authorities will never interfere with their plans anyway? The situation has resulted in many Saami communities not even attending the so-called consultations anymore. The situation is similar with regard to other extractive industries, such as mining and power plants. There are several examples of Swedish authorities during 2003 allowing establishments of mines in Saami traditional territories, even though it means the end of reindeer husbandry in the area. There are examples of Saami communities having to witness the establishment of a mine straight across the only reindeer migration path remaining after other extractive industries or railroads were established in the area. Such establishments simply mean the end of traditional reindeer herding in the area.

Leisure activities

During 2003, Sweden continued to allow leisure activities in the Saami traditional territories seriously disturbing traditional livelihoods. Under Swedish regulations, snow mobile traffic is supposed to be sensitive to Saami traditional livelihoods. Still, it is not uncommon that tourists are allowed to travel by snow mobile in reindeer herding areas. As a result, the reindeer are driven away from their pasture areas, and the Saami communities have to feed them artificially for weeks, causing costs and psychological harm.

Sweden retains control over the Saami people's small-game hunting and fishing rights confiscated in 1992, even though the Swedish government as late as 1981 had confirmed that these rights belonged to the Saami people. No explanation was ever offered as to how these rights came to be transferred from the Saami people to the state. Sweden retained control over these resources even though the government's own Reindeer Breeding Policy Committee concluded that the regulation constitutes an infringement in Saami hunting and fishing rights. During 2003 Swedish society increased its interests in the even more important moose hunt. Moose hunting is both an integral part of Saami culture and an essential source of income for Saami people trying to live on their traditional livelihoods. Swedish regulations govern how many moose can be hunted each year. During 2003, many Saami communities saw their share of moose reduced, in favour of non-Saami leisure hunters.

Language

The Saami Language Act constitutes a commendable effort to safeguard the cultural rights of the Saami people. However, the Act only applies to the four northernmost municipalities in Sweden, and thus leaves out substantial parts of Sápmi, where some distinct Saami dialects very close to extinction are spoken. The UN's Committee on the Elimination of Racial Discrimination (CERD) has urged Sweden to broaden the scope of the Act to cover all of Sápmi. No such action was taken during 2003. ❑

References

1   See Concluding observations: Sweden 24/04/2002, document CCPR/ CO/74/SWE para. 15. Compare also Concluding observations regarding Norway, See CCPR/C/79/Add. 112 (1999).
2   See *e.g.* Supreme Court NJA 1981 s. 1, the so-called *Taxed Lapp Mountain Case*.
3   See *"En ny rennäringspolitik – öppna samebyar och samverkan med andra markanvändare"*, Betänkande av Renärringspolitiska kommittén, SOU 2001:101, p. 235 and 239.

RUSSIA

*H*ow many and who are the indigenous peoples of Russia? Is being indigenous a question of race, lifestyle – or a question of where you live? Those were the main issues debated in 2003 following a national census carried out in 2002, which many said was chaotic and unprofessionally conducted.

Do the figures tell the truth?

Through the 1990s the death rate, average life expectancy, and birth rate were a major concern for the indigenous peoples. In *The Indigenous World 2002-2003* an example from Evenkia in Central Siberia, indicated a dramatic decrease in the number of indigenous people.[1] In 2003, new statistics suddenly showed the opposite picture, indicating a growth in the indigenous population. But do these figures tell the truth?

At the same time, the typical notion in Russia that "everybody is indigenous" because all citizens of Russia originally stem from some part of Russia, was used by the authorities to weaken the federal laws on indigenous peoples' rights. It also became an issue for internal discussions in the indigenous movement.

The indigenous peoples have been on the brink of extinction through the crisis in the 1990s. Therefore the results of the chaotic census in 2002 came as a big surprise and forced the indigenous peoples to ask themselves *if the number of indigenous people in the north of the Russian Federation has grown by 16.9%*.

Based on the coordinated efforts by the Russian Association of Indigenous Peoples of the North (RAIPON) and Minister of Nationality Issues of the Russian Federation, Vladimir Zorin, the results of the 2002 census, were finally published "unofficially", as the authorities did not want to publish the results. The results show that the number of indigenous peoples of the North grew from 181,517 in 1989 to 212,209 in 2002. Table 1 shows the figures for 26 indigenous peoples.

It is worth paying attention to the following five indigenous groups in particular: Ults, Aleut, Nganasan, Udege, and Chuvants. These peoples have decreased over the past 13 years according to the figures. Why are they the only ones? It is necessary to take a closer look at these census results. The growth of indigenous populations indicates a decent socio-economic situation in northern regions. However,

Indigenous peoples of the North, Siberia, and the Far East	1989	2002	+ growth - decrease
Total	181517	212209	+16.9%
1. Nenets	34190	41454	+21.2%
2. Evenk	29901	35377	+18.3%
3. Hant	22283	28773	+29.1%
4. Even	17055	19242	+12.8%
5. Chukchi	15107	15827	+4.8%
6. Nanaitsi	11883	12355	+4%
7. Koryak	8942	9077	+1.5%
8. Mansi	8279	11573	+39.8%
9. Dolgan	6584	7330	+11.3%
10. Nivk	4631	5287	+14.2%
11. Selkup	3564	4367	+22.5%
12. Ulchi	3173	3098	-2.4%
13. Itelmen	2429	3474	+43%
14. Udege	1902	1665	-12.5%
15. Saami	1835	2132	-16.2%
16. Eskimo	1734	1798	+3.7%
17. Chuvantsy	1384	1300	-6.1%
18. Nganasan	1262	879	-30.3%
19. Yukagir	1112	1529	+37.5%
20. Keti	1084	1891	+74.4%
21. Orochi	883	884	+0.1%
22. Tofalar	722	1020	+41.3%
23. Aleut	644	592	-8.1%
24. Negidalts	587	806	+37.3%
25. Ents	198	327	65.1%
26. Orok	179	432	+141.3%

Table 1. Population growth 1989-2002 for 26 indigenous peoples. Source: RAIPON Information Center, Palana, Kamchatka.

the picture in most regions of the Russian Federation is quite the opposite. The president of the Sobolevo region's Association on Kamchatka, Nina Orechova, states that the number of native citizens in this region went down by 127 people in the last few years. Table 2 shows how much higher the mortality rate than the birthrate is for indigenous peoples.

Year	Born		Died		Mortality rate compared to birth rate
	Total	Indigenous persons	Total	Indigenous persons	
2000	34	9	45	12	1.3
2001	19	4	56	11	2.7
2002	22	2	54	11	5.5
6 months of 2003	6	1	28	9	9

Table 2: Mortality rate among indigenous persons in Sobolevo region compared to birthrate. Source: RAIPON Information Center, Palana, Kamchatka.

In the Sobolevo region for example, statistics show that the primary cause of death for the past 3½ years has been alcoholism. Out of nine deaths in the first half of 2003, eight were alcohol related and only one was caused by illness. The indigenous peoples of Sobolevo turned to the Soviet of Peoples' Deputies and the regional administration for financial help in dealing with health issues among indigenous peoples. Considering this example, which is representative of the situation in many regions, the reason for the increase in the number of indigenous people must lie elsewhere.[2]

Why is the number growing?

It may be that more people dare to register as indigenous instead of Russian, as they feel that there is less cultural discrimination today than in the Soviet Union. Another reason could be that there are economic advantages through quotas for indigenous peoples in the education system, as well as for fishing and hunting rights and an earlier retirement age. At the Institute of the Peoples of the North in St. Petersburg the stipend for indigenous students is about 2000 rubles whereas ordinary Russian students get about 400. Still, when asked, some indigenous people say that they registered as Russian in the census out of "old habit". Many people have not forgotten that speaking your own language was considered "illiterate" in the Soviet period. Therefore, we cannot really say how many indigenous people there are in Russia.

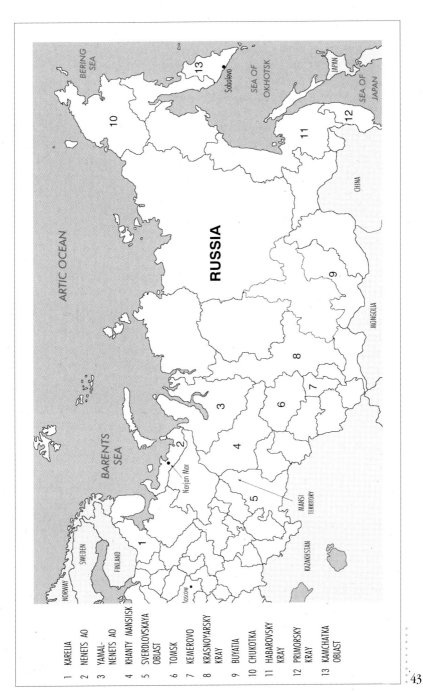

ARTIC OCEAN

RUSSIA

BARENTS SEA

BERING SEA

SEA OF OKHOTSK

SEA OF JAPAN

JAPAN

CHINA

MONGOLIA

KAZAKHSTAN

NORWAY

SWEDEN

FINLAND

Moscow

Naryan Mar

MANSI TERRITORY

Sobolevo

1 KARELIA
2 NENETS AO
3 YAMAL-
   NENETS AO
4 KHANTY MANSIISK
5 SVERDLOVSKAYA
   OBLAST
6 TOMSK
7 KEMEROVO
8 KRASNOYARSKY
   KRAY
9 BUYATIA
10 CHUKOTKA
11 HABAROVSKY
   KRAY
12 PRIMORSKY
   KRAY
13 KAMCHATKA
   OBLAST

43

Do indigenous people always live traditionally?

In spring 2003, long before the results of the census became known, the Russian Association of Indigenous Peoples of the North was challenged by the federal authorities who wanted to revise legislation on indigenous peoples' rights. For some time the Association had been considering a proposal from the authorities to change the legislation so it would cover only people living traditionally, or put in a more popular way, would only cover "those dressed in fur". The Governor of the Kamchatka Oblast summarized the position of the authorities by saying that there would be "no superiority by blood" as long as he was governor. Indigenous persons living in urban areas should be treated like any other citizens. On the other hand, representatives of the federal authorities expressed a wish to treat all people living in regions considered their traditional territories, as indigenous, arguing that indigenous peoples should not have special rights recognized as long as the nationality issue was not completely solved. Ordinary people however – as we can see in the results of the census – still believe that it makes a difference what nationality you have. Some people who would register as Russian in the past now register as indigenous.

As the automatic registration of nationality is being removed from the identification documents (internal passport) of all of the Russian citizens, many people fear that it will be completely impossible to prove your nationality in the future. Some deliberately "lose" the old Soviet passports, i.e. they hide it instead of handing it in for a new passport, to have some kind of official document left with a registration of their nationality. This can sound contradictory, but many people believe it to be important to have the possibility of claiming their rights as indigenous people in the future. In some cases it is even more complicated as some nationalities have now become officially recognized as peoples whereas they existed earlier as nationalities in passports, but were not included in the official statistics with the special rights that would go along with such recognition.

Information centers

While it seems unclear whether the indigenous peoples are about to disappear in reality – or on the contrary, grow in number - the indigenous movement all over Russia is consolidating and being strengthened from within. A young generation is beginning to use modern tools, such as the media, the internet, and international projects. A network of information centres is being expanded as capacity building programs begin to work. From St. Petersburg with its university environment, to Naryan Mar, Tomsk, Kemerovo, Habarovsk, Primorsky Kray, Kamchatka, Chukotka, etc. information on legislation and culture is being distributed, using the Internet, newsletters, and film. There is therefore an ongoing discussion about what being indigenous will mean in the coming years – as the movement seems to attract new people, as languages die out and traditions are being used in new ways, for special occasions, or even looked at as a commercial object (e.g. for tourism development) and not necessarily as a part of everyday life. For some there is a painful conflict in this, others see it as an opportunity for keeping a national identity, traditions and language alive.

Democratic representation?

In 2003 the debate about establishing an indigenous peoples' parliament in Russia was raised again. From a broader perspective this issue was also seen as a question of indigenous peoples' representation in existing democratic bodies. The federal Duma elections in December 2003 made some people hope that the indigenous peoples could be represented in Moscow by the end of the year, but their hopes were not fulfilled. On the contrary, the elections were a setback for pluralism in general, as President Putin's supporters ended up having an overwhelming majority after almost totally dominating the media before the elections. Even Putin himself "regretted" that the centrist parties did not even get represented in the Duma, leaving the Communists as the only opposition. No indigenous representative got elected to the federal Duma.

Some provinces have indigenous representation at a high level. For example, Hanty-Mansiisk and Yamal have specific quotas for indigenous representation in the provincial Dumas. In some areas in Buryatia an obligatory indigenous quota exists at the municipal level, which is seen as ideal by other provinces. It is also recognized that some regions can never have indigenous peoples represented with a special status for the simple reason that they are too few in numbers. Sverdlovskaya Oblast – the neighboring region of the Hanty-Mansiisky Autonomous Okrug - is a good example. Only a few hundred Mansi live in the province, just on the border of Hanty-Mansiisky Autonomous Okrug. How could they ever achieve representation in the local Duma with an indigenous representative?

A land-titling project in the area revealed some of the possibilities and problems in claiming back your traditional lands within the framework of the legislation of a modern state. By defining what families have traditionally inhabited the vast areas of the Siberian forests, referring to historic roots, traditional knowledge and lingustistic traces in the landscape it was possible to produce a set of treaties among the Mansi themselves, defining and dividing their lands. However, different opinions exist about whether to define this land as individual property, belonging to individual families, or to insist on collective rights to traditional lands. A solution could be to form a specific administrative unit covering the Mansi area, called "*rayon*" or "*volost*", comparable to a municipality.

Hunting issues

Such constructions can be found, for instance, in Buryatia (as mentioned) and in Karelia. The Mansi live in an area formerly dominated by enormous prison camps. Today the area is under pressure from poor people from the towns who are poaching to compensate for small salaries. This has meant a decline in the number of game animals. From time to time the local Hunting Inspector even tries to prevent the Mansi from hunting in their traditional areas, using the excuse that they have no right to bear arms. Under Russian law, membership in a hobby hunters' union is compulsory for carrying arms if you are not professionally employed as a hunter. Earlier the Mansi were officially employed by a State enterprise, but after the economic collapse in the Soviet Union they lost their jobs. Now they find themselves in a very difficult situation – relying on hunting for their subsistence life, but falling under the category of poachers, while being threatened by poachers from the cities. There have been attempts to arrest Mansi hunters, but an appeal by the local Association of Indigenous Peoples to the government's human rights representative of the area helped in that particular case, and the charges were dropped because of lack of evidence. The situation is therefore very complicated for the hunters. They are not sure what recognition they should aim to get with respect to land rights if they cannot get collective rights and be recognized as traditional hunters. In Habarovsky Kray, the Association proposes a change and an addition to the law "On the Animal Kingdom" to make long term licensing to individual representatives of the indigenous people possible. This solution would mean acceptance of state ownership to the land and would for some people in other parts of Russia seem too compromising.

Kranoyarsk

In Krasnoyarsky Kray the indigenous peoples of the small community of Sovrechka were ridiculed in the local press. The typical stereotypes were used about indigenous people sitting and waiting for support to continue living in a "hopeless" area. The local association of the indigenous peoples responded by visiting the areas and describing the situation from another angle. A long article in *Krasnoyarskaya Gazeta*[3] described how the people in Sovrechka are in the way of the big oil companies, which do not want witnesses or "victims" in the area. In Sovrechka there is still a small privately owned reindeer herd and clean lakes full of fish. The wild reindeer in the area are being shot by outsiders arriving by helicopter and snow scooter. People fear that the lakes and rivers will be emptied or polluted in the near future. The local people have experienced how an explosion at an oil field left the pipeline burning from autumn to spring last year with hundred metre high flames. The effects are believed to have caused psychological as well as physical health problems, but officially the statistics show only well-known causes for death and illness, e.g. cancer or infection diseases. In the article it is stated, however, that the biggest fear is now coming from the temptation of local people to sell off the land to the oil barons – after a possible future recognition of land claims.

Kemerovo

If people in Sverdlovskaya Oblast and Krasnoyarsky Kray are only witnessing the beginning of a new era, the Teleut of Kemerovo have already lost most of their traditional lands to coal mining. Words cannot describe the sadness of the enormous open pit coal areas where former grazing land for horses has been turned into dead black valleys full of dust and smog. Even though a part of the area belongs to a Teleut enterprise, the piles of waste from the coal mines are growing and taking up more and more of the land. Former grazing land is being turned into a swamp because of waste water seeping from the cliffs. Four small Teleut villages lie in the area. In 2003 the newly formed project organisation "Nabat" carried out a film project on their history and present situation, told in their own language. Some people in the area think that the time has come to sue the coal mining company for destroying the land, others think it better to try to find a compromise and get social and cultural support through compensation for the land loss. The situation has been discussed at conferences with scientists and even representatives of the authorities as mediators. In November 2003 it became the main theme at a conference devoted to the creation of a "regional nationality policy" at the Kemerovo University where plans to rehabilitate some of the coal mines were discussed with two purposes: (1) the restoration of land as a goal in itself and (2) the creation of jobs through such a project, which would be a positive side-effect that would benefit even the indigenous people. It might be a more realistic way to preserve at least part of the land rather than fighting for the rights to land, and also more interesting for the industry. A small people with a couple of thousand members would not stand a chance and might not be sufficiently united internally to take up the fight. ❏

Notes

1 The figures came from the Administration of the Russian President whereas the 2002 census was carried out by a number of official bodies.
2 RAIPON Information Center, Lach, Palana, Kamchatka. Electronic newsletter in English, December 2003.
3 Anatoly Buylov, *Krasnoyarskaya Gazeta*, 31 October, 2004.

ALASKA - U.S.A.

Nineteen percent of the people of Alaska are indigenous. This includes the major groups of Inupiat, Yupiat, Sugpiat/Alutiiq, Aleut/Unangan, Athabascan, Tlingit, Haida and Tsimshian. While the indigenous peoples of Alaska have made gains both economically and politically over the past three decades, new threats continue to emerge that keep them ever vigilant.

Alaska Natives have a special government-to-government relationship with the United States through their tribal governments. It is through this relationship that the U.S. government is obliged to deliver certain social and health services to the indigenous people. Federal legislation from the 1970s requires that the federal government provide the funding for indigenous tribes and organizations to provide these services themselves. The U.S. government itself decides which tribes are eligible for services through a designation called "federal recognition". Alaska currently has 231 federally recognized tribes.

Balancing economic and cultural development

Alaska's indigenous peoples continue to struggle to balance cultural values and traditional subsistence practices with opportunities for economic development. The political stalemate over exploration and development of the Arctic National Wildlife Refuge (ANWR) continues, with the U.S. Congress sharply divided on the issue. The state of Alaska, U.S. federal government, and a majority of Inupiat people of Alaska's North Slope support such development, while most Gwich'in Athabascan people in north-east Alaska and Canada, supported by conservationists, strongly oppose it. Proposals to open the refuge up to exploration recently failed in Congress by the narrowest of margins.

The Arctic National Wildlife Refuge is the only complete Arctic eco-system and undisturbed wilderness area in the world protected by law. The refuge is a land mass encompassing an area from the continental divide, separating the watersheds draining north and west into the Arctic Ocean from those draining west and south into the Bering Sea, to the Arctic Ocean and is home to more than 160 species of birds and 38 species of mammals, including musk ox, Dall sheep, grizzly and polar bear, beaver, lynx, porcupine and the famous Porcupine caribou herd. The refuge has remained undisturbed for thousands of years with little impact from the Gwich'in and Inupiat subsistence hunters. Those subsistence hunters today believe that oil development will threaten their way of life.

A national controversy surrounding the opening up of the refuge took place last year when a photo exhibition of the refuge by award-winning photographer and conservationist Subhanker Banerjee was scheduled to open at the Smithsonian Institution. Apparently because of political pressure, the exhibition was moved from its prime location to a basement hallway, causing an outcry from those opposed to the opening up of the refuge to oil development. Banerjee toured the refuge for his photography with Inupiaq guide and subsistence hunter Robert Thompson of Kaktovik. The result was a book, *Arctic National Wildlife Refuge: Seasons of Life and Land*, which became the center of national controversy when a member of Congress held up the book during a congressional session as evidence that the refuge should remain closed to oil development.

Those opposing oil development in the refuge would like to see low-impact development. Thompson, who has led a crusade to educate the public about the refuge said, "Sustainable development with recreational aspects such as eco-tourism, wildlife viewing, and backpacking should be encouraged, all that have low impacts and sustained the spirit of the land since time immemorial."

Less well-known but perhaps more pressing are issues of oil and gas development west of the refuge in the National Petroleum Reserve-A, known as NPR-A. The federal government is moving quickly to open up this vast area to leasing, creating opportunities for indigenous for-profit corporations and industry while also raising concerns about the growing cumulative impact on subsistence and other cultural values and practices. Unlike developments near Prudhoe Bay and Kuparak - location of the largest known North Slope fields - leasing in NPR-A could lead to development on the doorstep of villages such as Nuiqsut, Atqasuk and Wainwright. This could benefit the powerful Native-owned Arctic Slope Regional Corporation (ASRC), which owns significant surface and sub-surface rights and provides extensive oilfield services to industry. The Inupiat-controlled North Slope Borough could also benefit from tax revenues related to development.

The challenge for NPR-A development is how to balance potential economic benefits with the impact from oilfield infrastructure. As North Slope Borough Mayor George Ahmaogak, Sr. observes, "When development was contained in the Prudhoe Bay area, we didn't feel the disturbance. Now that some of us can see it from our homes, we

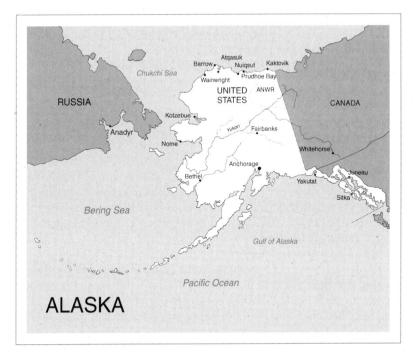

ALASKA

are reaching a threshold of awareness with potentially serious effects. [The federal government is] ignoring questions of social and cultural stresses on our people."[1]

A major new report by the National Research Council, *Cumulative Environmental Effects of Oil and Gas Activities on Alaska's North Slope* (2003), highlights the major effects of such development, including interference with subsistence, disruption of cultural values, environmental damage, roads, effects on animal populations, oil spills and abandoned infrastructure. It also demonstrates how the rising standard of living in North Slope communities depends on continuing income related to oil and gas activity.

The challenges of balancing development in NPR-A reveal the trade-offs involved for Arctic indigenous peoples in partnering with multinationals and distant governments in large-scale economic development. The National Research Council believes that trade-offs are inevitable. Benefits include jobs, tax revenues and a rising standard of living. Costs can include significant cumulative environmental, social and cultural impacts. The Gwich'in and a few North Slope Inupiat argue for a different form of sustainable development - more limited oil and gas activity combined with the expansion of eco-tourism and other recreational pursuits. This debate will only grow as indigenous for-profit corporations in Alaska seek to invest in a new gas line from the North Slope to southern markets. Key questions in this debate continue to be: who gets to decide which trade-offs are worth making, and how can indigenous peoples best protect their long-term interests?

Tribal funding threatened

Alaska's senior senator and chairman of the powerful U.S. Senate Appropriations Committee, Ted Stevens, has taken aim at funding for tribal governments, claiming that it is too expensive and inefficient to provide funding for all 231 federally recognized tribes. He has suggested that program funding go only to the regional Native non-profit corporations and not directly to the tribes in order to reduce administrative costs. Senator Stevens diverted funding for tribal law enforcement to the state of Alaska but changed it back to the tribes after much public outcry. Stevens has also said that he does not believe that Alaska tribes have the same jurisdictional authority as tribes in the "Lower 48" states.

Expressing his views in an interview on Alaska Public Radio, Stevens said,

> *The road they're on is the road to destruction of statehood because the Native population is increasing at a much greater rate than the non-Native population. I don't know if you realize that. And they want to have total jurisdiction over anything that happens in a village without regard to state law and without regard to federal law.*

Stevens has used his considerable influence in the U.S. Senate to fund millions of dollars of projects in rural Alaska. At issue is whether indigenous tribes should control the funding, making their own decisions about what is best for them and their communities.

20 years of higher education
for Alaska's indigenous students

The Rural Development Program of the University of Alaska Fairbanks celebrates its 20th anniversary in 2004. Housed in the Department of Alaska Native and Rural Development of the College of Rural

Alaska, the program offers both BA and MA degrees in Rural Development. There have been over 130 BA graduates since 1986. A postgraduate program that began in 2000 has seen seven graduates. Over 90% of the BA graduates and 100% of the MA graduates have been indigenous students. The program has allowed indigenous students to pursue their degrees, while living and working in their home villages throughout Alaska.

Most graduates are employed in positions throughout the state and, perhaps most importantly, in their own home villages in non-profit regional organizations, regional corporations, in management positions in their villages, tribal councils, with educational institutions etc. Alaska Native traditional knowledge is at the forefront of the program with Alaska Native Elders giving lectures, passing on knowledge and humor in classes and seminars similar to the way they were taught by their ancestors.

A majority of the students are active leaders in their indigenous communities, holding positions on boards of directors and tribal councils, local committees and key jobs. Most are also raising families while making valuable contributions to their communities. In some instances there are two generations who have completed RD degrees, being the first and second generation in their families to graduate from college. Student travel seminars in such places as the United Nations in Geneva and New York City, Indian Pueblos in New Mexico, and indigenous communities throughout Alaska have enabled students to broaden their view of the world and help understand how Alaska Natives fit into the global economy.

Twenty years ago, many villages in rural Alaska were only just being hooked up to telephone communications. While the telephone is still the main method of class delivery, new technology is making Internet-based classes a reality. As our ancestors traveled great distances in search of knowledge and food, today's generation combines their traditional knowledge with modern technology and western education, balancing tradition and academia to continue sustainability for future generations.

In memory of Peter John

Peter John, traditional Chief of all Interior Alaska Athabascans, was born on October 15, 1900 near Hess Creek in Interior Alaska. In the 1960s, he was a strong advocate of native land claims and was outspoken on issues of education, sobriety, leadership and integrity. As

Chief of Chiefs, Peter John's insights and contributions extended beyond his Athabaskan cultural experience to include the broader human realm of interaction between cultural systems. He was a leader whose cumulative wisdom, insights, integrity and lifestyle exemplify the values and beliefs with which the Athabaskan society as a whole identifies. His passing on August 8, 2003, at the age of 102, witnessed the loss of a most exceptional individual, one who was able to see beyond his own cultural upbringing and come to understand the human condition at a level that transcends conventional wisdom. For many of us, Chief Peter John seems to be our past, but is also our future. ❑

Note

1   *Anchorage Daily News*, 30.9.03, p. B3.

ARCTIC CANADA

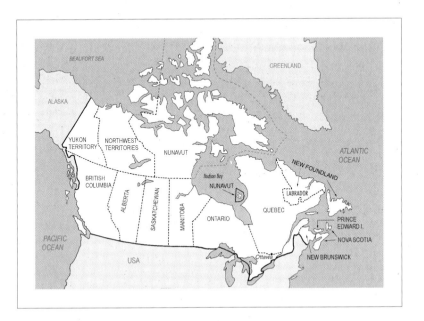

YUKON

T he Yukon Territory is located in Canada's extreme north-west region, bordering Alaska. Yukon First Nations represent a total of 10,000 members or about one-third of the Yukon Territory's population. There are fourteen separate Yukon First Nation governments. Their traditional territories encompass all lands within the Yukon Territory and spill over into the neighbouring jurisdiction of northern British Columbia and the Northwest Territories.

Today, eleven of the fourteen First Nation governments belong to the Council of Yukon First Nations (CYFN) the central political organization for Yukon First Nation governments. At international level, the Arctic Athabaskan Council represents CYFN, the Kaska Nation and the Dene Nation of the Northwest Territories in international environmental negotiations. The Arctic Athabaskan Council (AAC) has itself elected to be part of the Arctic Region group within the United Nations Permanent Forum.

10 years after signing the 1993 Umbrella Final Agreement

Under the terms of the *1993 Council for Yukon Indians Umbrella Final Agreement (UFA)*, Yukon First Nations hold surface title to 41,439 square kilometres of land or 8.6 per cent of all lands in the Yukon Territory. They exercise self-government powers over approximately one-third of these lands (including surface and sub-surface title). The remaining lands are cooperatively managed with the federal and territorial governments through a series of joint management agreements covering a broad range of subjects ranging from water management to heritage resources.

In 1968, Yukon Indians organized their first meeting to prepare their Statement of Claim to Canada for unsurrendered lands. In 1973, their claim was accepted for negotiation and in 1975 they formed the Council for Yukon Indians (CYI) to represent their collective interests in these negotiations. In 1993, the Governments of Canada and Yukon and CYI signed the *Council for Yukon Indians Umbrella Final Agreement.*

The 1993 UFA set a number of Canadian land claim precedents: it is the first framework for a land claim agreement in Canada not to require a blanket extinguishment of Aboriginal rights; the first to be concluded in a provincial or territorial jurisdiction where indigenous peoples do not constitute a majority of the resident population; the first to include provisions to completely replace federal Indian Act legislation in a territorial or provincial jurisdiction; and the first to empower First Nations to create and amend their own constitutions, define their own membership and establish self-governing First Nation governments exercising a broad range of municipal, territorial and federal government powers.

Self-government agreements

By the end of 2003, eight of the fourteen Yukon First Nation governments had concluded and were implementing Final and Self-Government Agreements negotiated under the 1993 UFA. Another four First Nations had finished negotiations and were preparing to ratify their negotiated agreements. Two First Nations, represented by the Kaska Nation as an umbrella organisation, are suing the federal government after negotiations reached an impasse. Despite this, the Yukon stands apart as the only region in Canada to fully embrace self-government and enter into a post federal *Indian Act*, post-colonial, 21st century partnership with the Canadian nation-state. CYFN continues to negotiate with Canada to provide the same constitutional status for self-government agreements that they have already obtained for their First Nation final land claim agreements.

Implementation of self-government

In 2003, the Council of Yukon First Nations and nine self-governing First Nations entered into discussions with Canada to begin a comprehensive ten-year review of the implementation of the first four Yukon First Nation land claim and self-government agreements. They also met twice with their federal and territorial government counterparts in a new, high-level political forum - the Intergovernmental Forum. The Governments of Canada (represented by the Minister of Indian Affairs) and the Yukon (represented by the Yukon Premier) meet twice yearly with the First Nation leadership to resolve outstanding issues. In 2003, these priority issues included education, economic development and fiscal relations.

In 2003, the eight self-governing Yukon First Nations continued to negotiate for the transfer of new federal programs to their jurisdictions under the Program and Service Transfer Agreement process. Negotiations were also underway to conclude new First Nation-Federal tax-sharing agreements with the Government of Canada. In 2000, Yukon First Nations formed the Yukon Indian Development Corporation (YIDC), representing 17 First Nations in the Yukon and northern British Columbia. The corporation operates at arms length from Yukon First Nation governments. In 2003, YIDC examined various development opportunities related to proposed natural gas pipeline and railway construction projects.

In early 2004, the Council of Yukon First Nations (CYFN) initiated a constitutional review process. The review includes provision for the creation of a constituent assembly to review ways and means of bringing Kaska Nation and Kwanlin Dun First Nations back into the central political body and to determine what self-governing powers and program service delivery should be delegated to the central political level. Kwanlin Dun First Nation, together with the Ross River Dene Council and Liard First Nation, function as independent First Nation organisations outside CYFN's regional representative body.❑

Sources

http://www.cyfn.ca/ourNations/index.html
http://www.cyfn.ca/
http://www.arcticathabaskancouncil.com

NORTHWEST TERRITORIES

T he indigenous peoples of the NWT include the Dene, the Inuvialuit and the Metis. The NWT is known by the Dene as *Denendeh*, and the high Arctic coastline and islands (Banks, Victoria, Melville, Prince Patrick, etc.) are known as the Inuvialuit settlement region. Denendeh, the land of the people, comprises the lands of 29 Dene communities in five regions: Gwich'in, Sahtu, Deh Cho, Tlicho and Akaitcho, totalling 21,000 Dene. The Inuvialuit Settlement Area comprises 6 communities of some 3,000 Inuvialuit. The Metis live throughout all the regions. This year we celebrated the accomplishments of each of the Aboriginal governments, as well as noting the challenges and opportunities ahead.

Following the signing of the Treaty of the Arctic Athabaskan Council (AAC - one of six Permanent Participants to the Arctic Council) in 2000, the Dene are now more circumpolar in perspective. AAC joins the Inuit, who are represented by the Inuit Circumpolar Conference, and the Gwich'in, who are members of the Dene Nation and represented internationally by Gwich'in Council International.

Gwich'in and Inuvialuit

The four Gwich'in communities, represented by the Gwich'in Tribal Council, which signed a "modern" land claim more than 10 years ago (1992), continue to negotiate an agreement-in-principle (AIP) for self-government. The AIP (initialled in 2003) is being implemented in collaboration with their Inuvialuit neighbours, represented by the Inuvialuit Regional Corporation. In the communities of Inuvik and Aklavik, Gwich'in and Inuvialuit share authority and responsible government. In 2003-2004, incredible development activity went ahead, particularly in the oil and gas fields of the Beaufort Sea. The Aboriginal Pipeline Group (a regional Aboriginal pipeline consortium), the Producers Group (Imperial Oil and others) and others are poised to enter into the environmental assessment process. This process precedes licensing and development of a gas pipeline down the *Dehcho* (Mackenzie River) valley.

Sahtu

The five Sahtu communities, signatories to the land claims agreement (1994), continue to prosper and grow. Recent oil and gas exploration has returned to deposits near Colville Lake, bringing with it development pressures. This remote fly-in community is yet to follow the boom and bust experienced in the 1940s in Norman Wells. In Deline, the community continues to recover from the lasting environmental/ social impacts of contamination by the Port Radium uranium mine, as well as other mines in and around *Sahtu* (Great Bear Lake). The Sahtu Dene are at a crossroads and one notable response, since the land claim has been community self-government agreements. To date, Deline has signed an agreement-in-principle (August 2003).

Deh Cho

Further up the Dehcho (Mackenzie River), the eleven Deh Cho First Nations, signatories to Treaty 11 (1922), are working to implement their Treaty. This work, known as the Deh Cho Process, has led to the establishment of a land-use planning board and the withdrawal of significant watersheds from development. Land-use planning is based on traditional use and ecological principles, creating the necessary buffer for sensitive areas from the irreparable damage of unfettered development. The Dene are striving for truly sustainable development - limiting economic development in line with the projected and matched growth needs of their communities. This is a rejection of past "staples traps",[1] with floods of southern labour following mega-project development, and alienation and displacement of Dene. The Deh Cho are faced with intense development pressure from a potential pipeline, as well as oil and gas developments near Fort Liard and the Cameron Hills (near the Alberta and British Columbia borders).

Tlicho

On the other side of the *Dehcho*, past the protected Horne Plateau, the Tlicho celebrated the signing of a land and self-government agreement (August 2003). The *Tlicho Agreement* establishes the rights and responsibilities of the four Tlicho communities within the context of responsible democratic government. The agreement gives the Tlicho the right to tax and deliver services to their membership. The Tlicho government (formerly Dogrib Treaty 11) participated in an environmental assessment of the DeBeers (Snap Lake) diamond mine. This is the third diamond mine after Diavik (Rio Tinto) and Ekati (BHP Billiton), which are both fully operating mines. The prosperity of diamond development and the signing of *Impact Benefit Agreements* (IBAs) mitigate some of the loss of traditional lands and resources. The Tlicho and some of the Akaitcho communities have signed IBAs with BHP Billiton and Rio Tinto, and we anticipate a similar agreement with DeBeers. The environmental impacts (social and biological) of the mines in the North Slave Geological Province are being monitored by the Independent Environmental Monitoring Agency (Ekati) and the Environmental Monitoring Agency Board (Diavik).

Akaitcho

Akaitcho Treaty 8 Council is made up of six Dene communities. Akaitcho is a diverse land of Chipewayan, Tlicho, South Slavey and Cree speakers. Metis also live in many of the South Slave communities. Intense development pressures, as in other parts of Denendeh, are being mediated by Akaitcho Territory Governments. For example, the Talston hydro-electric dam, built in 1948, is intended to supply power to the DeBeers Snap Lake mine. There are advantages to communities in that they will no longer have to rely on diesel generators but the potential for additional mercury leached into watersheds due to hydro-development may be a bone of contention for Lutsel'Ke, a community on the south-east arm of *Tutcho* (Great Slave Lake). The recognition by the federal government of Rocher River as a Band, both as a signatory to Treaty 8 and as a community in its own right, is gaining momentum under the leadership of the Dene National Chief. Rocher River people were dispersed into Deninu Kue, Lutsel'Ke, Dettah and Ndilo and, while they were signatories to Treaty 8 (1899), they did not coalesce into a sedentary community.

Band status has enabled the Dene to develop community infrastructure, it provides a framework and financing from the Department of Indian and Northern Affairs Canada (INAC) through the fiduciary responsibility and authority of the *Indian Act*. Last year, this piece of Canadian legislation was to be replaced by an array of reforms (C-7, the First National Governance Act) under the leadership of Robert Nault, INAC Minister. Nault's "self-government" reforms have mostly been dropped by the new Prime Minister, Paul Martin, who replaced Nault (who has since announced his retirement from politics) with Andy Mitchell as new INAC Minister. While political, administrative and financial reforms are essential to the Dene, and to all Aboriginal peoples in Canada, the sustainable use of human and natural resources is at the forefront of Self-Government negotiations (Agreements).

Coping with development impacts

The loss of fisheries and changes in caribou migration patterns are a warning of the unsustainable impacts of industrial development. Elders are increasingly talking about the many impacts of poorly managed human activities in Denendeh. The Dene sentiment for better management of human development recently came to the fore during public meetings of the MacKenzie Valley Environmental Impact Review Board (constituted by federal government legislation, the *MacKenzie Valley Act* mandates the Board to oversee development). Exploration in Wool and Drybones Bay shows deposits of diamondiferous kimberlite, 40 kilometers south of the City of Yellowknife. An environmental assessment of exploration has for the first time been carried out in the NWT. In the past, exploration and staking enabled by outdated mining legislation, undermined land and self-government agreements. Akaitcho is in the process of establishing an *Interim Measures Agreement* with INAC, establishing their own land-use planning board to oversee and regulate development.

A new Dene National Chief

During the summer, the Assembly of First Nations held a general election for the national Grand Chief. The incumbent, Grand Chief Mathew Coon-come had lost favour and political support and faced stiff competition from Roberta Jamieson and former AFN Grand Chief Phil Fontaine. Fontaine was re-elected Grand Chief at the AGM in Edmonton, Alberta. As the AFN Chiefs struggled with the question of electing a woman to the position, Dene Chiefs had no such qualms. In Aklavik, Denendeh, the gathered chiefs and the delegates of the 33rd Dene National Assembly elected the first woman National Chief, Noeline Villebrun. ❏

Note and sources

1   The expression "staples traps" was first used by Harold Innis, a Canadian economic historian, who noted that Canada's underdevelopment was a result of the export of raw, unprocessed resources, e.g. furs, timber, minerals, fish, etc.

The Dene Nation: www.denenation.com
The Assembly of First Nations: www.afn.ca
The Arctic Athabaskan Council: www.arcticathabaskancouncil.com

NUNAVUT

The last year in the life of Nunavut's first Legislative Assembly saw the government achieve one of its major goals, the passage of a new Wildlife Act. The first legislation to define Inuit cultural values within its text, the Act brought the rules governing the harvesting and management of wildlife into line with the 1993 land claim, which had resulted in the creation of the territory. Hunter and trapper organizations from Nunavut's one city and 24 hamlets gave their blessing to the legislation at a three-day workshop before the Act went before the legislature for final passage. The government also brought in a tough Tobacco Control Act, which it hoped would lower the territory's very high rates of smoking – especially among young people.

However, the achievement of a minor goal of the territory's young government sparked a controversy, which came to dominate Nunavut politics by the end of the year.

A cultural war?

Over the course of the year, some "regular members" of the legislature (i.e. those not in the Cabinet) became increasingly strident in their criticism of the government's performance. This criticism was frequently expressed in terms of the government – and sometimes the Cabinet Ministers themselves – not being "Inuit enough", despite the government's stated commitment to include *Inuit Qaujimajatuqangit* (Inuit knowledge and values, often referred to as IQ) in the operation of the government. A complicating factor was that several of the "regular members" of the legislature who were most critical of the government were also fundamentalist Christians, who sometimes equated IQ with their particular brand of Christianity. As a local newspaper editor observed, "It's a real culture war that's going on, and a real sort of a battle over what the Inuit identity consists of and what should the role of the Nunavut government be in asserting that identity".

Human Rights Act debates

By 2004 Nunavut had become the only jurisdiction at the provincial/territorial level, which had not passed a Human Rights Act. While federal human rights legislation prevails across the country, the 10 provinces and territories were expected to enact their own legislation affirming their governments' commitment to equal treatment under the law.

Controversy erupted over the fact that, like all similar legislation in Canada, Nunavut's proposed Human Rights Act would prohibit discrimination not just on the basis of ethnicity, gender and age but also on the basis of sexual orientation. This was too much for the fundamentalist politicians, who argued that homosexuality was foreign to Inuit culture and that prohibiting discrimination against homosexuals was an unwarranted imposition on a legislature that is supposed to be able to pass legislation that reflects its own values. The Minister of Education, Manitok Thompson, went so far as equate homosexuality with pedophilia – a statement both inaccurate and inflammatory, especially in a territory still suffering from the legacy of a number of pedophile priests and teachers.

After a tense debate in the Legislative Assembly the government's Human Rights Act passed into law by a narrow margin of 10 to 8, but as this occurred just prior to Nunavut's second election the question spilled over into the campaign.

Several prominent politicians chose not to seek re-election, including Jack Anawak (who accepted a patronage appointment from the federal government) and Manitok Thompson (who chose to run for office at the federal level). A strong challenge to the leadership of incumbent Premier Paul Okalik came from veteran Inuit politician Tagak Curley, who founded the Inuit Tapirisat of Canada in the early 1970s and led the early efforts to create Nunavut. Curley, a prominent figure in the territory's evangelical movement, pledged to re-open the debate over the Human Rights Act if elected.

Observers noted that any attempt to remove the Act's protection for gays and lesbians would be pointless, because the courts have deemed homosexuality a prohibited ground for discrimination under the federal Charter of Rights and Freedoms. In addition, many Nunavummiut asked why a political system trying to address a weak economy, high unemployment, overcrowded housing, poor health conditions, low levels of formal education and an increasingly bleak fiscal future was spending so much time debating whether or not to deny legal protection to a tiny subset of the territory's population. "But if you believe in your Creator, in your God, what does he say about [homosexuality]?" Curley said. "Is that acceptable to God?" Curley was also critical of the government's performance in economic and social matters.

While most Nunavummiut are relatively mainstream Anglicans and Roman Catholics, evangelical Christianity has been growing in popularity in recent years. The movement takes the Bible literally and believes that God speaks to them in signs and visitations. It is also millennial in character, believing that the prophesies about the end of the world contained in the Book of Revelations are about to come to pass, and has a fixation with the State of Israel. "We are organizing," an Inuit pastor told a newspaper. "The creation of Nunavut is our opportunity to demonstrate the true calling of who God called us to be. The signs are indicating that we need to prepare ourselves for the Second Coming."

Elections

The election held in February 2004 was something of anti-climax. Premier Okalik and all the members of the outgoing Cabinet who sought re-election were returned by the voters, while many of the "regular members" who had criticized them lost their seats. When the 19 members of second legislature met for the first time Okalik defeated Curley for the premiership, and Curley chose to sit as a "regular member" rather than serve in the Cabinet under Okalik. A number of other evangelicals were elected, but none of them ended up in Cabinet. Only two women were elected to the legislature, but both ended up with powerful positions in Cabinet – one as Deputy Premier and Minister of Health and the other as Minister of Finance. Overall, the second legislature appears to be a stronger and more thoughtful group than their predecessors. The Cabinet contains a number of men and women respected for their commitment to making Nunavut a better place to live, and the "regular members" include some sharp minds quite capable of asking tough questions of the government. Given the fiscal and other challenges facing Nunavut's second government, the next few years should be lively ones.

Suicide

While all of these events were taking place, a record number of Nunavummiut chose to take their own lives. Some 37 suicides were recorded in 2003, an increase of more than 50% over the previous year. By far the highest suicide rates were among Inuit men between 15 and 19 years of age (40 times the national rate for their peers) and between

20 and 24 years of age (25 times the national rate for their peers). The Legislative Assembly created a task force of community residents, which consulted widely and produced a series of recommendations. In response, the government helped launch a broadly based Nunavut Suicide Prevention Council, whose Inuktitut name *Isaksimagit Inuusirmi* means "Open your arms to life". ❑

NUNAVIK

2003 was the 25th anniversary of the Makivik Corporation, the Inuit birthright corporation created pursuant to the signing of the James Bay and Northern Québec Agreement. It represents the 9,800 Inuit of Nunavik, most of whom live in the 15 communities of Arctic Québec. In addition to being a significant political force, Makivik owns the regional airlines First Air and Air Inuit, a "country food" company, a fuel services company, and a stake in companies involved in fishing, maritime shipping, and other sectors. Pita Aatami was easily re-elected President in March, garnering 64 per cent of the vote in a three-way race.

On June 26, 2003 Makivik signed a framework agreement with the new Liberal government of the province of Québec, establishing

> *a formal process for arriving at a final agreement dealing with the merging of the main institutions of Nunavik into a single entity [...] and a new funding regime adapted to the merged organizations. Once the Kativik Regional Government, the Kativik School Board, the Nunavik Health and Social Services Regional Board and the Katujjinik Regional Development Council have been merged into one unified entity [...] negotiations [will begin] for a supplementary agreement for the creation of a new form of government in Nunavik.*

I.e. a more powerful and autonomous Nunavik government would be created by amalgamating all of the existing bodies into one larger one. Not all of the other organizations are comfortable with the way this process is proceeding. The Kativik School Board (KSB) went so far as to file a court challenge, asking for an injunction that would put negotiations on hold until its standing in the new order is clarified.

The KSB, which is elected by the Inuit of Nunavik, issued a press release stating that it *"disagrees profoundly"* with Makiviks' approach, *"in which signed agreements were cast aside and dissenting voices were not heard."* Makivik contends that it has the right to negotiate on behalf of all of the organizations. The judge hearing the case agreed with Makivik, and dismissed the school board's motion.

In other news, Inuit and Cree negotiators finalized an offshore agreement, signing a document covering wildlife management and resource use in the region's shared waters and islands.   ❑

Sources

Websites: www.makivik.org ; www.kativik.qc.ca ; www.krg.ca .

NUNATSIAVUT

The 5,300 member Labrador Inuit Association (LIA) and the federal and provincial governments initialled a comprehensive land claim agreement at the end of August 2003 - almost 20 years after the bargaining process began.

Key elements of the LIA land claim include:

- The establishment of a 72,500 km^2 Inuit settlement area known as Nunatsiavut ("Our beautiful land");
- The creation of an Inuit self-governing regional authority to be called the Nunatsiavut Government, and five Inuit Community Governments (in the communities of Hopedale, Makkovik, Nain, Postville and Rigolet);
- A $140 million cash transfer from the federal government to the LIA;
- A further $156 million federal transfer for implementation of the agreement;
- Inuit-owned lands totalling 15,800 square kilometres;
- Creation of the 9,600 km^2 Torngat Mountain National Park Reserve in northernmost Labrador;
- Greater Inuit economic benefits within a 44,000 km^2 zone of coastal waters; and

- A resource-sharing arrangement that gives Inuit a 25 per cent share in revenue from mining operations on Inuit-owned lands and a five per cent share in revenue from Voisey's Bay.

The LIA land claim differs significantly from the land claims signed by the Inuvialuit and the Inuit of Nunavik and Nunavut in that it provides for a form of explicit Inuit self-government. The Labrador Inuit Constitution - approved in 2002 to articulate the distinctiveness of Labrador Inuit and the need to preserve Inuit lands, language, culture and social structure - provides for the two levels of government (the Nunatsiavut Government at the regional level and five Inuit Community Governments) that will be implemented as a result of the agreement.

The Nunatsiavut Government will legislate for Inuit residents in matters such as education, health, child and family services, and income support. It will also have jurisdiction over its internal affairs, Inuit language and culture, the management of Inuit rights and benefits under the land claim, and may establish a justice system for the administration of Inuit laws. The community of Hopedale will be the legislative capital, while the administrative capital will be Nain.

A President of the Nunatsiavut Government and Members of the Nunatsiavut Assembly will be elected for four-year terms. As many Labrador Inuit live outside the settlement area, Assembly members will be elected to represent seven constituencies: the five communities in the settlement area, the Upper Lake Melville area (Happy Valley-Goose Bay and vicinity) and the rest of Canada. The President will chair both an Executive Council and the Assembly, which will have no fewer than 16 members. The President will appoint a First Minister from among the Members of the Assembly, and the First Minister will then appoint other Members of the Assembly to the Executive Council. Inuit Community Governments will replace the existing municipal governments, and may enact by-laws with regard to local or municipal matters. Inuit and non-Inuit residents will be able to vote for and serve as councillors in the Inuit Community Governments. Each Inuit Community Government will be headed by an elected official called *AngajukKâk*. The *AngajukKâk* will be equivalent to a Mayor, and must be an Inuk.[1]

The Canadian Charter of Rights and Freedoms applies to these Inuit governments and to matters under their authority, and federal and provincial laws will continue to apply to Labrador Inuit. Labrador Inuit will continue to be eligible to receive federal and provincial programs and services.

The Labrador Inuit ratification vote will be held at an as yet unspecified date in early 2004. Ratification requires approval by 50% plus one of the eligible Labrador Inuit voters and votes in both the Newfoundland and Labrador House of Assembly and the national Parliament before the land claim agreement can become law. If this happens, then all four Inuit regions of Canada will have settled their land claims.

The Inuit of Labrador never entered into a treaty with the British Crown, Canada or the province of Newfoundland and Labrador. LIA co-chief negotiator, Toby Andersen, who spent 17 years at the negotiating table with his provincial and federal counterparts, told the media that there were many times during negotiations that the push for greater Inuit control of their ancestral territory was like "banging your head against a brick wall. The ups and downs — you don't even want to hear about them. We've turned old and grey long before our time through this process". ❏

Note and sources

1 Inuk is the singular of Inuit. (Ed. note)

Web sites: www.nunatsiavut.com
www.labradorinuitratification.com

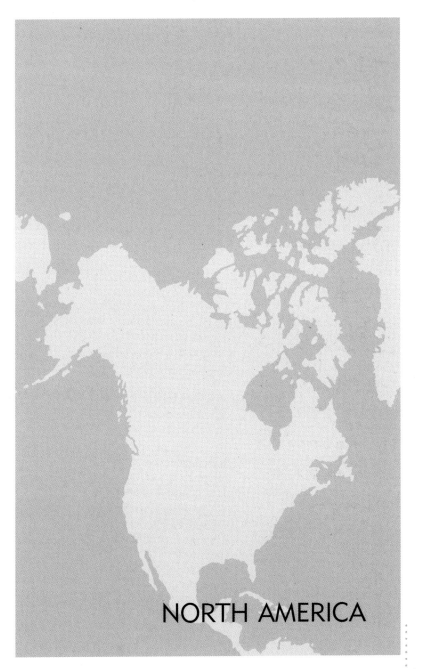

NORTH AMERICA

CANADA

First Nations Governance Act

The proposed *First Nations Governance Act* (FNGA), a proposal to modernize the colonial *Indian Act*, dominated dialogue between Canada's First Nations and the Liberal government of Jean Chrétien in 2003.[1]

The Indian Act of 1876 gave the federal government sweeping powers over the lives of First Nations people living on reserves, altered traditional systems of governance, and banned elements of traditional culture such as potlatch and some forms of dancing. The goal, baldly stated by the Superintendent of Indian Affairs in 1920, was "to continue until there was not a single Indian in Canada that has not been absorbed into the body politic and there is no Indian question and no Indian Department."

The Indian Act gave Aboriginal people the option of "enfranchisement" - trading their Indian status for full citizenship, such as voting rights. When few First Nations people opted for "enfranchisement" the government responded with more coercive measures, for example unilaterally "enfranchising" Indians who moved away from their reserves, joined the military, obtained higher education or, in the case of women, married a non-Indian.

The same goal - assimilation - was behind the Trudeau government's 1969 White Paper that called for the repeal of the Act and the elimination of special status for Aboriginal peoples. The proposal generated a groundswell of native outrage across the country. This Aboriginal militancy received unprecedented public support, and the anti-government backlash resulted in the White Paper being withdrawn - one of the great recent Aboriginal victories in Canada.

The Indian Act has been eroding under relentless legal challenges - a process that has been very costly to the federal government. This was one of the key reasons why the government set out to modernize it - not to create a legal regime that "works" for the First Nations, but rather to replace the existing outdated legislation with something that would be "bullet-proof" in the courts.

Indian Affairs Minister Robert Nault promised that the FNGA would be developed as a result of "input gathered from one of the most extensive consultations ever undertaken with First Nations people." Instead, the government failed to involve First Nations leaders in the process. In a manner, which surprised even the most cynical observers, Nault launched a sham consultative process. Less than 1% of First Nations people participated in the government's carefully managed meetings, online poll and questionnaire (critics noted that many First Nations have very limited access to the internet), or called the toll-free telephone number, and mailed in government forms.

After a consultative process which deliberately circumvented the First Nations leadership it came as no surprise that the proposed Act failed to acknowledge and reflect the fact that the First Nations have, and wish to strengthen, governance structures that work for them - structures that affirm, uphold and implement their values.

Critics argued that the FNGA would reduce First Nations to the legal status of municipalities; make First Nations leaders fiscally and politically accountable to the Minister of Indian Affairs instead of to their own communities; decrease the federal government's accountability to First Nations; abolish the right of First Nations to choose customary forms of governance; and, change some archaic sections of the Indian Act that are problematic to Ottawa but ignore the sections that the First Nations themselves have defined as the most problematic (such as recognizing the matrimonial property rights of First Nations women, and revising definitions of membership and "status").

The proposed legislation was preoccupied with the rhetoric of "public accountability for public funds," reflecting a stereotype of how First Nations' finances are currently being managed. A few high profile examples of corruption or mismanagement were generalized to portray Aboriginal peoples as a whole, the hypocrisy of which was proven by the massive accounting and corruption scandals that shook the governing Liberal party while debate over the FNGA took place. But the FNGA was not about accountability - it was about control. This is why the right-wing newspaper, *The National Post*, had no problem celebrating the fact that the FNGA was "really ... about assimilation".

Roberta Jamieson, Chief of the Six Nations of the Grand River, called the FNGA "little more than a new rule book... so fundamentally flawed, constitutionally and morally, that it can't be amended. It must be utterly rejected." She was outspoken in her assertion that First Nations "must take vigorous, principled and clear action" to ensure that the act is withdrawn. Many First Nations held demonstrations to accompany the protests that their national organizations made before parliamentary committees.

Protests against the FNGA reached their peak just as Chrétien was preparing to retire and be replaced as Prime Minister by Paul Martin. It became apparent that Chrétien was not willing to expend the political capital needed to force the unpopular legislation through parliament, and Martin let it be known that he thought that the FNGA had "poisoned" relations between Ottawa and the First Nations. Upon becoming Prime Minister in December 2003, Martin abandoned both the FNGA and the unpopular Minister of Indian Affairs, who had conceived it, and both were relegated to the history books.

British Columbia

> *Our history has shown, unfortunately all too well, that Canada's Aboriginal peoples are justified in worrying about government objectives that may be superficially neutral but which constitute de facto threats to the existence of Aboriginal rights and interests.*[2]

The Universal Declaration of Human Rights and the two Covenants affirm that all peoples have the right to self-determination. A people's self-determination is not possible without control over its lands and resources. In 1996, the Government of Canada agreed that indigenous peoples are peoples in international law and therefore have the right to self-determination. Since 1996, both federal and provincial efforts (internationally and in Canada) have been oriented toward limiting the right of self-determination for the Aboriginal Peoples of Canada.

One of the key problems faced by indigenous peoples in some provinces of Canada, and particularly in the province of British Columbia (B.C.), is that, under the terms of the original Confederation of the country in 1867, lands and resources fall under the jurisdiction of provincial governments, while under the Canadian legal system, fiduciary responsibility for indigenous peoples, their lands and resources rests with the federal government. By extension, it should also be borne by provincial governments, but in practice this extension has been customarily denied.

ILO Convention No. 169 (not ratified by Canada) affirms the right of Indigenous and Tribal Peoples to exert control over their own lands and resources, as does General Comment 23, paragraphs 3 and 5 of the CERD committee, the UNHCR monitoring body for the Convention on the Elimination of Racial Discrimination, which has been ratified by Canada.[3]

"Apology" and agreements

In its February 11, 2003 Speech from the Throne, the government of British Columbia made a formal apology to the indigenous peoples. It said,

> *Your government deeply regrets the mistakes that were made by governments of every political stripe over the course of our province's history. It regrets the tragic experiences visited upon First Nations through years of paternalistic policies that fostered inequity, intolerance, isolation and indifference.*

In the general absence of historic treaties, successive governments in British Columbia (B.C.) have been involved in the current treaty negotiations process for more than 11 years. During that time, only the Nisga'a Treaty has been finalized. Under discussion for over 100 years and under negotiation for 25 years, the Nisga'a Treaty was not a part of the current treaty negotiation process. To assuage public concerns, throughout the past 11 years of negotiations, First Nations in B.C. have assured the public that privately held lands would not be on the table. First Nations were looking to so-called "Crown" lands to make good their claims.

The Liberal government of B.C. is responding to the treaty negotiation imperative by selling Crown assets - lands, leases, licenses, tenures - at an accelerated pace before treaties can be negotiated to secure and protect these lands and resources for those who have historically owned them and who have never ceded or surrendered them. This alienation of indigenous lands and resources is being disguised through an elaborate system of interim measures and by supporting negotiations of indigenous partnerships with the corporate sector, which intends to exploit traditionally owned indigenous resources for corporate gain. Further, wording in agreements that relate to accommodation of Aboriginal rights now admits that such agreements are being negotiated *with prejudice* to Aboriginal title and rights.

The government of B.C. has developed economic measures agreements that aim to provide financial assistance to First Nations who are engaged in negotiations with government. It claims to have awarded over $25 million to First Nations for 113 projects. What it does not say is that these agreements prohibit the filing of any court action by the partner First Nation against the provincial government for any reason during the term of the agreement, or the agreement may become null and void.

Defining title and rights

In spite of the entrenchment of the rights of indigenous peoples, as peoples, in international law and in Section 35 of the Constitution of Canada, and in spite of the UN and OAS Draft Declarations on the Rights of Indigenous Peoples, the governments of Canada and British Columbia continue to insist that Aboriginal title and rights have, with the exception of a few domestic court cases, not been defined and that their definition is subject to domestic negotiation between the parties.

Duty to consult

The Delgamuukw decision[4] of the Supreme Court of Canada stated clearly that the State has three obligations: consultation, cooperation and compensation. The B.C. government's consultation policy is unilateral in that the government decides the scope of the consultation, the degree to which accommodation should be attempted, and what accommodation is workable. It questions the soundness and nature of the right or title being asserted, and may unilaterally choose to conclude the consultations.[5] This is in marked contrast to New Zealand case law, for example, which affirms, in part, that consultation is to be a two way process, is to be open-minded, is to be informative and ongoing, must balance the issues and must be given a sufficient amount of time.

Rather than working cooperatively to protect Aboriginal title and rights, the provincial government, in its consultation policy, is primarily concerned to know whether or not the right or title to be infringed has been proven in court. Secondly the government wishes to determine whether its infringement can be deemed justifiable. If yes, it will infringe. If no, it proposes to negotiate infringement through the application of "treaty related measures, interim measures, economic measures, programs, training, economic development opportunities, agreements or partnerships with industry or proponents or other arrangements..." On February 27, 2002, the B.C. Court of Appeal delivered a landmark decision regarding the duty of the Crown and third parties to consult with First Nations who have asserted, but not proved, aboriginal rights or title (Haida Nation *vs.* Minister of Forests and Weyerhauser). The court ruled that the province and the corporation have legally enforceable duties to consult with the Haida in good faith, and that the obligation extends to both cultural and economic interests.[6] The B.C. government is appealing this decision.

Denial and dispossession

In recent court actions, the government of British Columbia has argued that the provincial statute of limitations (section 3.5) applies to title claims arising from the Delgamuukw decision, indicating that any claims not filed by a six-year deadline (December 7, 2003) would be inadmissible. This, in spite of section 3 (4) which states "The following actions are not governed by a limitation period and may be brought at any time: (a) for possession of land if the person entitled to possession has been dispossessed in circumstances amounting to trespass."

This sudden, policy shift has caused many First Nations in B.C. to file writs of ownership in the courts to protect their title and rights. These writs, if inadequately represented, could be denied, with disastrous results.

> *Today, denial and dispossession continue in various forms, including non-recognition and non-implementation of the many court decisions which recognize and uphold Aboriginal and treaty rights in Canada. Governments instead interpret the cases to serve their own interests. In not implementing cases such as Sparrow, Delgamuukw and Council of the Haida Nation, governments deny First Nations that which they have won through the courts.* [7]

End of the Decade

2004 is the final year of the International Decade of the Indigenous Peoples of the World. The Government of Canada has said, in recent hearings in preparation for the UN Human Rights Commission meetings, that indigenous issues are a key priority. Under British, now Canadian law, the government of Canada is legally responsible, in a position of trust, for what belongs to First Nations in Canada. It remains to be seen whether the Government of Canada will live up to its fiduciary responsibilities to protect the assets of First Nations and to secure their right to self-determination through constructive, cooperative work on the Draft Declaration. It remains to be seen whether the First Nations of B.C. will have any recourse against the permanent alienation of their lands and resources that is now occurring through privatization in British Columbia, on which the Government of Canada remains silent. ❑

Notes

1 For earlier discussions on FNGA see also *The Indigenous World 2001-2002* and *The Indigenous World 2002-2003*.
2 C.J. Lamer and J. La Forest, Delgamuukw (Supreme Court of Canada)
3 Paragraph 3: The Committee is conscious of the fact that in many regions of the world indigenous peoples have been, and are still being, discriminated against and deprived of their human rights and fundamental freedoms and in particular that they have lost their land and resources to colonists, commercial companies and State enterprises. Consequently, the preservation of their culture and their historical identity has been and still is jeopardized. Paragraph 5: The Committee especially calls upon States parties to recognize and protect the rights of indigenous peoples to own, develop, control and use their communal lands, territories and resources and, where they have been deprived of their lands and territories traditionally owned or otherwise inhabited or used without their free and informed consent, to take steps to return those lands and territories. Only when this is for factual reasons not possible, the right to restitution should be substituted by the right to just, fair and prompt compensation. Such compensation should as far as possible take the form of lands and territories.
4 In Delgamuukw *vs* the Queen (1997), the Supreme Court ruled that "Aboriginal title is a right to the land itself". This recognizes extensive Aboriginal land rights not previously acknowledged. These rights include the "right to exclusive use and occupation of land" that is "inalienable" and cannot be extinguished unless ceded to the Crown.
5 Western Canadian Business Law, Nov. 2002: www.lawsonlundell.com
6 Bull, Houser and Tupper: Summary of BC Court of Appeal Decision in Haida Nation v. Minister of Forests and Weyerhauser and Implications for Local Governments, 2002.
7 First Nations Summit: Framework for Recognition and Reconciliation, 17 September 2003.

UNITED STATES

With the war in Iraq, upcoming presidential and local elections as well as the country's continual fight against terrorism, issues concerning Native Americans have not been at the forefront of national debates. As a result, Native peoples continue to strive for better protection of sacred sites, improved health care, education and employment opportunities, fairer gambling laws and a solution to the Indian Trust fiasco.

Sacred sites

Although the protection of sacred sites has been at the forefront of Native concerns, not all news has been dire in this realm. This has been particularly true in the case of the sacred sites noted in the last issue of "*The Indigenous World*".

Indian Pass, California, a Quechan site used for spiritual journeys and the Kerkuk Death Ceremony, have so far been protected from the Glamis Imperial Corporation of Canada. Although the Canadian company is appealing against the decision banning the area to open-pit mining at federal level, legally this outcome seems unlikely at the present time. Pressure brought upon the corporation by a coalition of Native peoples, local politicians and the National Trust for Historic Preservation has successfully staved off the corporation's desire to begin open-pit gold mining in the region.

Another successful win for Native sacred sites is that of Salt Lake, an important pilgrimage site for the Zuni peoples and others residing in the south-west. The Salt River Project relinquished its oil and gas leases to the region under pressure from local state officials and Native peoples.

A less clear fate faces the area near Bear Butte Mountain on the border with South Dakota and Wyoming. As noted in the last issue of *The Indigenous World*, private investors have planned to open a shooting range in the area. It is estimated that 10,000 rounds of ammunition will be used at the range every day. Currently, local politicians and business leaders in the area support the building of the shooting range. It is as yet unclear whether representatives of the Lakotas, Cheyennes, Kiowas, Crows, Mandans, Hidatsas and Arikiras will be able to halt the construction of this complex.

Along the Missouri River, numerous sites sacred to Native Peoples face potential destruction due to the management practices of the Bureau of Land Management. This region supports six dams and reservoirs. Its multiple users, such as farmers, weekend recreation users, river transportation interests and environmentalists often place conflicting demands on the Bureau of Land Management. In order to comply with some of these needs, the Bureau releases fluctuating amounts of water from the dams. As a result, many sites important to Native Peoples are in danger. Given the potential imminent destruction of these sacred areas, the National Trust for Historic Preservation has listed the region as one of the top eleven sites in the United States needing protection.

Two Congressmen, Nick Rahall and Dale Kidee, recently passed the Native American Sacred Lands Act HR 2419. This act, though vulnerable to interference from the executive branch of the United States government, is an important tool with which to aid Native peoples fighting to protect their sacred sites.

Health care

Medical care for Native peoples continues to be abysmal, especially on the reservations. Native peoples have the lowest life expectancy of any ethnic population in the United States. As a matter of fact, 13% of Native youths under 25 are three times more likely to die than the rest of the country's populace. A number one killer is adult onset diabetes. At present, 12.2 % of adults aged 19 and older contract Type II diabetes. The disease leads to blindness, kidney failure and a loss of circulation in the body's extremities. In April, the National Congress managed to extract 750 million dollars from the federal government to fight this disease. Unfortunately, however, this amount of money is a far cry from the necessary funding needed to increase the health of Native peoples. For example, in the last fiscal cycle, President Bush allocated 2.63 billion dollars for indigenous health issues. At a minimum, 2.87 billion dollars are necessary, according to healthcare workers among Native peoples. Including inflation, current funding is less than was available in 1977. These monies would only cover everyday medical needs and would not be used to update Indian Health Service facilities. Most facilities are in dire need of repairs since being upgraded 19 years ago.

Cancer rates and tuberculosis continue to rise among Native peoples. The mortality rate from breast cancer continues to be higher for Native women as compared with women from other ethnic backgrounds. In addition, tuberculosis occurs in higher rates among indigenous communities than other ethnic populations, with the exception of some immigrant groups.

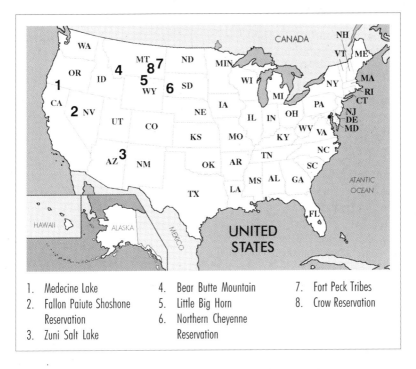

1. Medecine Lake
2. Fallon Paiute Shoshone Reservation
3. Zuni Salt Lake
4. Bear Butte Mountain
5. Little Big Horn
6. Northern Cheyenne Reservation
7. Fort Peck Tribes
8. Crow Reservation

Alcoholism remains a problem among many Native peoples on reservations and in urban areas. Earlier studies estimated that rates were as high as 80% among Native men, compared to a national average of 20%. Recent studies of the phenomena, however, have suggested that the rates for Native men may be as low as 30%. The higher rates may more than likely be related to stereotypes of drinking among Native peoples. A number of innovative treatment programs have been started by Native nations over the last decade. Although the use of *peyote* is considered illegal except within the context of religious ceremonies associated with the Native American Church, some of the more successful outcomes have come from the spiritual and religious healings offered by this sacred plant. To date, the federal government refuses to provide monies for these programs.

Indian Trust controversy

This case, dating from 1996 when Eloise Cobell, a Blackfoot from Montana, sued the United States Department of the Interior over the loss of monies from trust lands, has yet to be resolved. The Bureau of Indian Affairs, under the aegis of the Department of the Interior, manages 55.7 million acres of tribal lands. Cobell's class action lawsuit represents 300,000 landowners who claim that the government mismanaged their land assets. In many cases, lands were leased to extractive industries at a cost far below market value. Frequently, lease monies owed to the landowners were either not paid or underpaid. Because the problems date from the early 1900s, and literally 137 billion dollars are at stake, legal fights revolve around how far back to check records for fraudulent lease agreements made by government officials acting as go-betweens for Native peoples. The Interior Department is currently trying to limit its liability in this case by only considering leases granted between 1985 and 2000. In a controversial move, the Bureau of Indian Affairs has begun to hand over trust management to a newly developed agency, the Office of the Special Trustee. Many tribal leaders have criticized this reorganization plan and want the Bureau of Indian Affairs to continue to oversee trust lands. There is a concern that, because Native leaders have been ignored in discussions over the reorganization of the Bureau of Indian Affairs, this plan will diminish the governance role of Native peoples within their nations.

Educational issues

Approximately 50 thousand Native students attend the 185 schools funded by the Bureau of Indian Affairs. These schools serve 30 to 40% of Native children. As in the past, however, Native education continues to be woefully under funded. Educators tend to be underpaid, sufficient school supplies are lacking, and they frequently teach in substandard buildings. The lack of monies granted to Native students is reflected in high drop-out rates and few students attending universities. Only nine percent of Native students obtain university degrees. Yet 22% of white students and 20% of all other ethnic populations in the United States graduate from university.

Lack of employment opportunities

Residents of reservations encounter unemployment rates as high as 80%. Within urban areas, unemployment among Native peoples averages around 14.4%. Among the rest of the country's citizens, unemployment rates hover around 6.3%. Lack of educational and employment opportunities on many reservations are a major contributor to these grim statistics. Those that have jobs must often live on substandard amounts of money. On average, employed tribal members earn a yearly salary of approximately $8,232.00. Low-income citizens from other ethnic populations generally average an annual income of $14,420.

Involvement in presidential politics

One recent phenomenon has been the growing involvement of Native peoples in national and local elections. For example, Native voters proved critical in the Senate race in South Dakota and the governor's contest in Oklahoma. This year marked the first time that the National Congress of American Indians invited presidential candidates to speak to tribal leaders from around the nation. The political power of Native peoples has been fueled by profits from casinos. At this current time, 201 out of 562 federally recognized tribes operate casinos, which generate $12.7 billion in revenue. Although much of this funding supports tribal projects, some money is used to support candidates who support Native issues.

Controversies concerning the 2000 census

Many of the United States census administrators agree that Native peoples experience the highest population undercounts of any minority group in the country. Problems of this type can be attributed to frequent changes in household members, distrust of the government and differing definitions as to who is Native. In the 2000 census, 2.1 million individuals identified themselves as Native. However, their individual tribes officially recorded only 1.7 million people. More than 100 tribes are challenging the 2000 census results and conducting their own recounts. Each person counted brings in several hundred dollars a year in federal grant money. So far, 39 tribes have successfully challenged the numbers generated in the 2000 census. This will permit these communities to gain access to much-needed funding for education and other projects important to the viability of the Native communities.

Discriminatory housing policies

A government-sponsored study found that Native peoples are more likely than any other minority population to encounter discriminatory housing policies. The Housing and Urban Development Department studied three regional areas with high populations of Native peoples. These included New Mexico, Montana and Minnesota. Based on the results of their study, Hispanic renters were discriminated against 26 percent of the time when they applied for tenancies, while rates for African Americans amounted to 22 percent. Native peoples on the other hand, faced discriminatory practices 29 percent of the time. Hopefully, these findings will lead to fairer rental practices in the future.

Casinos

Native American gaming has been a bane for numerous tribal nations. In order to receive a gaming license, the Native community must enter a compact with the state in which the tribe is located. If the state allows gambling, then Native tribes may open casinos with little problem. In some areas, however, states do not allow betting, which prevents local tribes from participating in this source of revenue. This is the case in Nebraska, for example. During the last three legislative sessions, a number of politicians attempted to extend gaming rights to Native tribes. These efforts have failed for a number of reasons. One factor involves reservations on the part of some of the state's religious peoples. Another issue relates to the efforts of nearby states to keep casinos out of Nebraska. These other regions fear that gambling in Nebraska will diminish revenues in neighbouring states.

Native American artistry

With over 100 years of American cinema, it is only in the last five years that Native films have begun to earn the respect and distribution they deserve. In the early days of cinema, when over 100 movies a year were made about Native peoples, these cinematic events tended to either romanticize Native peoples or portray them as evil savages. Fortunately, this has changed with a new crop of Native filmmakers. In addition to the inroads in filmmaking, numerous Native writers are beginning to gain recognition for their work. These new voices will presumably help mitigate many of the stereotypes plaguing Native peoples in the United States. Films such as "Skins" and "Smoke Signals" have had a major impact on the public's perceptions of reservations. In addition, books such as *"Reservation Blues"*[1] and *"Songprints"*[2] have offered images of the hopes and dreams of Native peoples. ❏

References

1 **Alexie, Sherman. 1996.** *Reservation Blues*. New York: Warner Books.
2 **Vander, Judith. 1996.** *Songprints. The Musical Experience of Five Shoshone Women*. Champaign: Univ. of Illinois Press.

MEXICO,
CENTRAL AMERICA AND
THE CIRCUMCARIBBEAN

MEXICO

F our main events made 2003 an important year for indigenous affairs in Mexico: (1) the establishment in Chiapas of "*los Caracoles*" and "*las Juntas de Buen Gobierno*"; (2) the publication of a General Assessment of the Human Rights Situation in Mexico (*Diagnóstico General sobre la situación de los Derechos Humanos en México*) produced by the Office of the UN High Commissioner for Human Rights; (3) the June visit of Rodolfo Stavenhagen, UN Special Rapporteur on the Situation of Human Rights and Fundamental Freedoms of Indigenous People; and (4) the reform of the National Indigenist Institute (*Instituto Nacional Indigenista*).

Mexico: ten years of Zapatismo

The 10th anniversary of the uprising of the Zapatista National Liberation Army (*Ejército Zapatista de Liberación Nacional*) in Chiapas was celebrated on January 1, 2004. After 10 years of armed uprising, neither Mexico nor Chiapas are the same any more: there has been a Revolution of "Words" and most indigenous peoples can now make themselves "heard" at both national and international fora.

And yet, ten years on, there was a need for some reflection. It was time to look back over the achievements, the successes and failures that had taken place. Many indigenous people who originally formed the basis of the EZLN's support have now distanced themselves from the neo-Zapatista movement. Various factors have contributed to this: the military and paramilitary presence in the area, the public resources injected into the region, and EZLN decisions - such as the collectivisation of land and a prohibition on receiving government support. "Disillusionment" has set in.[1] Nonetheless, it has been a ten-year period during which indigenous people have been listened to. Their voices have been heard, and not only in the press releases of Sub-Comandante Marcos. The indigenous now make themselves heard, they want a Mexico that listens to them, that shares with them the wealth of their natural resources. It is for this reason that a response is needed from the federal government, along with the conditions necessary for re-establishing a dialogue.

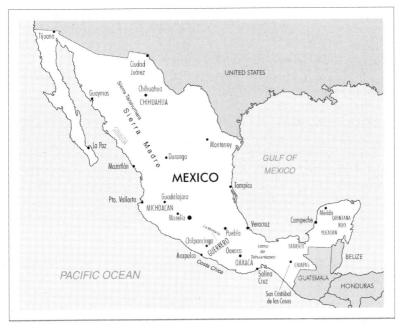

Chiapas: *Los Caracoles* and *Las Juntas de Buen Gobierno*

1	La Realidad
2	Morelia
3	La Garrucha
4	Roberto Barrios
5	Oventic

Source: www.ciepac.org

After a long period of silence, the EZLN command re-emerged once more in August 2003, announcing that "the indigenous peoples... organised in the EZLN, have prepared a series of changes with regard to their internal conduct and their relationship with civil society".[2] What emerged was "*Los Caracoles*", a Zapatista response to the 2001 Constitutional Reform of indigenous issues and the failure to comply with the San Andrés Accords. *Los Caracoles* substitute *los Aguascalientes*[3] and will form the headquarters for a new administrative body within Zapatista territory, the "*Juntas de Buen*

87

Gobierno" (Good Governance Committees - JBG).[4] There will be five committees, one in each of the autonomous regions (that is, Selva Fronteriza, Tzots Choj, Selva Tzeltal, Zona Norte de Chiapas and Altos de Chiapas) and they will comprise one or two delegates from the respective MARZ (*Municipios Autónomos Rebeldes Zapatistas* – Zapatista Rebel Autonomous Municipalities) Councils.

The role of the JBGs will be the following: to counteract inequities in municipality and community development; to mediate in conflicts between the autonomous municipalities, and between autonomous and non-autonomous municipalities; to handle complaints against the autonomous councils and their management structures or violations on their part; to supervise implementation of community projects and tasks in the MARZ; to meet with and encourage national and international civil society to visit communities, implement production projects, etc.; and, in agreement with the CCRI-CG (*Comité Clandestino Revolucionario Indígena - Comandancia General* / Indigenous Revolutionary Clandestine Committee – General Command) of the EZLN, to promote and approve the involvement of men and women from the Zapatista Rebel Autonomous Municipalities in activities and events outside of the rebel communities, and to elect and prepare these members.[5]

As Armando Bartra notes, it is significant that "through the JBGs, the autonomous municipalities become partly independent of the EZLN, as the politico-military authority is restricted to 'watching over' the committees and, where necessary, defending the population but, for everything else, the civil authority will be solely responsible".[6]

According to Hector Díaz-Polanco, "the JBGs result from the specific needs of the Indian peoples of Chiapas. As the Sub[-Comandante Marcos] has explained, in spite of a number of notable achievements, the development of the autonomous municipalities is also creating distortions. The JBGs will endeavour to resolve these and, what's more, create a leap forward in the exercise of autonomy. But there is reason to suppose that similar needs....will mean it is likely that peoples from other areas of the country, in turn, will find themselves forced to consider the regional coordination of their autonomies. The significance of the JBGs, as a regional organisation, revolves around the fact that they extend beyond, or could extend beyond, the particular reality of Chiapas. The support the Zapatista initiative has received from all kinds of indigenous organisations is an indication of this".[7]

An alarming assessment

At the end of 2000, the then High Commissioner for Human Rights, Mary Robinson, and President Vicente Fox signed a technical cooperation agreement. In 2002, an office of the High Commissioner was established in Mexico, charged with carrying out an assessment of the human rights situation. Four Mexican academics were appointed for this task. The report was published on 10 December, on presentation to President Fox.[8] One section considers the situation of the rights of indigenous peoples.

The assessment indicates that land is one of the main causes of human rights violations against indigenous peoples, particularly the problem of boundaries between *ejidos* (cooperatives), communities and small properties. In addition there are "conflicts over the use of collective resources, such as forests and waters; illegal invasions and occupations of communal lands and plots on the part of loggers, cattle ranchers or private farmers; the accumulation of properties in the hands of local landowners *(caciques)*, etc.".[9] In defending their lands, the indigenous have clashed with the forces of law and order (police and military), with peasant farmers and private landowners. The forest resources on indigenous territories are frequently exploited by timber companies, with the support of state governments. In defending their lands, the indigenous have frequently been harassed or imprisoned under unclear circumstances.

One such example is that of Isidro Baldenegro, an indigenous Rarámuri. In 1998, the Secretary for the Environment and Natural Resources in Chihuahua granted a forestry licence to Artemio Fortes to log 24,000 hectares of virgin forest belonging to the indigenous Tarahumara from Comunidad Coloradas de la Virgen, in the municipality of Guadalupe y Calvo. This community has initiated legal proceedings against the licence. As a result, many indigenous people have received death threats and, in March 2003, Isidro Baldenegro was imprisoned by bailiffs from Chihuahua state, accused of possessing arms and marijuana. Various NGOs maintain that his arrest is due to his role in defending his community's forest resources.

Many indigenous people find themselves defenceless at the hands of public prosecutors or judges because they do not speak Spanish. What is more, they have no access to interpreters or defence councils to help them through the proceedings. There are unjustified arrests, and torture is committed by elements of the police force (municipal, state and federal) and army. Another factor is the harassment of indigenous people and leaders because of the protests, complaints and demonstrations they are undertaking.

In Chiapas, more than 12,000 indigenous people have been displaced from their places of origin. Only a few families have returned. The government denies the presence of paramilitary groups but the assessment indicates the contrary, noting their existence through interference in the region's conflicts, assassinating, displacing and "disappearing" indigenous people. Various organisations complain that elements of the Armed Forces in Chiapas, Guerrero and Oaxaca are carrying out "patrols and checks on highways and roads, arbitrary detentions and arrests, body searches and searches of belongings, raids on communities and searches of properties, intimidating interrogations, death threats, extrajudicial or summary executions, sexual harassment and abuse of indigenous women."

The assessment notes the worrying situation of indigenous women, migrants and children (malnutrition levels amongst these latter being most alarming). With regard to the Constitutional Reform (see *The Indigenous World 2002 - 2003*), it recommends that the "Congress of the Union re-open the debate on constitutional reform of indigenous issues, with the aim of clearly establishing the fundamental rights of indigenous peoples in accordance with current international legislation and in accordance with the principles agreed in the San Andrés Accords."

Visit of the UN Special Rapporteur

The UN Special Rapporteur on the Situation of Human Rights and Fundamental Freedoms of Indigenous People, Mexican-born Rodolfo Stavenhagen, officially visited Mexico from 1 to 16 June.[10] There was controversy around his agenda and the places to be visited. He finally went to Mexico City to meet indigenous migrants and representatives from nearby native communities. In Sonora he met the Yaqui, in Jalisco the Huichol, in Chihuahua the Tarahumara, in Oaxaca representatives of various indigenous groups, and in Chiapas he held meetings with indigenous people displaced from their communities, religious leaders and representatives of civil, indigenous and peasant farmer organisations.

In Guerrero, a meeting was held in the town of Tlapa, Montaña region, to hear statements from Na savi (Mixteco), Nahua, Me' phaa (Tlapaneco) and Suljaa' (Amuzgo) who had been the victims of serious human rights violations. Particular emphasis was placed on the cases of indigenous women raped by soldiers; the El Charco massacre, when the army executed 14 indigenous Mixteco; the harassment and persecution of indigenous authorities and the denouncement of various land conflicts classified as "hot spots" due to their highly explosive nature. At the end of the meeting, the Rapporteur declared, "These are grave and serious violations of the human rights of the indigenous people of Guerrero.... particularly all the cases related to land conflicts, bad justice administration and militarization."

All the indigenous people Rodolfo Stavenhagen met during his visit stated their opposition to the 2001 Constitutional Reform. He also received complaints regarding the absence of health and education services and food, problems of land ownership and natural resource use, lack of access to justice, the presence of paramilitary forces, the effects of militarization on indigenous communities, etc. The Rapporteur's report of his visit will be presented to the Commission on Human Rights in April 2004.

Resisting in order to survive: the indigenous peoples of Guerrero

On 23 August 2003, various soldiers of the 48th Infantry Battalion raided three Me'phaa family homes in Encino Amarillo, Acatepec municipality. According to statements from the victims, the soldiers stole eight thousand pesos, two shotguns and attempted to rape two women, all under the pretext of seeking guerrillas and drugs traffickers. The community's response was to go to the military camp to identify those responsible, demanding they be punished and expelled from the region.

On the ninth anniversary of the Coordinating Body of Community Authorities of Costa Montaña, celebrated in Buenavista, San Luis Acatlán municipality, more than two thousand indigenous people from 60 communities gathered to demonstrate to the state government their determination to promote and develop their community system of justice and security.

On 20 November, the traditional authorities of the Suljaa´ (Amuzgo) people of Xochistlahuaca municipality celebrated their first anniversary as an indigenous municipal government, although it is not recognised by the *mestizos* of the area, the political parties or the state and federal authorities. It is a government in resistance, standing up to the discrimination, repression and scorn of the *mestizo* municipal power. Despite their longstanding financial difficulties, more than a thousand Amuzgo celebrated this struggle with a march and a festival. They denounced the fact that "the government has ignored our voice, it has used the law to imprison us, awaiting our demise, but this will not come because our people now know how to live in resistance."

Fourteen Me'phaa men from El Camalote, Ayutla municipality, decided to break their silence to denounce the fact that, in 1998, thirteen of them had been sterilized following deceit, pressure and threats on the part of medical staff from the state government's health department. The fourteenth was sterilized in 2001. This complaint is in addition to the 19 cases of fathers from the Na savi people in the communities of Ocotlán, Ojo de Agua and Fátima, Ayutla municipality, who were also forcibly sterilized in 1998, without the authorities having awarded any compensation so far.

INI becomes CDI

The National Indigenous Institute (*Instituto Nacional Indigenista* – INI) has now become the National Commission for the Development of Indigenous Peoples (*Comisión Nacional para el Desarrollo de los Pueblos Indígenas* - CDI). The official reason was that INI's "model of care was no longer viable; neither its method of operation nor its budget sufficient to fulfil the proposals and desires of the native peoples of Mexico".[11] The aim of the CDI is to "guide, coordinate, promote, support, encourage, monitor and evaluate public programmes, projects, strategies and actions for the integrated and sustainable development of indigenous peoples and communities [...]." However, this does not represent a true change in the State/indigenous peoples relationship but "reproduces the authoritarian and assistentialist relationship that the state has maintained with them".[12]

Portrait of a "Marvellous Country"

In November, Vicente Fox stated that, "Mexico is a marvellous country with a solid economy". Did this description include the rights of indigenous peoples? This article has depicted the difficult situation in which indigenous people live. There has been progress but there still remains much more to do. It is everyone's duty not to forget them and the conditions in which they live. It is difficult to see them falling within the "Marvellous Country" Fox mentions. It would be "marvellous" if, in 2004, they once more formed the focus of debate, a debate not limited to mere ideas but one in which real action is taken to begin to change their situation. ❑

Notes and references

1 **Juan Pedro Viqueira. 2004.** "Las comunidades indígenas de Chiapas a diez años del levantamiento neozapatista". *Letras Libres*, January 2004.

2 CCRI-CG EZLN press release, 19.07.03 quoted in *MEMORIA* No. 176, October 2003.

3 *Aguascalientes* were fora established by the EZLN in some rebel villages in the Lacandona forest to receive and meet with civil society. The name *Aguascalientes* comes from the fact that, in this northern town of Mexico, in 1914 – in the middle of the Mexican Revolution – the revolutionary factions met to promote an agreement and to build a revolutionary government, which Emiliano Zapata and Francisco Villa established that year by taking Mexico City. (Ed. note)
http://www.rojoynegro.info/aguascalientes/paginas/quees.html

4 See http://www.laneta.apc.org/sclc/ezln/2003ago09.htm

5 *La Jornada*, 29 July 2003. Chiapas, la treceava estela (sexta parte): un buen gobierno.

6 **Armando Bartra. 2003.** "¡Caracoles! Descifrando la Treceava estela". *Memoria* no.176, October 2003.

7 **Héctor Díaz-Polanco. 2003.** "Juntas de Buen Gobierno - ¿Una etapa superior de la autonomía?". *Ibid.*

8 *Diagnóstico sobre la situación de los derechos humanos en México.* 2003. Mexico: Office of the United Nations High Commissioner for Human Rights in Mexico. See
http://www.cinu.org.mx/prensa/especiales/2003/dh_2003/index.htm

9 During 2003, the Ministry for Agrarian Reform resolved some land conflicts that were considered "hot spots".

10 More information can be found in "México antes de Los Caracoles", *Asuntos Indígenas*, IWGIA, no. 3/2003.

11 Fox's words when he signed the decree creating the CDI on 19 May 2003. See http://www.ini.gob.mx/

12 Centro de Derechos Humanos Miguel Agustín Pro Juárez, A.C. 2003. *Informe Anual de Violaciones a los Derechos Humanos 2003.* Mexico. p. 8.

GUATEMALA

The most recent census, dating from late 2002, puts the Guatemalan population at approximately 11.2 million people, 43% of whom are indigenous. In reality, however, and in official circles, the figures is generally considered to be 60% or more. This 60% is made up of three peoples: the Xinca, the Garífuna and the Maya. The latter are the majority as the Xinca number no more than 100,000 inhabitants and the Garífuna 150,000.

Up until May 2003, there were 21 linguistic communities, fully and clearly recognised and defined amongst themselves and, subsequently, by the Guatemalan state. However, during that month, and without awaiting the recommendation of the Guatemalan Academy for Mayan Languages (*Academia de las Lenguas Mayas de Guatemala* – ALMG), a controversial decree issued by the Congress of the Republic added another.[1]

The indigenous struggle and elections 2003

During the last half of 2003, Guatemala held general elections to appoint the President and Vice-President of the Republic, the deputies to the Congress of the Republic and the Central American Parliament, and municipal mayors along with their respective councils.

Although the rhetoric of many of the political parties was that of full indigenous participation, few of them actually had many indigenous candidates on their lists and the figures show that this participation was really only effective at municipal level, that is, within the local authorities. Of 158 deputies to Congress, only 15 are indigenous, in other words 9% of the total number and, of these, only one is a woman. This is an outrageous figure because far from increasing, indigenous representation has actually decreased. The previous legislature was 12% indigenous. This means that, for those who win seats in Congress and most of the municipalities, their own personal or party political interests take priority over their people's struggle. It also highlights a need to transform not only the party political system but also legislation in this regard. There are democratic ways of electing authorities that are still practised by indigenous peoples but which, although recognised in the Political Constitution of the Republic of Guatemala, are not respected. The elections for the Totonicapán community mayors are perhaps a symbol of such democratic participation.

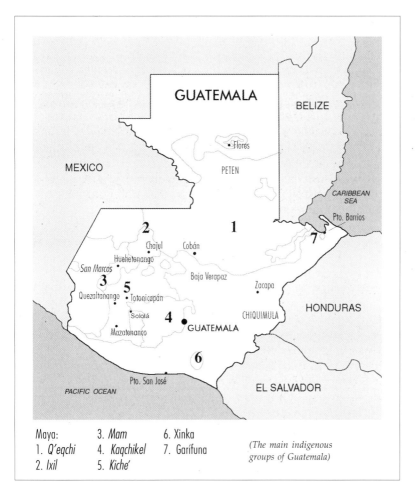

Maya:
1. Q'eqchi
2. Ixil
3. Mam
4. Kaqchikel
5. Kiche'
6. Xinka
7. Garífuna

(The main indigenous groups of Guatemala)

The following are some of the most important events that took place in relation to indigenous peoples during the elections.

For the first time in the country's history, an indigenous candidate stood for the post of President of the Republic of Guatemala: Rigoberto Queme Chay, Mayor of Quetzaltenango. Up to 15 January 2004, he sought alliances with three parties: one with some experience, the New National Alliance (*Alianza Nueva Nación* –ANN) and two more recently created: *Trasparencia* and *CASA*. Due to power struggles relating to the naming of candidates for deputies and municipal mayors, no coalition was forthcoming and Rigoberto Quemé had to withdraw from the contest. Although his withdrawal caused quite a stir, it was the right decision. It remains to be seen what form indigenous presence will take in future elections, both within the parties and within the institutions that most clearly represent them.

The two final contenders in the elections for President of the Republic, *Gran Alianza Nacional* –GANA- and *Unidad Nacional de la Esperanza* –UNE- stated throughout that indigenous peoples would form a priority for their government. In the case of GANA (headed by Oscar Berger, who won the presidency), a document was published on 12 October 2003 entitled: "*Gran Alianza Nacional*'s Commitment to the Indigenous Peoples of Guatemala". Recognising their condition of exclusion and constant discrimination in public spaces and state institutions, and within the political parties, the document undertakes, among other things:

- To implement the Agreement on Identity and Rights of Indigenous Peoples
- To include indigenous professionals within state structures.
- To create and strengthen public institutions so that they can effectively contribute to promoting the rights of indigenous peoples.
- To support indigenous peoples' organisation and participation, including the indigenous local authorities.
- To prioritise the state's fight against racism and discrimination.
- To gradually provide ongoing health and justice services in indigenous languages.
- To invest greater resources in bilingual education.
- To recognise the validity of indigenous customary law and
- To respect the freedom and plurality of religions and cosmovisions.

It remains to be seen whether these commitments will actually be honoured or whether, as with other governments, these issues were only raised because of the election campaign. During a TV news broadcast on 29 December, Rigoberta Menchú indicated that the President elect had offered her a position as special ambassador and plenipotentiary, provided this position did not prevent her from carrying out her role as Nobel Prize winner and UN goodwill ambassador.[2]

It should also be noted that the document fails to address a number of highly important issues such as land, natural resources and the rights of indigenous women. Even so, the composition of the elected Congress will have an impact on the rights of indigenous peoples.

The challenge of racial discrimination

Other events are causing the re-emergence of issues which, only a few years ago, would have been unthinkable.

Towards the end of 2002, a reform of the Criminal Code was decreed in which discrimination was categorized as a crime. This categorization raises a huge question for indigenous peoples given that the specific crime of racial discrimination, discussed and agreed upon for more than four years by the vast majority of indigenous leaders, has been postponed to a later date.

This decree was validated with the consent of various important national and foreign figures known for their racist stance. Rejection of the reform by large sectors of the indigenous population, through lack of sufficient consensus, was criticised by this non-indigenous elite who are moreover spreading the idea that it is they, on the contrary, who are discriminated against by the indigenous.

One symbolic case of discrimination was brought by Rigoberta Menchú against the President of the Republic (Alfonso Portillo), the President of Congress (Efraín Ríos Montts) and other public officials, including the former director of the National Civil Police and the Minister of the Interior. The allegation against these people is that hundreds of indigenous people were deceived into attending a violent demonstration held on 24 and 25 July 2003 with the aim of obtaining the fraudulent registration of Ríos Montts as presidential candidate. Although it was they themselves who had promulgated this decree, in an apparent act of compliance with the Peace Accords, it is also they that have hindered its fulfilment, petitioning four members of the Constitutional Court close to the governing party to get the case set aside. There has been no news as yet of the Constitutional Court's decision. Ríos Montts was unsuccessful in his attempt to become President of the Republic in the first round of voting on 9 November 2003.

It was not long before the Head of the United Nations' Mission in Guatemala – MINUGUA – recognised the lack of a specific law on racial discrimination and recommended the implementation of clear policies to overcome such a serious gap, indicating that, "discrimination is interpersonal, legal because the justice system is exclusively *ladino,* and institutional because of the minimal indigenous participation".[3] These policies undoubtedly form an historic challenge for any government in Guatemala, right through from those in local power, to the Congress of the Republic, to the Executive with all its departments, and to the judicial machinery in all its expressions.

Maya culture: some political successes

In May 2003, a law legalising the use of indigenous languages in basic services was promulgated. Although a reform of the Constitution would be needed to make indigenous languages truly official, this law would seem to be a step in the right direction.

In December 2003, the 10-year concession for Channel 5 Television was awarded to the Guatemalan Academy for Mayan Languages. This is undoubtedly a great opportunity, perhaps one of the most significant in 2003, but we do not yet know what budget will be allocated to this channel to enable it to function and be of benefit to the indigenous peoples. The challenge will be to make it not only an instrument of cultural dissemination, but also one that is capable of rising to the technological, thematic and motivational challenges ahead, as it will have to compete with other national and international channels broadcasting in the country. It will need to show the true nature of indigenism, not just in Guatemala but elsewhere too. Against this backdrop, an appeal is being made to the international community to offer it its unconditional support. At the same time, ALMG was awarded a 25-year concession over premises to be used as offices from which to run the Channel. These premises comprise what used to be a privileged military residence for former defence ministers.

The indigenous movement

Given the two mass protests that took place, one at the end of November and the other in early December 2003, one could be forgiven for thinking that the Guatemalan indigenous movement is relatively united. Nonetheless, despite the presence of more than 10,000 people at one demonstration and 15,000 at the other, the submission of more than a hundred extremely varied demands to the government quite clearly demonstrated the lack of consensus among the leaders who traditionally hold themselves up as Guatemala's indigenous representatives.

The task of developing a common strategy by which to produce a joint proposal still seems to be in its infancy, given that visions continue to be sectoral or individual. The presence of some indigenous people in Congress, others in government posts, and yet more running small organisations that are supported and backed by international funders with unclear aims, means that the spectre of division remains ever present.

A number of new indigenous organisations emerged during the 1990s around the peace process. Some have already disappeared and others now have only a weak presence. In 2003, the National Council of Indigenous Peoples (*Consejo Nacional de Pueblos Indígenas*) emerged out of the grassroots organisations of 20 of the 21 linguistic communities. The Council seeks, through the vision of the community and people, to influence all areas of work, ensuring a place for all organisations with a common goal, albeit with a diversity of issues.

Recurrent problems in Guatemala

The area of the Peace Accords that has been least implemented is that of the identity and rights of indigenous peoples. However, there are also other problems which, whilst they affect all of Guatemala's population in general, impact more heavily on indigenous peoples.

Impunity remains commonplace. The justice system has still not applied itself to clarifying the thousands of cases that as yet only emerge as horrifying figures in an unprecedented Latin American genocide. According to the Commission on Historic Clarification (Truth Commission), the victims number more than 200,000, 83% of them Maya. But instead of dealing with the cases of victims of the internal armed conflict, the government appears to prefer to reward many of those responsible, organised or re-organised in the Civil Self-defence Patrols or PAC.

Corruption is a social blight that has now taken root in the local authorities, in the villages with indigenous mayors or without, with some exceptions. But most corruption still takes place at central government level, and there are no clear indications that those involved will be brought to justice. Corruption certainly makes many indigenous people even poorer. Information suggests that more than fifty (largely indigenous) villages are suffering from famine. This is closely related to a lack of jobs, housing, health and better living conditions.

The failure to involve most of the population in the decisions of a "democratic" government makes the system look bad. Or perhaps democracy is built on exclusion? The state that persists in Guatemala is clearly still a feudal one, hiding behind a façade of democracy.

Ungovernability is another problem that is clearly leaving its mark. One example is the inexplicable deaths of many indigenous women and elderly people. This would appear to be part of a planned and defined strategy, but the state has yet to offer a solution to the problem. Violating human rights in order to instil terror in the population continues to define a counter-insurgency strategy in a country where there are no longer any insurgents: many of them are now well ensconced in government. This policy has the greatest effect among indigenous communities which, even now, continue to be terrorised by a resurgence of Civil Auto-defence Patrols. In addition to the right to life, the worst human rights violations relate to the right to land, to natural resources, to free organisation and to the practising of one's own spirituality.

There are so many problems that cannot be considered in this brief article but, as a final example, the lack of indigenous consultation is in flagrant violation of the law. One particularly enlightening example is that of the decision to authorise gold mining in one of the country's poorest municipalities, San Miguel Ixtahuacán, in the western department of San Marcos. The environmental impact of this will have dire consequences for the inhabitants of this area. Another is the way in which attempts are being made to distort concessions in protected areas which, in large part, comprise communal indigenous lands. This is quite clearly another way of robbing the indigenous of their lands, albeit by different means. ❑

Notes

1 The municipality affected is Aguacatán, in the department of Huehuetenango. Promulgated for political reasons, this decree will almost certainly have negative consequences for the inhabitants of the communities affected.
2 Rigoberta Menchú later declined the invitation, nonetheless maintaining her support for the new President.
3 *Prensa Libre*, 27.12.03. Interview with Tom Koenegs, head of MINUGUA.

NICARAGUA

T his year has been marked by the enactment of a series of laws that are extremely important for the indigenous communities and the autonomy process.

The regional autonomy process

Law No. 28, *The Statute regarding the Autonomy of the Atlantic Coast Regions of Nicaragua* was promulgated by the National Assembly of the Republic of Nicaragua and published in the *Official Gazette*, No. 238, on October 30, 1987. After an endless number of problems and a delay of 16 years, the National Assembly's Commission on Ethnic Affairs and Indigenous Communities issued the legislative decree for the "Regulation of Law No. 28, referred to as the Statute regarding the Autonomous governments for the Atlantic Coast Regions of Nicaragua."

Prior to the approval in the National Assembly plenary session, some indigenous leaders from the indigenous party Yapti Tasba Masraka Nanih Asla Taranka (YATAMA) disagreed with the passage of regulation of Law No. 28 without first undertaking a reform of the autonomy statute. However, their objections were not accepted because they were made after the official deadline. The approval of legislative decree No. 3584 in the National Assembly took place in a plenary session on July 9, 2003; all members of the Assembly attending the session that day voted in favour.

The formal procedures for due compliance with the provisions of the Autonomy Law, including the powers of the Councils and Regional Governments, are stipulated in the regulation. The Ruling Commission of the National Assembly also deemed it necessary to emphasize various aspects that are fundamental in the legislation, including the conceptualization of the Autonomy Statute as a system of government that is legally, politically, administratively, economically and financially decentralized, and establishes the powers of the Autonomous Regions of the Atlantic Coast and their administrative organs within the Nicaraguan state. The rights and obligations of their inhabitants to exercise their historic rights conferred by the Nicaraguan Constitution are also specified.

The decree also stipulates that the regional institutions must administer the health programs, education, culture, transport, public services, sports and infrastructure, in coordination with the corresponding entities and ministries so that the Autonomous Regions of Atlántico Norte (RAAN) and Atlántico Sur (RAAS) exercise their powers in an effective and real manner. The Autonomous Regions are also responsible for the promotion of the study, encouragement, development, preservation and dissemination of the traditional cultures of the Atlantic Coast of Nicaragua, as well as their historic, artistic, linguistic and cultural heritage.

Short-term prospects on the Caribbean Coast

Within the frame of broadening the autonomy process, there are favourable prospects for progress in the institutional decentralization of two high-priority strategic sectors - education and health. After many days of work, consultation and institutional efforts, two policy and strategy documents have been produced for these sectors in the Autonomous Regions: *Sistema Educativo Autonómico Regional* (SEAR) and *Modelo de Salud de la RAAN*. Various specific aspects of the Caribbean Coast have already been incorporated in the respective national documents, for example, the National Education Plan for 2001-2015.

In terms of decentralization and devolution, an advance in the transfer and delegation of functions and human resources is probable in the short or medium term, but without an adequate budget. One of the principal challenges will, therefore, be to resolve the fiscal gap between responsibilities and powers (to allocate public spending), on one hand, and income, on the other.

Process of formal legal recognition of communal lands

In January 2003, Law No. 445, *The Framework Law regarding the Communal Property of the Indigenous Peoples and Ethnic Communities of the Autonomous Regions of the Atlantic Coast of Nicaragua and the Bocay, Coco, Indio and Maiz Rivers*[1] was passed. Of special importance is the fact that in its first introductory paragraph the law stipulates that:

> *The State of Nicaragua has an unshirkable commitment to respond to the request for title to the lands and territories by the indigenous people and ethnic communities of the former Mosquitia*[2] *of Nicaragua, a right provided for in the international treaties signed between*

England and Nicaragua, such as the Treaty of Managua in 1860 and the Harrison-Altamirano Treaty of 1905. This right to the land is recognized in the Constitution of Nicaragua of 1987 and in the Statute regarding the Autonomous Regions of the Atlantic Coast.

Further on, in the fifth paragraph, it states: "Article 180 of the Constitution of Nicaragua guarantees the indigenous people and ethnic communities of the Atlantic Coast of Nicaragua that their forms of communal property will be respected and made effective". And in Chapter I, Article 2 (1) it states: "To guarantee the indigenous people and ethnic communities full recognition of the rights to communal property, the use, administration and management of traditional lands and their natural resources, through the demarcation and granting of title to them."

Chapter VIII, Procedures for Legal Recognition of Lands, contains the fundamental operative aspects for the implementation of the law. Its articles cover the procedure of legal recognition, the granting of communal property titles, the demarcation and legal recognition of the territorial property of the indigenous communities, full and direct participation by indigenous and multi-ethnic peoples, etc. It also institutes the creation of the National Commission on Demarcation and Granting of Land Titles (CONADETI), and three Cross-Sectoral Commissions for Demarcation and Granting of Land Titles (CIDT), each with clearly defined functions, and its own internal regulations and budget. Further, it establishes a range of technical, regional and territorial commissions.

In the context of Nicaragua's structural fiscal crisis, the provisions of Chapter XIV of the law, referring to the matter of financing are of transcendent importance; its article 62 establishes that:

> *The State, while the process of demarcation and legal recognition is being carried out, shall ensure the inclusion in the General Budget of the Republic each year the allocations necessary to finance the investments required by the work and activities of whatever nature that are needed for the purposes stipulated in this Law.*

In order to support financing of the relevant activities the law also establishes the creation of the National Fund for Demarcation and Granting of Legal Recognition of Communal Lands, which will be administered by the National Commission for Demarcation and Granting of Land Titles (CONADETI), under the supervision of the Ministry of Finance and Public Housing, through the Office for the Granting of Rural Land Titles (OTR).

First year of implementation of the law

As is all too common in Nicaragua, a year after the approval of Law 445, progress in implementing it is too slow and the Government of Nicaragua has not embraced as its own the huge tasks involved in the process of legal recognition of the communal lands.

The implementation of the law began in the third quarter of the year, with the elections of the ethnic representatives for the CONADETI and two of the three land titling commissions (CIDTs), under the supervision of the Regional Councils of RAAN and RAAS. The CIDT of the department of Jinotega was established at the same time. The main result of the efforts of these first months are two documents of norms approved in December 2003: 1) The Manual on Procedures for the Demarcation and Granting of Land Title for the Communally

Owned Lands of the Indigenous Peoples and Ethnic Communities of the Atlantic Coast of Nicaragua and the Coco, Bocay, Indio and Maíz Rivers, and 2) The Internal Regulation for the Functioning of the National Commission regarding Demarcation and Granting of Land Title.

Given the absence of a budget allocation from the Government of Nicaragua, most of the expenses of the bodies mentioned have been covered by contributions from two projects receiving international financing from the World Bank: the Biological Corridor of the Atlantic and the Project for Land Administration.[3]

The six indigenous territories located completely or partially in the BOSAWAS Biosphere Reserve, as well as the community of Awas Tingni, are the cases receiving the highest priority for exercising all the stages stipulated in the law. Three geographical zones are being given priority for the analysis of their land use and tenure. Two of the zones are located in RAAN: the northern coastal area of the municipality of Puerto Cabezas, populated by Miskitos, and the multi-ethnic geographical sector of Tasba Pri. A third geographical zone is the municipality of the Desembocadura de Río Grande, in RAAS, with a majority Miskito population.

According to some analysts, it is realistic to expect that the process of granting legal land title to communal lands may take 15 years.

International events organized in Nicaragua

The Forum on Indigenous Territory, Demarcation, Identity and Spirituality was held in Bluefields in October 2003 with participants from Honduras, Guatemala and Nicaragua, including experts in the subject of demarcation of indigenous territories. Hosted by the University of the Autonomous Regions of the Caribbean Coast of Nicaragua (URACCAN), the forum's principal objective was the exchange of experiences of demarcation and the granting of titles for indigenous lands in Latin America.

By virtue of the Statute of Autonomy, already regulated, and Law No.445 it is evident that Nicaragua sets a standard for countries in Latin America and the Caribbean in these two matters.

Forestry Law approved

The approval by the National Assembly of the General Law regarding Conservation, Promotion and Sustainable Development of the Forest

Sector (Law No.462), on August 28, 2003,[4] is another notable development in 2003.

Law No. 462 is aimed at establishing the legal framework for exploiting forests, and developing a sustainable forestry sector, using forestry management of natural forests, the fostering of plantings and the protection, conservation and restoration of forest areas as the fundamental basis for that process. Nevertheless, there is uncertainty about whether or not the implementation of this law really constitutes an effective brake on the logging and destruction of forests on Nicaragua's Caribbean coast.

Encouraged by the approval of the Forest Law, different municipal governments, most of which have territorial jurisdiction over the BOSAWAS Biosphere Reserve, have agreed to organize a coalition for institutional legal recognition of land title through a public land deed, in order to slow down the illegal traffic of wood. The municipalities of Matagalpa, San José de Bocay (Jinotega), Wiwilí-Jinotega, Wiwilí-Nueva Segovia, Waspam, Bonanza and Siuna have joined together in this effort. The municipal leaders have agreed that the National Forestry Institute is not fulfilling its functions and exercising its institutional powers satisfactorily, and that many of its officials tend to maintain close relationships with a sort of national timber mafia, who are the main beneficiaries of the extraction of wood on the Caribbean coast.

Conflicts over communal property

A strip on the border between the municipal boundaries of Prinzapolka, Rosita and Puerto Cabezas is the zone in Nicaragua where there is the greatest conflict over the issue of communal land ownership. The most significant case is the tension between a group of Miskito communities, especially Laya Siksa and Lagoon Kukalaya, and a growing number of peasant settlers. At the end of the year, the irresolute efforts of the different governmental and non-governmental bodies had not managed to counteract nor calm a situation, which appeared to be leading to an armed confrontation.

One noteworthy conflict, which received press coverage, is the reactivation in the middle of this year of an old land lawsuit between the "*bloque*"[5] of Diez Comunidades and the Karata *bloque*, whose community boards both have their headquarters in Bilwi. With the renewal of this lawsuit, there has been a resurgence of the dispute over the major part of the urban area of Bilwi and an annual rental income of almost US $1 million.

A third significant conflict during 2003 involves the Sumu-Mayangna community of Fenicia, in the municipality of Rosita, as a claimant against a *mestizo* family in a lawsuit over land. The community is requesting the return of 500 *manzanas* of communal lands, which it argues were unfairly appropriated through various legal procedures. This territorial area includes a strip 2.5 kilometres long where the Rosita airstrip is located. In this proposal the indigenous community has requested support from various judges and human rights organizations to recover these lands.

The main mobilization in defence of communal property of the indigenous communities of the Pacific and central areas of Nicaragua is being carried out by the indigenous community of Jinotega. Jorge González, president of the Council of Elders and the main leader of the indigenous communities of Jinotega, is the main spokesperson in the claim on land occupied by the company HIDROGESA, which is in the process of being privatized. The company has two hydro-electricity turbines, which generate 100 megawatts each.

The indigenous community is claiming approximately 10,000 *manzanas,* which were taken from them in the 1960s during the reign of the Somoza family dynasty through various methods, including threats and repression. The communities are also demanding back rent on the lands being claimed, which have been used by a State company for more than 40 years. This claim amounts to more than 20 million *cordobas* (about US $1.3 million).

Other problems related to communal ownership

Another event of particular importance, which was almost a scandal, was the offer made on internet in the middle of the year by the company Inmuebles de Nicaragua (INMONICA), to sell a 352.5-hectare piece of land composed of lots granted by the Nicaraguan government to former combatants belonging to YATAMA in the beginning of the 1990s. The land is located between the Miskito community of Miguel Bikan and the Ipritingni River, 70 kilometres northeast of Bilwi, in the municipality of Waspan. According to INMONICA's Web page, the value of the property is US $19,500, equivalent to US $55.00 per hectare. The sales offer emphasizes that the land includes virgin forests with abundant fauna and stands of precious wood such as mahogany and different kinds of high-quality cedar, among other species.

This case illustrates again a growing contradiction between the emerging private ownership of land by indigenous individuals and the recovery of territories claimed by *bloques* of indigenous communities. It also highlights the derisory value given to biodiversity and natural resources by some sectors of the population, with negative effects on the request for legal recognition of the lands and territories communally owned, as well as on the sustainable use of these resources.

Although somewhat unrelated to the matter of indigenous lands and communal ownership, another significant event this year should be mentioned: the revived threat of eviction of over 200 Miskito families living on Isla de Maíz (Corn Island), 70 miles northeast of Blue-fields, RAAS. These families are considered squatters, without any chance of being granted legal title to their lots. Generally the head of the family earns a living diving for lobsters for foreign or national fleets fishing in Nicaragua's territorial waters.

Current developments in the Awas Tingni case

During this year the Nicaraguan government continued to delay compliance with the decision by the Inter-American Court of Human Rights of the Organization of American States in favour of the Sumu-Mayangna community of Awas Tingni.

The main progress made this year was an analysis of land tenancy and use by the Awas Tingni, commissioned by the Project for Land Administration (PRODEP), with World Bank financing. This activity was carried out by a consortium formed of Alistar Nicaragua and the Centre for Research and Documentation of the Atlantic Coast (CI-DCA-UCA), from June to August 2003. The consultancy team was co-ordinated by Dr. Anthony Stocks, of Idaho State University, USA.

After the presentation of the draft of the final report by the consultants comes the difficult step of resolving the conflicts, which is the task of the bodies created this year under the provisions of Law 445. This process was still bogged down at the end of 2003 although the Awas Tingni had already presented a formal request for demarcation, delimitation and land title before the CIDT of the RAAN.

Final considerations

The results for 2003 are, in general, positive. Of particular importance is the significant improvement in the legal-institutional framework for regional autonomy, including the full and effective recognition of a range of collective and individual rights. Experience thus far indicates that the broadening and consolidation of the process to strengthen autonomy will depend on the political will of the state, and on the level of joint organization and action by the beneficiaries. Major efforts still must be made to achieve better use of the natural resources and to build local and communal institutional abilities to improve the material and spiritual well-being of the indigenous peoples and ethnic communities of RAAN and RAAS.

Greater progress has been made this year than in previous years in the process of legal recognition of communal property, although greater efforts and concrete achievements are also necessary to meet the expectations for communal property rights of the indigenous peoples and ethnic communities. ❏

Notes and references

1 Ley del Régimen de Propiedad Comunal de los Pueblos Indígenas y Comunidades Étnicas de las Regiones Autónomas de la Costa Atlántica de Nicaragua y de los Ríos Bocay, Coco, Indio y Maíz. *La Gaceta* Diario Oficial No. 16, 23 January 2003.
2 In English, known as the Mosquito Coast. (Tr. note).
3 *Proyecto de Ordenamiento de la Propiedad*, or PRODEP is a project that aims to foster agrarian reform by regularizing land rights and supporting peri-urban land titling. (Ed.note).
4 *La Gaceta* Diario Oficial No. 168. 4 September 2003.
5 A *"bloque"* is a group of communities that have joined together to present a common land claim. (Ed.note)

PANAMA

Brothers at war on the Panama-Colombia border

The murder by Colombian paramilitaries of four indigenous Kuna leaders from the communities of Paya and Pacuro, on the Panamanian border with Colombia, in early 2003 was to become, for the rest of the year, an issue of discussion and reflection around what happens to indigenous communities when they are forgotten by governments, particularly when they are located in the most inhospitable and dangerous places.

Autopsies on the bodies of leaders (*caciques*) San Pascual Ayala, Ernesto Ayala and Luis Ernesto Martínez de Paya following the attack indicated that they had been tortured before being executed.

The examination of the forensic pathologist, Juan Rosales, revealed that the paramilitaries had decapitated San Pascual Ayala and amputated his left arm above the elbow. His head has not been found. The body also presented wounds to the right side of the body consistent with the use of a sharp instrument. There were no bullet holes.

According to the autopsy report, Ernesto Ayala, traditional leader (*sayla*) of Paya, presented a wound from a projectile entering via his mouth and exiting through the right side of his head. He also suffered a cut to his abdomen. Luis Ernesto Martínez received four bullet wounds and his skull was completely shattered, possibly due to a sound blow with a blunt object or an effect known as cranial fragmentation, which can be caused by a high calibre firearm.

In the face of this atrocity, representatives from the different indigenous communities in Panama filed a criminal complaint against the perpetrators of these assassinations with the Solicitor-General's Office. This complaint was no more than a symbolic gesture, for they were fully aware that the paramilitary Colombian Self-defence Units (*Autodefensas Unidas de Colombia* - AUC) that crossed into Panamanian territory enjoy complete freedom to commit crimes and are rarely condemned by either the police or the judicial authorities in Colombia.

The plaintiffs demanded that the Panamanian government file the relevant complaints and request Colombia's immediate cooperation to bring those responsible to justice stating, "the Panamanian government must be emphatic in resolving this investigation". The complaint noted the fact that Panama was a signatory to the Inter-American Convention against Terrorism, and so was required to investigate

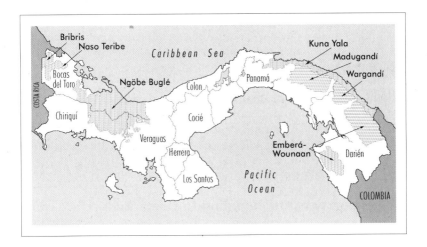

the case both nationally and internationally, as was the Colombian government.

The Tule of Colombia seek refuge

In early 2003, the Tule or Kuna of Arquía, some 400 people, requested refuge in Panama in the face of "the distress and terror" caused by the violence in Colombia.

The Tule of Colombia requested the Kuna General Congress (highest traditional and administrative authority of the Kuna in Panama) to give refuge to its people within the autonomous territory of Kuna Yala, given that the Kuna or Tule, though separated by a national border, had always maintained traditional economic, cultural and family ties.

This request was formally made at an ordinary session of the Kuna General Congress, held in the Yandup community (Kuna Yala) in April 2003. The Congress resolution referred to international humanitarian law and stated that the Kuna of Panama would be ready to give refuge to the Arquía community, "should they decide to move". For this reason, they requested "respect and support" – for the decision adopted by the Congress – from the government, the UN High Commissioner for Refugees (UNHCR) and other organisations working with refugees and the displaced.

The issue is still being discussed between the Kuna authorities of both countries. The Panamanian government has given no particular opinion in this regard but is warily watching what is going on.

However a government source, who wishes to remain anonymous, has suggested that any move would be emphatically opposed, despite the fact that the Kuna have autonomy within their own *comarca* or Indigenous Territory.

The conclusion of all the Panamanian indigenous authorities is that the continuing war along the border with Colombia is irrelevant to the demands of their peoples, and that the parties involved, the guerrillas and the paramilitary, are indistinguishable. Indigenous people would gain no benefit whichever side took political control of the country.

Indigenous workers migrating to Costa Rica

Another concerning situation is taking place along the Panamanian border with Costa Rica, specifically the cases of the indigenous Ngöbe-buglé, Bri-bri and Naso peoples. Because of a lack of sustainable and regular sources of employment in their areas of origin, these people regularly travel to Costa Rica with their families to work in the sugarcane harvest. An unspecified number of Panamanian indigenous children are born in that country, and there is no proper registration system. In other words, these children are in many cases "neither Costa Rican nor Panamanian". They are hence unable to enjoy the protection and guarantees of the Family Code in Panama. At the time of writing, we are unaware of any formal or systematic policy of assistance to resolve a problem that is preventing nationality, along with the right to a name, from being exercised. These are fundamental rights of the individual.

According to a report of the Panamanian Ombudsman and the United Nations Children's Fund (UNICEF), the situation is worrying because the size of the problem is unknown and statistics are assumed to be unreliable. The report concludes that the lack of security along the border areas has forced indigenous groups to move with their families, often with children who are not registered and adults who have lost their documentation.

The Kuna General Congress calls for unification

The Kuna people of Panama are currently settled within three duly legalized territories: Kuna Yala Comarca (1953), Kuna de Madungandi Comarca (1996) and Kuna de Wargandi Comarca (2000). Ta-karkunyala (Pucuro and Paya), which is in Darién Province on the border with Colombia, is still awaiting demarcation. Kuna Yala has autonomy within the territory it has always held on the Caribbean coast. Madungandi territory is in the eastern part of Panama Province whilst Wargandi lies within the boundaries of Darién Province. This being the case, the three Kuna regions have common borders that link them along various points of the Kuna Yala *comarca*.

For this reason, during the Kuna General Congress held at the end of April 2003, the early unification of the Kuna people was approved so that it would in the future be one single territory, one single nation. This is something the Kuna leaders have constantly dreamt of since the turn of the last century, one of its greatest supporters being *cacique* Nele Kantule.

In the Kuna people's declaration, its leaders stated that, "after centuries of colonial aggression, which led to the destruction and dispersal of our peoples throughout the rivers and forests, and after one hundred years of the Republic, which deepened this political division with national and provincial borders, we have joined to-gether to share our problems and initiate a process of coordination and unity in defence of our rights".

If unification of the Kuna territories were to take place, a large area of Panamanian territory would be Kuna self-governing. This is cur-rently the case with the Ngöbe-buglé *comarca*, which was established (1997) within the boundaries of what were previously the provinces of Bocas del Toro, Chiriquí and Veraguas.

Now that a possible and rapid reform of the 1972 Political Consti-tution of the Republic of Panama is being discussed at national level, indigenous people consider this to be just the right moment for the Indigenous Territories or *comarcas* to be constitutionally recognised as part of the country's political division, something that is not the case in the current constitution.

2004 general elections

On 2 May 2004 there will be general elections in Panama. And once more the different candidates from the traditional political parties will be approaching the indigenous communities in search of votes, enabling them to gain power. This year the elections hold more impor-tance for the indigenous communities because, in the case of the Ngöbe-buglé, two new seats have been added to the Legislative Assembly as well as a dozen or so *corregimiento* representatives (local counsellors) in that *comarca* and one in Madungandi.

However, as is the case throughout Abya Yala, indigenous peoples have no confidence in the established electoral system because, when traditional parties gain power, they simply stop listening to indigenous demands.

References

Daily newspaper *La Prensa de Panamá.*
Daily newspaper *El Panamá-América.*
Daily newspaper *El Siglo.*
Centro de Asistencia Legal Popular (Centre for Popular Legal Assistance - CEALP).
Comisión de Asuntos Indígenas de la Asamblea Legislativa de Panamá (Commission for Indigenous Affairs of the Panamanian Legislative Assembly).

TRINIDAD AND TOBAGO

A ccording to rough estimates, there are 12,000 people of Amerindian descent in north-east Trinidad. The Santa Rosa Carib Community (SRCC) in the Borough of Arima is the only formally-organized group of people with an Amerindian identity. Its membership consists of several related families of indigenous ancestry.

Direct political representation creates ambiguous situation

One of the striking features of the Santa Rosa Carib Community is that it has for some time had direct access to the centre of political power through direct representation at the local level. Ricardo Bharath Hernandez, the President of the Carib Community, contested the Arima West constituency as a candidate for the ruling People's National Movement (PNM) during the local government elections of 14 July 2003. For the fourth time, he was elected to a three-year term as the representative of an area that encompasses the Church lands on

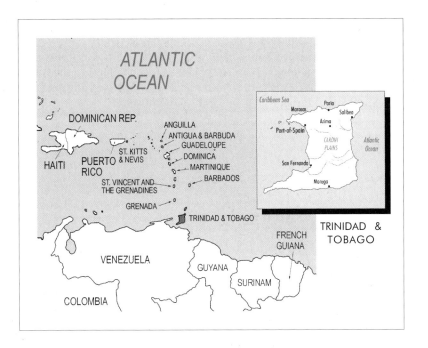

which the Santa Rosa Carib Community Centre is based. As a consequence of his latest electoral victory, Bharath Hernandez was selected by the PNM to serve as Deputy Mayor, the highest political post ever held by a leader of the Carib Community. He was chosen on the basis of his long service to his constituency, which includes a Carib-descended minority within a larger multi-ethnic population, as well as for his service as the leader of the Santa Rosa Carib Community for most of the last thirty years.[1]

This appointment continues a long tradition of linkage between the Carib Community and local government in Arima, helping the Caribs to project themselves in a manner that is out of proportion to their actual numbers in the Borough. On the other hand, being responsible for issues that go well beyond the concerns of the Carib Community, and having to represent a constituency in which Caribs are a minority, places significant demands on the Carib leader in having to also attend to many interests and concerns not specific to his community. It is perhaps one of the ironies of direct political representation that access to the centres of decision-making have been increased while, at the same time, opportunities for representing exclusively Carib interests have declined.

Quest for land: defining rights

The quest for land continues, following promises by both past and present governments to grant a substantial piece of land to the Carib Community. The promise of a land grant was renewed in June 2000 by then Prime Minister Basdeo Panday, who stated:

> ...The Caribs have petitioned the Government for the grant of State Lands for the establishment of a Carib Village, together with land for the establishment of a Carib Forest Reserve. I support those aims, in principle... There can be no objection to the grant of ceremonial lands to our Carib brothers and sisters. [2]

When the People's National Movement, under Prime Minister Patrick Manning, took office in 2001, renewed commitments were made. Then Minister of Community Development, Joanne Yuille Williams, referred to assistance provided to the Carib Community in the form of funds for a Resource Centre as part of a process of "reparation for a community that has lost a lot.... we need to pay a lot more attention to this group here, to facilitate them".[3] On 18 November 2002, a letter from the Office of the Prime Minister indicated that the government had received, and were processing, a Carib request for State lands on the Blanchisseuse Road, north of Arima. Another letter came from the Lands and Surveys Division in early December 2002, indicating that they were processing the request, lands were available, and the next step was simply to allocate them. At that stage it seemed as if the land grant would proceed smoothly and quickly.

In actual fact, the purported grant is being officially treated as a lease, with possible property taxes applicable. Being a 300-acre plot, the tax could be substantial. In addition, as the application has passed through the hands of various levels of bureaucracy, it has come to be treated as profit-making land, designed purely for commercial purposes. The Carib Community was then instructed that it would have to secure a private land surveyor to formally survey the intended property. The lowest price quoted to them for such a survey was $75,000 TTD, approximately $12,000 US and more than twice their annual operating budget. The struggle of the Carib Community has now turned into one of securing funding for these costly exercises and ensuring that the land is treated as a grant and not as a commercial lease. Once the survey has been concluded, the final step is for a recommendation to allocate the land to be passed to Cabinet for final approval.[4] The consequences of a potential misdirection of the grant could be very serious for the Carib Community, as they have been in the past. In the mid-1970s, under the pretext of another promised land grant, the Santa Rosa Carib Community was obliged to register itself as a limited liability company. That entailed restructuring internal positions of authority within the Community, state surveillance, demands for tax returns even when no revenues had been earned, and a series of other bureaucratic impositions that had no relevance to the actual structure, internal relations and aims of the Caribs. The Carib Community is hoping to construct a village for its members, most being dispersed throughout Arima. In addition, the intention is to focus on indigenous horticultural practices and to create a hospitality centre that will house visiting delegations of Amerindians from across the Caribbean and the South American mainland. Clearly, a great deal is at stake and the process of obtaining the said lands remains as incomplete as it is fragile.

Strengthening regional relationships

Developing and deepening ties with other indigenous communities and organizations across the Caribbean has long been a central aim of the Arima Caribs in their own projects of cultural exchange and solidarity. In 2003, the Carib Community sent three of its members, headed by Cristo Adonis, to the Caribbean Festival of Arts (CARIFESTA VIII) held in Suriname from 24 August to 5 September. Events that brought together indigenous representatives from across the Caribbean Basin were held in a collective Amerindian Village designed to be a showcase of Amerindian traditions and to provide a location for religious rituals in which various representatives participated. A "smoke ceremony" was led by Adonis, a shaman of Trinidad's Carib Community.

On 14 October, Trinidad and Tobago's official "Amerindian Heritage Day", the Santa Rosa Caribs were accompanied by a delegation of eight individuals from Suriname and two from Dominica's Carib Reserve. A ceremony was held at the statue of the legendary Chief Hyarima in Arima, followed by a procession to the Town Hall with a formal reception prepared by the Mayor. The gathering of delegates from Suriname and Dominica was funded by the Trinidadian Ministry of Culture and an Amerindian non-governmental organization in Suriname. The Surinamese are in turn planning to hold a week-long series of workshops at the Carib Centre in Arima starting on 16 January 2004, designed to cater for youth interests and skills development.[5]   ❑

Notes and references

1   **Forte, Maximilian C. 2003.** Trinidad Carib Leader Appointed Deputy Mayor of Arima. *The CAC Review* 4 (2) August 2003. www.centrelink.org/August2003.html
2   Prime Minister of the Republic of Trinidad and Tobago, the Hon. Basdeo Panday at the launch of the International Indigenous Gathering, 29 June 2000.   www.kacike.org/srcc/Panday.html
3   **Forte, Maximilian C. 2002.** The First Nations Resource Centre in Arima, Trinidad. *The CAC Review* 3 (7-8) August-September 2002. www.centrelink.org/Sept2002.html
4   For more details, please see: **Forte, Maximilian C. 2002.** Lands for the Arima Caribs. *The CAC Review* 3 (10) December 2002. www.centrelink.org/Dec2002.html; and idem. **2003.** Interview with Ricardo Bharath Hernandez on the Quest for Carib Lands in Trinidad. *The CAC Review* 4 (2) August 2003. http://www.centrelink.org/August2003.html. For background history on the original alienation of Amerindian lands in Arima, see **Forte, Maximilian C. 2003.** How the Amerindians of Arima Lost Their Lands: Notes from Primary and Other Historical Sources, 1802-1880. *Issues in Caribbean Amerindian Studies* 5 (1) June 2003. www.centrelink.org/landreport.html
5   Bharath Hernandez, Ricardo and Cristo Adonis. Personal telephone communication, 10 January 2004.

SOUTH AMERICA

COLOMBIA

After one year in office, President Álvaro Uribe Vélez continues to enjoy a high level of popularity. Surprising perhaps, given that his supporters believe their lives have shown no improvement. Never in the country's political life have Colombians graced an incumbent with such a long "honeymoon" period, all the more incomprehensible given his government's poor results.

The struggle against poverty

Colombia is experiencing its worse economic and social crisis of the last four decades, a crisis demonstrated by a breakdown in productive activity that has forced almost 60% of the economically active population into the informal sector and one quarter of the Colombian population into poverty. This crisis is also evident in the growing concentration of wealth and in the violent eviction of more than two million people from their lands, one of the world's greatest human tragedies of our time.

Violence and drugs trafficking have undoubtedly contributed to a collapse in production investment and the abandoning of Colombian agro-industry. And it is also clear that corrupt civil servants have looted the nation's coffers, squandering the Colombians' heritage. Álvaro Uribe's government is obviously not responsible for this chaotic situation. The roots of the problems lie in previous administrations, and have accumulated over many years of state inefficiency. As noted in studies carried out by the Office of the Comptroller General (*Contraloría General de la Nación*), this economic crisis is due primarily to a lack of true entrepreneurial spirit in the country, brought about by a "culture adverse to investment and capital accumulation, and inclined to consumption".[1]

Under such circumstances, it was only to be expected that the economic liberalisation that took place during the 1990s would increase inequality, bringing the number of people in absolute poverty to more than two million (not counting the displaced), and would lead to the country's de-industrialisation. Over this period, almost one million hectares of agriculturally productive lands were taken out of production and environmental degradation increased. If this was the result of an incipient liberalisation, we can but imagine what implementation of the FTAA (Free Trade Area of the Ameri-

1. Paece
2. Embera
3. Uitoto
4. Inga
5. Nukak
6. Kankuamo
7. Cogí
8. Tule (Kuna)
9. Bari

cas) – fervently supported by our head of state – may do. Most analysts doubt the capacity of our businesses, given that they are still geared towards competing with or resisting competition from imported goods.

To persist then, as Uribe is doing, in speeding up the move towards a more open economic model as a strategy by which to improve the living conditions of the most disadvantaged Colombians is not only an error, it is a crime.

The policy of "Democratic Security"

For Álvaro Uribe's government, "the focal point of the Democratic Security policy consists of achieving complete control over the country in order to ensure the full rule of law, governability and a consequent strengthening of democracy." According to Álvaro Uribe, as the violence is defeated, there will be "more possibility of carrying forward simultaneous policies of security, increased state income, and economic and social recovery."

The democratic security policy has thus become an essential strategy with which to achieve the objectives of a Community State, guaranteeing public order, creating a climate favourable to increased productive investment, attracting foreign capital, increasing growth, lowering unemployment levels and hence bringing poverty to an end. The government is thus sparing no efforts or resources to establish what some analysts consider to be the most costly and ambitious law and order policy the Colombian state has ever known.

Despite the fact that, at the end of 2003, the government was able to present eloquent figures on the progress of its democratic security policy (a 45% reduction in terrorist attacks, 30% reduction in kidnappings, 20% in extortion, 25% in murders, 33% in the blowing up of electricity pylons and a harsh blow dealt to the military structure of the Revolutionary Armed Forces of Colombia, the FARC, with some leaders captured), it had not managed to weaken the insurgency, despite the fact that during 2003 most of its resources went into fighting these illegal armed groups. The country's monetary, social and economic crisis has become a real obstacle to financing the Armed Forces' growing budget. Further resources from abroad are not a certainty, given that the scandal created by irregularities in the handling of the Plan Colombia's funds has hardened the North American government, whilst the European countries do not view Uribe's bullish policy in a positive light.

Hence there is disenchantment with Uribe in this area and a fear that if the second year of government does not manage to weaken the FARC enough to force it to the negotiating table then the FARC - having withdrawn its forces, biding its time and waiting for Uribe to "pay the price" - will return the country to the nightmare of the battle field, increasing the already massive numbers of dead, displaced and kidnapped.

An end to corruption

Wasted public resources and tax evasion have been two further factors contributing to intensifying the Colombian social crisis. The problem was raised by Álvaro Uribe on gaining office when he spoke clearly, condemning state corruption, stating that Congress would be revoked (reducing it and unifying the Senate and the Chamber in order to save money and make them more functional and efficient) and threatening to put anyone in the administration or state companies behind bars if they defrauded the Colombians of their heritage. But none of this took place. The anticorruption "Tsar" resigned from his post claiming a lack of commitment on the part of the government's own staff. With this resignation it became clear that this office had been created to give the impression that corruption was being tackled but that, in reality, it did not have government backing and hence no power to do anything.

But whilst the Uribe administration has not yielded positive results in these three areas, so important for tackling the social crisis in Colombia, it has also not had much luck in implementing unpopular policies, namely a series of initiatives that run counter to the construction of a democratic, pluralist and participatory state. Some analysts see this as the turning point in the Colombian people's enchantment with Álvaro Uribe. We are talking of the referendum, the presidential re-election, the creation of an "Uribist" party and the adoption of a law on "an alternative to prison" that offers members of armed groups their release from prison if they abandon force, even if they have committed crimes against humanity.

The referendum

The referendum called by Uribe was held on 25 October. After several months of hard bargaining between the government and the legislature, the referendum – which was to have contained three or four questions – ended up being a long and inconsistent text, incomprehensible to the ordinary voter, and introducing irrelevancies such as punishment for personal consumption of marijuana and cocaine but leaving aside the revocation of Congress, one of Uribe's flagship issues. Many questions, such as that of the "political death of corruption" and other anti-corruption measures were no more than "gimmicks" to get the electorate to the polling booths, given that they already exist in current legislation. The most difficult thing to swallow in the referendum was approval of the adjustment plan required by the International Monetary Fund (a two-year salary freeze, abolition of the comptrollers, cuts in social spending, etc.). In order to gain the support of the locally-elected authorities in promoting the referendum, these were granted a two-year extension period of their term in office.

The most important issue was that the referendum should be approved by a wide majority because the president's prestige was at stake: the referendum had become a plebiscite on his "Democratic Security" policy. Uribe did not sense that the social organisations, including the indigenous organisations, were encouraging people to abstain. His strategy to endeavour to polarise public opinion into friends or enemies of the referendum was very clumsy, implying that anyone not for the government was for the terrorists. His worst error was to turn on the human rights organisations, accusing them of assisting the terrorists through their critical analysis of his first year in office.[2]

The votes gained did not reach the threshold necessary for approval. As Camilo Castellanos said: "Such intolerance highlighted the risk of writing the government a blank cheque".[3]

"It never rains but it pours"

The fiasco of the referendum over, thoughts turned once again to the fact that, as Uribe's prestige still remained unscathed, it would be worth amending the Constitution to allow for presidential re-election. The argument was clear: there was a need for continuity in the democratic security policy, which was on the right path, and in the economy, whose upturn indicated that the course was the correct one.

It is clear that Uribe Vélez is ready to put his prestige on the line once more. But the organised forces are also unifying. Uribe's supporters are organising a political party that will unite the remains of the two traditional parties (liberal and conservative), whilst the democratic sectors are joining force, creating a new political phenomenon in Colombia: the dawn of a pluralist and democratic Left that explicitly rejects any reference to gaining power by violent means in its programme.

More of the same: the anti-terrorist law

At the end of 2003, the bill presented by the Uribe government to reform articles 15, 24, 28 and 250 of the National Constitution was approved. With the reform of these articles, the bill – better known as the "anti-terrorist law" - establishes restrictions on rights to privacy, the inviolability of correspondence, freedom of residence and movement and other individual freedoms. The government argued the need to provide the President of the Republic and state institutions with mechanisms able to play a preventive role in the war on terrorism. The strongest criticisms of this law have been directed at the fact that the security forces, who even without a security law have committed many outrages, are now being given the powers of criminal investigation.

Birds shooting at the guns

A bill on "an alternative to prison" is currently under discussion, which envisages the release from prison of members of armed groups who, having committed crimes (even atrocities and crimes against humanity), decide to demobilise and return to civilian life. This process is already underway with the Colombian Self-Defence Units (AUC). The Peace Commissioner, Luis Carlos Restrepo[4] and other government representatives are pushing for this bill to be sped up and are even talking of pardons and amnesties, arguing that the eradication of paramilitary groups is the most important step towards peace and overcoming the terror. This view runs counter to that of many human rights organisations, people close to Uribe and even the Bush administration, the government's main ally, who state that there can be no impunity for atrocities. An Amnesty International report (2002) indicated that, in Guatemala, a "corporate mafia state" was being established due to the fact that strong networks of demilitarised and amnestied paramilitaries and soldiers had entered the state institutions, forming mafias of drugs traffickers with almost invulnerable powers, who carry out all kinds of fraudulent business. Something similar is feared in Colombia, all the more given that links between paramilitary groups and international drug rings have been noted.[5]

What is clear, and is another gauge of the strength of the Uribe government, is that neither the State nor those in the armed conflict who committed the atrocities should be entitled to grant general or unilateral pardons, given that any legitimate act of pardon must be rooted in a process that involves all of society, including the victims' families and the communities affected by the violence. But the process has barely begun, with hearings of the so-called "social consultation to overcome the paramilitary phenomenon" in progress in the Congress of the Republic despite 850 members of the *Cacique Nutibara* front of the AUC plus an indigenous self-defence group in Cauca department having already been hurried into demobilising.

New democratic institutionality

On 26 October, the day following the referendum, the Colombian people went to the polls once more, this time to elect governors and mayors. In an event unprecedented in the country's history, the candidate for the *Polo Democrático Independiente* (Independent Democratic Pole) and sectors comprising the *Frente Social y Político* (Social and Political Front), Luis Eduardo Garzón, won the Bogotá Town Hall, beating the Uribist alliance candidate by a wide margin. Similarly, Angelino Garzón won the governorship of Valle del Cauca, the largest department in south-western Colombia.

The building of this new democratic institutionality has been made possible by the efforts and maturity of many movements in breaking away from the grey and ambivalent game of arms versus electoral and socio-political democracy.

This is perceived as being the turning point in the Colombian people's infatuation with Uribe. They are beginning to realise that Uribe is not the "best catch". The referendum results demonstrated this. The collapse of the referendum marked the breaking point and, in so doing, hindered the introduction of a new right-wing party within society. With the elections the following day arose a new movement of the alternative and democratic left in organisational, political and policy terms.

It is on this new institutionality that the country's main indigenous organisations are pinning their hopes, given that they have long - and at a high cost in life - rejected all armed strategies as political tools. And also because they share the idea that political citizens are built through struggles and demonstrations.

Human rights in indigenous areas

Below we present sections from the report produced by the National Indigenous Organisation of Colombia, ONIC, on the human rights situation in indigenous areas of Colombia. Many of the problems mentioned here have long histories. Some have worsened under the government of Uribe Vélez, and more concretely with the policy of democratic security. The document states:

...That the internal armed conflict in the country and the policy of "Democratic Security" being implemented by the current government have put at risk the lives of many indigenous peoples in the Sierra Nevada de Santa Marta, Arauca, Cauca and Putumayo, to mention only those territories in which the violation of human rights and international humanitarian law has been the most evident. Guerrilla forces, paramilitaries and the state's armed forces subject and abuse entire communities with their armed arrogance and ideology, disrespecting their traditional authorities, territories and the culture of many indigenous peoples.

That the internal armed conflict has had devastating effects on indigenous areas. These are very vulnerable peoples who, although not involved in the country's armed conflict, are its main victims. Peaceful by nature, these peoples are often forced by the armed players to participate in a war they do not understand and is not theirs. This violates their rights to life, autonomy, to their own culture and territory, free from violence. This can be observed in massacres, selective crimes, threats, intimidation, "informing", collective forced displacements or confinements, forced recruitment, restrictions on the entry of food and medicines to their communities and attacks on the communities' cultural and spiritual objects.

We wish to highlight the significant responsibility of the Colombian state, through its action or omissions, which have constituted human rights violations and particularly its responsibility in the ethnocide being perpetrated against some of Colombia's indigenous peoples, insofar as the abandonment, lack of protection, political, cultural and socio-economic exclusion to which the Colombian state has condemned its indigenous peoples is systematic. The National Development Plan, the aim and fundamental priority of which is to achieve a highly questionable "democratic security" establishes no public policies to guarantee and achieve the rights of indigenous peoples. It relegates as dead letter article 7 of the Fundamental Principles of the National Constitution, by which the State recognises and protects the ethnic and cultural diversity of the Colombian nation.

Through the government, the State does not establish how the right to life – particularly of their leaders -, and the right to their ancestral territories and sacred sites, which are fundamental to the very existence of indigenous peoples, should be truly and effectively guaranteed and protected; it does not protect universal assets such as biodiversity, it exploits - without listening to our concerns – the mineral and energy resources; encourages no care or strengthening of the health and education of our communities; is not interested in the food security of almost one quarter of the Colombian population living in the most abject misery. The lack of public policies in land (granting, titling, extending, regularising), health and education, demonstrate the exclusion to which we indigenous peoples are subjected, along with our peasant farmer and afro-Colombian brothers.

In violation of international humanitarian law, the government directly involves the rural population in the armed conflict by means of programmes such as the "peasant soldiers", the "informants' network" and the recruitment of indigenous people into their armed forces. It also puts us in danger when state employees "inform" on indigenous organisations and leaders, claiming they belong to or are involved in particular armed groups.

In implementing megaprojects on indigenous territories, undertaken with national and transnational capital, the State takes no account of the ILO's requirement to duly consult indigenous peoples and their organisations before handing over the exploration and exploitation of hydrocarbon and other natural resources on indigenous territories to voracious companies, without considering the environmental and social consequences these activities cause, with the aggravating circumstance that multinational companies are involved in human rights violations.

Likewise, the reforms made to the Mining Code, without considering our objections, give a free rein to the indiscriminate exploitation of resources on the part of transnational companies, without establishing any protective measures for indigenous peoples. The Colombian state is thus violating rights recognised in the American Human Rights Convention and other international instruments it is required to comply with.

Impunity and an absence of justice

The same document denounces the Colombian state:

...For not protecting the life and existence of indigenous peoples, the full and free exercise of our human rights, our own organisations, territories, ancestral natural and cultural goods, which have determined our survival as peoples. In our opinion, the State and the privileged classes defend economic interests that are damaging to the vast majority of Colombians.

It is this ruling class, powerful and arrogant, which – as noted by the UN delegate for Colombia, James Lemoyne - "has great responsibility for the aggravation of the armed conflict in Colombia". And it is directly responsible for the fact that there are more than 26 million poor Colombians, of which 13 million live in misery and 2 million are displaced, most of them peasant farmers, afro-Colombians and indigenous. These figures, together with the inequitable land ownership and concentration of wealth in the hands of a few, form a favourable environment for a further outbreak of the war in Colombia.

The indigenous organisations state that, during 2003, 139 indigenous people were murdered. This figure surpasses that of the previous two years. Some of the people most affected are the inhabitants of Sierra Nevada de Santa Marta. Despite protective resolutions and the implementation of precautionary measures to protect the indigenous peoples of the Sierra Nevada, 61 indigenous Kankuamo and 5 Wiwa were murdered and more than a thousand indigenous people forced to abandon their land.

The Embera, for their part, particularly those living in Chocó department, this year recorded 86 homicides, disappearances and injuries.

ONIC's document demands that the State:

...Fulfils obligations and commitments accepted before the national and international community. And we will continue to resist and fight in defence of our life, territory, autonomy and cultural identity. In this respect, we are making progress in various specific initiatives, for which we require the determined support of the Inter-American community and its legal and political instruments. These initiatives include: a) establishing Indigenous Peace Councils with leaders of renowned experience; b) communication and support networks to implement the Indigenous Early Warning System in coordination with the government alert system; c) methods of protection and areas of refuge for leaders at risk, based on an exchange between reserves and other forms of humanitarian assistance aimed at guaranteeing the life and sustenance of threatened communities; d) meetings for discussions between armed players at regional, national and international level; e) formulation of an Emergency Plan and Resistance Plans in the face of the armed conflict and forced displacement...

Notes and references

1   **Garay L.J. 1999**. *Construcción de una nueva sociedad*. Tercer Mundo Editores, Santafé de Bogotá.

2   **Plataforma Colombiana de Derechos Humanos, Democracia y Desa-**
    rrollo. 2003. El Embrujo Autoritario. Primer año de gobierno de Álvaro
    Uribe Vélez. Bogotá. www.plataforma-colombiana.org
3   Entre la Democrácia y el Autoritarismo: Colombia se debate entre un
    país que no acaba de nacer y otro que no termina de morir. *Asuntos*
    Indígenas, 2003 (4), IWGIA.
4   A well-known Colombian psycho-analyst known affectionately as "Dr.
    Tenderness" for his excellent essay "on the right to tenderness" and
    now, for the occupational hazard of defending the government's law on
    an 'alternative to prison', also known as "Dr. Torture".
5   During the course of the anti-drugs operation "Take Off", the Italian
    police established links between the AUC's number two, Salvatore
    Mancuso, and the Italian mafia via deliveries of cocaine to the fearsome
    Ndrangheta calabresa. El Espectador newspaper 1.02.2004.

VENEZUELA

D uring 2003, Venezuela was immersed in a reconsolidation of
both its economic and political spheres. This was the path
chosen by the government to create the conditions enabling, firstly,
democratic governance in the face of an inflexible and powerful opposition in economic and media terms and, secondly, the provision
of appropriate and fitting responses to the people in terms of health,
education and jobs.

The political climate

Among the important decisions taken during 2003, both structural
and short-term, it is worth noting the government intervention in the
functioning, structure and policies of the oil company, *Petróleos de*
Venezuela (PDVSA). This company had historically been seen by Vene-
zuelans as a first-rate organisation in terms of its resource production
and distribution. During the first half of the year, PDVSA, or rather the
former members of its senior management team, were responsible for
a stoppage that threatened rights established in both the Constitution
and the law. Venezuela being a virtual mono-producer, this halt
immediately and seriously affected the country's economy. Intervention in PDVSA took place with public knowledge and revealed infor-

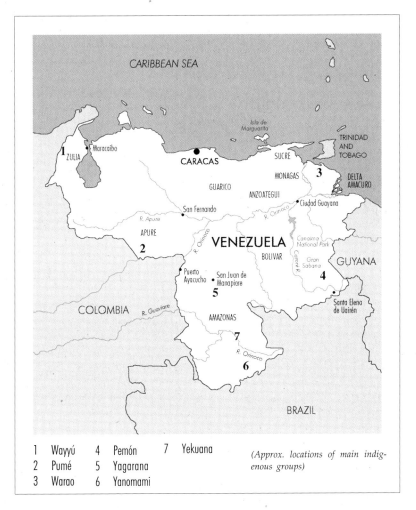

1	Wayyú	4	Pemón	7	Yekuana	
2	Pumé	5	Yagarana			
3	Warao	6	Yanomami			

(Approx. locations of main indigenous groups)

mation that was to destroy its "company of excellence" image. Among other things, it transpired that only around 20% of its income was actually entering the state's coffers while the remainder went on operating costs and, more particularly, senior management salaries. The government considers this intervention to be one of the most important processes for creating structural change.

Another important decision was to design immediate intervention policies to provide effective and appropriate responses to the problems being suffered by the population. "Missions" were therefore created, aimed particularly at tackling issues related to health and education. These are being implemented through the creation and official appointment of a Working Commission, whose job is to create a specific programme for the area in question. The Missions have ministerial status and their own budget, reporting directly to the President of the Republic.

Indigenous organisations support the government

In this process of national level socio-economic change and recon-solidation, the indigenous peoples of Venezuela are of the opinion that the government is demonstrating an attitude of respect, guaranteeing the rights enshrined in the Constitution of the Bolivarian Republic of Venezuela. It is therefore the responsibility of the grassroots organisations to work conscientiously to create proposals and to undertake the necessary political lobbying to enable them to be included as state policies.

In this complex political situation, the National Indigenous Council of Venezuela (CONIVE) is maintaining its unrestricted support of the government of President Hugo Chávez Frías.

One area in which CONIVE is actively involved is policy and programme design, such as the establishment of the Guaicaipuro Mission. This is a policy-focused "mission" the general aim of which is to provide an immediate response to the most acute problems being suffered by the country's indigenous peoples. It was created early in the second half of 2003, in line with the State's rapid intervention requirements. It is a bipartite commission, made up of representatives of both indigenous peoples and the National Executive, and has ministerial status. To date, agreement has been reached on the priority issues: health, intercultural education and land titling.

Another example is the review of bilingual intercultural education programmes: the Ministry of Education has invited regional organisations to carry out this review, and this work is still in progress.

CONIVE also participated in monitoring the year's electoral processes, particularly the action days when petitions were signed with regard to a decision on a referendum of legislative and presidential posts.

It should also be noted that CONIVE and its regional organisations were actively involved in the demonstrations held during 2003 in support of constitutionality and President Chávez.

Participants at the ORPIA Congress

Photo: Pablo Lasansky

ORPIA's 4th Congress

Amazonas is the southernmost state in Venezuela. Its territory covers 180,000 kms^2, and it has a population of 108,000 people,[1] 60% of whom belong to one of the 20 indigenous peoples living there.

In September 2003, ORPIA held its 4th Congress to coincide with the 10th anniversary of its establishment. The Congress was attended by 400 delegates from the Amazonian indigenous communities, and the following strategic lines were agreed for the indigenous movement during 2004:

- The right to collective ownership of ancestral lands
- Training for indigenous leaders to analyse and negotiate their demands
- Formal education as a real tool of empowerment. (Review of the bilingual intercultural school and its real effects)
- The protection and re-cycling of traditional knowledge
- A review and reform of indigenous public health care.

Political situation in Amazonas state

Amazonas state is currently run by an indigenous governor elected with the support of the indigenous movement. Nonetheless, after two and a half years of struggling to gain real indigenous participation in government decisions on public policy design and implementation, ORPIA and its political wing, the "United Multi-ethnic People of Amazonas" (*Pueblo Unido Multiétnico de Amazonas* or PUAMA) movement, decided to withdraw their support from the current governor. The crisis in living conditions of our people and the impossibility of negotiating the policies that were being established by the regional government were the causes of this.

During PUAMA's last congress, held in May 2003, the ideal model of indigenous government was discussed.

Beyond the importance of electoral success and the need to gain political power in local government spaces, PUAMA is based on a philosophy that governs its members' actions. This can be summarised as follows:

> *To unite the indigenous peoples of the Amazon to demand participatory democracy, to develop autonomy and indigenous governance in order to build a truly pluricultural and multi-ethnic state.*

Its mission has been built on this philosophical basis, which is "to gain access to local and national government under conditions of legitimacy, transparency and participation".

In line with the above, the mobilising principles of both the leaders participating in this first meeting and the leaders who were elected to PUAMA's Board of Directors must be highlighted. These are:

Unity of the indigenous movement of Amazonas state in order to guarantee the building of a consensual indigenous political project.
Consultation with indigenous peoples, organizations and communities on the future of the PUAMA political movement.
Political participation as a means to gaining respect for the rights of indigenous peoples.

In line with these principles, their stated objectives were:

- To create spaces for the political participation of indigenous peoples in defining their own future and in decision-making.
- To create spaces for reflection and training on the criteria required for good local indigenous government, adapted to the cultural, social, economic and political realities of the multiethnic and pluricultural state of Amazonas.

The demarcation process

During 2003, the National Demarcation Commission, CND, chaired by the Minister for the Environment and Natural Resources, worked towards obtaining basic agreements around the technical procedures to follow for the presentation of territorial titling requests. For this, various workshops were organised involving indigenous representatives from throughout the country and mapping experts. As a result, regulations for presenting applications are being drawn up which, in line with what was agreed, aim to guarantee flexibility and agility in the technical aspects of this process. In spite of such agreements, the President of the Republic has highlighted the need to begin the process of submitting applications and maps, even though these regulations are not yet complete, as some indigenous organisations are well advanced in the work in their region. Such is the case of the Ye'kuana "Kuyujani" organisation in Bolívar state, and also that of ORPIA.

Throughout 2003, progress in the process of Demarcating the Habitat and Lands of Indigenous Peoples and Communities so that they obtain the collective title to their land has been an area of significant work for ORPIA. This process can be considered in two stages: self-demarcation and demarcation.

Self-demarcation is an initial and prior internal stage in which 1) the communities manually draw sketches of their territories by sector, 2) the anthropological files justifying the territories required by each sector are produced and 3) the information in each of the sketches is transferred onto official maps. This stage of self-demarcation is being carried out by ORPIA and the indigenous peoples and communities of Amazonas state, and is justified on the basis of various articles of the Demarcation Law – a law that defines the constitutional right of Venezuela's indigenous peoples and communities to obtain the collective ownership of their lands.

ORPIA held community assemblies throughout Amazonas state from the end of 2002 and throughout 2003, attended by elders, shamans, community leaders, *comisarios* and elected indigenous authorities, during which the people themselves produced the sketches of their territories. The participants at all assemblies enthusiastically took part in producing these sketches. This course of action was ratified during ORPIA's 4th Congress, at which the delegates decided that ensuring the right to collective ownership of their territories would be an organisational mandate for 2003-2006.

With regard to the other elements of self-demarcation (the production of files for each sector and the transfer of information from sketches onto maps), ORPIA has - since the second half of 2003 - begun to define the theoretical context and methodology that will enable both the preparation of the files along with experts in the socio-cultural reality of the indigenous peoples and communities of the Amazonas, and the transfer of the community-drawn sketches onto official maps.

Once the self-demarcation has been completed, the second phase of the process will begin: the demarcation. This is when the maps of each sector are submitted, with their respective files, to the Regional Commission for Demarcation in Amazonas State and the National Demarcation Commission for their consideration. A negotiation process then begins within these bodies, between indigenous and state representatives in order to approve the planned indigenous self-demarcation. Demarcation is jointly undertaken by the Ministry for the Environment and Natural Resources (MARN) and the indigenous peoples, communities and organisations. To some extent, the demarcation phase has been taking place alongside self-demarcation.

No indigenous organisation has yet formally submitted files for negotiation and so no title has yet been approved.

The health problem

Serious health problems continue to affect the Venezuelan indigenous population. Although indigenous peoples' right to health and to respect for their traditional medicine are formally and constitutionally recognised, there is still a gaping hole between what "should be" and the reality, which is the result of centuries of marginalisation. Although Venezuela is a middle-income country, Amazonas state is remarkably less well off. This state, which includes 20 different indigenous ethnic groups, is "another world", as confirmed by its inhabitants. The human development index, levels of environmental health and the percentage of population with access to drinking water are significantly lower than for the rest of the country.

As a consequence, infant mortality, which is nationally 19 per thousand births, rises to 43.9 in Amazonas[1] and the mortality rate through malnutrition is almost four times higher in Amazonas than in the rest of the country.[2] The difference in infant mortality rate is primarily due to nutritional problems and transmissible diseases, which are among the main causes of morbidity and mortality for the indigenous population.

It is noteworthy that, for 2001, the rates of diarrhoea-based illnesses, pneumonia and tuberculosis in Amazonas state were double those of the rest of the country and, over the past year, the incidence of malaria has been seventy times higher![3]

The situation in Delta Amacuro state, populated largely by the indigenous Warao population, is very similar to that of Amazonas. Indicators of health and water access are similar to Amazonas and less than half those of the capital's region. The incidence of diarrhoea, related to the level of environmental health, is double that of the capital's region, and the incidence of measles, which reflects the coverage of immunization programmes, is 0.9 per hundred thousand inhabitants in the capital region but 4.4 per hundred thousand in Amazonas and 9.0 per hundred thousand in Delta, a rate thirty times higher than that of the country's capital.[4]

For 2003, the five main causes of illness in Amazonas state were infectious diseases: malaria, diarrhoea, viral syndrome, helminthiasis and acute rhinopharyngitis.[5] General causes of mortality during 2003, on the other hand, show a combination of deficiency and infectious diseases characteristic of the developing world (malnutrition, diarrhoea, pneumonia, tuberculosis, malaria, HIV / AIDS) and illnesses more generally associated with the industrialised world (cardiovascular disease, cancer, accidents, diabetes, suicide). A similar situation can be seen among the indigenous Warao population in Delta, with levels of diarrhoea, pneumonia and measles being significantly higher than in states with a higher level of "development" although also with the presence of systemic and metabolic illnesses more characteristic of urban stress and lifestyle changes. For example, high blood pressure and diabetes are twice as common in Delta.[6] This "double load" of illnesses of both "poverty" and "development" is being increasingly observed in the countries of the South.[7]

The malaria problem

Malaria is a sensitive indicator of the efficiency of the health system. Last year, the rate of malaria in Amazonas doubled, reaching a high of 87.7 cases per thousand, the worst rate in the country and seventy times higher than the national average (1.2 per thousand). This makes it the main cause of illness in the state and the seventh cause of death among children less than 12 months of age.[8] Three indigenous municipalities in Amazonas (Atabapo, Autana and Manapiare) presented the highest rates of incidence in the country. Delta Amacuro state experienced a 298% increase in the number of malaria cases, many of them caused by *Plasmodium falciparum*, which affected the indigenous Warao population. Other states with large numbers of indigenous people, such as Bolívar and Zulia, also showed increases in case numbers of between 55 and 545%.

With regard to Amazonas state, this noteworthy change in the transmission dynamic seems to have been influenced by three important factors:

- The incomplete decentralisation of the health sector which, on the one hand, weakened the central body responsible for malaria control with the aim of including control activities within horizontal programmes of Integrated Health Care and, on the other, led to a decline in the financial independence of bodies responsible for control at regional level, thus affecting service efficiency.
- The influence of illegal gold mining on the appearance of malaria, firstly in San Juan de Manapiare municipality and then, with much greater force, in Atabapo municipality, where an

incidence rate of 303 per thousand was reached, predominantly caused by *Plasmodium falciparum.*

- A marked drop in Gross Domestic Product (GDP) during the first quarter of 2003, as a consequence of the oil stoppage in December 2002. This led to a lack of resources in Amazonas state with which to mobilise health personnel responsible for malaria control.

Although the decline in GPD affected the whole country and had negative consequences for the whole health system, the figures indicate that the oil stoppage hit disadvantaged sectors disproportionately. One notable case is that of the Yanomami population, who present the worst indicators in Amazonas state, with infant mortality at between 76 and 250 deaths per thousand births, way above the average for Amazonas state. Being further from the capital, these people were worse affected by shortages of petrol, food and logistics.

The causes of the current health situation are many, ranging from structural causes determined by the spatial distribution of the indigenous population and the health system's resources, the absence of an indigenous health sub-system, geographic and cultural barriers, the impoverishment of people at highest risk, processes of migration and cultural change, low indigenous participation in resource management to more immediate causes, linked to the country's extreme polarisation, which interferes with the functioning of services and programmes, and which finds its expression in an oil stoppage or in the far less apparent - but equally important – slower rate at which resources flow via institutional channels. ❑

Sources

1   United Nations Development Programme (UNDP). 2001. Annual Human Development Report in Venezuela.
2   ibid. 2000.
3   Ministry of Health and Social Development (MSDS). Epidemiology Department, Amazonas. 2004. Malaria eradication programme No 53, 2003.
4   Human Development Report 2000. Venezuela: UNDP
5   Ministry of Health and Social Development. 2003. Amazonas Epidemiological Report. Caracas: Epidemiology Department
6   Human Development Report. 2000.
7   **Brundtland, Gro. 2002.** The World Health Report 2002 "Reducing Risks, promoting healthy life". Geneva: WHO.
8   MSDS. 2004

ECUADOR

After decades of strengthening, of struggle on the part of indig enous peoples, of uniting the country's social movements (public sector, peasant farmers, old Left, etc.) with a view to building a plurinational and multicultural state in Ecuador, the national indigenous organisation, CONAIE, finally became involved in Ecuadorian party politics through its political wing, Pachakutik (PK). And, in alliance with the *Sociedad Patriótica* (PSP) party, CONAIE reached the pinnacle of power, occupying senior government posts for the first time in Ecuador's history.

Given the previous corrupt regimes that had driven Ecuador to its deepest ever economic crisis, CONAIE was the answer to the people's desire for political change within the country. At local level, the Amazonian indigenous communities believed and hoped that this situation would benefit their land rights claims, support their plans to develop and build autonomous peoples, promote oil policy reforms, etc.

CONAIE, rather like the Titanic, set about navigating the dark and dangerous waters of power, *power* archaically being understood as depicted by corrupt Ecuadorian party politics.

"The sinking of the Titanic, also known as CONAIE"

On 15 January 2003, ex-military officer Lucio Gutiérrez of the *Sociedad Patriótica* party became the President of Ecuador, with strong support from his Pachakutik-CONAIE alliance partners.

A spirit of optimism quickly engulfed Pachakutik, mixed with surprise at their "rapid rise to power", along with the immediate challenges this implied in terms of the risk of failure.

The new government was, according to Llucu Miguel, PK coordinator, an "opportunity, but not the great moment the indigenous had been proclaiming for the past 20 years".

The question was whether Pachakutik could, by launching itself into politics, suddenly transform the years of indigenous struggle through this opportunity, given that in Ecuador political manoeuvring takes place under the concept of turning such "opportunities" to one's advantage, the typical logic of politicking. Their confidence that they would be able to turn circumstances to their advantage could, then, have been their first mistake.

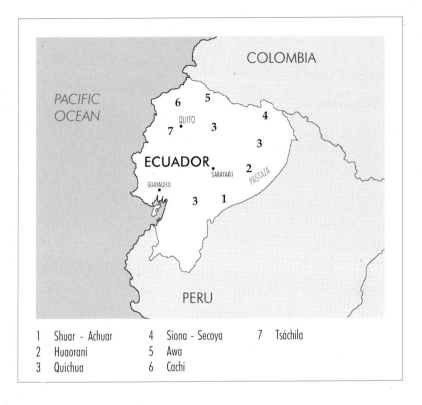

1	Shuar - Achuar	4	Siona - Secoya	7	Tsáchila
2	Huaorani	5	Awa		
3	Quichua	6	Cachi		

Convinced of their own strength and that they were the "political alternative", CONAIE and PK believed with the utmost innocence in "strengthening this government, strengthening the alliance and hence "fulfilling" the slogan of "*Ama shua, ama llulla, ama quilla*" which, in Quichua means "Do not steal, do not lie, do not be lazy".

However, this naivety lasted no more than a couple of weeks, until the Gutiérrez government announced the possible implementation of economic measures that CONAIE had long opposed, such as increases in the price of fuel, gas, diesel and electricity.

This first decision on the part of the government, which threatened the economy of the poorest sectors of society, was one of the main factors fuelling the conflict between CONAIE and Gutiérrez, and was later to become one of the causes of the alliance's breakdown.

CONAIE had always formed part of the opposition, the alternative, uncontaminated and pure. But once in power, it realised that Gutiérrez's political project ran counter to the indigenous organisation's ideals. It found itself in a position where power embarrassed it, and Pachakutik found itself trapped in the dilemma of being in power but not wishing to become contaminated by exercising it; of supporting the president whilst asking him to explain himself, of being responsible for decisions whilst at the same time criticising them. This dilemma made it difficult for Pachakutik to view its own political objectives with any maturity, to outline new positions or have any great desire to govern and raise the alternative proposals for which indigenous peoples had been fighting for decades and on which CONAIE had built its position in opposition.

The economic policy agreements with the IMF, accepted in advance by the government behind Pachakutik's back, clearly demonstrated that joining the political mêlée under neoliberal economic policy structures only led to disillusion and a series of contradictions with the social sectors.

At this point, CONAIE - like the rebellious child turning on its father - began to organise a number of protests against the government.

What did CONAIE gain from these demonstrations? Perhaps it needed to be in power to be able to organise a demonstration of its opposition?

The picture was clearer than the muddy waters of the Machángara: while Gutiérrez was playing the role of "best friend", giving the Indians an opportunity to visit the seat of government whenever they wanted, he was taking decisions behind their backs. My right honourable members of the Government, this is what is known as hypocrisy!

Could the president's attitude be termed treason? CONAIE leaders had known Gutiérrez from years back, they had fought side by side in the events that were to overthrow President Mahuad. The reason for this hypocrisy? Did they believe that the PSP's former military officers were going to admit that "Indians" were governing the country? To embark on a mistaken political adventure, to believe that the indigenous movement's relationship with the former Colonel was going to guarantee the trust and honesty of both government and governed, was perhaps a misguided strategy.

On 25 July 2003, the government signed a political agreement with CONAIE in which it made the following commitments:

- The government would rule out implementing any projects that included privatising strategic areas of the state.
- The government would undertake to review and evaluate various oil and energy contracts, promoting the so-called "People's fora to discuss the oil and energy policies to be implemented during its term in office".

- The government would agree not to increase the price of domestic gas.

CONAIE also presented the Head of State with other issues to be discussed at "a further meeting".

This political agreement calmed things down within the alliance, but only until August.

The alliance breaks down

In August 2003, the Pachakutik block decided not to support approval of the Law on Civil Service and Administrative Careers in the National Congress, a law that formed part of the agreements with the IMF. In addition, President Gutiérrez distanced himself from the principles that had been agreed upon with his "urgent economic packages", which were detrimental to the vast majority of Ecuadorians. This became another point of conflict to be added to the disagreements CONAIE had regarding foreign policy issues, such as the Plan Colombia and the FTAA. All this triggered a breakdown in the government alliance between Pachakutik and *Sociedad Patriótica*.

Only six months after Pachakutik and CONAIE had embarked upon the adventure of government, initially commenced by Antonio Vargas (ex-president of CONAIE), they had been shipwrecked. Shipwrecked in their efforts to understand and outline a new Ecuadorian foreign policy that would respect the sovereignty and right of the peoples. According to Leonidaz Iza, current president of CONAIE, "There was no effort on the part of the government to make our proposals viable or change our country's direction. There is great corruption in the corridors of power... ."

The search for true representation of the people was a failure due to the weakness shown by Pachakutik, its great political naivety and its lack of concrete political proposals.

No longer in government, Pachakutik now has no choice but to take full responsibility for its actions over the past few years. The weakening of CONAIE that has been witnessed has destabilised other Amazonian and highland indigenous organisations.

The consequences of this breakdown have taken a dangerous form, in the desperate action to "punish" the "anti-patriots", as seen from the authoritarian and military logic of the Gutiérrez government which, apparently, is involved in persecuting and attacking CONAIE leaders, imprisoning and murdering its opponents.

Sarayacu: autonomous territory

While at a national level CONAIE and Pachakutik are once more taking to the streets to continue their struggle in opposition, the territorial conflicts in the Amazon have intensified to such an extent that they are endangering the region's social stability and, as a consequence, the integrity of the indigenous communities.

The situation in Sarayacu

On 5 May 2003, the IACHR (Inter-American Commission on Human Rights) requested that the Ecuadorian government take preventive measures in the conflict between the CGC-Chevron Oil Company and the Sarayacu community.

The following examples demonstrate that this request was heeded little, if at all:

- Respect for the physical integrity of community leaders and members. There are still arbitrary lawsuits and criminal cases against them.
- The lack of will on the part of the authorities to investigate the events that took place in January 2003.
- The open threats by government officials, such as the Governor of Pastaza, who warns that, if the work stoppage continues in blocks 23 and 24, the areas will be militarized.
- The persistence of military units operating out of the nearby communities of Jatun Molino and Pacayacu under the pretext of preventing clashes between the communities.
- The breakdown in river traffic along the river Bobonaza, which prevents communication within the Sarayacu territory itself.

On 16 October 2003, at a hearing at the IACHR in Washington, community head Marlon Santi once more presented a complaint relating to the deteriorating situation in Pastaza following the failure to comply with the Commission's requests.

While waiting for the international human rights bodies to put pressure on the Ecuadorian government to intervene in the affair, the CGC-Chevron-Sarayacu conflict worsened. On 2 and 5 December 2003, members of the Sarayacu community were attacked by civilians supporting the oil company whilst travelling to Puyo to protest at the government's threats of militarization.

Faced with this situation, in December 2003 the IACHR attempted once more to protect the rights of Sarayacu and demanded measures to guarantee the safety of the community's inhabitants.

However, government statements, its arrogant attitude and lack of will to dialogue destroyed all possibility of precautionary measures. With an attitude reminiscent of former military dictatorships, the Ecuadorian government is thus in violation of the constitution and international law protecting the rights of indigenous peoples. This was confirmed in Amnesty International's recent demands made to the Ecuadorian state in response to statements made by the Minister for Energy and Mines, Carlos Arboleda.

Sarayacu and the proposal for self-determination
In the face of these events, Sarayacu has opted for the possibility of self-defence by declaring itself an Autonomous Quichua Territory. It is thus reaffirming the right to establish itself as a people and to freely manage its territory and the use of its natural resources, along with the right to administer its own justice and govern its territory.

In the proposal, Sarayacu suggests that the Ecuadorian state should redefine the oil map, and consider economic, social, environmental and cultural variables on an equal footing. It also demands, among other things:

- The removal of the CGC Oil Company and compensation for damage caused in the community.
- An independent international audit of the oil projects for blocks 10 and 12 and an assessment of their benefits for the communities in Pastaza province.
- That Sarayacu be declared a territory free from oil activity.

An uncertain future

The country's current political climate indicates that the pluricultural and multilingual nation of Ecuador is still far from embarking upon new democratic paths that will enable the indigenous peoples to define their own self-determination. And it will be impossible to do so while the country continues to apply a corrupt oil policy, enabling companies such as CGC-Chevron to invade indigenous territories and wreak havoc.

In addition, the rhetoric of indigenous autonomy can only become a reality when it is taken up by the communities themselves and "their own household is put in order". The divisions that exist within the communities (caused by the oil companies themselves), the absence of community leadership, the impoverished quality of life caused by a massive explosion of epidemics, the breakdown of the *ayllus* family, are all indicators of a serious situation that requires the players themselves to redefine and prioritize urgent actions by which to strengthen the essential conditions for their life plans.

Failing this, we will continue to embark upon political projects that are alien to the vision of being RUNA. Projects such as the great CONAIE-Pachakutik Titanic only serve to destroy our vision of who we are. ❑

Sources

Ecuadorian newspapers: *Hoy, El Comercio, Expreso.* January 2003 to December 2003.
De la Torre C. Nacionalismo y autoritarismo. *Hoy.* 31.01.2004.
Viteri C. Autonomía y gobierno. *Hoy.* 02.2001.

"Minga Informativa de Movimientos Sociales":
pasalavoz@movimientos.org
Sarayacu Web page: www.sarayacu.com

PERU

The Truth and Reconciliation Commission

T he Report of the Truth and Reconciliation Commission (*Comisión de la Verdad y la Reconciliación* - CVR) was one of the most important events in Peru for indigenous people, given that it confirmed the serious structural divorce between official Peru and the real tragedy that took place in the lives of indigenous peoples and communities. The internal armed conflict that devastated Peruvian society from 1980 to 2000 was responsible for 69,280 deaths, of which 75% were indigenous Quechua or Asháninka.

The report considers Shining Path to be "*the principle perpetrator of crimes and human rights violations*", being responsible for 54% of recorded fatalities. Referring to the action of the armed groups, it indicates that the generalised and systematic violation of human rights constituted a crime against humanity. It also condemns members of the Armed Forces for having propagated sexual violence against women.

The report particularly highlights the critical situation of the indigenous communities of the Selva Central who suffered severely, at the hands of subversive groups and through state abandonment. The Asháninka people were the victims of murder, destruction and devastation of their communities and the kidnapping of entire families by Shining Path, who later took over the Selva Central as their operations area. During 2003, dozens of malnourished and anaemic Asháninka re-appeared who had, for the past 17 years, been fleeing from or in the captivity of small columns of this armed group, hidden in the wooded Vilcabamba mountains in the upper forests of Junín. An EFE wire states that, according to police sources, as of 20 July 2003 there had already been 59 armed raids in Satipo province. For this reason, the pacification process has yet to be fully completed and there is a fear that terrorist action may re-emerge in that area.

As a result of the report, the adoption of reparation measures is still a pending issue on the government's agenda and, for the CVR this "has profound ethical and political implications and is an important component of the national reconciliation process". The report states:

> *The overwhelming majority of victims of the conflict were poor indigenous farmers, traditionally discriminated against and excluded, and they are the ones who should receive preferential treatment from the State.*

The crisis in CONAPA deepens

During 2003, the relationship between the government and the indigenous organisations suffered a serious deterioration due to the failed model of the National Commission for Andean, Amazonian and Afro-Peruvian Peoples (*Comisión Nacional de Pueblos Andinos, Amazónicos y Afroperuanos* - CONAPA).

Following the dissolution of the Technical Secretariat for Indigenous Affairs (*Secretaría Técnica de Asuntos Indígenas* - SETAI), the Executive provided no opportunity to discuss the proposed institutional system approved by the Indigenous Consultation of 12 to 14 April, deciding instead to re-establish CONAPA with temporary indigenous representatives chosen by the government itself. The Coordinator of the Indigenous and Afro-Peruvian Peoples' Development Project (*Proyecto de Desarrollo de los Pueblos Indígenas y Afroperuanos* - PDPIA) was dismissed in June with no justification. Unlike his predecessors, he had been selected via a public process with indigenous supervision.

Faced with these events, on 14 August a broad coalition of indigenous organisations held a press conference to present the Public Declaration of Indigenous Peoples of Peru in relation to the institutional crisis within CONAPA. This document represents a breakdown in the relationship between the state and indigenous peoples and solidly questions the existing lack of institutionality. Among the arguments given, it states that CONAPA is an inefficient institution, with no institutional hierarchy, whose decisions are binding to no one. It lacks legal status, and its own budget conceals decisions that have been taken behind the backs of the indigenous organisations. It has lost its legitimacy. The signatory organisations ratified their institutional proposal (see *The Indigenous World 2002-3003*), rejected the re-establishment of CONAPA and demanded direct dialogue with the Executive.

Strengthening of the national indigenous organisation

The Permanent Coordinating Body of Indigenous Peoples of Peru (*Coordinadora Permanente de los Pueblos Indígenas del Perú* - COPPIP), an umbrella organisation for many important organisations such as the Inter-ethnic Association for Development of the Peruvian Forest (*Asociación Interétnica de Desarrollo de la Selva Peruana* - AIDESEP) and the National Coordinating Body for Communities Affected by Mining

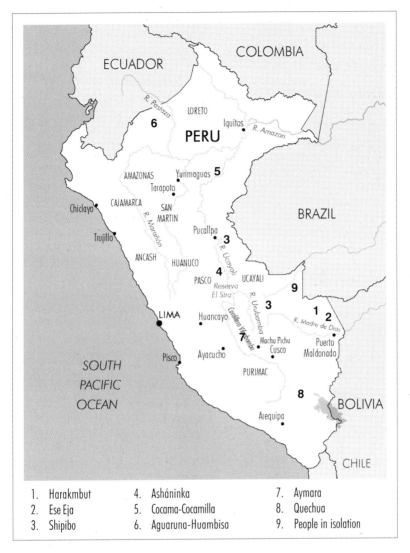

1. Harakmbut	4. Asháninka	7. Aymara
2. Ese Eja	5. Cocama-Cocamilla	8. Quechua
3. Shipibo	6. Aguaruna-Huambisa	9. People in isolation

(*Coordinadora Nacional de Comunidades Afectadas por la Minería* - CO-NACAMI), was very active this year in promoting important events. One such event was the National Indigenous Consultation on Constitutional Reform, in April, at which a joint proposal to include the rights of indigenous peoples and communities within the Political Constitution was approved together with other organisations. Unfortunately, the driving force behind the campaign came to a halt when

Congress decided unexpectedly to suspend drafting of the constitutional reform bill, which was 80% complete. One reason behind this halt was the parties' fear of experiencing a serious political reverse in the referendum on this bill, due to insufficient consultation and debate. However, the joint proposal has been retained as a policy contribution of the national indigenous movement and is being disseminated and discussed with the grassroots.

From 27 to 29 October, COPPIP held its National Assembly – Indigenous Consultation on Institutionality under the slogan: In defence of the Rights of Indigenous Peoples with Identity and Autonomy. The national meeting came to the following agreements:

- To withdraw CONAPA's authority to speak on behalf of Peru's indigenous peoples and to immediately initiate a lawsuit against the Peruvian state requesting that resolutions of this body be annulled.
- To submit a request for precautionary measures to the OAS Inter-American Commission on Human Rights.
- To approve and support the Proposal for an Institutional System for Indigenous Peoples, approved by the Indigenous Consultation held from 12 to 14 April 2003, which proposes creating a Decentralised Public Body for Indigenous Peoples at ministerial level, a Development Fund as executing agency and a real space for dialogue and consultation at a high level between the state and indigenous peoples as equals.
- To request that the Project for the Development of Indigenous and Afro-Peruvian Peoples (PDPIA), supported by the World Bank, be halted once and for all as it violates the dignity of indigenous peoples and serves only for corruption and embezzlement.
- To request the suspension of mining concessions on indigenous territories in Madre de Dios and other regions of Peru.
- That the draft Law on Languages and its regulatory texts should form the object of adequate consultation with indigenous organisations.
- That the Action Plan for Education produced by the indigenous peoples should be considered.

Main problems in the Amazon

Camisea: proven impacts

On 25 August, COICA, AIDESEP, COPPIP, CONACAMI, ARPI and COMARU published a statement entitled: Declaration of Indigenous Peoples in Defence of Life, Territory and the Environment. In this important document, the grave and serious impacts of the Camisea mega-project on the Urubamba forest were highlighted. This area is home to, among others, indigenous Machiguenga, Yine Yame and Caquinte communities, along with peoples still in isolation.

In June, an investigation team that visited the indigenous communities affected by the Camisea project, comprising COMARU (the Machiguenga Council of the River Urubamba) and various US environmental NGOs, presented a summary of its findings. The team members observed numerous serious environmental and social problems. They indicated that the four issues of most concern documented during the visit were the following: (a) massive soil erosion and multiple land slides, causing serious damage to the clean water ecosystems, (b) local food and health being affected by the decline in fish and water quality, (c) flawed compensation negotiations exploiting the lack of community preparedness, and (d) the existing monitoring plan being neither effective nor transparent and being ignored by the company.

Plot 57 and the Nahua problem

Last May, the Nahua sent letters to the government requesting the exclusion of plot 57 from their territory as a solution to the permanent invasions of illegal loggers and the titling of their territory. Despite the Nahua's dramatic request, they received no response. This forced them to send a delegation to the capital in November to dialogue with various authorities and to insist on their demand.

The Nahua have lived an undetermined length of time in a state of voluntary isolation at the headwaters of the rivers Manu, Mishagua and Serjali in the departments of Cusco, Ucayali and Madre de Dios, without any regular contact with other peoples, far less with the wider society. They sought refuge in this distant zone through fear of illness, slavery and genocide. But, since 1950, groups of loggers have been entering their traditional territory, felling trees and encroaching ever closer to their villages.

Following the explorations carried out by Shell for the Camisea project, groups of loggers took advantage of the abandoned access paths to make direct contact with the Nahua population and unleash, from 1984 on, an epidemic of respiratory illnesses that caused the deaths of more than half the population.

Protection for peoples in isolation

An important step forward for AIDESEP has been the creation of the Special Programme for Indigenous Peoples in Voluntary Isolation, Sporadic or Initial Contact, and the formulation of their Strategic and Operational Plan, through which they are implementing various actions such as the drafting of legal proposals, requests for territorial reserves, technical studies and so on.

AIDESEP brought a public interest action against Supreme Decree 028-2003-AG of 26 July, which entrusts CONAPA with the provisional guardianship of the peoples in voluntary isolation located within the extraction area of the Camisea project. AIDESEP considers this guardianship to be a step backwards in legal terms as it treats the indigenous peoples as if they were minors and denies them the capacity to represent themselves.

The organisation expressed its concern that the State was overstepping the mark in the use of its public powers, virtually appropriating representation of the indigenous peoples in isolation for itself. This was taking place whilst the legitimate representation of Amazonian indigenous organisations, who have been actively defending the peoples in isolation for decades and with whom they share ancestral contact and membership links, was being sidestepped.

AIDESEP maintains that, even in coordination with the National Institute of Natural Resources (INRENA), CONAPA is in no institutional position to exercise control mechanisms to protect the territorial integrity of the reserve or formulate contingency and emergency plans in case of contact, as provided for by article 5 of the noted mechanism. A bipartite State/indigenous peoples commission should be established to coordinate efforts and to ensure the protection of peoples in isolation who are located in very remote areas inaccessible to the state but not to the Amazonian indigenous.

Article three validates the violation being perpetrated by the Camisea mega-project through its extraction of gas from within the Territorial Reserve that was established by the state on behalf of the ethnic Kugapakori and Nahua people. It states that, "The right to exploit the currently existing natural resources should be exercised following the greatest of considerations, guaranteeing that the rights of the indigenous peoples inhabiting the area will not be affected". It

Achuar leaders from Pastaza. Photo: FECONACO/Racimos de Ungurahui

does not, however, specify what such considerations consist of or how they should be applied.

In addition, AIDESEP submitted claims of unconstitutionality against the Peruvian government for its inaction in the face of the social and environmental impacts caused by the Camisea Gas project on the Matsigenka, Nanti and isolated peoples of the area, and for the impact of oil operations in Plot 8X on the Achuar and Kichwa peoples of the river Corrientes in Loreto.

Forest concessions
Another ongoing problem denounced by AIDESEP is the superimposition of forestry concession contracts on the territories of native communities. This caused numerous conflicts in many parts of the Amazon during 2003, particularly in the Ucayali region. The Aidesep Ucayali Regional Organisation (*Organización Regional Aidesep Ucayali* - ORAU) has denounced alleged irregularities in the concessions in favour of corrupt sectors, with the complicity of INRENA employees.

AIDESEP is also denouncing the persistent discrimination in neglecting requests for the physical-legal regularisation of the communities affected by the forestry concessions. They emphasise that the state, through the Special Project for Land Titling and Rural Land Registry (*Proyecto Especial de Titulación de Tierras y Catastro Rural* - PETT) and INRENA, is telling them that it has no budget, and yet it is granting preferential title to settlers and concessions to logging companies.

For its part, the Regional Coordinating Body of Indigenous Peoples - San Lorenzo (*Coordinadora Regional de los Pueblos Indígenas San Lorenzo* - CORPI-SL), in the Province of Alto Amazonas, Loreto, is denouncing the manipulative action of the OXI-Burlington Recurse oil consortium which, with the complicity of the Ministry of Energy and Mines, is trying to enter the Acuar people's territory. They reject the campaign of information workshops by which it is trying to justify its compliance with the requirement for consultation. They state, for example, that the workshop of 20/21 July was held without the prior knowledge of the communities and their organisations, using unrepresentative pseudo leaders with the aim of justifying their intention to invade their territory.

Problems in the Andean coast area

The impact of mining on the communities

Three hundred delegates participating in the International Forum on Mining, Society, Environment and Development, held in Cajamarca in September 2003, signed a public statement in which they indicated that the decision to impose mining as a priority economic activity ignored the rights of the communities to decide their own development, given that mining activities impact negatively on the eco-system, society and culture of the communities. A global economic model was in this way being consolidated that would assign our economies the role of raw material production and destroy traditional ways of life.

In addition, in October, the National Coordinating Body of Communities Affected by Mining (*Coordinadora Nacional de Comunidades Afectadas por la Minería* - CONACAMI) held its Second National Congress and continued its campaign of complaint against the impacts of mining on the lives of the communities.

This organisation maintains that, over the last decade, mining in Peru has had the consequence of contaminating large water basins and poisoning thousands of people living in areas neighbouring the mines, with more than 300 communities being displaced from their territories and more than 600 leaders arrested and tried for defending their rights.

CONACAMI claims that the current government is continuing the same economic and mining policy that was commenced in the 1990s under Alberto Fujimori, who offered opportunities for foreign investment, particularly in mining. Between 1993 and 1996 alone, the Peruvian government signed 153 tax incentive agreements, of which more than 40 were in the mining sector. Despite the promises of and expectations for change, the current government has conceded the Ministry of Energy and Mines to the business sector.

The organisation is denouncing the threat of 239 mining projects, 122 of which are for gold and which, if implemented, would cover more than 60 million hectares with an investment of more than 8 billion dollars to 2008. Meanwhile, the State is failing to guarantee respect for the communities' rights in terms of consultation and participation, rights that are protected by ILO Convention 169.

The indigenous communities living in areas neighbouring the mining operations are the victims of their impact. These operations disrupt their right to life, they contaminate their environment and natural resources, displace them from their communal territories, and change their cultures and subsistence methods. They damage their right to health, contaminating the water and air with mercury, arsenic, lead and other heavy metals. Analyses carried out in La Oroya, Cerro de Pasco, Choropampa (Cajamarca), Ilo, San Mateo de Huanchor and Callao all demonstrate the presence of metals in people's blood.

CONACAMI's Congress agreed to demand the government's immediate compliance with the Commitment Act of 19 July 2002, signed by the Ministries of Energy and Mines, Agriculture and Health and which agreed to establish - by means of Supreme Decree - a High Level Tripartite Dialogue Commission with the aim of resolving the various conflicts caused by mining activity in Peru. This commission has not been established due to delays on the part of the Executive itself. CONACAMI is also calling on the Ministries of Justice and the Interior to put a stop to police and court actions aimed at terrifying and persecuting national leaders and the leaders of the communities affected by mining (CORECAMI) in Huancavelica, Pasco, Junín, Piura, Apurímac, Moquegua and other regions.

Contamination in Yanacocha

Yanacocha is one of the largest mining projects in Peru and is located at the head of the Cajamarca valley, in the highest part, which is the source of three micro-basins. In June, the Colombian company, INGETEC, submitted an Environmental Audit and Environmental

Assessments on the operations of Minera Yanacocha in Cajamarca, Peru. This document states that:

- The impermeability system is vulnerable, as demonstrated by the detection of a relatively high cyanide content in the waters released by the sub-drainage systems.
- In order to lower costs, Minera Yanacocha is overloading the leaching areas. The results can be observed in cyanide escapes detected in waters under the leach pads.
- Given its magnitude and location in an area of high vulnerability, in which the sources of various waterways of regional importance are to be found, considerable negative impacts have been observed on the physical, biotic and social environment.

The audit states that "the main sources of alternative water for the future supply of Cajamarca would be influenced by mining operations". To these problems was added Minera Yanacocha's continual abuses of the surrounding farming communities (Tual, Apalina, Quishuar), the invasions of lands for exploratory studies, the reduction in channels supplying water to the communities, the arbitrary closure of roads, etc.

Prospects for 2004

The Report of the Truth and Reconciliation Commission (CVR) contains a number of proposals for institutional reform that the government must consider when adopting an integral reparations plan. These include, in particular: recognition and inclusion of the rights of indigenous peoples and their communities within the national legal framework and the creation of a state institution or body for indigenous and ethnic affairs.

According to Recommendation A.10. of the CVR, the proposal for the rights of indigenous and Afro-Peruvian peoples must include, among other things, recognition of the following individual and collective rights:

- *The inclusion of individual and collective rights within the constitution;*
- *The definition of the Peruvian state as a multinational, pluricultural, multilingual and multi-faith state;*

- *Interculturality as a state policy;*
- *Their legal existence and status as peoples and their communal ways of organising;*
- *The inalienable, imprescriptible, non-seizable and inexpropriable nature of their lands and territories;*
- *An indigenous law and justice administration system in accordance with human rights plus access to the ordinary justice system with judges specialised in indigenous issues;*
- *Recognition of traditional mechanisms of alternative justice.*
- *The creation of a state institution or body for indigenous policy.*

In Recommendation A.11, the CVR states that

> *In compliance with a number of international obligations, the Peruvian state must develop and strengthen an institutional system appropriate to caring for and promoting the development of indigenous and Afro-Peruvian peoples and communities.*

Only in this way will it be possible to begin to overcome the conditions of structural exclusion, abandonment and age-old marginalisation to which significant sectors of the population have been subjected and which makes them particularly vulnerable to action on the part of violent groups. It also states that:

> *The creation of a body with sufficient strength and technical, administrative, economic and financial autonomy, which can draw together the responsibilities, programmes and projects of various public sectors, with the power to regulate, direct and implement development policy, plans and programmes should be explored.*

In addition, on 7 January 2004, Law 28150 was published creating the Committee to Review Legislation on Peasant and Native Communities, which has a period of six months as from its establishment to produce a draft Law on Peasant and Native Communities in Peru. This means that the communities of the coast, mountains and Amazon will have a common agenda to support in the face of attempted reforms. COPPIP has rapidly established a coordinating body to set up a Working Group and organise consultation on this issue.

There is also concern in indigenous circles at the planned consultancy being organised by the Special Project for Land Titling and Rural Land Registry (*Proyecto Especial de Titulación de Tierras y Catastro Rural* - PETT) of the Ministry of Agriculture, by which it intends to promote individual titling within the peasant communities. Specialists consulted are of the opinion that the terms of reference for this consultancy, which will receive funding from the Inter-American Development Bank (IABD), are biased towards privatisation as they do not propose dealing integrally with the issue of the communities' territories and the main priority is to establish regulations for article 11 of Law 26505 and Law 26845 on individual titling in favour of settlers and third parties in possession of peasant communities' territory. This conceals a serious threat to the territorial integrity of the communities.

Another threat hanging over Peru's indigenous peoples is implementation and possible approval of a Free Trade Agreement (FTA) with the United States or the FTAA, for which the government established a negotiating committee early in 2004. Despite protests at continental level and also, timidly, within Peru, the government is showing no signs of sensitivity to the dangers of such commitments, given the existing inequalities in the country. ❏

BOLIVIA

T he country has been in a state of complete social turmoil since the beginning of 2003. The economic model has come with a high social price, while the political system has focused decisions excessively on the political parties. This has all led to a deepening of the crisis.

The new social crisis broke out in January and February 2003 when the government tried to implement an income tax that would cause even more hardship for the poorer sectors. The police mutinied and the armed forces, acting on government instructions, confronted them causing dozens of casualties. The state was split from within. The mob, with no political direction but a wealth of accumulated fury, attacked various offices of the three branches of the state along with the headquarters of the traditional political parties, and looted a number of shopping centres.

The October events

On Friday 17 October 2003, television images focused on President Sánchez de Lozada, his senior ministers and allies briskly climbing into helicopters on the air force runway in La Paz to be taken to the El Alto international airport to board commercial flights to other countries. The strong men of the regime were fleeing.

The wave of popular protest had been expressed through a number of events. On 8 September around 200 peasant farmers, headed by the Aymara leader, Felipe Quispe, declared a hunger strike on the San Gabriel radio station (bastion of popular education and alternative communication in the town of El Alto, department of La Paz). They justified their action on the basis of the list of 72 demands that had accrued since the 2001 demonstrations in the *altiplano*.

On 19 September, called upon to do so by their leader, Evo Morales, the organisations allied within the Movement to Socialism *(Movimiento al Socialismo)* held protests in almost all of the department's towns in opposition to the government's proposed gas exportation terms, gas being one of Bolivia's most important resources. At the same time, peasant farmer blockades were being set up in the *altiplano*[1] by grassroots organisations with various demands but no visible leadership. On 20 September, the Minister of Defence, Carlos Sánchez, the evil face of the regime, led an operation to "rescue the

159

tourists held in Sorata area". Their transfer through the area of Warizata in buses led to a clash between soldiers and peasant farmers, leaving a balance of 7 dead and 17 wounded.

The protests were becoming localised in the *altiplano* around La Paz and the government's strategy was to crush them militarily. However, the urban sectors came onto the scene in October. On the 8th, the Regional Workers' Union (*Central Obrera Regional*) and the neighbourhood committees of El Alto declared an indefinite civil strike, in relation to which the Bolivian Workers' Union (*Central Obrera Boliviana*) called various national demonstrations.

The evening of 9 October plunged the country into mourning once more. A clash between miners and police in Uyania had left 3 dead and 21 wounded. By now, the protests were spreading throughout the highlands. The strategy in El Alta was to seize the Senkata petrol and gas distribution plant in order to cut off fuel supplies to La Paz. In Santa Cruz, a peasant farmer march to the city set off from Yapacani, and blockades were established on the San Julián roads.

The worst massacre of the gas war was to take place on 11 and 12 October. The army violently intervened in El Alto in a frustrated bid to regain control of the Senkata plant, leaving dozens dead and hundreds wounded. Not only did they fire on the protestors but also on private homes. The military strategy was intended to instil terror in the people and, through militarization, to isolate the conflict in this town. But the government failed once more.

On Monday 13, mass protests made their way to La Paz, from El Alto, Las Yungas, the *altiplano* and the mining centres. The people of La Paz also joined in the demonstrations. Throughout the country, the popular sectors had changed their demand: instead of continuing to oppose gas exports, they were now calling for the President's resignation. That same day, Vice-President Carlos Mesa declared himself independent from the Executive Power, whilst remaining in the Vice-Presidency of the Republic.[2]

On Wednesday 15, a march that had started in Oruro was surrounded by army troops in the area of Patacamaya, causing the deaths of two miners. Immediately, urban protests and peasant blockades took place throughout the country. That evening, the ex-Ombudsman and a group of intellectuals went on hunger strike demanding the constitutional succession of the Presidency. Two days later, almost one hundred middle class people were on hunger strike. By Thursday 16, the cards were down: more than 200,000 people had assembled in the Plaza de San Francisco in La Paz demanding the President's resignation.

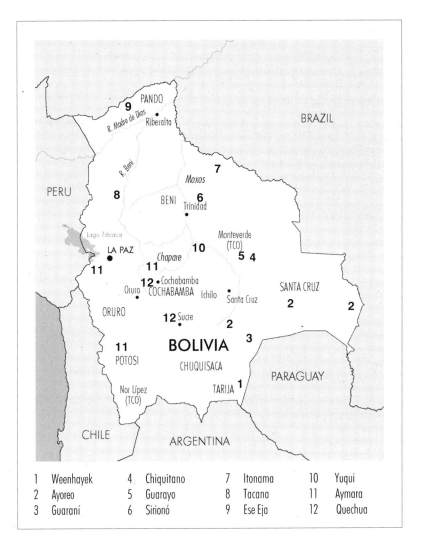

1	Weenhayek	4	Chiquitano	7	Itonama	10	Yuqui
2	Ayoreo	5	Guarayo	8	Tacana	11	Aymara
3	Guaraní	6	Sirionó	9	Ese Eja	12	Quechua

On Friday 17 October, the regime's Minister of Education and Culture, still in office, appealed to the coalition's allies to leave in an organised fashion rather than to stampede out. Later that night, Parliament voted to accept the President's resignation. People from virtually all corners of the country were seized with jubilation.

Meanwhile, in Santa Cruz, a Yapacaní settler demonstration that had joined up with another headed by the department's Peasant Farmers' Federation, commencing two days previously in El Torno, had entered the main square. Against the above backdrop, the peasant farmers were fenced in and brutally attacked by regionalist groups, stirring up racist tendencies the aim of which, deep down, was to prevent the popular protest from affecting the privileged position of the lowlands power groups. The popular sectors' message was also clear: the premises on which the elite based their power would be disputed and resisted.

The popular uprising had a clear indigenous identity along with an issue of national agreement: the defence of gas and the President's resignation. Nonetheless, it lacked coordination in terms of its policies/demands and in terms of unified political direction.

The country's structural problems

Bolivia has a population of 8.4 million people and an annual growth rate of 2%. The Bolivian people are largely indigenous, with one of the highest poverty levels in the region. According to the 2001 census, 63% of the national population live below the poverty line and 14% survive on less than 1 dollar a day. 90% of the rural population struggle in poverty whilst 60% suffer situations of extreme poverty.

The annual growth in population demands economic growth of at least 5% of GDP. Nonetheless, the current fiscal deficit stands at 8% of GDP. Exports are at very low levels, representing only 19% of GDP. As for direct foreign investment, this is very far from national expectations. In 2003 it totalled 1,044 million dollars, with no impact on job creation. The country's economically active population numbers 3 million people, of whom 83% work in the service sector while 11.95% (almost 300,000 people) are unemployed.

The above typifies the economic crisis and the enormous imbalances existing within Bolivian society. In our opinion, the main structural problems are ethnic, class and regional conflicts, and economic and political dependence. The most immediate expression of these structural problems at national level can be seen in the different voices, actions and clashes of interest around the gas and hydrocarbon issue, the land issue and the call for a Constituent Assembly.

Gas in the history of Bolivia

Energy resources form the basis of a country's industrial development and so their possession and control are determining factors in public policies and international relations.

Santa Cruz de la Sierra, October 2003. Photo: IWGIA archives

The country's energy policy – that of privatisation – has organically incorporated the hydrocarbons sector into transnational capital. *Yacimientos Petrolíferos Fiscales Bolivianos* (YPFB) was dismantled in two stages. Firstly (1996), the then President, Sánchez de Lozada disposed of the oil fields and pipeline networks at a "bargain price": 843.9 million dollars when proven reserves alone were worth 13,000 million dollars. Secondly (2000), his successor in the presidency, General Banzer, sold off the refining complex and marketing networks for only 122 million dollars, despite this being the area that was creating the greatest profit.[3]

Prior to the State companies' privatisation, hydrocarbons being extracted and/or discovered were owned by the YPFB, a body that could sign operating or partnership contracts, retaining 50% of the proceeds. Marketing and transportation were a State monopoly. The legal framework adopted after privatisation broke the production chain, restricting state ownership of hydrocarbons to fields that were not declared commercial, and reclassifying reserves as existing or new, with state participation being reduced from 50% to 18% in the new ones.

Between 1985 and 1996, YPFB contributed an average of 339 million dollars per year to the General Treasury of the Nation (TGN), thus forming an essential pillar of the country's financial stability. Since privatisation, transfers to the TGN have fallen from more than 363 million dollars in 1996 to only 15.2 million dollars in 2000, contrasting with the rate of export growth.

The size of Bolivia's gas reserves, 54.9 cubic feet tons (both proven and probable), makes it number one in South America with 42% of reserves, followed by Argentina with 20.8% and Venezuela with 16.6%. Such potential is an opportunity to produce a national development strategy based on natural gas industrialisation.

The Anglo-Spanish consortium, Pacific LNG, has been pressuring for Bolivian gas exports to California to go via Chile. Its plan was to win the project and invest 6,000 million dollars in order to gain a return of 20,000 million dollars over 14 years (selling 23 million cubic metres of gas per day at a price of 0.70 dollars per BTU). Of this total investment, only 20% would take place within Bolivia. The profits to Bolivia over the same period would have totalled 50 million dollars per year by way of taxes and royalties (a total of 707 million dollars over 14 years).

To commence exporting Bolivian gas, Pacific announced a consortium with Sempra Energy, a holding company that distributes energy to the United States, Mexico and Chile and which has various deals negotiated in this neighbouring country through its partner CMS Energy, owner of 50% of Gas Atacama and Nopel in Tocopilla. There are historic problems still unresolved between Bolivia and Chile: the 1904 Treaty by which Chile cut off Bolivia's access to the sea, the mining of its borders, the arbitrary diversion of the waters of the rivers Mauri, Lauca and Silala, creating a deep-rooted anti-Chilean sentiment among the Bolivian population.

The land issue

Making the collective rights of indigenous peoples a reality has an inescapable price: access to and return of their ancestral lands.

In Bolivia, indigenous peoples' territories have been encroached upon by people linked to the power base who stockpile land and who, in many cases, have fabricated land titles superimposed on areas occupied by the indigenous and even on each other's lands. The land ownership structure of the country is one of the most concentrated in the region. Estimates indicate that businessmen own 8 times more land than indigenous and peasant farmers, despite representing only 1% of the population. The greatest inequities are to be found in the country's lowlands, where 76,000 businessmen own 22 million hectares, whilst 78,000 smallholders own only 3 million hectares.

Land tenure shows a bipolarity between smallholdings and large estates, both enemies of rural development. In fact, levels of productivity do not even guarantee internal self-sufficiency, and they are also damaging to management of the ecological floors. Consequently, the current land ownership structure not only represents an unfair distribution of lands but is also creating poverty, low productivity and soil erosion.

The current Bolivian agrarian process, initiated with the promulgation of the new Agrarian Law of 1996, has as its fundamental pillars the clarification of agrarian rights and prioritisation of the titling of native community lands in favour of indigenous peoples. This titling is conditional upon regularisation, so indigenous peoples can only obtain their lands once others who hold illegal plots within them have been removed.

On the basis of the historic demands of 1990,[4] the indigenous peoples requested the titling of 158 Native Community Lands covering a total area of 35 million hectares from the state. During more than seven years of implementing the new Agrarian Law, only 3 million hectares (less than 10% of the total requested) have been titled and many territories have been wiped out.[5] This is because, in applying the land regularisation procedures, the same irregularities are being committed that caused the 1953 Agrarian Reform to fail, in terms of an equitable distribution of land.

The indigenous and peasant farmers are aware that as long as the actions of those involved in the agrarian process depend upon the political interests of power groups, it will not be possible to gain the true independence of the public authorities, nor to comply with the law. The Political Constitution therefore has to be reformed by means of a participatory Constituent Assembly.[6]

Constitutional reform

Against the background of the deep social crises that have occurred since 2000, a debate on constitutional reform was embarked upon. In July 2001, the political parties - through the Church - undertook to institutionalise the Electoral Court and promote reforms that included the widest possible social involvement, even contemplating the possibility of a Constituent Assembly. Several months later, they appointed a number of "important" citizens to form the People's Council in order to gather together social expectations. This task was restricted to fora, workshops and exchange events with little civic participation and no social agreement.

In March 2002, the People's Council's proposal for constitutional reform was published. In its preliminary recitals, it declared its supposedly neutral character, concealing its neoliberal nature. In its general section it declared the social nature of the state but, in the special regulations, it restricted state ownership of natural resources, and it eliminated agrarian reform as a state role, the subjection of agrarian rights to work and the social nature of peasant farmer ownership. It included institutions of semi-direct democracy as political rights: the citizen's right to propose new legislation, the referendum and the plebiscite, the first robbed of its binding nature and the second and third subject to the will of Parliament and the Executive to organise them and establish their conditions. The proposal was the object of great criticism and was thus abandoned.

In May 2002, the parties holding a parliamentary majority agreed to a new proposal. This expanded fundamental rights but constitutionalised the system of superintendencies, which would have *carte blanche* to continue natural resource privatisation. It accepted the citizen's right to propose new legislation, subject to regulations to be approved by Parliament, recognised civic groups for popular representation provided they fulfil requirements similar to those demanded of political parties, included the power of Parliament to repeal the President's mandate and vice versa, provided he then also resigns, thus tightening the dependence between the two and, finally, agreed to the referendum as a measure to adopt constitutional reforms approved by Parliament but no more. The proposal was rejected: Parliament could not approve it and national elections were imminent. Previously, the "politicians" had promised the indigenous that they would include a Constituent Assembly in the law for constitutional reform.

On 31 July 2002, Parliament approved the law for constitutional reform, including most of the content agreed between the parties in May but including three new issues: eliminating the Congressional and Presidential right of repeal, establishing an absolute majority for organic laws, (that is, those that regulate the way in which the organs of public power and the electoral system are run), thus marginalizing the strong indigenous/peasant farmer group elected at the elections on 30 June of that year and, in addition, envisaging the creation of new bureaucratic anti-corruption bodies dependent upon Parliament and the President. In other words, the political system was establishing control over itself. This law lacks legitimacy, it reproduces the framework of power, does not include a Constituent Assembly and does not make civic participation and social control a reality, nor does it safeguard the independence of the public authorities from traditional political party control. In any case, this too failed as a constitutional reform due to the national conflict that was to occur.

The future

The new government is still very slow in taking steps to implement the national agenda (hydrocarbons, land, Constituent Assembly). The dominant tendency within the new regime seems to be one of liberal restoration in both economic and political terms. With regard to the new hydrocarbons law, the official proposal focuses on regaining ownership of the resources, substituting shared risk contracts with other operation and partnership contracts, regaining some the YPFB's functions, enabling it to become a manager and operator, creating an additional tax on hydrocarbons that would vary according to production levels and the size of the fields, and creating a National Energy and Hydrocarbons Council (CNEH) to establish the sector's policies.

These changes would be in addition to adopting measures aimed at changing the national energy matrix and promoting the industrialisation of gas.

In terms of the land issue, the government has not yet given any clear signals. The structural problems in the agrarian process relate to a lack of transparency in land regularisation; the implementation of technical regulations that run counter to the spirit of the law and counter-reform measures that infringe upon indigenous and peasant farmer rights; the lack of definition in distribution of state lands; unfulfilled state commitments; and the systematic collapse of the sector's institutionality. The President has appointed a Land Delegate and a new interim National Director for INRA. Nonetheless, their actions have thus far been limited to dealing with specific conflicts and smoothing over others that have threatened to escalate into violence. No political will to tackle the structural problems in the agrarian process has been evident, despite the rekindling of the scandal involving a deputy, a businessman and two Chilean nationals who defrauded the state of half a million dollars, expropriating vast areas of land in Santa Cruz.

In terms of the Constituent Assembly, Parliament has approved a law of constitutional reform, which includes a constitutional text along with the binding referendum, ruling out the path of the interpretative law of popular sovereignty to constitutionalise them. The difference between these procedures relates to the scope attributed to the Constituent Assembly, given that via the path of interpretative law it is characterised by an exercise of popular sovereignty whilst via the path of planned reform it is subjected to the will of Parliament which, in turn, will legislate on its workings. In addition, the constitutional reform has included 15 of the 45 articles that formed part of the law requiring a constitutional reform, and incorporating changes: it defines the type of government as a representative and participatory democracy, this latter being expressed via mechanisms for popular deliberation and government, such as the Constituent Assembly, the citizen's right to propose legislation and the referendum. In terms of popular representation, it also recognizes civic groups and indigenous peoples in addition to political parties. However, the conditions for implementing the above are subject to special laws, and so they will be subject to the will of those who still exercise a legislative monopoly.

Uncertainty continues with regard to the political and social situation. This forces us to raise the need for a wide national debate to tackle the most urgent problems, and a true social and political pact to guarantee the viability of the Constituent Assembly and to banish the ghosts of 'partidocratic' manipulation that haunt it. ❏

Notes and references

1 Altiplano is the name of the Andean highland region of Bolivia. (Ed. Note)
2 Carlos Mesa is a prestigious social communicator who was invited by Sánchez de Lozada and his party –the MNR- to form part of the 'binomial' that fought the election and gained power.
3 See Petróleo y gas en Bolivia, in the CEJIS journal *Artículo Primero* Nº 12, "Gas para todos los bolivianos", Santa Cruz, March 2003.
4 That year, the indigenous peoples of Beni were instrumental in the march for "Territory and Dignity" from the town of Trinidad to La Paz, having achieved great national and international backing and the recognition of 5 indigenous territories via decrees promulgated by President Paz Zamora.
5 Particularly in the Guaraní area, some indigenous communities maintain their condition of captivity; land regularisation has not affected the cattle ranches, as a number of them have been consolidated through the mere presentation of certificates of cattle vaccination. Indigenous demands have therefore not been met.
6 In May 2002, the indigenous peoples and peasant farmers of the east of the country organised the 4th March of the lowlands demanding that the authorities and political system organise a Constituent Assembly, making known their sectoral demand for a reorganisation of the country as a prior step to achieving their own demands.

BRAZIL

W ith the inauguration of Luiz Inacio Lula da Silva as President of the Republic on 1 January 2003, Brazil's indigenous peoples began the year hopeful that important changes might take place in the country's policy on indigenous peoples. This was because President Lula and his Workers' Party had historically presented themselves as defenders of the rights of the oppressed, including indigenous peoples. Before Lula's election, Workers' Party MPs had, on various occasions, come out in defence of indigenous peoples within the National Congress and Lula had presented himself as the indigenous peoples' ally, attending various indigenous assemblies as guest of honour. Once Lula and the Workers' Party came to power, it was believed that this would be an excellent opportunity for guaranteeing indigenous rights in practice.

And what of the "Commitment to Indigenous Peoples"?

Lula had already undertaken to support land demarcation, adopt special public policies in the areas of health and education, promote the culture and sustainable economic development of indigenous peoples and reform the National Indian Foundation (FUNAI), the body responsible for indigenous affairs. Lula's proposals could be found in a document entitled "Commitment to Indigenous Peoples" which, if it were to be implemented, would represent a significant step forward for Brazil's indigenous peoples.

However, President Lula's first year in office has shown that, as with previous governments, protecting indigenous rights is not one of his priorities. Instead of promoting indigenous rights, Lula's government has focused on building alliances with sectors opposed to indigenous peoples, in order to guarantee a majority in the National Congress. In this regard, Governor Flamarion Portela and Senator Mozarildo Cavalcante, both from Roraima state and both opponents of indigenous rights, were welcomed into the government fold.

In addition to a lack of federal government attention, crimes perpetrated against indigenous peoples increased during 2003. According to information from the Missionary Indigenist Council, CIMI, 23 indigenous people were murdered between 3 and 6 November 2003 as a consequence of land conflicts.

In the face of government inaction, indigenous leaders and organisations publicly stated their dissatisfaction. During the First Perma-

1.	Cinta larga	3.	Macuxi	5.	Guaraní	7.	Guajajara
2.	Yanomami	4.	Xavante	6.	Ticuna		

nent Forum of Indigenous Peoples of the Amazon, organised by the Coordinating Body of Indigenous Peoples of the Brazilian Amazon, COIAB, which took place from 3 to 6 November with the participation of 350 leaders from the Amazonian region and guests from the rest of the country, the federal government (in attendance at the event through the person of the General Undersecretary of the Presidency of the Republic) was severely criticised.

The Executive Secretary of the Socio-environmental Institute, Marcio Santilli, who acted as the event's advisor, presented an analysis of the political environment criticising, among other things, the tendency for

Lula's government to get bogged down in the search for market confidence and centralised power, adopting a slow rate of action and a vertical understanding of civil society, underestimating the social movements' capacity to exert pressure and relegating the indigenous and indigenist movement to obscurity. He also criticised it for abandoning the Workers' Party programme and institutionalising FUNAI's indigenist policy.

The indigenous leaders at the event criticised the federal government for its failure to implement measures recognising their lands and to develop health, education and sustainable development policies for indigenous peoples.

Jercinaldo Satere, COIAB's General Coordinator, highlighted the fact that his organisation had provided the government with various papers, and had received no response, "not a word to say that the government was going to resolve the problems affecting our peoples. In the face of this silence, we took a decision to burn the document. Perhaps this is how to get the government's attention." In fact, on the last day of the meeting of the Permanent Forum of Peoples of the Amazon, a public ceremony took place in which the indigenous participants set fire to the document "Commitment to Indigenous Peoples", thus demonstrating their dissatisfaction with Lula's government.

Land

Raposa Serra do Sol

The conflicts over the indigenous lands of Raposa Serra do Sol must be mentioned, this being the last of the large territories to be demarcated in the country. It relates to 1.67 million hectares located in the north of Roraima state and inhabited by the Ingarico, Panamona and Wapixana peoples. The area includes 152 communities totalling 15,000 people.

The indigenous peoples of Raposa do Sol have been fighting for their territorial rights for more than 30 years but the demarcation process has been moving very slowly and with many difficulties, due to pressure exerted by people who have settled there, along with the deputies and governors of Roraima state. The delay in concluding the demarcation process has led to various conflicts and violations of indigenous rights. According to information from the Roraima Indigenous Council, CIR, between 1981 and 2003, 21 indigenous people were murdered due to land conflicts in this region.

According to FUNAI, around 700 people are illegally settled on the Raposa Serra do Sol indigenous lands. These settlers are demanding that the demarcation be carried out in pockets, excluding the rural areas occupied by non-indigenous settlers and the highways.

The CIR has also denounced the presence, since 1998, of a Border Patrol in Uiramuta community. This military presence is having a negative impact on indigenous culture and organisation. The women are the main victims of human rights violations on the part of the soldiers.

In addition, in January 2003, an indigenous man named Aldo Mota was shot dead, having disappeared two days previously during a conflict between indigenous communities and landowners. Mota's killing led to an uprising on the part of the indigenous and the whole year passed under a cloud of conflict.

On 23 December 2003, the Minister of Justice, Marcio Thomas Bastos, announced that the indigenous lands of Raposa Serra do Sol would be recognised in their entirety. At the same time, a group of indigenous people, being manipulated by rice producers, and who were occupying 18,000 hectares of the land, reacted in opposition to the approval, organising various public demonstrations. In January 2004, these groups kidnapped three missionaries linked to Roraima Diocese (which supports demarcation of the indigenous lands of Raposa Serra do Sol), holding them captive in private prisons. They also blocked the highway linking Boca Vista, capital of Roraima state, with Venezuela. The missionaries were freed and the road re-opened following the intervention of the armed forces but fierce controversy continues over the demarcation of Raposa Serra do Sol. We believe the President of the Republic should issue a decree ratifying the lands in order to conclude the demarcation process and thus put an end to conflict in this region.

The Guaraní-Kaiwa

The situation of the Guaraní-Kaiwa is also worthy of special note. They inhabit 28 territories covering a total area of approximately 50,000 hectares in Mato Grosso do Sul state. The population numbers around 2,000. The Kaiwa have repeatedly appeared in the news due to the suicides that have been taking place as a reaction to their lack of land. Tired of hoping the government might respond to their demands, in January 2004 around 3,000 indigenous Kaiwa, who live on very small plots, occupied 14 estates covering some 9,000 hectares which, in actual fact, form part of their traditional territory. The case is being considered by the courts, but it has already been decided that the indigenous should withdraw from the estates. The Kaiwa are threatening to resist and it is possible that clashes may soon be observed between the police and the indigenous. ❏

PARAGUAY

A ccording to the preliminary results of the 2nd National Indigenous Census, held within the context of the National Population and Housing Census 2002,[1] the indigenous population grew from 38,703 in 1981 to 85,674 in 2002. The figures establish a constant percentage of 1.5 to 1.8 in relation to the national population. According to the same census, these peoples are keeping their traditional subsistence practices alive, 78% of indigenous people producing handicrafts and 98% devoting their time to hunting, fishing and gathering.[2] This information ratifies the entry into force of indigenous territoriality as a concrete act, but also shows that the indigenous population is to be found within the lowest income bracket in the country.

New government – same indigenist policy

The general elections of 27 April 2003 meant a change in qualitative terms within the state bureaucracy and have perhaps constituted the greatest variable in the state of affairs examined in the previous report for *The Indigenous World*. Some of the cases that were symbolically held up in testimony to the poor level of human rights enjoyed by the indigenous have remained unchanged, with their corresponding negative balances. You only have to look, for example, at the legislature's failure to allocate funds for the return of indigenous lands; the failure to comply with the duty to guarantee life and health; the continual complaints of corruption in the Chaco provincial government; or the indigenous exodus to urban centres for socio-economic and environmental reasons.

Of course, it would be impossible for any state to bring about the changes necessary to destroy what is a structural denial of rights within the space of one year, all the more so given the previous period (of ex-President Luis Ángel González Macchi) of virtual absence of public management.

Under these circumstances, reflections must focus on the starting points that can be identified in order to visualise the state's direction under the leadership of this new government. Will there be progress or a backwards slide in terms of its human rights obligations? Are the bases in place on which improvements can be made or will they need to be built?

To begin with, if we look at the government programme put forward by the President elect, we can see that it does not include indig-

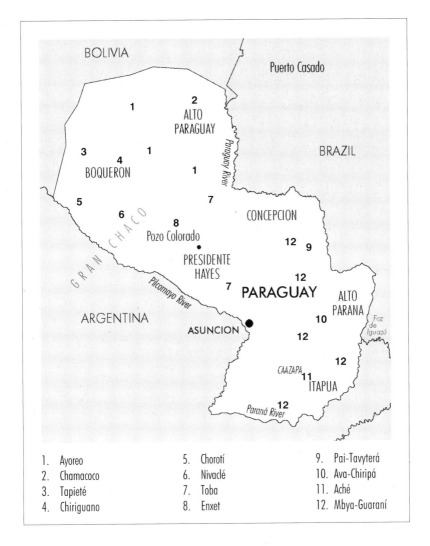

1. Ayoreo	5. Chorotí	9. Pai-Tavyterá
2. Chamacoco	6. Nivaclé	10. Ava-Chiripá
3. Tapieté	7. Toba	11. Aché
4. Chiriguano	8. Enxet	12. Mbya-Guaraní

enous peoples as one of its main themes. Indeed, only a brief mention is made of them in the education proposals. This absence of indigenous rights within the government's agenda is not exclusive to the Colorado Party. None of the other political parties that gained parliamentary representation (*Partido Liberal Radical Auténtico*, UNACE, *Patria Querida* and *País Solidario*) had any proposals to make in this area.

This policy vacuum suggests that the new government's indigenist policy will be produced "off the cuff". In this context, a number of important reference points should be borne in mind, such as Colonel Oscar Centurión's continuing position as head of the Paraguayan Indigenous Institute (INDI), confirmed in post by the President of the Republic, Nicanor Duarte Frutos. In this respect, it should be noted that part of Centurión's platform of work during the previous government was to attempt to fulfil the state's international commitments with regard to the indigenous communities of the Chaco, which are under the supervision of the Inter-American Human Rights System.[3] This relates essentially to the obligation to return land.

The State, indigenous peoples and civil society

In terms of indigenous organisations and their own political proposals, the Commission for the Self-Determination of Indigenous Peoples (CAPI) held an Indigenous Congress from 11 to 15 October in Asunción. CAPI is an initiative of various indigenous organisations, created to respond to the Paraguayan state's intention to unilaterally repeal the Statute of Indigenous Communities (Law No. 904/81) without the full and effective participation of all indigenous peoples, as established by current legislation. The participants themselves considered the Congress a success, issuing a press release at its conclusion. We have chosen to highlight a number of its points here.

Firstly, the indigenous participants considered the Congress to be an important step forward in the process of uniting and strengthening their organisations and peoples, emphasising that there was a firm decision to continue to work for the effective achievement of the event's slogan: "Unity, Dignity and Respect".

Secondly, and with regard to the draft proposal for a new indigenous law drawn up by CAPI following country-wide consultations, the 1st Congress assessed the resulting document and decided to keep it as a proposal to be further fine-tuned as a regulatory alternative to any new government attempts to modify or abolish Law No. 904/81. Lastly, the participants unanimously decided to hold a 2nd Indigenous Congress and to request that the state respect indigenous consultation and participation rights in relation to any initiative affecting them.

It is clear that whatever programme the state implements in favour of indigenous rights – and there is little certainty in this regard – the future can no longer be one of unilateral government measures that do not involve the indigenous.

In relation to the indigenous peoples of the Chaco, various cases of human rights violations on the part of the court authorities have been recorded in recent years, such as that of the Yakye Axa community, which was harassed and even subjected to eviction and removal from their houses.

In September of this year, a similar case of eviction was noted in an Enxet community, Puerto Colón. There, the indigenous were forced to abandon their ancestral lands, which now form part of a cattle ranch. The procedure was carried out without a search or eviction warrant. Representatives of the Attorney General's office were accompanied by police officers, along with lawyers and employees from the Algarrobal S.A. Company, the titleholder of the property.

Because of the illegal actions of the Attorney General's representatives, the indigenous community abandoned their houses and were left exposed to the elements on the banks of the river Paraguay. More than 60 children, suffering from hunger and many of them sick, along with 50 women, some of them sick and elderly, were among the victims of these actions. One elderly woman died some days later.

Although these serious actions on the part of state officials should be investigated by the relevant court-appointed organs of justice administration, there has to date been no information on the initiation of any investigations into the acts perpetrated against Puerto Colón community. On the contrary, legal action was taken by the company that owns these ancestral community lands against the people who offered the community legal assistance following the eviction, employees of the NGO Tierraviva. This legal action would appear to reveal the same pattern of persecution and harassment of human rights defenders that was noted in other cases during 2003, and which the country's human rights community should remain alert to.

The right to property

According to INDI's estimates, published in the daily newspaper, *ABC* (January 2003) there are currently 4,000 indigenous families in the Chaco and 3,000 in the Eastern region who do not own land. In spite of this, there is no state budget allocated for land purchases. According to INDI's president, the legislature granted 18,000 million guaranís (3,000 dollars) in bonds at the end of 2002 to buy lands within the context of international commitments but did not leave sufficient time for their use. According to the new government's statements, it will provide all necessary support to ensure the legislature allocates the funds requested by INDI.

In addition, data from the private sector indicates that indigenist institutions within the *Foro de Entidades Indigenistas del Paraguay* (FEPI) had already produced an inventory of the lands guaranteed to indigenous peoples and communities in 1995, some 487,522 hectares in total (446,305 in the Chaco and 41,217 in the Eastern region) along with lands claimed and pending restitution, some 1,396,886 hectares. Of the 56 cases of indigenous property rights in the Eastern region presented to the state by FEPI, only 17 have been resolved to date, and not all in accordance with the community's original claim. In other words, the state purchased lesser areas than those claimed. The remaining 39 cases have been waiting 6, 10 even 20 years for their claims to be satisfied. It should be noted that around 106 communities in the Eastern region with little or no land and no process underway – and with no INDI process likely to commence – still require 97,699 hectares to be able to continue their particular way of life on an area of "sufficient size and quality", in accordance with article 64 of the National Constitution.

With regard to the Western region, FEPI presented 19 cases. Six of these were fully resolved, 2 partially resolved and 11 are still waiting. Some of them have been waiting more than 10 years, having exhausted not only all administrative but also all legislative recourse, with negative responses to all requests (Yakye Axa, Sawhoyamaxa, Xakmok Kásek and Totobiegosode cases in the Veragilma S.A. land claim).

According to information from the last census, there are 496 indigenous communities recorded in Paraguay but processed information on their title and ownership of land is only available for 394. Nonetheless, this information is of recognisable reference value. Of the 394 communities that were questioned on the possession and title of their land, 247 had titled lands, 56 held lands but with no title and 91 had no land. These partial results do not indicate whether the guaranteed lands conformed or not to the basic legal parameter of restitution.[4] On the other hand, the disparity of criteria for data gathering means that, for example, where there is one land title, one single community will be noted but, in reality, there may be various communities living there (generally denoting a lack of land) and it may be that some of them have a claim underway (for example, the Kemha Yaksepo community, which is located within the lands of the La Esperanza community, in the Chaco). In fact, information on existing claims was not noted, and so the situation of a generalised failure to fulfil territorial guarantees and rights in the country is of unavoidable severity.

Social rights

Since the beginning of the year, numerous cases of serious illness have once more arisen due to the state's abandonment of health provision in the indigenous communities. This was the case of the Chaco communities struck down - in the midst of a food and water shortage - by various respiratory and pulmonary ailments, malnutrition, diarrhoea, vomiting and skin complaints.

As in 2002, 2003 continued to record various cases of teenage mothers and young indigenous girls and boys who, displaced from their communities of origin for socio-economic reasons, settle on the outskirts of urban centres to make a life from begging and/or who end up being exploited for their labour.

In terms of the state's response, at the beginning of the year INDI stated that - for lack of a sufficient budget - it had not been able to bring indigenous migration to a halt. A two-stage community re-integration plan was implemented: the first stage aimed at reintegrating members of the Nueva Esperanza, Campo 9 and Caaguazú communities, the second at community strengthening through self-sufficiency etc. The plan failed for lack of funds.

In this context, the procedures for forced returns have not changed. In the case of the indigenous living around Market 4 in Asunción, INDI requested the Juvenile Court to authorise the return of the children to their communities. The Court decided that, prior to any decision, the Ministry for Children and Youth (CODENI) should intervene to verify the situation of the indigenous children. In spite of this, various indigenous Avá Guaraní families from Canindeyú department finally returned to their communities in an Armed Forces truck at INDI's request, without the Juvenile Court having authorised such a measure.

Three complaints before the IACHR

The Yakye Axa community

On 11 April 2003, within the context of a march organised by the indigenous of the lower Chaco in the capital, the first case of a Paraguayan indigenous community to go before the Inter-American Court of Human Rights (IACHR) was made known to the general public: the case of the Yakye Axa community against Paraguay.

The Yakye Axa community is situated 80 kms along the road linking the towns of Pozo Colorado (President Hayes department) and Concepción (Concepción department) in lower Chaco, a settlement of unstable housing on a strip of public land. Since 1993, it has been demanding the return of part of its traditional territory from the state, lands taken from them by means of continual acts of eviction. To date there has been no effective protection of their fundamental rights through the mechanisms of domestic law, that is, through INDI or the legislative, even judicial, powers.

For this reason, in 2000, the community turned to the Inter-American Commission on Human Rights, suing the Paraguayan state for not guaranteeing their fundamental rights, in violation of the American Human Rights Convention.

Having considered the complaint, at the end of last year the IACHR ruled that Paraguay had violated Yakye Axa's rights to life, to ownership of their ancestral lands, to legal guarantees and protections, and had failed in its duty to guarantee the rights of the Convention and adopt measures of domestic law. It also asked the state to adopt a series of measures in reparation of these violations, including measures aimed at land restitution, health care and education provision, and legal reforms to prevent a repetition of such occurrences.

As the state did not comply with these recommendations, earlier this year the IACHR referred the case to the Inter-American Court, for this body to ensure justice is done in this concrete case.

The Sawhoyamaxa community
On 24 December 2002, the community informed the IACHR of its decision to withdraw from the process of amicable settlement that had been initiated with the State in 2001, given the lack of results achieved, the time passed and the absence, insufficiency and inoperability of the measures and initiatives to provide reparation of the community's rights implemented by government representatives to date.

The IACHR approved Admissibility Report Nº 12/03 on 20 February 2003 during its 117th ordinary period of sessions, in which it declared the Sawhoyamaxa community's complaint against the Paraguayan state admissible in relation to the alleged violation of ownership rights (art. 21), legal guarantees and protections (arts. 8 and 25), the adoption of measures of domestic law (2) and the duty to guarantee the rights enshrined in the American Convention (1.1), establishing a period of two months for presentation of additional observations on the case as from the date of notification – 13 March 2002 – and offering to mediate between the parties in order to reach an amicable settlement of the case. With the approval of this report, the claim became known as Case N° 12,419.

Following further conversations with the State, and no favourable results for the Sawhoyamaxa community being forthcoming, its members and the petitioners decided to continue the lawsuit with the presentation of pleadings on 14 July 2003.

The Xakmok Kásek community

This complaint on the alleged violation of articles 2, 8(1), 21, 25 and 1(1) of the American Convention was declared admissible by the IACHR on 20 February, establishing a two-month period for the presentation of additional observations on the case as from the date of notification. With the approval of this report, the claim became known as Case N° 12.420.

Via a note dated 13 March 2003 sent to the petitioners, the Commission made itself available to the parties (the community and the State) to reach an amicable settlement. On 27 March, in response to this offer, Marcelino López, Xakmok Kásek leader, communicated to the IACHR the community's decision to hold a preliminary meeting with the government before giving an answer.

In this context, various meetings were held between the indigenous community's leaders and state representatives.

The results of these conversations were considered unfavourable to the community's rights and unlikely to lead to a procedure for amicable settlement, and so the victims and their representatives decided to give up trying to reach an agreement with the State and agreed with the INDI president, Colonel Oscar Centurión, to accept the purchase of a property offered by the state to the community (3,200 hectares) on the understanding "that this plot forms part of the greater area of 10,700 hectares claimed by this community since 1990" and that "acceptance neither implies nor should be understood as a relinquishment of the rights claimed before the Inter-American Commission on Human Rights in Case 12,420, or that the action is being dropped".[5]

Unfortunately once more, this land purchase on the part of the State did not materialize because the current owners (Mennonite co-operative Chortizer) withdrew from the sale.

As a final measure in the case before the IACHR, the pleadings were presented jointly with the Sawhoyamaxa on 14 July 2003. ❑

Notes and references

1   Dirección General de Estadísticas Encuestas y Censos (DGEEC). 2002. Censo Nacional de Población y Viviendas 2002.
2   *Noticias*, January 2, 2003.
3   We refer to the cases of the Sawhoyamaxa and Xakmok Kásek com- muniites before the Inter-American Commission on Human Rights, and of Yakye Axa before the Inter-American Court.
4   A parameter which, in the National Constitution (art. 64) is determined by providing that the lands must be of a "sufficient area and quality for the preservation and development of their particular ways of life". In the Statute of Indigenous Communitie it is established that "it will be determined according to the number of people settled or to be settled in a community, such as to guarantee the economic and cultural viability and expansion of same" (art. 18).
5   Note dated 22 May 2003, signed by the leaders of Xakmok Kásek community and sent to the President of INDI.

ARGENTINA

D uring these past 12 months, the country appeared to awaken from the long nightmare that began several years ago and reached fever pith with the fall of President De la Rúa in December 2001. The heated social demands for a complete renovation of the political class, that cast doubt on the value of democracy and its ability to respond to citizens' needs, showed a tendency to ease. Although this year was the 20th anniversary of the restoration of the democratic system, Argentina is a country devastated by corruption and plundering. Social exclusion has reached heights previously unseen. More than half the population lives in poverty and illiteracy; the laws and the judicial system, far from defending citizens, are the main allies of corruption and of the perpetuation of impunity.

Fresh air but the socio-economic crisis continues

The swearing in of a new government elected by the people in May 2003 brought some fresh air to this scenario. In many ways, the social climate during the first months of Néstor Kirchner's administration was similar

1. Ona	6. Huarpe	11. Chulupí
2. Tehuelche	7. Diaguita-Calchaquí	12. Toba
3. Mapuche	8. Rankulche	13. Chorote
4. Mocoví	9. Kolla	14. Qom
5 Mbya-Guaraní	10. Wichí	15. Pilagá

to the one that followed after the last military dictatorship (1976-83).
Among other reasons, because the President's first measures focused on
the restoration of the judicial and institutional system, and of human

rights: the renewal of the national Supreme Court of Justice, changes in the military command, the derogation of the decree that banned the extradition of members of the Armed Forces accused of state terrorism, the approval with constitutional rank of the Convention on the Non-Applicability of Statutory Limitations to War Crimes and Crimes Against Humanity, and the legislative annulment of the Due Obedience and Full Stop laws.

Unfortunately, these necessary political actions have not been matched by effective measures to change the living conditions of citizens: according to official measurements, in May 2003, 26.3% of the population lived under the poverty line and in November unemployment reached 16.7%.

In a different vein, although the national government proclaimed that if there is a fiscal surplus it will be applied to the payment of the internal debt, the commitments made to the International Monetary Fund and pressure from multinational firms set a limit on social spending and restricted the possibilities for new social programmes. For these reasons, although the new administration has taken some fundamental steps, the political gestures "for the public" are still greater than the intense and systematic work towards the construction of state policies that are the essential elements of life in a democracy.

Social assistance or policies for indigenous peoples?

The indigenous world was not left out of the scenario presented by the Kirchner administration. The National Institute for Indigenous Issues (INAI) continued its routine work during the year, without any news that would indicate change in the relationship between the indigenous peoples and the State; rather, it was quite the opposite. The first political action of the Minister for Social Development and Environment, which is the ministry that administers state policy regarding indigenous peoples, appeared to mimic the policies of the early state of the late 19th century, when there were attempts to settle the "savage and untamed" inhabitants of Chaco and turn them into rural workers. An article published in national newspapers noted:

> In the Paraje Campo Medina in the Chaco district of Pampa del Indio, where "nothing has been planted" for the last nine years, Social Development Minister Alicia Kirchner yesterday handed out tons of cotton seeds and heard the [Toba] people's demands regarding issues such as health, education and land... [and] she once again clarified

that she did not visit the province to "sell false hopes but to accompany the transformation of this town with commitment and work".

The minister's action was part of the "Manos a la Obra" (Hands to Work) National Plan for Local Development and Social Economy, whose main objective is the development of productive enterprises and does not address the indigenous peoples' constitutional rights or the ILO's Convention No.169. Years ago the Argentine Chaco region stood out in international trade as a producer of cotton. The region's indigenous people, trained as harvesters, sold their labour to local businessmen for part of the year, and during the rest they sustained themselves with the food collected in the bush and the rivers. But in the 1960s, when harvesting became mechanical, the work came to an end. Later, when Argentina could no longer compete on the international market, the cotton storehouses closed down and planting cotton ceased to be a profitable business. So the indigenous people remained in their communities attempting to live off the natural resources they could get from their territories, which became more and more diminished. Even if the tendency today is to substitute local products for imports, it is doubtful that this is the best place to start. To whom and for how much would a small indigenous producer sell his meagre harvest? What businessman – if any – is willing to face unequal competition with multinational firms?

This single example is sufficient to illustrate the tone of state policy towards the indigenous people during the year. Is the national government unaware of the needs and demands of the indigenous people?

The INAI still does not abide by the court ruling that orders the participation of indigenous people in its team through the creation of the Council of Indigenous Peoples. It lacks a programme or an activity plan and has failed to establish goals or strategic lines of action to develop its mission. Why such carelessness? Why so little interest for such a specific sector of the national community as the native peoples? This administration, perhaps more than others, views indigenous peoples as citizens who are undifferentiated from the rest of the population or, at best, are seen as "the poorest of the poor". Thus, when social policies are proposed or executed, historical and cultural differences are not taken into account. In such a context, this first action of state policy should not be seen as an isolated event, but rather, as the nucleus of current indigenist policy: that is, providing assistance to indigenous communities according to a common assistance plan for all underprivileged population groups.

Lack of clarity and political inaction

There has also been political inaction regarding the most urgent need of the indigenous peoples: the identification and registration of their territories. The INAI has not given the slightest indication of what criteria should be followed, nor has it issued a grounded opinion on the matter. Despite the existence of plenty of cases that could be used for a global analysis of the situation of indigenous lands and could enable the design of a reasonable federal titling programme, the responses have been infrequent and opportunistic. Each demand is being dealt with as if it were unique. As an example, we will take two concrete situations that could be considered excellent material for the formulation of this policy.

Lhaka Honhat lawsuit at the IACHR

Against the backdrop of the Inter-American Court of Human Rights' ruling in 2001 on the Awas Tingni case, the INAI has wasted an opportunity to introduce principles and criteria to be followed in the case of indigenous lands in Argentina, some of which were precisely elaborated by the Inter-American Commission and Court for the identification of the Awas Tingni community lands.

Furthermore, in the context of the process of the friendly resolution of the Lhaka Honhat case, where the INAI is responsible for elaborating a proposal for handing over lands that takes into account the traditional land use of the affected communities, its attitude has been that of a mere observer at the negotiating table, without a voice or the political will to ensure – with rigorous technical-legal arguments – the territorial rights of the social sector that ensures the survival of all the officials and technocrats that are part of the INAI.

National Plan for the Regularisation of Indigenous Lands

This plan was created in 1996 and to date not a single property deed has been granted to indigenous communities. After more than seven years since its spectacular launching, the INAI has not addressed this plan as something that could be a national land granting programme. On the contrary, as a result of its inefficiency, it has allowed each province to "do as it pleased" according to the mandates issued by local politicians. As a result, what we have today are three isolated "cases"; fragments of what should have been the launching of a cohesive national plan. Hence the following results:

Jujuy: In 2003, the third instalment of 70,000 US$ was paid for the demarcation, measurement and subsequent granting of deeds of indigenous community land. Of a total of 1,200,000 hectares, only three deeds, for an area totalling 630,000 hectares, are ready to be handed to the communities in the department of Susques. As more time goes by without the completion of this phase, the alienation of indigenous lands continues.

Río Negro: The process of recognition of lands began in the Lipetrén community, where three communities were identified. In this case, the demarcation phase was completed, covering approximately 600,000 hectares. For 2004 the province has requested 83,000 US$ to carry out the corresponding measurements. In the meantime, the Coordinator for Development in Indigenous Communities (the province's agency for indigenous issues) is working in two areas with communities that had a decree for the reservation of lands, on the first phase of the process (information regarding their new rights). However, no work is being carried out in critical areas where there is alienation of public lands.

Chubut: Although the Autarchic Institute for Colonisation, which is in charge of executing the programme, has funds available to carry out its task, they claim that no progress has been made because of a "lack of human resources". The question in this case is then to ask why some of these funds are not used for the relevant training.

Some indigenous initiatives

Organisation of Indigenous Nations and People in Argentina (ONPIA)
On October 11, 2003, a group of indigenous organisations and leaders finally formed an organisation to represent them at the national level. The initiative began to take shape during the meeting of the Fund for the Development of the Indigenous Peoples of Latin America and the Caribbean that took place in Buenos Aires in April. However, not all the communities and organisations in the country are part of it because − its founders say − they have communication problems that prevent them from reaching everyone.

Project for the inclusion of the rights of indigenous peoples

During an official ceremony in the city of Bariloche, some Mapuche leaders approached President Kirchner to demand a genuine state policy for indigenous peoples. These leaders reject the social action policy that is being implemented and wanted a direct dialogue with the President in order to get him to give this policy a 180-degree turn. As a result of this, some leaders from the Mapuche, Kolla and Diaguita Calchaquí communities met with the Social Development Minister and proposed the creation of a Working Commission on Indigenous Policy. The Commission will be formed by indigenous leaders and officials from certain public institutions, and aims to elaborate a working document for each of the following areas: land and territories; biodiversity; multi-culturalism, and customary law. In the next stage the working documents will be debated in six regional workshops and ultimately in a national workshop to be called the Parliament of the Indigenous Peoples of Argentina 2004. The result of all these workshops will be expressed in a series of juridical and legislative initiatives that will be presented to national authorities for their consideration. ❑

CHILE

A ccording to the 1992 census there were 1,200,000 Mapuche in Chile distributed between the VIII, IX and X regions, and including 500,000 Mapuche currently living between Santiago and Valparaiso.

In the last census carried out in 2002, these numbers suffered a dramatic change. According to the National Statistics Institute (INE), the institution in charge of carrying out the census, there are now only 600,000 Mapuche in the whole of Chile.

This fact, which has been considered by many leaders as a "statistical genocide", finds no logical explanation among analysts of Mapuche issues. Many consider that this is the outcome of the following census question: "Do you consider yourself as belonging to any of the indigenous peoples of Chile?" That is, determining their belonging by self-definition and not by the characteristics typical of the Mapuche: having a different surname, living in a community, speaking the language, etc.

This statistical "fact" is significant because decision-makers within government may feel Mapuche issues should not be given great importance, as this is a relatively reduced segment of citizens.

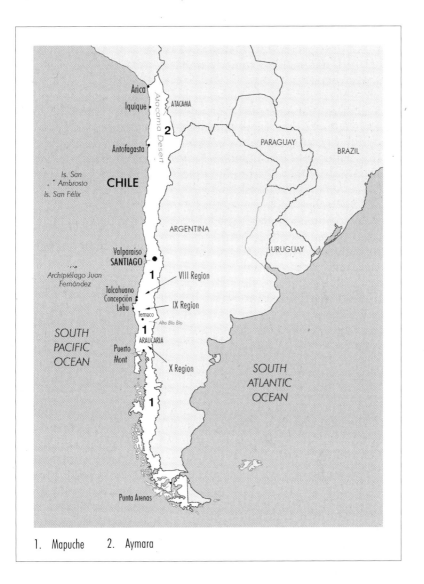

1. Mapuche   2. Aymara

The grassroots organisation of the Mapuche world

The traditional grassroots organisation of the Mapuche people is the *Lof*, the family, which grouped with other families of the same sector forms a *Lofche*. Several *Lofches* form a *Rewe*, which then join to form an *Aiya-Rehue*. These, in turn, will join in a *Butalmapu*, the supreme unit of a whole Mapuche territorial identity. The *Butalmapu Lafkenche* – people of the sea – of Arauco formerly existed under this form in the current VIII region of the country, and at present there are attempts to reconstruct it.

After the military occupation of the Mapuche territory by the Chilean state (known as the "Pacification of the Araucania" 1881-83), the Mapuche were legally confined to "*reducciones*", or reserves, losing their traditional form of organisation.

The "Titles of Mercy" handed out until the 1940s were the result of the Law of Southern Property, a process that is known as that of the "*reduccionismo*" of the Mapuche. The current community stems from the old "*reducción*" and receives legal recognition through integration laws aimed at making the Mapuche participate in national life. This process of "communitarisation" is still taking place and is regulated by the Indigenous Law 19.253, passed in 1993 during the government of President Patricio Aylwin.

According to this law, the state's interlocutors are the indigenous communities and associations that have their own internal statutes and are registered with the National Corporation for Indigenous Development (CONADI). The number of communities changes rapidly from one year to another, because, according to Law 19.253, a new community may be formed with only 10 families, a phenomenon that has provoked a rapid decomposition of the old communities, which have divided themselves systematically over the last few years.

In the province of Arauco alone, which comprises seven communes (Curanilahue, Arauco, Los Álamos, Lebu, Cañete, Contulmo and Tirúa), there are 120 communities and some 50 Mapuche Lafkenche associations.

The community associations

In certain sectors there are associations of communities that are created with an economic interest, to obtain greater assistance from the state. These associations are recognised through the Indigenous Law and thus defined as interlocutors by the authorities.

In Arauco, this practice has been accelerated by the current government's application of the Origins programme, which consists of a 130 million US$ loan from the Inter-American Development Bank (IDB) to the Chilean government to accelerate the development of indigenous communities.

There are now some 20 sectoral associations in the province that group communities around economic initiatives and who benefit from this programme.

The IDB loan agreement explicitly stipulates that the money may not be used to purchase land and, therefore, many communities view this programme as being based on a populist welfare approach (*asistencialismo*).

Political organisations

The current recognition of communities through Law 19.253 does not allow them to raise political demands such as the recognition of territorial rights, constitutional recognition, and even less, the right to autonomy and self-determination.

In the face of this legal vacuum, a group of Mapuche organisations have been established to link the communities with the aim of raising political demands. They have thus become bodies of social pressure on the government.

Most of these organisations are critical of the purely economic approach on which the Chilean state bases its action and recognition of the communities.

At present there are three important organisations that seem to have the ability to articulate the political and territorial claims and demands of the great majority of Mapuche communities and the urban associations of Santiago and Valparaíso despite the organisations' lack of official and legal recognition by Chilean authorities. The organisations are the following:

El Consejo de Todas las Tierras
(The Council of All Lands, CTT)

This is the oldest organisation and was established in 1991, when many of its members abandoned the Ad-mapu organisation (of Communist origin) to found the "Fifth Centenary Commission", a group that in 1992 became the CTT.

Its activities are largely at the national level and the organisation is present in Mapuche communities of Valdivia, Temuco and Santiago. The Consejo de Todas las Tierras' main areas of influence are Panguipulli, Lago Ranco, Coñaripe, and Pocura, in the X region of Los Lagos (Valdivia). In the IX region, it is present in Lumaco, Carahue, Imperial, Victoria, Temu cui-cui and Curarrehue. In the VIII region it is strongest in the mountainous area of Alto Bio-Bio, the valley of Queuco, and Trapa-trapa. And in urban areas, its strength is visible in associations in Temuco and Santiago.

The CTT bases its action on the strategy of "ungovernability" of the Mapuche areas and the community territories. It regularly mobilises its grassroots and negotiates – mainly on land issues – in the sectors where it is influential.

Politically, the CTT does not appear as part of any of the traditional Chilean political currents. It has gained institutional support as a result of its ability to question public policies, to renew its discourse and to persist over time.

La Coordinadora Arauco Malleco
(The Arauco Malleco Coordinator, CAM)

This organisation was born in the Province of Arauco in 1994. Its creation sprung from the "*pegun-dugun*" group of Mapuche students from Concepción. Its consolidation took place between 1995 and 2002 when it was active in the recovery of land and the assertion of rights, which it carried out through its strategy of "territorial control".

Its influence within communities is relatively small, but its "spectacular" actions give it a greater importance than it really has. In the last two years it has been the group that has suffered the most repression. Its spokespersons and activists have been taken to court for violating the law of internal security.

Currently, it is strong in the IX region in the areas of Collipulli, Traiguen and Lumaco. In the VIII region, in the province of Arauco, it carries out activities for territorial recovery in Rukañanco, southern Tirua, Lleu-Lleu and Cullinco.

Its activities and strategies have been systematically influenced by Chilean political forces, as many of its activists come from the Communist parties, the Movement of the Revolutionary Left (MIR) and the Manuel Rodríguez Patriotic Front, organisations that opted for armed struggle during the military period. This political approach brought about the first internal fracture in 2002, from which two currents of opinion have developed. This division has greatly weakened its activities and actions.

La Identidad Lafkenche de Arauco
(The Arauco Lafkenche Identity, ILA)

The ILA was formed in 1999. Its main members split from the CAM and initiated a regrouping of communities throughout the province of Arauco, creating a grassroots solidarity related to their Lafkenche (people from the sea) identity.

The ILA is not an organisation, but a movement formed by communities. These are grouped in two currents: those that opt for institutional action, and are led by the Tirúa municipality; and the provincial coordination of communities, which is working for territorial autonomy, their main demand being territorial restitution and the subsequent valorisation of these lands.

The ILA presented its Lafkenche proposal in 2000 and the current government has drawn from some of these proposals, mainly the creation of the Commission of Truth and New Treatment of Indigenous Peoples, as well as from its current proposal for the creation of special territories, the first step towards a form of autonomy.

The ILA only functions at the provincial level in Arauco and does not aim to be a national organisation, although it does influence the national Mapuche debate. It calls for the reconstruction of territorial identities in the whole of Chile, contrary to the CTT and the CAM, which act more like Western-style organisations.

This is how it maintains and forms part of the Coordination of Territorial Identities, an entity that is not recognised by the authorities, but which has a voice in many conflicts.

The current government's institutional choice

The current government authorities also have their organisations (whether this is recognised or not), which consist mainly of Mapuche activists from the parties in the ruling coalition " *la concertación*".

Thus, the communities represented by these organisations are mainly oriented towards state institutions, among them the CONADI, and they generally benefit from programmes and schemes that the state distributes among the Mapuche.

This is being strongly criticised, as government authorities are seen as applying the system of "political clientelism" among the Mapuche – an attitude aimed at the coopting of communities, lead-

193

ers and associations through the concession of "favours" that are then being translated into support for their political parties during election time.

Conclusion

All the Mapuche communities in Chile are currently involved in the organisations outlined above; the different declarations, opinions, communiqués, proposals, etc., are inscribed within one of these currents.

The demands for territorial and political rights are more marked in the non-institutional organisations that are not recognised by the law or by the authorities. However, on many occasions the authorities are forced to negotiate with them, which validates the organisations and makes them spokespersons and counterparts in the general conflict.

The government's criminalisation of the Mapuche movement has had profound repercussions within the communities, as the laws that are applied to Mapuche leaders stem from the juridical framework of the dictatorship. The anti-terrorist law is a law for a state of emergency and for this reason, there are many researchers and analysts that conclude that in the Mapuche case there are areas and territories that live under the state of emergency, a fact that becomes visible due to the presence of the police and the control the police exercise on the Mapuche.

The extra-judicial actions of the Mapuche in some symbolic cases, especially those of the CTT and the construction of the Ralco central by ENDESA Spain, are signs that "judicial appeals" by the affected parties may be filed at an international level – for example at the Inter-American Court of Human Rights – as a response to inadequate internal legislation and as a way of forcing the current political authorities to approach the Mapuche conflict from a different perspective, particularly from the perspective of the rights of the peoples. ❑

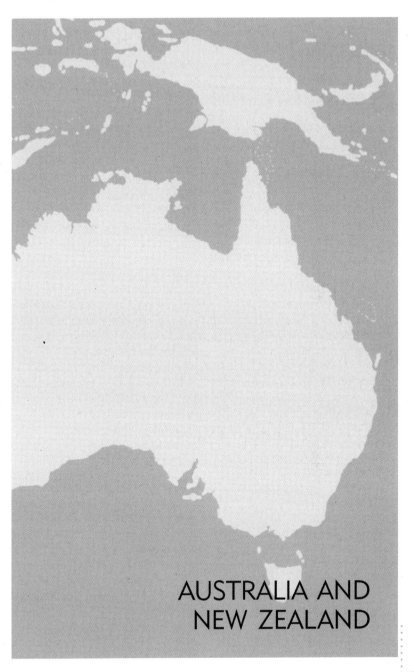

AUSTRALIA AND
NEW ZEALAND

AUSTRALIA

Sound and fury

A ustralia's year in indigenous politics and policy was "full of sound and fury, signifying nothing", as Shakespeare might say. The noise, rhetoric and disinformation nationwide were inversely proportional to the progress. But indigenous *self-determination* and indigenous-white *reconciliation* continued as underground currents, and important publications appeared.

One real event was the loss of indigenous control over national indigenous administration. The Aboriginal and Torres Strait Islander Commission, ATSIC, was created in 1990 as a combined national government administration and network of elected regional indigenous councils with a national indirectly elected commission or board. That moral obligations to its indigenous voters and official duties as part of the public service would conflict should always have been obvious, and were not the only deep conflicts that afflicted it.[1] Any indigenous body would be pressed to respond to wider issues than its mandate, funds and staff allow, so great are client needs and marginalisation. From the outset, when Prime Minister John Howard took office in March 1996, his Coalition (of Liberal and National parties) took full advantage of failed expectations among blacks as well as whites to condemn ATSIC, while using it to symbolise supposed waste and indigenous "privilege" for uninformed or racist voters, a handy scapegoat for white anxieties about globalisation and social change. Back in 1988, as party leader, he had sponsored a wide crypto-racist attack in Parliament on the federal indigenous administration and its indigenous head, but investigations turned up little.[2] For Howard and his Coalition, race is the issue, not maladministration. He has even advanced a defence that one may do racist things but not be a racist – not an excuse international war crimes tribunals would accept.

When ATSIC's elected head, Geoff Clark, became a personal target and political distraction in June 2001 following press reports of alleged rapes 20 years earlier, the conventional wisdom called for Clark to step aside so as not to discredit ATSIC.[3] His deputy and would-be successor, Ray Robinson, was similarly pursued by rumours and criminal charges. The two men were political rivals and both remained in office, running for re-election and winning in late 2002. The media have followed their difficulties, and sometimes contributed to them. Finally, Robinson stood down as deputy. However, in mid-2003

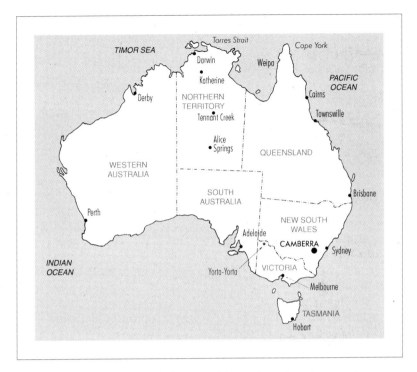

the government removed almost all ATSIC staff and funds from the board's control.

Dismantling indigenous autonomy

At that moment another issue arose. In the days before the second meeting of the United Nations Permanent Forum on Indigenous Issues, in May 2003, ATSIC's elected board were afraid to send their chief, Geoff Clark, to New York. The UN Forum has an energetic North Pacific member, but no one from Australia, New Zealand or the South Pacific. With ATSIC and indigenous illusions of autonomy already shattered, before the government's own appointed review inquiry had even reported, the indigenous affairs minister Philip Ruddock added insult to injury by musing aloud about whether to allow Clark's UN travel.[4] By any measure, it was important that Clark attend. The Australian government itself had submitted an unhelpful proposal to the Forum,[5] urging that it not "burden" governments with demands but confine itself to UN in-housekeeping. Perhaps thinking they had

nothing left to lose, the ATSIC Commissioners unanimously supported Clark's trip and he went, with or without the approval of
minister and officials.

In one of his typically able UN contributions, Clark said,

> We say it is no coincidence that the health status of Indigenous
> peoples in countries similar to ours – the United States, Canada and
> New Zealand – is improving more rapidly. All of these countries have
> signed Treaties which have given official, legal and constitutional
> recognition to their first peoples. As part of the Treaty processes in
> these countries there has been a sustained commitment to addressing
> social and cultural needs while ensuring Indigenous peoples have
> greater control over their own lives. An Australian Treaty would
> allow us real self-determination on policy development, service im-
> plementation and the allocation of funds for health resources. A
> Treaty would enable our peoples to have a fair and equitable share of
> the vast resources wealth in our lands and seas as enjoyed by our
> brothers and sisters elsewhere. It is well past the time for our political
> leaders to face up to their responsibility to make a fair and just
> settlement with the dispossessed and rightful owners of our country's
> lands and seas.[6]

In August, Clark was removed from ATSIC's chair by the government
(see cartoon of minister Philip Ruddock executing him). As 2003
draws to an end, he is demanding his chair back after a recent trial
regarding his role in a pub brawl. Robinson faces charges of financial
mismanagement of the Aboriginal organisations he built up to em-
ploy many people and provide many services in south-west Queensland. A new minister, Amanda Vanstone, promises ATSIC reform in
2004. She says she wants to focus more federal effort on rural and
remote areas while pressing state governments to take up their city
roles; to devolve more ATSIC control to local and regional bodies; and
to encourage more women in leadership, adding that, "If you go to any
community that is working well, women are involved in the running
of the community."[7] Howard rejects indigenous autonomy and political community, and rejects indigenous *consent* in politics and policy,
so little progress is possible. As for his so-called "practical reconciliation"[8] – as if universally available social services were remarkable
in "first world" countries! – this is insufficiently funded and befogged
by Howard's moralising and scolding.

"I'm warning you...I'll appeal" Source: Danny Eastwood in Koori Mail, 2003

War is hell, war is swell

Howard and his government subscribe to far right ideas of American exceptionalism and unilateralism, while denying an international community. Howard rushed into an invasion of Iraq alongside Bush and Blair, glorying in his chance to be a war leader posing with troops, or mowing and aping solemnly at the mention of war dead. He has even, belatedly and since 2001, used the Commonwealth of Nations (former British Empire), and UN on some days, when they can give his paranoid parochialism a photo opportunity as world statesman. President Bush has called Howard "a man of steel" as the latter claims a "deputy sheriff" role to America and has promised preventive military action in the world, a doctrine causing disquiet in South-East Asia, with some leaders unkindly recalling Australia's murderous indigenous history.

In July, Howard found a vast new indigenous empire to dominate. Having earlier avoided or humiliated the Forum of South Pacific countries, i.e., Papua New Guinea and the many smaller island countries and home rule territories, now:

John Howard [has] unveiled an ambitious plan to create a South Pacific economic union to head off terrorism, corruption and decay, [e.g.,] ...Australia's contribution to a 2200-strong force to restore law and order in the Solomon Islands. The Prime Minister ...said he would urge barely viable Pacific nations of fewer than 100,000 people to move to pool resources such as airlines and policing, because they were simply uneconomic.[9]

Speaking to Australian and mixed South Pacific troops gathered in North Queensland bound for the Solomon Islands the next day, Howard told them in cinema Cowboys-and-Indians dialogue:

[W]e in the Pacific are your friends, we understand you need help, we understand you want conditions of law and order and peace and hope for your people in the years ahead, and you've reached out your hand and asked us for help and we have come together in a friendly Pacific way, under the appropriate codename of "Operation Helpem Fren" we've come together, all of us, to help you.

As 2003 ended, Howard was sending troops and police to Papua New Guinea.

Northern Australia

Positive steps have been Ms Clare Martin's Northern Territory government working with Aborigines to write a new regional constitution.[10] However, a 2004 election might bring back an anti-indigenous populist Right government. In Torres Strait, a series of thoughtful articles by Kevin Savage in the regional newspaper has explored the issue of *decolonisation* in the region and the need to resolve outstanding identity, governance and indigenous rights issues.[11] Such articles and debate should help Australia and Torres Strait Island leaders to speed up agreement on an overdue regional autonomy plan. Elsewhere, much talk of "partnership" in government-indigenous community relations and modest self-management in local government guise may bring some results or experience useful for resolving wider issues of indigenous political futures.

History and identity

The History Wars, by Stuart McIntyre and Anna Clark (2003),[12] is a good introduction to another phenomenon. Howard, his government and various right-wing allies deny much post-war social and cultural cosmopolitan change in Australia and the world, seeking to reinforce nostalgia for mid-20th century British hegemony as the "official" culture of the continent. This crusade, achievable perhaps on the Falkland or Pitcairn Islands, has benefited from intellectual apathy and has marginalised people in some parliamentary seats. Howard regularly likens Aborigines to failed immigrants who have not been absorbed into the "mainstream" or its economy. But the attack has gone much further. Howard's men on the Board of the new National Museum have denounced that institution's Aboriginal and Torres Strait Islander exhibits, demanding more "dead white males," and have had the museum's Aboriginal director removed. His government encourages or sponsors denial of the history of murderous white-indigenous relations and the Stolen Children (known to the world through the movie, *Rabbit-Proof Fence*). No, we were a nice Christian people who wouldn't do nasty things, says denier-in-chief Keith Windschuttle, author of *The Fabrication of Aboriginal History* (2002),[13] even though the Aborigines were a nasty brutish lot. White Australian identity had long been built on nasty brutish British ways in military and convict society. For a reply to Windschuttle, see *Whitewash,* edited by Robert Manne (2003).[14]

Meanwhile, historian Henry Reynolds' *North of Capricorn* (2003)[15] reveals the multi-racial Aboriginal-Islander-Asian north of Queensland, Northern Territory and Western Australia. Non-Europeans honourably and industriously built Northern Australia, only to be rewarded with removal and dispossession upon Federation in 1901, a constitutional movement based strongly on white racism and production of the White Australian Policy. The book will change the way Australians see their country. *Dancing with Strangers* (2003)[16] by historian Inga Clendinnen, meanwhile, affectingly and intimately re-examines relationships between the first white and black leaders in Sydney after British settlement in 1788, a book likely to be an international landmark in cross-cultural relations. Of special interest to *The Indigenous World* readers is a small book, *Mr Ruddock goes to Geneva* (2003),[17] in which law professor Spencer Zifcak examines the Howard government's war against the United Nations over indigenous and refugee issues.

A gesture

One bizarre 2003 moment came on July 23 in the Cabinet room when Howard invited and co-chaired a "summit" with Aboriginal academic, writer and political leader, Ms Jackie Huggins, together with various ministers and Aboriginal and Islander spokespersons (ostentatiously excluding ATSIC head Clark), to discuss violence against indigenous women. This is Howard's ideal issue because it makes Aborigines look bad and makes him look good, caring, concerned. For about 72 hours before, during and after he said not a word out of place, an unprecedented performance in tact and indigenous decorum. (At the very same time he was talking down to Pacific Islanders before his forces went ashore at Guadalcanal!). His motive soon became clear. July 26 was his 64th birthday, long heralded by himself as a decisive moment for determining his future. The weekend newspapers would have been full of articles saying how successful Howard had been but what a shame it was that he could not do the right thing *vis-à-vis* the Aborigines! The violence summit pre-empted this. The gullible presented it as a triumph for reconciliation but Jackie Huggins, herself national co-chair of Reconciliation Australia, wrote succinctly of the meeting in *The Australian* (30.7.2003):

> *These symbolic acts of reconciliation can have meaning across cultures, but if they are not linked to social change or practical improvements in living standards they run the risk of being seen as empty gestures. True, we are operating in the context of a federal Government that has limited the reconciliation agenda and set aside issues that indigenous people have identified as being central to the process. Those of us involved in reconciliation have a responsibility to keep the rest of the agenda alive. These issues will not go away.* ❏

Notes and references

1   See **Sullivan, P. (ed.). 1996**. *Shooting the Banker: Essays on ATSIC and Self-Determination*. Darwin: ANU, North Australia Research Unit.
2   In "First World" countries, few opposition leaders would allow supporters to mount such an attack, nor would the broadsheet press give it much respectability, so I was surprised at the time.
3   A year later, police investigators said no charges would be laid against Clark.
4   *The Australian*, 7.5.2003. Clark rebuffed...
5   Document E/C.19/2003/20, 4.4.2003.
6   Speeches & Transcripts. http://www.atsic.gov.au/default.asp 20.5.2003.
7   *The Australian*, 23.12.2003.
8   See **Crough, G. 2002**. A Practical Critique of Practical Reconciliation. What is the Reality of Indigenous Funding? Australian Universities

Review, Vol. 45, 1: 4-10. **Jones, Nicky. 2003**.*Wrongs and rights: the economic, social and cultural rights of indigenous peoples in Australia.* Brisbane: School of Political Science and International Studies, University of Queensland. **Kauffmann, Paul. 2003**. A Social Indicator Comparison Between Indigenous People in Australia and Canada and the Approaches to Redress the Balance. Indigenous Issues and the Nation. *Australian Canadian Studies,* Vol. 21, 1: 75-99.

9   *The Australian,* 23.7.2003. PM's new Pacific solution.

10 For more see **Jull, P.** Why the Northern Territory matters. http://eprint.uq.edu.au/archive/00000649/ and Reconciliation Constitutions: Canadian & Australian Northern Territories. http://eprint.uq.edu.au/archive/00000322/

11 See **Jull, P.** Decolonisation…. http://eprint.uq.edu.au/

12 **Macintyre, Stuart, and Anna Clark. 2003.** *The History Wars.* Melbourne: Melbourne University Press.

13 **Windschuttle, Keith. 2002.** *The fabrication of Aboriginal history.* Sydney: Macleay Press.

14 **Manne, Robert (ed.). 2003.** *Whitewash: on Keith Windschuttle's fabrication of Aboriginal history.* Melbourne: Black Inc.

15 **Reynolds H, 2003.** *North of Capricorn: the untold story of Australia's North.* Sydney: Allen & Unwin.

16 **Clendinnen, Inga. 2003.** *Dancing with Strangers.* Melbourne: Text Publishing.

17 **Zifcak, Spencer. 2003.** *Mr Ruddock goes to Geneva.* Sydney: UNSW Press, University of New South Wales.

AOTEAROA - NEW ZEALAND

The struggle to preserve Māori customary rights over the seabed and foreshore has been the defining issue in New Zealand politics over the past year. The current debates about Māori access to the foreshore and seabed were fuelled initially by concerns expressed by tribal authorities that they were being excluded from a share in the potentially lucrative marine farming business.

In 1997, Te Tau Ihu, which "represents" the *iwi*[1] at the top of the South Island (Ngāti Apa, Ngāti Koata, Ngāti Rauru, Ngāti Tama, Ngāti Toa, Rangitane and Te Atiawa) were concerned about the way in which marine farming, or aquaculture, was developing in the Marlborough Sounds. They argued that they were effectively being shut out of the burgeoning marine farming industry and took legal action in the Court of Appeal (at the time, the highest legal court in New Zealand) claiming "customary title" of the Marlborough seabed and foreshore (the land between the high and low water mark). The assertion of customary title was, however, principally a legal strategy that arose out of anger that the Government was reaping the financial benefit from the tendering of marine space while Māori commercial interests were being excluded from the aquaculture industry. In June 2003, a Court of Appeal decision challenged the Crown's long-held assertion that it owned the foreshore and seabed, and found Māori may have customary interests in the foreshore which could lead to the granting of private title. In that court decision, the Te Tau Ihu iwi won the right to present a legal case before the Māori Land Court, to determine the extent of their customary rights in the foreshore and seabed.

Backlash

Against a background of growing public anxiety, fuelled by media sensationalism and deliberate misinformation, a number of politicians have claimed that if Māori were awarded customary title to the foreshore and seabed they might block off public access to the beaches or sell them. Bill English and the conservative National Party, the main opposition party in the legislature, see this issue as an integral part of their "one standard of citizenship" campaign which they hope will revitalise the National Party and their prospects at the general election next year. They are promoting the issue as a "racially" divi-

1. Taitokerau
2. Tainui
3. Arawa
4. Mataatua
5. Taira Whiti
6. Takitimu
7. Te Upoko O Te Ika
8. Manawatu
9. Whanganui
10. Taranaki
11. Te Tau Ihu

Regional *iwi* groupings. Source: www.takoa.co.nz

sive one that institutionalises the rights of one "race" over another. The National Party has pledged to work with other political parties to introduce legislation to confirm exclusive Crown title of the beaches, foreshore and seabed and to extinguish any claimed customary title.

It has found a willing ally in the right-wing New Zealand First political party which is likewise campaigning vigorously on the basis of "one law for all New Zealanders" and are gaining increasing media publicity for their drive to repeal all Treaty of Waitangi principles in New Zealand laws. Under their banner - "Immigration's up, Treaty Costs up, Crime's up: had enough?" - Winston Peters and New Zealand First are using the foreshore and seabed debate as part of their broader political platform to justify putting an end to the Treaty of Waitangi claims or what they pejoratively call the indigenous "grievance industry". They are generating some populist support for the idea that New Zealand's future as a nation is being increasing undermined by "racial divisions". This is why they've publicly declared their opposition to the Māori customary rights over the foreshore and seabed on the basis that legal rights should not be expanded to recognize title to these resources on the basis of "race".

The pro-business political party ACT (Association of Consumers and Tax Payers) is also linking the seabed and foreshore issue to the idea that indigenous rights are undermining harmonious "race relations". They are building their campaign around the "principle of liberal democracy" that all New Zealanders should be equal as citizens and that all should have the same rights under the same laws. This quote from the ACT Party web site encapsulates their position:

> Another risk to harmonious race relations in New Zealand comes from the threat to the rule of law posed by claims relating to partnership and sovereignty. The government of New Zealand is not a partnership between one racial group and the rest. It is inconceivable that New Zealand can have harmonious race relations built upon principles of divided representation or privilege based on race.

This is why right-wing political parties such as NZ First, ACT and National are threatening to repeal all laws that permit or require any central or local government agency to recognise the rights of Māori under the Treaty of Waitangi (some also intend to abolish the Māori seats in Parliament).

These appeals to "one standard of citizenship" or "one law for all New Zealanders" are classic themes in racist, right-wing discourse. The idea that Māori claims under the Treaty of Waitangi are inherently divisive has in fact a much older ideological legacy in New Zealand politics. The "one nation, one people" myth -with its direct appeal to nationalist sentiments- has been at the heart of popular racism for many years. Its infamous catch cry, "We're all New Zealanders" has frequently been employed to deny the legitimacy of Māori struggles for the return of land, a greater share of society's resources and an active role in formal decision-making.

It is convenient that the brutal and violent history of colonisation, the systematic appropriation of Māori land and resources, the economic and social inequalities that generally exist between Māori and non-Māori in contemporary New Zealand society, the constant grind of racism and police violence experienced by working-class Māori communities throughout the country, miraculously vanish from these accounts. In fact, the arguments often go deeper than this. Māori are frequently represented by some groups as a privileged sector of New Zealand society directly benefiting from special access to resources and a range of targeted initiatives: special educational programmes, separate political representation and even special rugby teams are all seen as the product of invidious separatism.

The strident calls for "one law for all" directly appeal to an underlying racist current within New Zealand society. These views are given respectability by current politicians because they promote the idea that racism and discontent are essentially stirred up by a few Māori extremists on the fringes of an otherwise harmonious society who are acting against the "national interest". "Ordinary New Zealanders" on the other hand, are presented as passive victims whose rights are being trampled on in this process.

Who "owns" the foreshore and seabed?

The idea that Māori customary rights in the foreshore and seabed will lead to the exclusion of non-Māori from access to New Zealand beaches conveniently ignores the reality that the public has no right to stroll along more than a third of New Zealand's beaches. In fact, large chunks of the foreshore are already privately owned. This is even revealed in two reports prepared for the Government recently which debunk myths about the public's rights to enjoy the land next to most lakes, rivers and the sea. A land access reference report found that more than 30 per cent of land adjoining bodies of water is in private hands, and the New Zealand coast is the least accessible. It shows there is no such thing as an uninterrupted Queen's Chain - usually understood to be a 20m strip of public or reserved land ringing New Zealand waterways. Unfortunately, for many New Zealanders it is acceptable to override Māori customary rights that do not restrict access to the coast, while at the same time ignoring private exclusive title held by non-Māori that restricts public access to the New Zealand beaches.

Government's policy proposal

Although the Māori Land Court has legal jurisdiction to determine "aboriginal" or "customary rights and title", the Government immediately announced it would legislate to block due process by giving ownership of the foreshore and seabed to the "people of New Zealand". The racist hysteria whipped up by the media coverage of the case, the sensationalist response of ACT, NZ First and National politicians, together with the widespread speculation that the Government would legislate to extinguish Māori customary rights, have generated widespread anger in Māori communities throughout the country.

In August 2003, the Government released a number of policy options to address the foreshore and seabed issue in a "consultation document". Those proposals perpetuated the myth that Māori would deny public access to beaches unless the government extinguished their title and limited their traditional rights. Despite the misinformation and provocative statements, Māori communities unanimously rejected the proposals in a consultation process with Government Ministers and public servants. Many saw the underlying principles of the document as an effective extinguishment of Māori rights and a denial of due process.

Despite this rejection, the Government has stuck to the policy framework outlined in its initial proposal and in December 2003, indicating that except for those areas that are already in private hands, ownership of the foreshore and seabed will be vested in all the "people of New Zealand" and the government will be responsible for managing and regulating it on behalf of everyone.

This new "people of New Zealand title" extinguishes indigenous rights long recognised in both common law and within Māori communities. Furthermore, by advancing a framework that upholds public rights of access to, and use of, the coastline and marine environment, while "recognising" in a very limited and restricted fashion Māori customary rights and "ancestral connections" to the seabed and foreshore, the government's policy proposals abrogate key aspects of international law pertaining to the rights of indigenous peoples. To make matters worse, for all intents and purposes the policy framework prevents Māori from presenting their claims in the courts to have those customary rights and interests clarified and defined.

The Crown has acknowledged that its proposals involve extinguishing Māori rights but have argued that this is merely a "theoretical extinguishment" because under the government's plan, the Māori Land Court would be empowered to issue a new customary title to those indigenous communities with "ancestral connection" over the foreshore and seabed. Crucially, however, this customary title would NOT represent an ownership interest in the foreshore and seabed but sit alongside the "people of New Zealand title" and as such would not affect public access. Furthermore, the test used to determine the new customary title will be defined by law to prevent the Māori Land Court taking an "expansive approach" to customary rights. In this way, the government has acknowledged a vague set of Māori interests in the seabed and foreshore but has adopted an extremely limited definition of those customary rights and interests. This is why the Government has stated that the right to undertake a new activity which was not a feature of a traditional practice - "development rights" - such as the right to harvest a newly discovered resource - will not be part of customary rights.

A statutory commission - of five to seven commissioners - would receive applications from Māori who wanted to have a customary title. The commissioners would tour New Zealand holding regional inquiries to establish which groups hold customary rights in the different regions. The commission would then make recommendations to the Māori Land Court. Holders of such titles would have enhanced opportunities to participate in the management of coastal marine areas. It is significant that the proposals encapsulate the Crown's attempt to redefine the essence of *tino rangatiratanga* (Māori self-determination) as little more than the ability of Māori communities to exercise a quasi-management role in areas which it chooses. ❏

Note

1   *Iwi* is the largest descent based socio-political unit in Māori society. It literally means "bones" and an iwi is considered metaphorically to be an extension of oneself. Iwi are generally grouped in regional groupings like Te Tau Ihu.(Ed.note)

EAST AND
SOUTHEAST ASIA

JAPAN

There has never been any official census of the Ainu population in Japan but it is reported by the Hokkaido government's research into the actual daily conditions of Hokkaido *Utari* (*Utari* means Ainu in Ainu language) that the Ainu number around 24,000. However, according to the 1985 Tokyo Metropolitan government research, the figure is 2,700. It is worth noticing here that the Japanese government has never held exact demographical information on the Ainu population, who live in several different areas of the country.

No recognition of the Ainu as an indigenous people

The Japanese government has acknowledged the Ainu as a minority population but has never officially recognized them as an indigenous people. The Japanese government stated in an incidental vote in the National Assembly on "The law for the Promotion of the Ainu Culture and for the Dissemination and Advocacy for the Tradition of the Ainu and the Ainu Culture" (*Ainu Shinpo*), enacted in 1997, that they would consider the issue of whether the Ainu are indigenous or not when the issue of indigenous peoples is resolved in the United Nations Draft Declaration on the Rights of Indigenous Peoples. So far, the Japanese government has insisted that there is no definition of indigenous peoples.

The Ainu Association of Hokkaido is the biggest Ainu organization and has about 15,000 members. The Association has functioned since 1972 under the jurisdiction of the Hokkaido government, receiving funds from the state according to its *Utari* welfare policy. This welfare policy has been ongoing, but it has been defined from the beginning as a welfare policy with regional limitations in the sense that it covers only Hokkaido, and is not a minority policy that applies to Ainu living elsewhere. The same limitation was crucial in the process of enacting Ainu Shinpo, since a government ordinance declared that only the Hokkaido government had the right to submit a fundamental plan of the law, thereby excluding Ainu who lived outside Hokkaido.

Discrimination

There is still discrimination and a financial gap between Japanese and Ainu. The Japanese government has still not recognized the

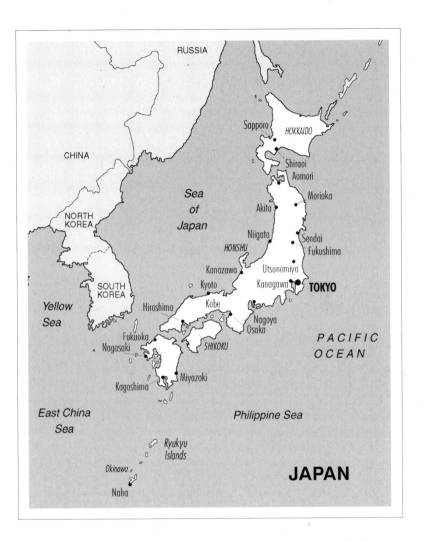

RUSSIA

CHINA

Sea
of
Japan

NORTH
KOREA

Sapporo
HOKKAIDO

Shiraoi
Aomori

Morioka

Akita

Niigata

Sendai
Fukushima

HONSHU

Kanazawa

Utsunomiya

SOUTH
KOREA

Kyoto

Kanagawa

TOKYO

Yellow
Sea

Hiroshima

Kobe

Nagoya
Osaka

PACIFIC
OCEAN

Fukuoka

Nagasaki

SHIKOKU

Kagoshima

Miyazaki

East China
Sea

Philippine Sea

Ryukyu
Islands

Okinawa

JAPAN

Naha

level of discrimination. There is no official recognition of the long
history of oppression of the Ainu. In the history curriculum in schools,
for example, the past is presented in such a way as to legitimize the
current power structures in society. In conclusion, these factors have
been an obstacle that has created inequality and discord among the
Ainu. ❑

TIBET

I n recent decades, growing Chinese immigration to Tibet has led to increased marginalisation of Tibetans in their own country, because the immigrants, their culture and economy dominate developments in Tibet. If no acceptable solution is found for Tibet in the near future, the Tibetans may well end up in a similar position to other indigenous peoples around the world. In China, they are defined as an "ethnic minority" along with other indigenous groups in the country. It is because of this similarity between the Tibetan population and indigenous peoples that IWGIA has chosen to include Tibet in *The Indigenous World*, bearing in mind that the Tibetans do not want to be identified as an indigenous people. They see Tibet as an occupied country, and one that is increasingly being colonized by China.

Following the visit of the Dalai Lama's envoys to Beijing and Lhasa in September 2002, there was hope among international observers that China would consider serious negotiations with the Tibetan Government in Exile on the issue of Tibet. It therefore came as a shock when a young Tibetan was executed in January 2003 for his alleged participation in bomb attacks in eastern Tibet. Together with his Buddhist teacher, he was accused of "terrorism" and "sabotage against the unity of China". The death penalty against his teacher was postponed for two years and is still pending.

Human Rights

Another young Tibetan died in hospital while serving a 9-year sentence for "separatist activities". He was arrested in 2001 for putting up posters demanding Tibetan independence. The exact reasons for his death are not known but he is said to have been tortured in prison. He is one of 52 political prisoners who have died since 1987, either during or shortly after their imprisonment.

There are indications that the number of political prisoners is again increasing. According to the independent British news service, *Tibetan Information Network* (TIN), this is particularly due to a large number of arrests in eastern Tibet. Among those arrested in 2003 were four monks, accused of participating in "long life" prayers for the Dalai Lama. Two other monks were arrested for being in possession of his books.

The whereabouts of the young boy, who was identified by the Dalai Lama as the incarnation of the Panchen Lama, remains un-

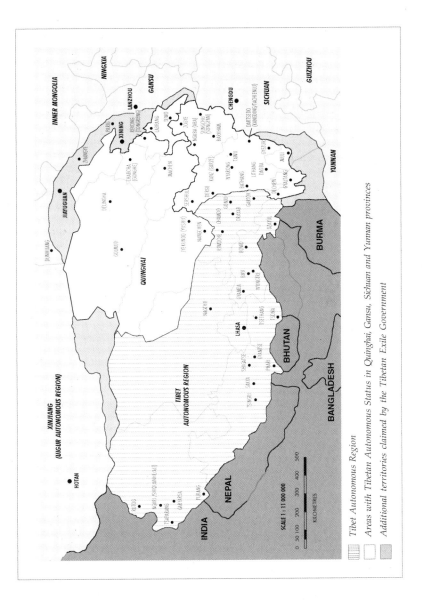

Tibet Autonomous Region

Areas with Tibetan Autonomous Status in Quinghai, Gansu, Sichuan and Yunnan provinces

Additional territories claimed by the Tibetan Exile Government

SCALE 1 : 11 000 000

0 50 100   200   300   400   500
KILOMETRES

known. The Chinese authorities refuse to allow international human rights organisations or any others to meet him.

The situation of Tibetan refugees in Nepal continues to deteriorate. On May 18, Tibetan refugees were handed over by the Nepalese authorities to the Chinese police and returned to Tibet. China claims

215

to be working to end the "unauthorized movement" of Tibetans into Nepal. One of the measures taken to make it difficult for Tibetans to enter Nepal is the recent construction of a new road close to one of the most common crossing points for Tibetans. The road makes it easier for the border police to control the area. Western tourists and the local police in Khumbu have confirmed that Chinese border police shot at 34 Tibetan refugees in October and penetrated into Nepalese territory. A young Tibetan woman died in September as she fell into a crevasse while trying to flee from the border police.

In its latest report on China, Amnesty International expresses concern for the human rights situation in Tibet, where at least 100 Tibetans are in prison for political reasons. Ongoing reforms of the legal system in China have not visibly improved the situation in Tibet. The Tibetans' right to assembly, freedom of speech and religion and their right to self-determination continue to be suppressed. Despite the Chinese invitation to the Dalai Lama's envoys to China, it continues to be forbidden for Tibetans to pay reverence to the Dalai Lama.

Political developments

The Tibetan Government in Exile sent two special envoys from the Dalai Lama to China in May at the invitation of the Chinese authorities. Despite high expectations for this second visit within one year and China's apparent interest in improving its relationship with the Tibetan Government in Exile, nothing much seems to have come out of it. Upon their return, the envoys remarked upon the positive attitude of the Chinese government officials but could or would not give any "road map" for negotiations in the near future. China's new leadership, under president Hu Jintao, has not yet shown an open interest in solving the issue of Tibet.

The attitude in China towards Tibet seems to remain virtually unchanged. In November, the Chinese foreign minister accused the Dalai Lama of making false propaganda in the international community. This is but another example of the Chinese refusal to listen to the Dalai Lama, who continues to stress that he does not seek independence for Tibet but "meaningful self-rule" as the best guarantee of the preservation of Tibetan culture and environment. The definition of Tibet, and whether this includes Tibetan areas now incorporated into Chinese provinces, remain points of dispute.

The annual U.S. Congressional-Executive Commission on China Report for 2003 states that the repression of Tibetans continues under

Chinese rule. The report spotlights the repression of religious freedom, intolerance of political dissent, strict controls on the media and Internet, and a lack of autonomy for Tibetans. In Tibetan areas, official controls continue to limit the practising of Tibetan Buddhism. Authorities often characterize the religion as backward and its practice as a burden on society.

Parliamentarians from across Europe and from the European Parliament have called on China to drop all preconditions for negotiations with the Dalai Lama and again requested that an EU Special Representative for Tibet be appointed to facilitate the dialogue between China and the Tibetan Government in Exile. They recommended that if no progress were made with constructive negotiations in the immediate future, EU member states should reconsider the European Parliament's resolution of July 2000, which proposed recognising the Tibetan Government in Exile as the legitimate representative of the Tibetan people. Tibet Support Group representatives participating in the Group's Fourth International Conference in Prague in October also signed a letter urging the European Commission to appoint a Special Representative on Tibet. However, the EU remains vague in its relationship with China. In a 2003 policy paper on China, EU ministers encourage the continuation of dialogue between the Chinese authorities and representatives of the Dalai Lama but do not come up with a concrete plan of action.

Living conditions in Tibet

The situation for the Tibetan population under Chinese occupation remains largely unchanged. The growth in Chinese population in Tibetan areas is substantial, and many Tibetans believe that this influx is the most serious challenge facing Tibetan culture. In addition, there has been tremendous growth in the number of Chinese tourists visiting Tibet. In a recent report based on official Chinese census figures from November 2000, TIN analyses the population composition in Tibet Autonomous Region (TAR) and other Tibetan areas. The Tibetan population remains overwhelmingly rural while Chinese immigrants live in the cities. The number of Chinese immigrants in TAR has risen from 4% to 6% or maybe even 10% since 1990. The growth in the Chinese population is primarily due to immigration, while the Tibetan population has one of the highest levels of natural population growth in China. Tibetans number approximately 5.5 million, excluding Tibetans in exile. TIN argues that the numbers may not be as significant as the fact that the Chinese are concentrated in towns where most of the economic development takes place, while the majority of Tibetans live in rural areas and have little opportunity to participate in the development process. The level of education continues to be low and Tibetans find it hard to compete with the Chinese.

Chinese officials point to years of surging economic growth in Tibetan areas but unofficial reports show that most Tibetan incomes are trailing regional economic indicators. Observers say that the engine of growth is central government funding of large-scale infrastructure construction projects and the service sector, which is dominated by government-run work places, and not local production. Unofficial reports show that the gap between urban and rural incomes has doubled over the past decade, leaving the majority of Tibetans increasingly disadvantaged.

The destruction of the environment in Tibet continues to be an issue of concern. One of the latest worrying developments is the local government's plan to build a road around the holy mountain, Mt. Kailash, which would allow tourists to drive round the mountain. Environmentalists and Tibet supporters around the world have launched a campaign to stop the project, which would have serious implications for both Tibetans and the environment. In its 2003 report on the State of the Environment in Tibet, the Central Tibetan Administration in Exile expressed its concern over China's large-scale "Western Development Program", initiated by the Chinese government to exploit the resources in the region. It calls upon the Chinese government to reconsider the large projects and replace them with small-scale ones that do not undermine the integrity of Tibet's eco-system.

However, an article in a prominent party journal featured a recent senior official declaring that "Development is the last word". Recognizing the social risks he continued: "We should correctly handle the relations between reform, development, and stability". The paper outlined a vision for a reconfigured demographic landscape, calling for herders and farmers to be resettled in compact, urbanized communities.   ❏

TAIWAN

In memory of Faki Tiwai Sayun, father figure of the Pangcah people.[1] He devoted his life to the education of indigenous children and fought for the future of the indigenous peoples of Taiwan. His death is a great loss for the Pangcah and all indigenous peoples in Taiwan.

Tribal identity

Taiwan's indigenous peoples constitute only 1.7% of the country's total population. Those classified as indigenous, however, constitute only some of Taiwan's indigenous peoples. Since the period of Japanese colonization, the indigenous peoples have been categorized into "*Ping- pu*"[2] (those who live in the plains) and "*Kao-sa*"[3] (those who live in the mountains). The "Ping-pu" indigenous groups were largely assimilated by Chinese settlers. Today, a few "Ping-pu" members are still classified as indigenous but only because they have been mistakenly categorized as neighbouring "Kao-sa" tribal groups.

Officially, those classified as indigenous peoples are divided into 9 tribal groups (the 9 groups that were categorized as the Kao-sa groups). In 2001 a Ping-pu group, Thao, (categorized as a part of Cou), gained recognition as the 10th group. The official recognition of the Thao has fired up the group identity issue among other tribal groups.

By the end of 2002 the Kavalan, another Ping-pu tribal group, was recognized by the government as a "new" group (the 11th). Despite their distinct language and culture, the Kavalan had been classified as part of the Pangcah people, and had been fighting for recognition of their existence as a separate group since the mid 1990s. The Kavalan regained its status as a tribal group but, ironically, only those who were once mistaken as Pangcah are now recognized as Kavalan. This year, more than 600 of those who had not been classified as Pangcah and had thus lost recognition of their indigenous identity, claimed Kavalan heritage. In light of the preferences given to indigenous peoples, such as the indigenous land management system, social welfare and affirmative action, it is unlikely that the government will readily grant these "non-indigenous" people indigenous status.

Group identity is also a serious issue among some kao-sa groups that have been recognized officially. This year, the Truku, who were categorized by a Japanese anthropologist as a subgroup of the Atayal (a kao-sa group), tried to claim separate existence. They organized local public hearings as well as organised a petition signed by the Truku people. Their claim angered the Atayal and the Sedeq (another subgroup of the Atayal, itself claiming a distinct heritage and claiming that the Truku are Sedeq). Academic categories created decades ago have thus taken on political implications. After long discussions, on January 14 2004, the Executive Yuan[4] announced that the Truku was now the 12th officially recognized tribal group[5] but the dispute between the Atayal, the Sedeq and the Truku remains.

The group identity issue is expected to become even more controversial over the coming years, especially since the draft indigenous self-government act and related political structure will be granting "tribal groups" unprecedented political significance.

The Cou and the honey case

The Cou indigenous tribal group, located in the Mt. Ali area in the middle of Taiwan, enjoys fertile land and abundant natural resources. Since the mid 1980s, the Cou village Tanayiku has started to protect its natural resources, without any help from state institutions. Initially, the Tanayiku River was being over-fished, sometimes through illegal means such as poison or electricity. The families who owned different parts of the Tanayiku River voluntarily turned their privately owned parts of the river into village commons and organized volunteer patrols to stop the over-exploitation and make sure the ecosystem of the river had a chance to revive. After more than a decade, the Tanayiku has evolved into a living legend as a model for environmentalists and a draw for tourists and money.

Tanayiku not only brought in money and opportunities but also raised social capital and encouraged the rediscovery of the nation's long lost pride. Although with no official status, the Tanayiku community has been working like a small state, executing its village pact, exercising certain policing powers and running its own social welfare programs. Tanayiku has become a model not only for environmentalists but also for indigenous activists who have been claiming the right to govern themselves. The Cou tribal group as a whole have now followed the example of Tanayiku, with more villages beginning their own social engineering and placing the Cou in an active and leading position in the discourse of, and recent developments in, indigenous self-government.

As the Cou have become more assertive in their autonomy, tensions between the Cou and the neighboring Chinese settlers' commu-

1. Yu–shan National Park

2. Shei–pa National Park

3. Taroko National Park

Cou people protest against the opening of the new Temple in honor of the Martyred Lord of Mt. Ali, Wu-feng. Photo: Yapasuyong E. Niyahosa

nity have developed. The following two examples highlight the lurking tension. In February 2003, an elder of the Cou community, the *Peyonsi* (headman) of Tapangu village was charged with robbery. The Peyonsi had confiscated a barrel of wild honey from a Chinese Taiwanese, who the Peyonsi believed was stealing honey from Cou territory. Since the Peyonsi's claim to self-policing was not sanctioned by the Taiwanese legal system, the Peyonsi was found guilty of robbery and sentenced to 6 months in jail, with two years' probation.

Although the indigenous peoples' right to self-government has been intensively discussed and an Indigenous Self-Government Act (ISGA) has been tabled in the Legislative Yuan, the honey case indicates that the Chinese Taiwanese, the police, and the court did not look at the Peyonsi's claim in the light of the indigenous peoples' right to self-government. Although the Peyonsi thought continuing the legal process was futile, his people raised funds and persuaded him to appeal to a higher court, hoping the case would help highlight the indigenous peoples' right to govern themselves. On January 11, 2004, however, the court of appeal ruled that the jail sentence should be upheld.

Continuing veneration of Wu-feng

A second case, exemplifying the tension between the Cou and the neighbouring Chinese, traces its origins back through the history of the Cou. Almost all Taiwanese know the story of Wu-feng, included in official text books as part of the history syllabus. In the story, the kind and generous justice fighter Wu-feng sacrifices his life to prevent the Cou from continuing the barbarous practice of headhunting. The moral of the story is that the Chinese settlers enlightened the barbaric indigenous peoples and brought civilization to Taiwan, even at the cost of sacrificing their own life. In memory of Wu-feng's greatness, the local administrative area was named after him, and he has become an important deity, the Martyred Lord of Mt. Ali, venerated by the Chinese settlers from the surrounding areas.

From the Cou perspective, however, Wu-feng was far from a sacred figure, and instead took the form of an unscrupulous trader. The Cou killed Wu-feng as a result of his serious transgressions against the Cou. Textual research in recent years has established that Japanese colonizers[6] invented the legend of Wu-feng's self-sacrifice as part of a program to civilize indigenous inhabitants. In 1988, indigenous activists tore down the bronze statue of Wu-feng, in a landmark act in the indigenous movement's reinterpretation of Taiwan history. The local administrative area has been renamed, and the Wu-feng story has been removed from the text books.

The Wu-feng story has not been forgotten by Chinese settlers. The veneration of Wu-feng never really passed away, and the opening of an enormous newly-built Martyred Lord of Mt. Ali Temple in April 2003 suggests that the vitality of the Wu-feng myth continues. The whole ceremony was even broadcasted nationally by one of the largest TV stations, re-telling the Wu-feng story. The Cou people protested against the spectacle in a quiet and peaceful way, with banners in their hands. The enormous new Wu-feng Temple now stands high in the Cou region. Although freedom of religious belief and freedom of speech constitute basic human rights, indigenous activists demand that some consideration should be given before supporting and promoting symbols that many deem repressive and hurtful.

Indigenous Self-Government Act

As President Chen Shui-bian promised, indigenous self-government has figured high on the agenda for the past 3 years. After lengthy discussions, the draft of the Indigenous Self-Government Act (ISGA) was approved by the Executive Yuan and sent to the Legislative Yuan for approval. The draft, first prepared by the Aboriginal Peoples' Council (APC, the highest administrative body for indigenous affairs under the Executive Yuan) in 2000, has changed in several important respects since it was conceived.

As mentioned in *The Indigenous World 2002-2003*, the first draft was more like a special version of the Municipal Governance Act, with detailed articles regulating the form of indigenous government and its powers. The second draft differed from the first in that it reflected input from an influential non-indigenous minister without portfolio. The articles in the second draft were more like principles than settled rules, allowing indigenous governments to form themselves in traditional ways, and allowing flexibility regarding the manner in which they choose to exercise their powers.

The Final Draft adopted the spirit of the second draft, allowing the indigenous peoples to adopt their traditional political practice as their system of governance, but made other controversial changes. The decision on the Final Draft was made in the cabinet of the Executive Yuan, of which the APC is not a member and thus has no voting rights. The Final Draft deleted the articles regarding preparatory procedures for the establishment of an indigenous self-government. While the new draft seems to be radical in many ways, it requires the APC to implement follow-up decrees and makes no mention of the responsibility of other Ministries and government bodies to facilitate negotiations for indigenous self-government. By reducing the burden and responsibility of the other government institutions, effectively implementing the proposals for self-government without the resources of the central government is going to be difficult. The APC, by itself, is unlikely to be able to implement the self-government systems that have been established.

Moreover, although the Final Draft deleted the articles on preparatory procedures, it added an article requiring that, after the APC and the preparatory committee for an indigenous government have come up with a draft basic government law, the draft has to be promulgated by the Legislative Yuan (i.e. the Parliament). The Final Draft was silent as to whether the Legislative Yuan would have powers to make any substantial changes to the draft of the basic law. If "normal" legislative procedure is followed, then the Legislative Yuan, with only 8 indigenous representatives (tribes are not represented individually) among the 225 seats, will have the final and ultimate power to decide the structure of the indigenous governments. Although the Final Draft adopted the radical rhetoric used by indigenous activists, and the Preamble states that the essence of the draft is to respect the volition of the indigenous peoples, the Final Draft seems unlikely to deliver results with regard to such lofty aspirations.

Presidential elections

With the presidential elections coming in early 2004, parliamentary members from different political parties have been preparing their last grand show of their term. In addition to the ISGA, there are several important indigenous bills dealing with issues such as indigenous land and intellectual property rights. Different interest groups will try to push through versions of the bills that meet their interests. For example, the Association for the Right of Non-indigenous Inhabitants in Indigenous Areas, who calls itself the *Ping-quan-hui*, serves as the greatest reactionary power in opposition to the indigenous rights movement. Made up of non-indigenous inhabitants and investors in indigenous areas, the Ping-quan-hui stands strongly in opposition to indigenous rights claims. As one of the most influential interest groups in elections, since it provides significant funding for local politicians, the Ping-quan-hui has always been successful in lobbying to boycott indigenous rights bills. In 2003, they already expressed their dissatisfaction with the ISGA Draft and started their lobbying.

In light of the forthcoming elections, the rhetoric and practice of the indigenous rights campaign is expected to be very chaotic. During one of his recent campaign speeches, President Chen Shui-bian once again asserted his respect for indigenous peoples. In his previous campaign, in 2000, he promised to build a new "partnership" with the indigenous peoples, a partnership that fell short of its goals in his first three years in office. During this recent speech, he announced his plan for a New Taiwan Constitution, including a suggestion that the Constitution should have a special chapter on indigenous peoples, and should enshrine a "quasi" "state-to-state" relationship between the Taiwan government and its indigenous peoples. As with the 2000 election, these inspiring words could very possibly turn out to be mere slogans. Since the indigenous peoples are only a small percentage of the population, little attention will be focused on indigenous issues. And yet, because they form a decisive minority in an evenly divided country, it is certain that the indigenous peoples, including their organizations and activists, will again be inevitably drawn into the heavily-mobilized political games of 2004. ❑

Notes and references

1 Pangcah, with its total population of 155,000, is the largest indigenous ethnic group based in the eastern part of Taiwan.
2 Researchers have different categorizations of the tribal groups that constitute the "Ping-pu". A prevalent study identified 9 tribal groups: Kavalan, Ketagelan, Taokas, Pabura, Hoanya, Pazeh, Babuza, Thao and Siraya.
3 The 9 "Kao-sa" tribal groups include Atayal (including the Sedeq and Truku subgroups), Saisyat, Bunun, Cou, Pangcah, Puyuma, Paiwan, Ruikai and Tao.
4 The Executive Yuan is the administrative body of the government. The Executive YuanBoard is the decision-making body of the Executive Yuan.
5 The 12 tribal groups now officially recognized include the 9 groups that were categorized as Kao-sa, and 2 Ping-pu groups: the Thao (recognized in 2001), the Kavalan (recognized in 2002). In 2004, finally, the Truku, a tribal group originally categorized as a subgroup of the Atayal, gained independent group status.
6 Taiwan was colonized by Japan from 1895 to 1945. (Ed. note)

PHILIPPINES

The Philippines is the only Asian country to have officially adopted the term indigenous peoples. According to estimates of the National Commission on Indigenous Peoples (NCIP), between 12 and 15 million of the country's total population of 70 million are indigenous. Roughly 60% of them live in the southern island Mindanao, a third on the main island Luzon in the North, and the rest are scattered over the other islands of the archipelago. In October 1997, the Philippine government passed the comprehensive Indigenous Peoples Rights Act (IPRA) as mandated by the Constitutional Provision, by which the Philippine State must recognize and promote the rights of indigenous peoples.

Implementation of the IPRA

Seven years after its promulgation, the National Commission on Indigenous Peoples (NCIP), the government body established to oversee the government's programs on indigenous peoples including the implementation of the IPRA, is still in the process of drafting special orders to bring about some of its provisions. It was only in the past three years that the Commission came up with policy guidelines on how to secure Certificates of Free and Prior Informed Consent, on its quasi-judicial powers, on how to deal with ancestral domains recognized by previous government policies, and on the formation of a Consultative Body of indigenous leaders. The strong advocacy and participation of the civil society have been vital not only in the passing of the IPRA, but also in its implementation.

Ancestral domain titling and the issue of the survey guidelines

From 2001 to 2003, when the majority of the present Commissioners took their oath of office, the NCIP awarded one Certificate of Ancestral Land Title (CALT) and 11 Certificates of Ancestral Domain Title (CADT). The previous Commission had not awarded any. For the year 2004, the NCIP promises to award 68 CADTs, of which 56 will be funded by the NCIP and another 12 will get financial and technical assistance from NGOs. However, there is a glaring absence of NCIP-

promulgated survey guidelines.

The discussion on the promulgation of survey guidelines by the NCIP started in 2001. There was a clamor for their release, since ancestral domains and lands cannot be treated as public lands. Neither could they be dealt with as private lands, and therefore should not necessarily be subjected to the same requirements with regard to titling.

A major bone of contention in the discussion on the survey guidelines was the level of accuracy needed, and thus the type of equipment to be used in the survey of ancestral domains, as well as who should certify such accuracy. Geodetic engineers expressed their doubts on the applicability and appropriateness of the combined use of Mapping Grade and Survey Grade Global Positioning Systems (GPS) in the conduct of surveys. Their main contention was the probable accuracy error that will arise with the use of Mapping Grade GPS. Mapping grade survey equipment produces less accurate results than survey grade equipment. Although there seems to be a preference for the latter in terms of the output to be generated, survey costs are expected to be higher if survey grade equipment is used. Also, unlike in the lowlands' farmland and real estate, survey grade accuracy has little relevance in the delineation of the large ancestral domains, which are mostly located in the rugged uplands with boundaries usually following natural landmarks.

Representatives of the NCIP, indigenous peoples and NGOs who have established a Forum on Ancestral Domain mapping and titling, worked together to harmonize the issues pertaining to the survey of ancestral domains. The results of their endeavors were presented to the NCIP, which partially incorporated them in its draft guidelines. But there is still considerable resistance within the government, among academics and above all among geodetic engineers against adopting a more flexible approach that would allow for the use of both mapping and survey grade GPS equipment according to the nature of land to be surveyed, and thereby would allow NGOs to conduct surveys. The geodetic engineers maintain their authority as the legally authorized officers to conduct surveys as mandated by RA 8065.

The current NCIP Chairperson, Atty. Reuben Dasay Lingating, reiterated the NCIP's legal mandate to oversee all surveys and delineation of Ancestral Domain including the quasi-legislative authority to promulgate special rules that would cover mapping in ancestral domains. He welcomed most of the comments and concerns raised by the geodetic engineers but maintained that NCIP is committed to issue titles to qualified indigenous communities as mandated by the IPRA.

While waiting for the final decision on the survey guidelines, the commission pushed through with the survey of ancestral domain using the Department of Environmental and Natural Resources-Department Administrative Order 1998-12 or the Revised Manual on Land Surveying Regulations in the Philippines. This was prompted by a strong order from the Philippine President, Gloria Macapagal Arroyo, who promised the titling of more than 100,000 hectares of CADT in her state of the nation address in July 2002, as well as strong demands from the various indigenous communities who have already complied with the various documentary proofs of their ancestral domains.

A Consultative Body of indigenous leaders

Among the rights that indigenous peoples in the Philippines have been struggling for is the right to a voice strong enough to be heard. The IPRA's response to this is to provide for the establishment of the Consultative Body, which it defines as "the body consisting of traditional leaders, elders and sectors of the different Indigenous Cultural Communities /Indigenous Peoples". As with the other promises that the IPRA has offered, it was some time before this body got off the ground.

How to constitute the Consultative Body, and in particular how to select the indigenous leaders to become part of it, was one of the issues that the Office of the Presidential Assistant on Indigenous Peoples Affairs tackled in 2001. When the new NCIP Commissioners were appointed in the second half of that year, the clamor for the formation of the Consultative Body was one of the urgent calls of indigenous peoples and support groups. It was in October 2003 that the Commissioners came up with the guidelines on how to constitute the body through an administrative order (AO 1, Series of 2003).

Among the functions of the Consultative Body that the guidelines stipulated are the following:

1. To deliberate on important indigenous peoples' issues and concerns and give input or make recommendations on policies for adoption by the Commission;
2. To recommend programs and projects to the Commission;
3. To act/serve as a monitoring body for the implementation of policies, projects and programs of the Commission and other government agencies affecting indigenous peoples; and
4. To assist in the management and resolution of conflicts/disputes in accordance with customary rules and processes.

To undertake these, the administrative order calls for three tiers of consultative bodies – provincial, by ethnographic region (under IPRA the country has been divided into seven ethnographic regions) and at the national level. While such levels were not defined in the IPRA, they were based on consultations with indigenous leaders since 2001, wherein they consistently stated that, since there was still not a widely accepted way to represent the numerous indigenous peoples in the Philippines equitably, representation should be as complete as possible, at least at the provincial level.

The selection process is to proceed as follows. A National Coordinating Committee (NCC) consisting of national-level indigenous peoples' organizations and NGOs will oversee the formation of Ethnographic Regional Coordinating Committees (ERCCs). The ERCCs in turn oversee the formation of Provincial Coordinating Committees (PCC).

The PCCs will hold provincial peoples' caucuses where representatives of indigenous peoples organizations and NGOs will be encouraged to reach out to as many indigenous communities and organizations as are known to exist within the province on the matter of the formation of the Consultative Body. Each ancestral domain and resettled indigenous community will select five representatives for the Provincial Consultative Body (PCB). Every municipal-level and provincial-level indigenous peoples' organization and Tribal Council is entitled to one representative. The PCC will designate a time and place when these representatives will select or elect five representatives for the Ethnographic Regional Consultative Body (ERCBs). In turn, the ERCCs shall designate a time and place when these representatives will select/elect ten representatives for the National Consultative Body (NCB). All coordinating committees will cease to exist with the formation of the NCB. The administrative order ensures the inclusion of women and youth representatives, even though men dominate the political leadership structures of most of the indigenous peoples in the Philippines.

Civil society organizations that have been involved in the process of drawing up the Consultative Body's guidelines had serious criticisms of some of the provisions (among others that the government-created pseudo-leaders in the so-called Tribal Councils are to be represented on the provincial level body). However they agreed on a compromise to allow the NCIP to try these out, mainly in response to NCIP's own accommodations.

By the end of 2003, the project was at the stage of forming the ERCCs and the NCC was firming up its role as the policy-making body of the process. It is expected that the whole process will be completed within 2004. The establishment of the Consultative Body is currently receiving financial support from IWGIA. The critical support offered by IWGIA has been complemented by incessant lobbying of indigenous peoples' organizations and support groups.

The process of forming the Consultative Body is still riddled by critical questions: In the first place, how are indigenous groups and communities defined? How can the selection of truly genuine indigenous leaders or representatives be assured? How can one equitably yet in a manageable manner represent the indigenous groups in the Philippines, which vary greatly in size, language, geographical location, political structure, etc.? How can more local logistical and financial support be harnessed?

Both civil society and the National Commission on Indigenous Peoples (NCIP) have agreed that if they waited for these questions to be answered satisfactorily before making moves regarding the Consultative Body, it may never be formed. And meanwhile, the indigenous peoples in the country have expressed their desire to have a body of genuine indigenous leaders and representatives as soon as possible. This Consultative Body is a first serious attempt to accomplish this within a government context, i.e. mandated by a law. The tri-partite arrangement of NCIP, indigenous peoples' organizations and NGOs must continue to cooperate to keep the process moving. There is mistrust of the NCIP's honesty and efficiency, there is the jostling of indigenous peoples' organizations and NGOs for their own political or ideological interests, there are worries of the NCIP and indigenous peoples' organizations that NGOs will take over.

However, there may never be a more opportune time than now to accomplish the constitution of the Consultative Body for indigenous peoples. With presidential and local elections taking place within the year 2004, there are grave fears that it will be difficult to avoid political interests influencing the selection/election of Consultative Body leaders at the expense of the indigenous peoples' interests. Yet postponing the process until after the elections leads to the dilemma that by that time, the term of the present Commissioners (who are supportive of the body's formation) will end. There is no guarantee that any new Commission will take up the cudgels for a Consultative Body formation. And looming in the future as a significant threat, is the potential diluting or even abrogation of the IPRA and its provisions if the proposal for changes in the Philippine Constitution is seriously taken up.

Ongoing human rights violations

A National Workshop of Indigenous Peoples on Human Rights is planned for February 2004 in Manila. The aim of the workshop will be to assess the human rights situation of indigenous peoples since the visit of the UN Special Rapporteur on the Human Rights and Fundamental Freedoms of Indigenous Peoples, Prof. Rodolfo Stavenhagen, in December 2002 (see *The Indigenous World 2002-03*). More than 100 indigenous representatives from all over the country are expected to participate.

According to reports prepared for the workshop the situation of human rights and fundamental freedoms of indigenous peoples has not improved and, in most regions, has deteriorated even further. Militarization and aggressive development have worsened in all parts of the country. These are the two main causes of violations of civil, political, economic, social and cultural rights and freedoms of indigenous peoples.

Between January 2002 and December 2003, 702 cases of human rights violations were documented in the Southern Mindanao Region alone. Around 300 of these occurred in indigenous peoples' communities. Violations ranged from forced evacuations, food blockades, arbitrary arrests and illegal detentions to massacres, murders, and torture. All remain unsolved and no justice has been brought to the victims and their relatives. Warrants of arrests were served but no arrests have yet been made.

In the Cordillera 1,296 cases of human rights violations were documented during 2003. With the military counter-insurgency operations continuing, the Cordillera remains one of the regions where human rights violations are most rampant. Such incidents include arbitrary killings, arrests and harassment, and the disruption of livelihoods due to military bombing in Bontoc and Sadanga, in Mountain Province. More aggressive recruitment of indigenous men into the notorious paramilitary forces, like the Civilian Auxiliary Force Geographical Units (CAFGU), was conducted by the armed forces of the Philippines in Mountain Province and Kalinga. Human rights violations by such paramilitary forces have also been rampant in Mindanao.

Another region suffering severely from the ongoing militarization is Mindoro Island where massacres, arbitrary killings and torture have been conducted by military elements against innocent non-indigenous and indigenous civilians. There, the indigenous Buhid people, who have always abhorred any form of violence and whose lives are severely disrupted even by the mere presence of people carrying arms, demand that all armed groups, i.e. both the military and the leftist New People's Army leave their territory for good.

The national workshop on human rights will come out with a final document including a number of demands to the government and plans for action by indigenous peoples themselves aimed at promoting and protecting the Human Rights and Fundamental Freedoms of indigenous peoples.[1]   ❑

Note

1   The final document of the workshop will be posted on the IWGIA website under International processes / UN Special Rapporteur.

TIMOR LOROSA'E

A lmost two years after Independence, Timor Lorosa'e is still struggling to get the country and a well-functioning democracy on its
feet. The challenge is enormous and the problems vast. Much, however, is going in the right direction. The main concern is what will
happen when the UN leaves the country in May 2004.

Building democracy on the ruins of war

When the Indonesians left Timor Lorosa'e in 1999 they left a country
in ruins, and the new regime has been faced with the huge task of
reconstructing it.

Since the struggle for liberation, the gap between the elected politicians and the local population has grown. Previously, they fought
side by side against the Indonesians but, once the Indonesians were
thrown out, contact between the rural population and their leaders
deteriorated. Everything indicates, however, that the politicians are
taking their role seriously. In 2003, in an effort to re-establish contact
and simultaneously disseminate information about democracy, President Xanana Gusmão initiated his "Open Presidency" programme
and parliament continued with its "Open Governance" initiative.
One of the objectives was to instigate local visits and discuss relevant
issues with the population. Both initiatives are intended to create
commitment to the political process among the population.

The problem is that the population has a long list of basic needs that
have not been met, and therefore little time for political commitment. The
people need food on the table, better health conditions and construction
materials to rebuild their ruined houses. Democracy comes second.

The risk, in the short term, is that if there are no improvements in
the wretched conditions they are suffering, people will lose faith in
the government. It may, however, be seen as an important sign for
democracy that the local people now have the possibility of speaking
directly to the politicians without fear of reprisals.

Democracy calls for patience

Eighty per cent of the East Timorese population live in the country-
side, where there are often no newspapers, radios or TVs. This pre-

vents many of the locals from receiving information from the government, thus impeding their commitment to and understanding of the new democracy.

Moreover, the East Timorese have never experienced democracy before and they do not have a basic understanding of what it is. "People in Timor Lorosa'e have been oppressed for a long time so we need time to explain to them again and again and again what it is all about. That calls for patience," says João M. Saldanha from the East Timor Study Group, an independent think tank carrying out development research in Timor Lorosa'e.

Another project that has attempted to build democracy in Timor Lorosa'e is the Community Empowerment and Local Governance Project (CEP). The World Bank was behind this project, which ran from 1 February to 31 December 2003. Some 20 million USD were spent on the project and one of its main aims was to involve the local population in decision-making processes. People had to decide themselves where they needed help, and the project thus tried to strengthen local democracy.

The project came up against a number of problems, as it had not taken the country's traditional leadership structures into account but, all in all, it seems as if the project has sown some seeds of democracy in Timor Lorosa'e.

The public administration is short of personnel

Great progress was made in Timor Lorosa'e during 2003 but it is obvious that the country will not be able to manage in crucial areas once the UN mission to the country – UNMISET – withdraws in May 2004. This was the conclusion reached by the UN in its biannual report from October 2003.

One major issue is the shortage of people to fill crucial posts in the public administration. According to the UN, only 86 per cent of the 13,082 budgeted positions in the public administration have been filled, and in some crucial areas international assistance is required to ensure that tasks are carried out satisfactorily.

Another huge problem is the judicial system, with the courts of law seriously short of qualified people. There was not a single lawyer remaining in the country when the Indonesians left, and the recruited judges, public prosecutors and defence counsels still need training. The handling of cases is characterized by chronic delays, and more money is needed for this purpose. The lack of qualified staff within the judicial system can also be seen in the legal proceedings being taken against individuals who committed serious crimes in relation to the conflict in 1999, where a backlog of cases is piling up. If these problems are not resolved, there could be problems creating an acceptable reconciliation within the country in the long run.

When the UN mission leaves the country, it is anticipated that several donors will also leave, while others will reduce their support. If funding disappears, the country will be hard pressed to handle the situation and develop democracy, nor will it be able to continue to train and advise public servants, politicians and lawyers.

The free press is alive

One of the truly positive developments in Timor Lorosa'e has been the blossoming of a free press. For the first time in the country's history, a free and independent press has emerged, one that is not afraid of criticizing the government. The editor of the country's widest circulation newspaper has even received threats from the prime minister but still the newspaper continues undaunted. The newspaper's major problem is – according to its chief editor Salvador Ximenes Soares – its economic situation

The radio station Radio Falintil is also endeavouring to develop democracy. "It is important that someone keeps an eye on the government. If a politician accepts bribes or the police behave badly, then my radio listeners need to know about it. But I also try to explain to them why we have political parties, and why it is important that children attend school," says radio presenter Anito Matos.

The NGOs are lagging behind

When the UN leaves Timor Lorosa'e, it will be important that a well-functioning civil society is in place to take over. The local NGOs play a central role in this but, unfortunately, many of them have huge problems. "Many of the local NGOs have a name only, and no programme," says Joaquim da Costas Freitas, director of the NGO Forum, an umbrella organisation for the NGOs working in the country.

Following independence, numerous NGOs emerged. The NGO Forum states three reasons for this: the great need for help, the free rein now the Indonesians had gone and the large amount of donor funding available. The main problem, according to the NGO Forum, is that the UN and international organisations have not been sufficiently adept at getting the local organisations involved. "When they leave the country, they will leave nothing behind for the local NGOs. They have not received the necessary capacity building and the donors have not ensured that the programmes in the country are sustainable," states Joaquim da Costa Freitas.

This may mean several NGOs having to close down. The NGO Forum fears that this will, in turn, deprive many East Timorese of a crucial channel of communication with the government. ❏

INDONESIA

In September 2003, the indigenous peoples of Indonesia held their second congress or national gathering known as *Kongres Masyarakat Adat Nusantara II* (the Second Congress of the Indigenous Peoples of the Archipelago). Six hundred indigenous representatives from various places throughout Indonesia attended the meeting. The Congress was the culmination of a long process that included local and regional meetings of AMAN's member organizations.

The first Congress (1999), and the overall "*reformasi*" movement that has been taking place in Indonesia since late 1998 (after Soeharto's fall) have stimulated the growth of a new perception of indigenous peoples in the country. There is also a growing recognition of the existence of indigenous peoples, although such recognition largely still exists on a symbolic level only. This symbolic recognition, which can be found in the amended Constitution of 1945 (2000), and in some of the new laws and in draft bills and regulations, unfortunately does not automatically result in a changed attitude on the part of the State apparatus.

The State apparatus has maintained the same violent attitude as during President Marcos' New Order regime. While there were indications during 2000 and 2002 that the State was willing to show more respect for its people, including indigenous peoples, some human rights violations did once more occur in 2003. The cases reported in this article are examples of these.

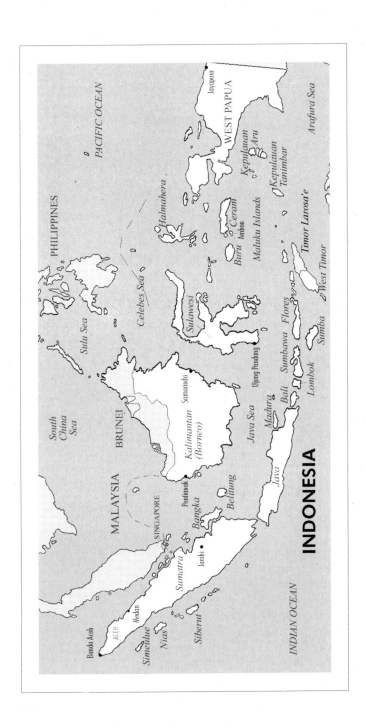

Policy and legislation

As in previous years, legal recognition of indigenous peoples and their rights during 2003 was still restricted to legislation and policy instruments. The other authority, the judicial power, was not able to bring about significant improvements in its deficient legal status. Most court rulings were unfavorable to indigenous peoples - a situation that seems to have become more and more institutionalized. In response to this, the Supreme Court issued a new decree on Court Connected Mediation this year, which actually could provide more room for customary courts.

There were no significant developments in legal recognition of indigenous peoples and their rights during 2003. The 2nd amendment to the 1945 Constitution, passed in 2000, and which articulates indigenous peoples' rights,[1] maintains the tradition of constitutional recognition. This amendment has stimulated the reformulation of laws and bills on natural resources and citizens' rights to include articles on indigenous peoples. This includes bills on Natural Resource Management; Water Resource Management; Coastal and Small Island Management; Plantation, Mining, Genetic Utilization and Preservation; Revised Laws on Fishery and Criminal Code; Proposed Amendment to the Law on Population and Family Prosperity Development; and Law No. 22/2003 on the National Education System. All this legislation recognizes indigenous peoples and their rights although most still contain some conditionality.

The fall of the authoritarian New Order regime altered the previous centralized and monopolistic legal politics. Although a number of regional administrations still continue to apply the New Order's style of conditional recognition of customary rights, some have been trying to pass more responsive regulations. In June 2003, the Regent of Merangi agreed to legally recognize a customary forest in Batu Kerbau village, in the vicinity of Sungai Manau sub-district, encompassing approximately 2,000 hectares, through Decree No. 287 Year 2003. The initiative, which was supported by a local NGO called KKI Warsi, was the second in the province of Jambi, after the Regent of Bungo issued a similar decree in 2002 on the recognition of a customary forest of approximately 800 hectares. Also in 2003, the district administration of Kutai Barat passed Perda (Regional Regulation)[2] No.12 Year 2003 on Community Forest Management, which explicitly recognized indigenous peoples' rights to forest resources.

The situation is very different in Pasir district, East Kalimantan. Controversy is inflaming the province. This began on 3 December 2003 when the district administration of Pasir submitted 12 proposed regional regulations to the regional parliament, one of which was on the *Hak Ulayat*, i.e. the traditional right of indigenous communities to their land. The draft of the regulation concluded that no community groups in the district complied with the criteria for being recognized as indigenous peoples. This conclusion was based on research carried out by academics from the University of Hasanudin (Makasar, South Sulawesi) and commissioned by the district administration of Pasir: the research concluded that there were no indigenous peoples in the district and, logically, there was therefore no *ulayat* land either.[3]

This action on the part of the district administration of Pasir is representative of the conservative politics used by the State and its local authorities to deal with indigenous peoples and their rights. The State establishes criteria and conditional recognition of indigenous peoples, while the local authorities follow them up in different ways. Activists have observed that there are four ways in which administrations deal with indigenous peoples: (1) they try to legally recognize indigenous peoples as they are; (2) they legally recognize indigenous peoples on some conditions; (3) they appear to legally recognize indigenous peoples but are actually taking commercial and political advantage of them; and (4) they *do not* legally recognize indigenous peoples.

The second and third ways were dominant throughout 2003. The Megawati regime's way of dealing with West Papua is an example of the third way. In 2001, some of the West Papuans were pleased with the enactment of Law No. 21/2001 on Special Autonomy for the West Papua Province, which recognizes the indigenous peoples of West Papua, their rights over the land and other natural resources, their human rights and the establishment of a regional truth and reconciliation commission. At the same time, the President issued a decree speeding up the process of dividing the province into three by 2003. The fourth way identified above is expected to become more prevalent over the years to come, particularly if the 2004 national elections produce a pro-market and repressive regime. Some district administrations, which have legally recognized indigenous peoples and their rights, are facing problems in implementing these decisions.

Everything indicates that, thus far, legal recognition of indigenous peoples and their rights has been on paper only. The indigenous movement's apparent satisfaction with what has been obtained seems to convince the State that it has gone the right way about lessening the radical movement among indigenous peoples. It is not surprising that it is reluctant to seriously implement such legislation. This policy will not change until all advocates of indigenous rights start to seriously question this lack of implementation.

Re-emergence of violence

Local Autonomy has had an unpredictable impact on the relationship between people and the State at local level. Most local governments are driven largely by the political and economic interests of local political elites and local government bureaucracy. On the one hand, the local governments always defend their political power through control of their district's economic resources by military and police force, as well as the Court apparatus. On the other, the economic resources are almost never used for the peoples' needs but for various development projects that are of no real benefit to the people. Even worse, the process of implementing these projects has led to serious human rights violations. The two cases described below show how local governments have been neglecting people's basic rights. The human rights violations described reflect the situation in many other parts of the country, where the people are confronted with various forms of political domination and repressive measures by local governments.

Bonto Mangiring, a village in Bulukumba District of South Sulawesi Province, has a long history of conflict between the people, particularly peasants, and a big plantation corporation, PT Lonsum. The violations the people have suffered so far come not only from the company but also from the State apparatus, since both military forces and the Indonesia Police Guard are involved on the side of the company.

According to Agrarian State Ministry/Head of National Agrarian Body Decree,[4] it is clear that the villages now in conflict with the PT Lonsum do not fall within the concession of PT Lonsum. The Decree was issued as a result of unsettled conflicts in the region dating back to the 1980s when PT Lonsum began to consolidate its company and extend its concession thanks to its collaboration with central and local government and the Armed Forces. In reality, most of the people's land was appropriated during the 1980s and 1990s: the collaborators decided the price of land and the people had absolutely no say in the process. As a result, the compensation the people were offered was useless because the land was only valued at a few hundred rupiah (less than a dollar).

The people protested and took the case to court in order to get their lands back. In 1999, the Supreme Court delivered a judicial decision[5] in favour of the people. But this did not end the conflict. The state court of Bulukumba (a lower court) later ruled that the land area owned by the people as stated in the Supreme Court decision was larger than it should be. The villagers were subsequently evicted from the land with the help of 50 mobile police brigades and 100 military personnel. Villagers and civil society organizations complained to the Supreme Commander of the Indonesian Police Guard in Jakarta. He sent them a short reply stating that he would send an official letter to his inferior officers in South Sulawesi arguing that in the current era of decentralisation a problem like this should be settled in the region by the officers responsible for the respective area. Looking at this as an example of how the Armed Forces organise their institutions, indigenous activists fear that the people will suffer increasing violations on the part of local government and Armed Forces in the name of decentralization.

During 2003, the case developed as follows: in March (5-8) 2003, PT Lonsum brought some 500 people to destroy the houses and garden plots of Bonto Mangiring village. 700 hundred people responded to this harmful action by marching on the District House of Representatives and remaining there until March 10 when they obtained the agreement of the local government that PT Lonsum would no longer appropriate people's lands. To balance the decision, it included a clause that people were no longer allowed to carry sharp weapons such as knives, swords, etc. (not even in their own houses). This clause proved to have serious consequences when the company came back with soldiers, destroying the villagers' houses and appropriating their land on May 28, 2003. The people were left with no means to defend themselves. A July 18, 2003 Head of District Decision claimed that 200 ha of the lands in the area belonged to PT Lonsum. This area was included in the area won by the people according to the Supreme Court Decision of 1999. They now have nothing with which to defend their lands. It is clear that the agreement reached in March is merely a tactical way for the collaborators to minimize the people's space for protest.

The height of the conflict so far was reached on July 21, 2003 when the people reclaimed the lands that PT Lonsum had already planted with rubber trees. 1,500 people were involved in this action. They were met with gunfire from the police mobile brigade. Five persons were shot (two of these later died from their wounds) and four were imprisoned.[6] Since this incident, the Armed Forces have been more repressive and always stay in the area and fire at anybody who passes nearby. The people can no longer work safely in their gardens, and they fear going to the forest to hunt or collect other food sources.

For civil society, this conflict has highlighted how local government and all state institutions (House of Representatives, State Court,

Armed Forces) have collaborated with big corporations and have been more eager to follow agreements with these than to follow state policy in terms of governing their regions. The same tendency could be seen in the case that is taking place in the District of Manggarai, Flores, Nusa Tenggara Timur Province. Here, the conflict is between indigenous peoples and the local government. The people's lands have been claimed by the local government as a Protected Area. The indigenous people of Meler Kuwus have for many years been cultivating their garden and fields in the area claimed, planting commercial crops such as coffee, cocoa and commercial timber. This has now been destroyed by the local government and State apparatus. Three people were arrested and many others wounded during this conflict. What is surprising is that, in court, witnesses for the local government could not prove that the indigenous people's land was included in the area claimed as protected area. Nevertheless, development of the lands as a protected area continues under the local regulations.

Indigenous peoples' consolidation

The Second Congress of the Alliance of the Indigenous Peoples of the Archipelago (AMAN) was held in implementation of organizational decisions taken during the First Congress in Jakarta in 1999 and in response to the external situation. AMAN's members are indigenous communities and organizations at local and regional level. There are currently 777 communities verified as members whilst 927 have registered with the aim of becoming members. Aside from this, there are 18 indigenous organizations at local level and 11 at regional level allied to AMAN. All members have the right to send one or more representatives to the Congress. In the preparations for the Second Congress, 12 regional (provincial) indigenous meetings and many local meetings were held as a means of organizational consolidation as well as a way of choosing representatives to the National Council.

The main goals of the Second Congress were: (a) to draw lessons from the implementation of the decisions of the First Congress over the past four years; (b) to consolidate organizations of indigenous peoples and to develop a synergy between all indigenous actions at regional level; (c) to mobilize broad-based support for the indigenous peoples' movements through strengthening and broadening the alliance with other pro-democratic groups; (d) to develop organizational structures that are more responsive to all developments and more effective in serving their members; and (e) to sharpen the platform of movements by developing strategic guidelines for organization and programmatic frameworks that accommodate the aspirations and demands of the indigenous peoples in Indonesia. All these goals are aimed at creating a broader space for strengthening the indigenous movement for social transformation in Indonesia.

The biggest challenge to a just and prosperous social transformation in the future lies in the efforts to rehabilitate the social and ecological systems. Indigenous institutions, as well as their social, legal and political systems, and natural resource management need to be revitalized and empowered. The basis for a repositioning of the relationship between indigenous peoples and the state was formulated during the First Congress of Indigenous Peoples of the Archipelago, held in 1999. The Second Congress produced some important results with regard to the work programme for the coming years, organizational structure (new regional division), etc.[7]   ❑

Notes

1 Article 18B paragraph 2 and Article 281 paragraph 3.
2 "Regional regulation" is the authors' translation of "*peraturan Daerah (perda)*".
3 Articles 10, 11, 12 and 13.
4 Decree No. 111/HGU/BPN/1997.
5 No. 2553 K/PDT/1987.
6 At the end of 2003, they were still in prison.
7 The Resolution and other news of the Congress can be found at http://dte.gn.apc.org/AMAN/

MALAYSIA

Malaysia's nearly 22.7 million multi-ethnic population includes around 2.6 million indigenous peoples or 11.5 % of the total population. The majority of the indigenous peoples are found in East Malaysia, with around 1 million in Sabah and around 1.5 million in Sarawak. Indigenous peoples in peninsular Malaysia total 106,131. In Peninsular Malaysia, indigenous peoples are known as the *Orang Asli*, a collective term introduced by anthropologists and administrators for the 18 sub-ethnic groups generally classified for official purposes under Negrito, Senoi and Proto-Malay. In Sarawak, the indigenous populations are the *Orang Ulu* and the *Dayaks*. They are also very diverse, with the Dayaks forming a majority of about 50 percent of the total number. Officially there are 25 indigenous groups today listed in Sarawak. However, there are at least 37 known groups and sub-groups. In Sabah, they are termed natives or *Anak Negeri*. They are also very diverse and are estimated to comprise 39 different ethnic groups.

Land rights and court cases

Throughout 2003, the community of Tongod, Sabah, continued its struggle to assert its rights over lands taken by oil palm companies. After filing a court case in November 2002, in June 2003 the High Court in Kota Kinabalu ruled that the community's application was justifiable as a case and the defendants' application to strike out the case was dismissed with costs. The court case will continue in 2004. Communities in the area are in the process of collecting and disseminating information on the case (all of which is available only in English) through workshops. In the meantime, representatives from Bundu, Sabah, where the Dusun community was affected by logging upstream, filed another court case at the High Court. The communities have been successful in preventing logging since 1987 but, despite their strong resistance, a company encroached into the watershed and caused devastation in the area under the guise of building a piped-water project.

In Sarawak, the court case that was taken up by the Penan in Ulu Baram could not proceed due to numerous complications raised by companies, which have divided the communities (for an introduction to the case see *The Indigenous World 2002-2003*: 252). However, since

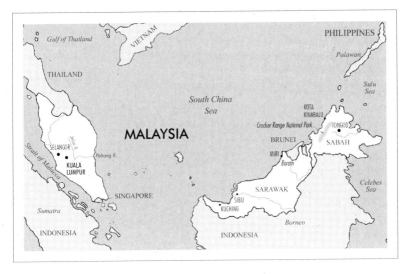

September 2003, these communities have renewed their efforts to blockade timber companies that have encroached into their native customary land. Leaders from the Penan communities have, over the past few
years, been meeting ministers and officials in state and central government to stop logging in their native customary land. In another
Penan area, in Pa Tik, the Shin Yang Group of timber companies was
reported to have threatened communities with arrest if they started a
blockade. The Penan community has been preserving this area as
their community forest. Numerous attempts by the community to
appeal to the company through letters have fallen on deaf ears.

The use of community mapping as a strategy to defend native
customary land faced a serious threat with the introduction of the
Land Surveyor Rules 2003 in Sarawak. Such a move by the government, rendering community maps invalid, is seen by the communities
as yet another obstacle to indigenous peoples' assertion of their land
rights. Nevertheless, indigenous organizations are not deterred and
continued throughout the year to learn GIS and GPS techniques to
enhance maps of customary land. In Sabah, Sarawak and Peninsular
Malaysia, the Indigenous Peoples Network of Malaysia (IPNM, also
known as JOAS) and other community mapping experts worked with
communities to draw up their own maps. Such maps are used as
evidence in court and also for coming up with strategic plans for the
communities.

Indigenous knowledge and biodiversity conservation

In Sabah, indigenous peoples continued to work in a holistic manner, linking biodiversity conservation with recognition of indigenous peoples' rights. Work on policy implementation and change related to various government departments in the state, such as the Drainage and Irrigation department (on watershed management), Wildlife department (on traditional hunting areas) and Sabah Parks (on customary lands within national parks). Communities were able to interact and dialogue with the respective departments and, even though this often resulted in frustrating experiences, it was found to be necessary in order to explain indigenous peoples' perspectives.

Elsewhere in Malaysia, communities have become involved in various activities to change policies on protecting indigenous knowledge and biodiversity. Organizations in Sabah, Sarawak and Peninsular Malaysia have been actively involved in discussions, particularly in preparation for the Seventh Conference of Parties to the Convention on Biological Diversity, to be held in Malaysia in February 2004. Although the Sabah and Sarawak Biodiversity Law has been in place since 2000, the issue of free, prior and informed consent of indigenous peoples has not been further acknowledged. Efforts to revitalize indigenous knowledge and practices of natural resource management have been one of the major activities of many indigenous organizations in Sabah.

Education

Another important aspect of the work of indigenous peoples in Malaysia in 2003 took place through the national Indigenous Peoples' Early Childcare and Development (IPECD) network. The network links organizations within the existing IPNM, thus contributing towards strengthening this national level network. Education of pre-school children has helped communities to consider and develop a curriculum that reflects and promotes the inter-generational transfer of indigenous values and knowledge to the younger generation. Through the community preschools, teachers and community members also found that women's participation and capacity enhancement significantly increased. In 2003, the IPECD network facilitated exchanges between indigenous peoples in Thailand, Kenya and within Malaysia. This was found to be effective in terms of giving women opportunities for exposure and learning.

National campaigns

In 2003, indigenous communities in Malaysia stepped up efforts to establish better relations with the Human Rights Commission in Malaysia (SUHA-KAM). During an annual gathering in conjunction with the World's Indigenous Peoples Day in Sabah in August 2003, indigenous peoples decided to submit memoranda to the state government and SUHAKAM. Through its own effort to organize a series of talks in different parts of Malaysia, SUHA-KAM has recommended that the government take the land issue seriously, particularly in the forthcoming general elections.

The Orang Asli of Peninsular Malaysia have also produced their own memoranda outlining the issues they are facing and have submitted these to the different government departments. In June 2003, the government amended the Orang Asli Act by increasing the fine from RM1,000 to RM10,000 (around USD 2,600) for any company found cheating in relation to projects involving Orang Asli land. This amendment was made in light of numerous cases of fraud, which the government itself found costly when it lost a landmark case involving Orang Asli land in 2002.

Promoting recognition of traditional institutions was another strategy to secure indigenous peoples' rights. Research into indigenous peoples and local government was conducted in Peninsular Malaysia and Sabah during 2003. The research was followed by a national indigenous workshop and a one-day seminar with government representatives and other non-governmental organizations held in June 2003 in Sabah by the Indigenous Peoples Network of Malaysia to discuss strengthening indigenous institutions and governance. The workshop and seminar highlighted the need to rebuild indigenous institutions that have been replaced in Malaysia by a government administrative structure. The workshop also recognized not only the need to protect village leadership structures from interference by political parties but also the need to restructure governmental institutions such as the Department of Orang Asli Affairs (JHEOA). Indigenous organizations also felt the urgency to involve women in all activities in the community in order to further enhance their capacities. In October, indigenous delegates from Malaysia attended an international workshop on local governance and indigenous peoples in the Philippines. A parallel process of research and national level seminars had taken place in the Philippines prior to the workshop, and the workshop as such provided an opportunity for indigenous peoples from both countries to further discuss strategies to promote the involvement of indigenous peoples and traditional governance institutions at local government level. ❏

THAILAND

T hailand is a country of great cultural diversity, traditionally a source, transit point and destination for large movements of peoples. Both ancient and recent history have ensured that this has been an enduring pattern, and today there is a wealth of divergent traditions and life patterns within the country. At the same time it is a country whose political and social leadership have created an inclusive national identity for generations, and many cultural groups in Thailand identify themselves simply as Thai. However, the indigenous and tribal peoples of the north and northwest of the country have fought for recognition of their dual identities as both Thai and as members of their own distinct peoples. These peoples, including the Karen, the Iu Mien, the Hmong, the Akha, the Lahu and the Lisu – among others - represent a range of cultural histories and migration paths, including groups indigenous to the nation, those indigenous to the region, and those that have traditionally migrated over large areas.

A disadvantaged position

Despite these historical differences, indigenous groups share a disadvantaged social and economic position within Thai society, stemming from physical distance from urban centers of power and a traditional separation between the Thai lowland wet rice cultivation and the highland dry swidden farming systems. Improving roads and infrastructure lessened this distance in the latter part of the twentieth century and the Thai State, in response to the turmoil facing neighboring countries, sought to extend its control over the previously relatively autonomous border areas.

The image of indigenous peoples presented to the Thai public during the course of the government's extension of administrative control into border areas was one of a sense of threat: a threat to national security through "contamination" by neighboring conflicts; the threat of narcotic drug production and trade; and a threat to the natural resources viewed as the property of the State. This threat mentality has lowered the social and economic position of the peoples viewed as threatening "others".[1] A collective movement for recognition of their rights to land, resources and political participation has developed in response to this disadvantaged political and social

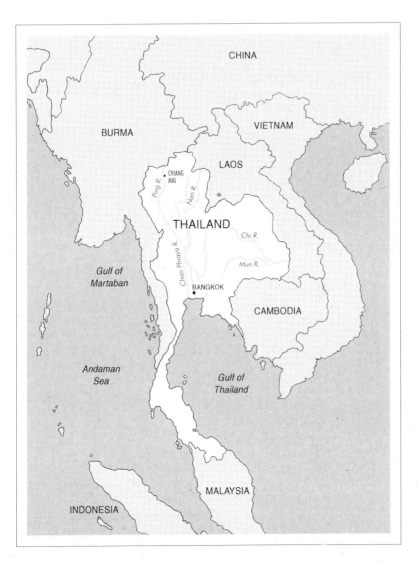

position. This is emerging in the form of widening and increasingly powerful networks between communities and peoples, and in the establishment of the informal institution of the Assembly of Indigenous and Tribal Peoples of Thailand (AITT) and support networks such as the Friends of Highland Peoples.

The political and social challenges faced by these organizations and peoples are significant, and the beginning of 2003 saw communities in the highlands reeling under a "drug suppression" policy introduced by the Thaksin government, which resulted in more than 2,000 extra-judicial killings in the three months of its implementation. The cause of this enormous death toll is hotly debated, with different groups blaming drug traders, corrupt government officials, soldiers involved in the drug trade, and even migrants from Burma. The only universally accepted fact, many months after the policy was brought to a close, is that these killings occurred outside of the justice system, and were a result, whether indirect or direct, of the government drug suppression policy. Within highland areas and in organizations established by indigenous peoples, it is widely seen that the policy was another instance of making a vulnerable section of society the scapegoat.

However harsh its impact, this policy was a short-lived phenomenon. For indigenous and tribal peoples in Thailand generally, it is the long-term policies and policy frameworks that discriminate against highland communities that are of the greatest concern.

Imposition of a "Master Plan"

In 2003 the government continued to ignore the articulated political, social and economic aspirations of highland communities, the majority of indigenous and tribal peoples in the nation, and indeed the right to articulate such aspirations. The Thai government (like many governments in Southeast Asia) structures national policy in the framework of "National Social and Economic Development Master Plans" – five-year programs that have been instituted in Thailand for almost 40 years. In 1992 the government issued the first of another range of policy frameworks, called the "Master Plans for Community Development, Environment and Narcotics Control in Highland Areas." In them they repeated the three negative stereotypes of highland areas that have dogged government policies for years – as underdeveloped, as environmentally destructive, and as the source of the drug problems in Thailand. The first two of these highland master plans were instituted with no community or public participation in the drafting process – something that was common under previous Thai governments. However, in 1997 the Kingdom of Thailand adopted a new Constitution that enshrined, for the first time, the rights of local communities and the rights of "traditional communities" to be consulted and involved in all and any decisions affecting their lives. The relevant sections, sections 59 and 76, state:

Section 59. A person shall have the right to receive information, explanation and reason from a State agency, State enterprise or local government organisation before permission is given for the operation of any project or activity which may affect the quality of the environment, health and sanitary conditions, the quality of life or any other material interest concerning him or her or a local community and shall have the right to express his or her opinions on such matters in accordance with the public hearing procedure, as provided by law;

Section 76. The State shall promote and encourage public participation in laying down policies, making decisions on political issues, preparing economic, social and political development plans, and inspecting the exercise of State power at all levels.

The expectation from this new constitution was that the policy frameworks that outline the practical work of government agencies – the Master Plans – would henceforth be drafted with a far higher level of community consultation. However, this did not happen and the draft 3rd Master Plan Community Development, Environment and Narcotics Control in Highland Areas was unilaterally adopted by government agencies. The Master Plan for 2002-06 proceeded despite strong civil society protest, a protest that called attention to the lack of review of previous master plans, and the lack of public participation in the drafting process. The response from civil society, and from the Assembly of Indigenous and Tribal Peoples of Thailand (AITT) was a mass rally in front of the Chiang Mai city hall, demanding the suspension of the Master Plan until civil society groups had conducted a review of the policy.

The result has been the establishment of a series of sub-committees to study the applicability of the current Master Plan in highland areas, on issues such as citizenship and forest / land rights – both issues of central concern to indigenous and tribal peoples in Thailand. These sub-committees, involving both government officials and representatives of civil society groups, have met throughout 2003 and are distinguished by a lack of progress on any of the major issues at hand. In the latter part of the 2003, however, clear plans emerged from the civil society groups involved. A full "pilot plan" of alternative community development and land / forest management has been drawn up, involving some 60 communities, in which civil society groups and community organizations will lead all policy making within the communities. It is proposed that the government allocate funding for this plan, the "Sustainable Highland Development Plan," and the government has been receptive to this idea.

Citizenship

The right to a voice and a presence in the political life of the nation is fundamental to long-term recognition of indigenous peoples' rights to land and resources. For almost a third of the indigenous and tribal population in Thailand who continue to lack citizenship, this right is denied. There are more than 290,000 individuals living within the highland areas of Thailand without secure legal status, divided into those recorded on previous surveys as residents, but without official status (134,000 individuals) and those without any documentation to use in applying for citizenship (157,000 individuals). These statistics are drawn from the official government numbers, published in the Master Plan for Highland Development, Environment and Narcotics Control in Highland Areas, and many individuals working on these issues consider these numbers unrealistically low.

Lack of citizenship papers among highland peoples in Thailand is a serious problem that has received the attention of community organizations and civil society for some time. The government response has been mixed, as the laws and policies regarding the recognition of citizenship are complex and the fluid borders between Thailand and its neighbors mean that population movements are small but constant. The development of citizenship law in Thailand has been complex and has resulted in a confusing series of conflicting laws. Although the government recognizes in its constitution and many of its laws the right of every person in its borders to a legal status, and the right of every child born to a birth certificate and citizenship, the practical reality is that these rights are not translated into secure legal status for many people. Many efforts have been made to address this problem and indigenous and tribal peoples have been active in community training on citizenship law, on advocacy and lobby work with the relevant government agencies, and in the task of collecting and reviewing the often complex array of documents required for a successful application.

Land and forest rights

The Community Forest Act - the first piece of legislation proposed to the Thai Parliament under an innovative provision in the 1997 Constitution, which allowed bills to be presented for consideration by peoples' movements - has not progressed in the course of 2003. The bill was passed through the House of Representatives in 2002 and was subsequently considered by the Senate. During Senate deliberations changes were made to the text that removed all realistic use of the bill to prevent violation of basic human rights to community resources in any area of land declared "protected". The bill went back to consideration by a joint sitting of both houses, scheduled to take place sometime in 2003. At the close of 2003 hopes were not high that the sitting would happen anytime soon.

Protected status of land in Thailand is a contentious issue – as in many other countries – and involves all land not covered by legally issued private land title being declared the property of the state. All State land is then declared "forest lands", with the presence of trees not considered an important criterion. These lands are then divided into a series of categories of protected areas with an equally complex range of legally allowed activities. The activities allowed in protected areas do not include residence or cultivation, and therefore the legal implication of a protected area is that all inhabitants become illegal squatters when a declaration is made. The only exceptions to this are those few communities given special status, on the bequest of the King, or by a special declaration of Parliament.

To exacerbate this situation of conflict and insecurity, the Thai government, through the Royal Forestry Department, drafted a five-year forestry policy in 2003 (to be implemented from 2006) that aims to increase protected areas in Thailand from an estimated current 15% of the total land area of Thailand to a target of 40% by 2011. Given that the estimated area currently under "protected" status is significantly larger than the actual area, the target will be difficult to achieve. Worse, the protected area law does not allow for the continuation of sustainable traditional use – or indeed continued settlement – and any increase in the size of protected areas without these fundamental questions resolved will result in the continued "criminalization" of highland settlements.

Future outlook

However there are many positive signs in Thailand for the realization of the rights of indigenous peoples, and of local communities, to the lands and territories traditionally occupied by them. The civil society and indigenous peoples representation in the sub-committees established in 2002 is a positive sign of increased involvement at a policy-making level with real impacts for communities in the north and northwest, and the pilot plan drafted by them is the first form of "alternative" or community-led development to be accepted by the government. Cooperation with local government agencies is also being maintained, and in some places strengthened, as communities go through the process of registering members for citizenship. Despite the significant issues remaining, notably discrimination against traditional occupants in protected areas, there is much to be hopeful about in the trend of increased and effective participation by indigenous and tribal peoples in the political life of the country. ❏

Note

1   **Suphachai Jawongsri and Prasert Trakansuphakorn. 2001.** Chao kao: Satana Kwam Pen Khon Thai thi tuk Luem (Hill peoples: the forgotten Thai peoples). *Sayam Rath Weekly Review*, 28 March-4 April.

CAMBODIA

Indigenous communities in Cambodia have their ancestral domains in the largely forested areas of the north and north-eastern part of the country. The Royal Government of Cambodia formed the Inter-Ministerial Committee (IMC) for Highland Peoples Development in 1994. This body developed a General Policy for Highland Peoples Development in 1997. This document still only exists in draft form. The National Poverty Reduction Strategy (NPRS) contains a number of brief points with regard to indigenous peoples in terms of their lack of representation at the management and legislative levels, language barriers, lack of access to law and rights, the historic exclusion of ethnic minorities in policies, decision-making and development processes and the ensuing disadvantage in terms of status, position and living standards.

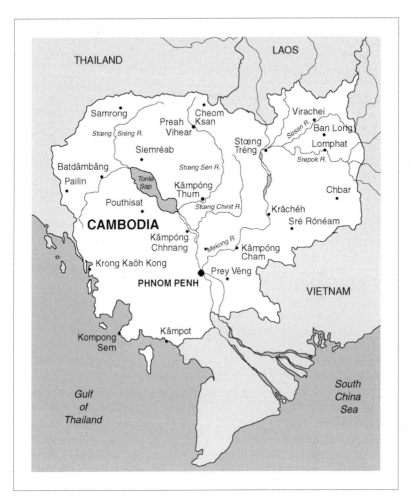

Land rights

Numerous studies have shown that most indigenous peoples operate a well-developed land allocation and land management system that relies on communal decision-making through traditional structures. Individual land titling and land sales bypass this system, threatening the collective nature of indigenous communities, leading to resource loss and creating poverty.

Provincial governments in Ratanakiri and other provinces have been working with partner organizations on programs to promote land security through community-based natural resource management. In Ratanakiri, this has resulted in provincial recognition of many community natural resource management areas. This is a positive step for initial land security – but it is offset by the national policy of rapid immigration of non-indigenous people into areas traditionally occupied by indigenous people. Roads and airports are being rapidly developed and the provincial and national vision is directed towards industrial agriculture and tourism, both of which are likely to disenfranchise indigenous peoples if implemented too quickly, which is what is happening.

In 2001, the Royal Government of Cambodia passed a new Land Law that contains provisions for indigenous communities to gain title to their land, either in the form of individual titles or as a communal title. In this law, indigenous community land can be defined as residential land, agricultural land or land kept in reserve as part of the traditional rotational cultivation system. There is also a chance that small areas of forest in the agricultural land complex can be included. Sub-decrees that define the requirements for legal recognition of communal land ownership have yet to be written. In order to inform the development of these legal instruments, a project commenced in 2003 whereby 3 communal land titling areas are being piloted, 2 in Ratanakiri and 1 in Mondolkiri. These pilot areas need to be monitored closely to ensure that bureaucratic constraints and vested interests do not strangle the process.

Despite these initiatives, land alienation remains an alarming and growing problem. Of concern is a proliferation of "land concessions" issued by the government in provinces such as Kompong Thom, Stung Treng and Kratie. These land concessions aim to establish industrial agricultural rubber or cashew nut plantations. They destroy native forest and reduce indigenous people to positions of subservience and poverty, their natural resources being excluded from their management and use.

Also of concern is the continuing growth of land "sales" involving misinformation, coercion, threats, bribes to officials and other illegal mechanisms. With these factors operating, a number of villages in Ratanakiri are now close to being completely landless. This is a growing concern and is being exacerbated by large infrastructure developments that fuel land speculation. Information about basic human rights, land rights and contract procedures is an urgent need. This information needs to be delivered in indigenous languages with the active involvement of indigenous peoples and their organizations. Likewise, independent legal representation on land cadastral commissions and court processes is needed. Many see strengthening of cultural and community identities as an important strategy for combating the trend of land sales by community people who feel disempowered or do not respect traditional community management structures.

Forestry issues

Like all communities using forest for livelihood support in Cambodia, indigenous peoples do not have secure management rights over the forest areas they traditionally use and manage. Land alienation means that indigenous peoples have to shift their agricultural areas into the forest. They are then blamed for forest clearing. Forest concessions intimidate indigenous communities and deprive them of developing their own secure and sustainable livelihood support.

Indigenous peoples are not entitled to extract timber for sawing, even by hand, "because this is not customary use". Indigenous peoples are establishing community regulations to protect the forest and feel discriminated against by the "customary use" provisions of the forest law and its interpretation.

A Forest Law (2002) and a Sub-decree on Community Forestry were recently passed (2003). This has created the legal instruments necessary for indigenous peoples' management and use rights. There is a strong need to carefully monitor the process and ensure that this sub-decree is passed and actually serves the needs of poor communities. It is imperative that it includes traditional community management rights over mature forest and not just degraded forest. Many forest areas, especially spirit forests, burial forests and small areas of forest among agricultural lands need to be included in communal land titling if indigenous land management and culture is to be protected. Excluding these forest areas will also have the effect of drastically slowing down the mapping required for communal land, thereby reducing the land security of indigenous communities in general.

Education

Despite the slow progress of education reforms in Cambodia, education for indigenous peoples has seen a number of positive developments. There is now a Draft Law on Education (March 2003) in which ethnic minorities are cited as having special educational needs and the right to formal education in their mother tongue. The Education For All (EFA) National Plan (May 2003) also includes specific mention of ethnic minorities as deserving and having the right to mother tongue education.

There have also been significant developments in the area of bilingual education programs, both in the formal and non-formal sectors. The Cambodian Ministry of Education, Youth and Sports officially approved scripts for five languages in 2003, with an official launch ceremony attended by senior government officials held in Ratanakiri in August 2003. Four of these scripts are for languages in Ratanakiri Province, and one for Mondolkiri Province. All use the script of the national language, Khmer, as a base, so Khmer literacy is also strengthened.

Non-Formal Education (NFE) – both bilingual and monolingual - continues to return positive results, possibly reinforced by the deficiencies within the formal education system. This form of education remains literacy based and has had much success, as indigenous communities have been given the flexibility to manage classes at the times most suited to their seasonal and daily lives. Another feature of the NFE has been that the teachers have been indigenous and have been able to use indigenous language to support Khmer literacy.

There continues to be a strong need for post-literacy NFE materials and classes. Various initiatives are needed to support people in developing their literacy skills past very basic Khmer and mother tongue literacy, especially those linked to development efforts. Many organisations, government departments and NFE programs still use non-indigenous language materials and staff for community education and extension.

In the formal sector, NGOs are working in close cooperation with the Ministry of Education, Youth and Sports to create a model for bilingual education in formal education in Ratanakiri. A Highland Children's Education Project operates against the backdrop of a prevailing attitude that indigenous people are not interested in formal education. It has shown that people are interested if education is provided in a culturally appropriate way. Ownership and interest on the part of the communities is high because of a system of school boards that allows community people a sense of ownership and control over their community's primary education.

Elsewhere in the formal education sector, however, many schools remain under or even non-staffed and therefore non-functional. In many cases, non-indigenous people are sent to teach in indigenous schools without adequate consideration of the practicalities. Isolation from their families and culture, language problems and cross-cultural barriers fuel the huge levels of teacher absenteeism. In areas where there is no Non-Formal Education, little or no effective education is available to indigenous peoples. This is within an environment of very rapid social and economic change and there is a very real danger that marginalisation will become further entrenched.

Health

Health indicators among indigenous peoples in Cambodia are still among the worst in the country. Indigenous peoples continue to report frequent incidents of corruption and abuse at the hands of non-indigenous health staff. This has led to indigenous peoples being very mistrustful of the health system and less likely to follow its directions and services. Many of the attempts to rectify this situation have been frustrated by inefficiency in the public health system. Recent moves to outsource health services may offer a short-term solution to this but reform of the national health system will also be required in the longer-term in order to develop health assistance that is responsive to indigenous peoples' needs.

Hydro-electricity dams

In previous years, extreme problems have been reported as a result of hydro-electricity dams located on the Sesan River in Vietnam, which flows through Ratanakiri province in the north-east of Cambodia. The dams have resulted in deaths from flooding and irregular river flows.

While these problems continue, they are likely to be exacerbated by more dams that have already been commenced or are being planned in Vietnam, on the Sesan River and on the Srepok River. These dams are being planned or built without adequate assessment of past impacts, any rectification of existing problems or first conducting serious future environmental and social impact assessments. International donor agencies and multi-lateral banks continue to support and validate their construction by supporting associated projects such as power line construction. In this way, large international institutions such as the Swedish International Development Agency, the Asian Development Bank, the World Bank and the Vietnamese government effectively undermine the lives of indigenous peoples in north-east Cambodia. There are very strong local concerns that industrial power generation and the model of industrial development that it supports have profound and long-term negative impacts on the lives of indigenous people.

Tourism

The Cambodian, Laos and Vietnamese government have signed a "Triangle Development Plan", which proposes opening the north-eastern provinces of Cambodia up to rapid, and large-scale road access and extensive tourism development. The Asian Development Bank has funded, via loans, the development of an international airport in Ratanakiri on the premise that rapid economic and tourism development will reduce poverty.

In relation to tourism, however, this model is based on the assumption that indigenous peoples will have access to and want tourism development. Without access to education and training services, it is unlikely that indigenous peoples will be able to have sufficient voice in tourism management or access to tourist incomes. In this context, tourism could further contribute to the marginalisation of indigenous communities. Tourism development needs to be controlled and managed until barriers to sustainable and equitable tourism development are removed. Current policies of rapid tourism expansion are misplaced and potentially highly destructive.

Decentralization: dependency or self-management

Much is made of the decentralization processes now underway within the Cambodian Government, and it is claimed that these developments offer real opportunities for promoting indigenous peoples' self-management. However, in many indigenous peoples' areas, much money is being directed into "development" without adequate support for true community development or human development support. In many predominantly indigenous areas, people in government and NGO projects deliver services in non-indigenous languages. In this scenario, per diems and similar financial support is being used to obtain participation in the activities of development agencies.

The effects of this are starting to be seen in the form of dependency, loss of community self-management and community disempowerment. If indigenous peoples are not actively involved in their own development and if there are no local alternatives to the industrial development models now being promulgated, many severe social and economic problems may be expected to arise, as they have in other indigenous communities around the world in similar conditions.

Concluding remarks

The Royal Government of Cambodia should take steps to adopt the General Policy for Highland Peoples' Development, drafted by the Inter-ministerial Committee (IMC) in 1997, as soon as possible. This is essential as Cambodia needs a national policy to allow indigenous peoples to guide their own development. The impediments to ratifying this policy need to be identified and openly debated.

Donors have developed guidelines on the treatment of indigenous communities and the impact of projects on indigenous communities. It is important that the donors remind the different actors and the general public that these guidelines and operational directives exist and need to be followed.

In accordance with their Operational Directive 4.20, the World Bank undertook an Indigenous Upland Minorities Screening Study in Cambodia in 2002, as the Bank was preparing a loan for the Rural Investment and Local Governance Project to support the Royal Government of Cambodia's expansion of the Seila Program. It is important that the content of such studies is disseminated widely throughout the country and that the findings are taken into consideration when making development decisions in indigenous peoples' areas.

The Minister for Land Management Urban Planning and Construction started to pilot communal land titles in three communities in Ratanakiri and Mondolkiri provinces in 2003. Donors, NGOs and indigenous organisations need to play a prominent role in ensuring that Indigenous Peoples' rights to their ancestral lands are not compromised in this process. ❏

VIETNAM

I n Vietnam, the term "Ethnic Minority" is routinely used rather than the term "Indigenous Peoples" as this latter is a complex concept in a country that has been subject to a range of migrations over a long period of time. Ethnic minorities are those who have Vietnamese nationality and reside in Vietnam but do not share the identity, language and other cultural characteristics of the Kinh (majority) people.[1]

There is a high degree of diversity amongst Vietnam's 54 ethnic groups (including the Kinh) in terms of language, land management practices, kinship systems, lifestyles and beliefs.

The ethnic minorities of Vietnam make up around 14% of the population (around 10 million people) but around 29% of the poor. 75% of them live in mountainous areas – mainly in the north and central highlands, which cover three quarters of Vietnam's territory. In some of these areas, the ethnic minorities actually constitute the majority population, and/or several minorities together outnumber the Kinh. However, there has been an increase in Kinh migration into some areas over the last 25 years. This has, in some cases, destabilised the local livelihood systems, especially in areas where agricultural land is in short supply, or where New Economic Zones have been established and cash cropping has been encouraged (e.g. coffee in the Central Highlands).[2]

Political and legislative developments

Vietnam is a country in transition. As a result, a large number of policies, as well as the institutional context for ethnic minorities, are changing. Recent summaries of the policy context within Vietnam have been produced by the government and by the Asian Development Bank (ADB).[3] A number of opportunities are presenting themselves in terms of livelihood development, improved education and other social service delivery, as well as administrative decentralisation. However, as Vietnam integrates into the international economy – including possible WTO membership in 2005 – there are some areas of increasing concern in relation to ethnic minorities. These include (collective) land rights, intellectual property rights over biological resources, employment in public services and administration, repre-

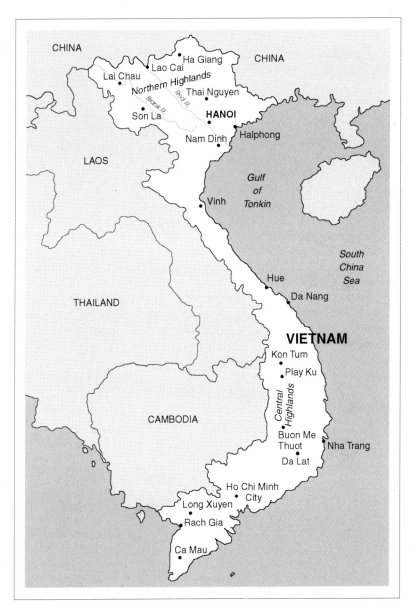

sentation in local, national and regional forums, as well as the key overall issue of poverty/food security, discussed in more detail below.

Poverty

Poverty amongst ethnic minorities is higher than amongst the majority population (using both national and international measurements). However, a recent World Bank report[4] indicates that poverty rates vary considerably from group to group. The variation in food poverty is most striking, with more than 86% of the Bana (Central Highlands) not being able to afford the consumer food basket, compared to 21% among the Tay (Northern Mountains). In the Northern Mountains, ethnic minority poverty continued to decrease over the period 1998-2002, although at a pace slower than poverty reduction amongst the total population. However, in the Central Highlands ethnic minority poverty has increased during the same period, which is thought to be at least partly due to the collapse in the price of coffee.

Monitoring poverty reduction and social development

Based on its social and economic development strategy for 2001-2010,[5] the Government of Vietnam produced a Comprehensive Poverty Reduction and Growth Strategy (CPRGS) in 2002.[6] This contains a number of indicators based on the Millennium Development Goals as they were interpreted for Vietnam, for example, on poverty, school enrolment and access to clean water. It is, however, not clear whether progress according to these indicators will be reported for specific ethnic groups, in order to track the growing gaps (despite general progress for nearly all ethnic groups). The government's first CPRGS progress report does not dissagregate data in this regard.[7]

Specific indicators in the CPRGS that relate to ethnic minority development include issues of land-use certificates for agricultural and forest land (taking place at a much slower pace in the areas with high levels of ethnic minorities) and increasing ethnic minority staff in public services and government administration, and in elected bodies at different levels. The first CPRGS progress report fails to report on change in this respect.

Tackling poverty reduction

The CPRGS acknowledges that the ethnic minorities suffer from higher poverty rates than the majority but it does not set specific targets for ethnic minorities' development, other than on representation issues within the general system of service delivery. Recent research shows that there is a need to target activities more carefully and make target programmes appropriate to the conditions in which ethnic minorities live (mountain agriculture rather than lowland rice cultivation).[8]

The Government of Vietnam has a range of programmes to reduce poverty in general and also some targeting the areas where ethnic minorities predominantly live.[9] Most of these programmes have capacity building components. However, these components are modest and not specifically targeted at ethnic minority people. The main programme that focuses on ethnic minority areas relates to small-scale infrastructure, from which all (local) citizens benefit. The average annual investment is significant.[10] There are also programmes supported by the Asian Development Bank and the World Bank, which focus on small-scale infrastructure but without specifically addressing ethnic minority issues.

The government has made significant efforts in developing local classrooms, and aims to build around 67,500 over the next few years based on "model" designs.[11] The education sector is supported by grants and loans from the donor community, often with a focus on remote and mountainous areas with ethnic minorities. Healthcare is improving, especially in the poorest communes and for the poorest households, who are entitled to free basic health care through a system of health cards.[12] This is a good development for large groups of ethnic minorities but some still have problems in accessing the recently improved local health facilities because of distance and language barriers.

Administrative decentralisation and streamlining is happening but the results of the "public administration reform" in ethnic minority communities are still very limited.[13] It should focus on appropriate capacity building to facilitate local involvement in planning and budget monitoring. This includes changes to the roles of the local administration (People's Committees) and supervisory bodies (People's Councils), partly under the State Budget Law.[14] Strengthening of grassroots democratisation has been encouraged since 1998 and was reinforced in 2003.[15] However, the first reports on the impact of grassroots democratisation show that, in the remotest and poorest areas, and especially in communes dominated by ethnic minorities, improvements in service delivery, public management and civic participation are still very modest. This is primarily attributed to the low educational achievements of the local population and the low capacities of local officials (of all ethnicities). Particularly slow progress is being made in women's participation. This is because many ethnic minority women do not speak Vietnamese (Kinh language) and the female literacy rate is particularly low. Even with the increase in primary schooling for girls in remote areas, there is insufficient post-school opportunities for young women to retain their command of the national language.

New resolution on ethnic minority affairs

The Vietnamese government addresses ethnic minority issues through a range of official bodies, including the Commission on Ethnic Minorities within the National Assembly. In addition, there is the Committee on Ethnic Minorities. In March 2003, the Communist Party of Vietnam issued the first ever comprehensive resolution dealing specifically with a number of ethnic minority issues, and defining how the most challenging issues for ethnic minorities in mountainous areas would be addressed.

The indigenous movement

Vietnam has a range of mass-based organisations,[16] operating from national to village level. None of these organisations focuses directly on ethnic minorities, but they operate in all communes and provide important sources of information to the grass-roots level. Training for ethnic minority women is often provided through the Women's Union.

In 2003, the new Law on Associations[17] was passed. The law presents some new opportunities for organisations to be set up at local level, although within some relatively strict conditions. This may facilitate the development of new local groups – especially associated with the development of forestland management.

A number of national NGOs operate in Vietnam with a focus on ethnic minorities, poverty reduction and the environment. These NGOs are often linked to research organisations and operate within a detailed policy framework.

There is increasing recognition of the role ethnic minorities and indigenous knowledge play in relation to biodiversity and agro-biodiversity conservation. In May 2003, a National Workshop on Biodiversity Conservation and Poverty Reduction in Mountainous Areas was held in Sapa, in the northern mountains, sponsored by SIDA (the

Swedish government's agency for international development). In September-October 2003, the Asian Regional Conference on Indigenous Knowledge and Biodiversity was held in Hanoi. This conference was hosted by the Center for Sustainable Development in Mountainous Areas (CSDM), together with the Asia Indigenous Peoples Pact Foundation (AIPP). The conference was co-funded by the Ford Foundation and the Swedish Society for Nature Conservation (SSNC). Forty delegates from fourteen countries and territories gave presentations at the conference.

A range of international organisations operate in Vietnam and a recent meeting was held in Hanoi to celebrate 10 years of INGO cooperation with the government. INGOs often operate in the poorest areas with ethnic minorities, but rarely do they operate as direct advocates for ethnic minority rights. Many INGOs have links to the Ethnic Minority Working Group, based in Hanoi, which focuses on bringing together experiences of organisations that work with ethnic minorities. Current rules and regulations do not facilitate formal linkages at this level between INGOs and Vietnamese NGOs although cooperation around key activities is growing.

Vietnam is a key member of the Montane and Mountains of South-East Asia's (MMSEA) network on Indigenous Knowledge and Peoples (IKAP) and the International Alliance of Indigenous and Tribal Peoples of the Tropical Forests. The fourth MMSEA meeting is currently being planned for early 2005. An organising committee has been set up in Hanoi and the proposed focus of the meeting is "The Sustainable Management of Natural Resources and Poverty Alleviation in the Uplands of South-East Asia". ❑

Notes and references

1 **Poverty Task Force/UNDP.2002.** Localizing Millennium Development Goals in Vietnam: Promoting Ethnic Minority Development. UNDP, Hanoi.
2 *Ibid.*
3 **Government of Vietnam. 2000.** *Chinh Sach va Phap Luat Cua Dang, Nha Nuoc ve Dan Toc* (Policy and Laws of Party and State about Ethnic Groups). Hanoi: Nha Xuat Ban Van Hoa Dan Toc. **ADB. 2002.** *Indigenous Peoples/Ethnic Minorities and Poverty Reduction in Vietnam.* Manila, Philippines: Environmental and Social Safeguards Division, Regional and Sustainable Development Department, Asian Development Bank. **Friberg, E. 2002.** *Ethnic Minority Participation in Public Life in Vietnam.* A Minor Field Study of the minorities' *formal* participation in the legislative

process at the national level and in the implementation of state law and policies at local levels; and the minorities' *informal* participation through the emerging civil society of Vietnam. Lund, Sweden: Faculty of Law, University of Lund.

4 **World Bank. 2003.** – Vietnam Development Report 2004 – Poverty.
5 **Government of Vietnam. 2002.** The *Comprehensive Poverty Reduction and Growth Strategy'*. Approved by the Prime Minister as Document No. 2685/VPCP-QHQT, dated 21 May 2002.
6 *Ibid.*
7 As part of the background papers for the **World Bank. 2003.** Vietnam Development Report 2004 – Poverty.
8 *Ibid.*
9 Decision No 133/1998/QD-TTg of July 23 1998 Ratifying the National Target Program on Hunger Elimination and Poverty Alleviation in the 1998 – 2000 period. Decision No. 135/1998/QD-TTg of July 31 1998 to Approve the Program on Socio-economic Development in Mountainous, Deep-lying and Remote Communes with Special Difficulties.
10 Decision No 159/2002/QD-TTg of November 15 2002 Approving the Scheme for Implementation of the Program on Solidification of Schools and Classrooms.
11 *Ibid.*
12 *Ibid.*
13 Decree No. 29/1999/ND-CP of May 11 1998 Promulgating the Regulation on the Exercise of Democracy in Communes.
14 Order No. 21/2002/L-CTN of December 27 2002 on the Promulgation of the State Budget Law.
15 *Ibid.*
16 Including the Women's Union, Youth Union, Veterans Association and Farmers Association, coordinated by the Vietnam Fatherland Front.
17 Government Decree 88/2003/ND-CP. Issuing the Regulations on the Organization, Operations and Management of Associations.

LAOS

L aos has the most ethnically diverse population of mainland South-east Asia. The ethnic Lao dominate the country both politically and economically, but make up only around 30% of the population. People, whose first language belongs to the Lao-Tai linguistic family, probably make up 66% of the population. The first languages of the remaining population mostly belong to the Mon-Khmer, Sino-Tibetan and Hmong-Mien linguistic families. These latter groups are often considered to be "indigenous peoples" of Laos, although officially the ethnic groups of Lao-Tai language speakers have equal status to other ethnic groups. The concept of "indigenous peoples" is thus confusing in Laos.

The largest policy-based threat to "indigenous peoples" in Laos appears to be opium eradication, followed by swidden agriculture eradication, land and forest allocation, village consolidation, and the construction of large infrastructure projects such as dams.

Subtle shift in shifting cultivation policy

Over the last two years there has apparently been a subtle shift in government policy regarding its efforts to eradicate shifting cultivation (see *The Indigenous World 2002-2003*). Although the government is officially sticking to its plans to eradicate shifting cultivation by 2005, there was a definite fall in news reports on this policy during 2003. This shift may be linked to the recognition that it will not be possible to meet the government's target, just as it was impossible to eradicate swidden agriculture by 2000. In addition, the government is continuing to review its Land and Forest Allocation Programme, which has been the main government mechanism for reducing shifting cultivation. Various reports have stated that attempts to eliminate shifting cultivation have led to increased poverty amongst indigenous people, as well as environmental degradation associated with serious disruptions in livelihoods (*ibid.*). Although the enthusiasm for land and forest allocation has generally waned, this has not always resulted in changes in practice at the provincial and district levels, and in some parts of the country the government is continuing to push hard for the eradication of swidden agriculture. In others, government officials have sometimes redefined shifting agriculture into "pioneer" and "rotational" swidden agriculture, with the latter being considered more acceptable than the former. This is good news for most ethnic groups, who have long practised various forms of rotational cultivation (*ibid.*)

Opium eradication campaign

Over the last two years, the Lao government has markedly stepped up its efforts to eradicate opium production by 2005,[1] and in 2002 and 2003 there was a significant increase in government propaganda associated with this campaign. For example, in June 2003, the *Vientiane Times* reported that, "The Lao Government is firm in its resolve to eliminate opium production by 2005."[2] Indigenous mountain-dwelling peoples in ten provinces and one special area, in central and especially northern Laos, are the main opium cultivators.

Since 2002 there has been a dramatic increase in the number of opium fields destroyed by the government before harvest time. Official government statistics state that opium production in Laos declined from 112.4 tonnes in 2002 to 78.5 tonnes in 2003,[3] and that the area under opium poppy cultivation declined from 42,130 ha in 1989 to 7,847 ha in 2003.[4] For example, in Nong Het District, Xieng Khouang Province, once one of the main opium growing areas in the country, production reportedly declined 93% between 1999 and 2003.[5] Government officials have, however, admitted that the task of eliminating opium production in Laos is extremely challenging,[6] but they still hope to cut opium cultivation by more than half, to 3,500 ha in 2004.[7]

In 2002, there were especially intense efforts to reduce opium production in Long District, Luang Nam Tha Province, another important opium producing area. However, these efforts are having grave consequences for the indigenous population, since many communities have been relocated to the lowlands by the government as a part of this programme. Some NGOs and bilateral funders are very concerned, as the recently resettled population has not adapted well. Despite the serious problems, it appears that efforts to eradicate opium production in Luang Nam Tha province continued to be intense in 2003. Similar circumstances, including human rights abuses and forced relocations, have been reported in other parts of northern Laos, and the situation is particularly serious due to poor swidden harvests over the last two years, leaving vulnerable populations with few options for survival.

Despite the serious impacts of the opium eradication programme, a number of Western governments continue to support Laos' efforts to eradicate opium production, especially the U.S. government, which agreed

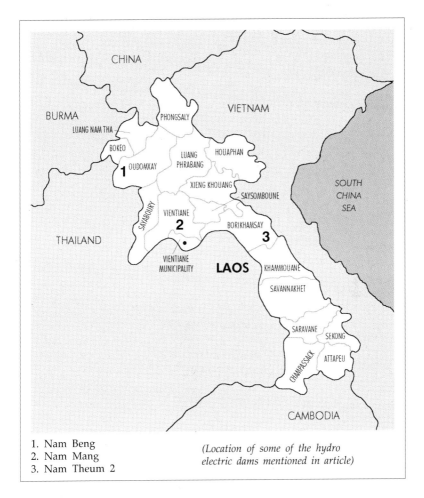

1. Nam Beng
2. Nam Mang
3. Nam Theum 2

(Location of some of the hydro electric dams mentioned in article)

to provide over US$ 1.9 million to the Lao government's drug control programme for 2003-2004. International organisations, including the United Nations Office on Drugs and Crime (UNODC) and its predecessor, the UNDCP, have also played key roles in supporting the opium eradication programme in terms of planning, policy and implementation.[8]

Millenarian movements

In 2002 and 2003, there appear to have been at least two messianic movements amongst indigenous people in northern Laos. The first occurred in Phousavang village, in Nam Nyou Special Zone of north-eastern Bokeo Province. Although details are sketchy, in December 2002 almost all of the approximately 200 ethnic Lahu Aga inhabitants of the community fled en masse. Members of a French NGO working in the village reported that "Phousavang has disappeared." A few days later, the Lao army was sent into the forest to search for the people, who they soon found and forced back to the village. The official explanation was that the villagers had fled to militarily organise against the Lao government, possibly with American and/or Thai support. However, in actual fact they were following an ethnic Lahu hermit who lived in a cave near the village of Thamprabat, which is also in Nam Nyou Special Zone. The hermit apparently came to Phousavang to announce that a messiah would arrive to feed and take care of them. The people followed him to the forest to clear an area and wait for the arrival of the messiah. Some reported waiting for American airplanes or helicopters to land in the cleared area ("the Americans are back"), or waiting for planes to drop sacks of rice into the area, like Air America[9] did during the war. Perhaps they were also waiting for guns and money to be dropped. Some may have believed that a real Lahu messiah was coming from heaven, and that they needed to move their village to the place where the messiah would arrive. The hermit was arrested as a rebellion leader, and jailed in the provincial capital of Bokeo. Since then, there have been no reports of this messianic movement spreading to other Lahu villages.

The most recent millenarian movement occurred in Houaphan Province, in northern Laos, and appears to have been led by ethnic Hmong people. In August 2003, when the movement apparently became active, a "group of robbers" opened fire on a bus traveling from Samneua to Viengsay District, killing five passengers. The incident was reported, in the Lao press, to have arisen due to business conflicts and illegal trade[10] but this was probably not the case. There have been various reports that the Hmong rebels are not part of typical anti-government groups but are instead part of a messianic cult involving both anti and pro-government Hmong elements. There may also have been small numbers of people from other ethnic groups involved. Although details are sketchy, the movement may have begun in northern Vietnam and spread to Houaphan and northern parts of Xieng Khouang Province. Like the Pa Chay rebellion of 1918-1921, which was also based in Houaphan,[11] the rebels apparently had their own flag with unusual symbols on it. Poorly armed, the group attacked an armory of the Lao government but failed to overwhelm it. One thousand soldiers from the Lao army were then sent to the area, roads were blocked and the provincial airport was shut down. Some provincial officials were arrested as sympathizers. Hmong people in Houaphan were apparently "corralled" into small areas so that they could be controlled. By October or November, calm had reportedly returned to the province, but the leaders of the movement are apparently still at large.

This incident, and a number of other rebel activities apparently instigated by Hmong insurgents, have created a very negative attitude towards the Hmong in Laos. In response to this trend, the Vice-President of the Lao Front for National Construction, H.E. Tong Yeu Tho, himself a Hmong, wrote an article for the Lao press on "the good and the bad Hmong".

Although it is unclear why these messianic movements flared up, history tells us that in the past they have often occurred during times when people felt extremely oppressed.[12] It may be more than a coincidence that the opium eradication campaign has intensified in Houaphan recently. In early 2003, the Houaphan government announced that their priority was to resettle villagers to the lowlands in order to reduce opium production.[13] Houaphan reportedly produces 25% of all the opium grown in Laos.[14]

Foreign journalists arrested and released

On June 3, 2003 two journalists from France and Belgium, and their ethnic Hmong translator, a US citizen, were arrested in Xieng Khouang Province. The journalists entered the country to meet with ethnic Hmong rebels, and were organising a night meeting with rebels near Khai Village, Phoukout District, when a group of local village militiamen encountered them. A fire fight ensued, resulting in the death of one of the village militia. Some of the rebels fled and others were arrested, along with the journalists and their translator.[15] After being incarcerated in Xieng Khouang, the journalists and their translator were each sentenced, on June 30, to 15 years in prison. However, in early July, all three were suddenly released and expelled from Laos. The Lao Minister of Foreign Affairs stated that the three were released "based on the humanitarian policy of the Lao government, in response to the proposals of Foreign Ministers of the three countries whose nationals were involved". Fines applied by the Xieng Khouang court during sentencing were paid before the three were released,[16] resulting in the end of what was a tense diplomatic situation.

Large hydropower dams

There was little activity associated with the construction of large dams in Laos during 2003, except for the continued building of the widely criticised Nam Mang 3 dam in central Laos (see *The Indigenous World 2002-2003*). It was, however, a troubled year for Laos' largest and most controversial dam, the US$1.2 billion 1,070 MW Nam Theun 2 project, which has been in the planning stages for years. In July 2003, the largest partner in the Nam Theun 2 consortium, Electricité de France (EDF) abruptly announced that it would be withdrawing its support for the dam. The decision was apparently largely due to the financial problems that EDF has been facing, along with political pressure at home to withdraw from overseas interests. But in October 2003, EDF reversed its decision and decided to proceed with the project. Since then, the power purchase agreement for selling power produced by the project to Thailand has been signed,[17] although details of the agreement have not been made public, raising concerns over transparency. The World Bank, which has been approached to provide a political risk guarantee for what would be Laos' largest dam to date, and whose support is critical for obtaining private financial support from European banks, has not yet decided whether or not to support the project. It is believed that many inside the Bank continue to have concerns regarding the expected severe social and environmental impacts of the project, especially along the Xe Bang Fai River. One of the most controversial developments in Laos relating to plans to build large dams was the announcement that the Vietnam Laos Investment and Development Company, a Hanoi-based consortium of Vietnamese dam-builders led by Electricité de Viet Nam (EVN), intends to invest more than US$ 1 billion in building six large dams in the Xe Kong River basin in the southern provinces of Xe Kong and Attapeu, both of which are populated largely by Mon-Khmer language-speaking ethnic groups. These dams include the Xe Kong 4 and Xe Kong 5 dams, both planned for the mainstream Xe Kong River in Xe Kong province, the Xe Kaman 1, Xe Kaman 3 and Xe Kaman 4 dams, and the Xe Pian Xe Nam Noy dam,[18] which was abandoned by the Korean company, Dong Ah, in the late 1990s after the Asian Economic Crisis set in. All are expected to have a serious impact on the livelihoods of indigenous people living in the Xe Kong basin in Laos, and the dams will also cause serious downstream impacts along the Xe Kong River in Stung Treng Province, north-east Cambodia.

New list of ethnic groups still to be approved

The Indigenous World 2002-2003 reported that the Lao National Assembly was expected to officially approve the new list of recognised Lao ethnic groups, which includes 49 groups, including at least 149 sub-groups, in February or March 2003. In 2003, the new list was presented to the National Assembly for comments but members had many questions, not all of which the Lao Front for National Construction was able to answer immediately. The National Assembly has therefore not yet officially adopted the list but will probably do so in March 2004.❑

Notes and references

1   *Khao San Pathet Lao*. February 20, 2002. Long District farmers destroy their own opium poppy plantation.
2   *Vientiane Times*. June 13-16, 2003. More firepower needed in war against opium.
3   *Ibid.*
4   *Vientiane Times*. August 26-28, 2003. Laos to meet opium eradication deadline.
5   *Vientiane Times*. December 19-22, 2003.Poppy fields become pumpkin patches.
6   *Vientiane Times*. May 20-22, 2003. Poverty eradication plans in the north.
7   *Vientiane Times*. October 24-27, 2003. Opium growth to be halved.
8   *Ibid.*
9   Air America, an airline secretly owned by the CIA, during its operations in Laos in the 1960s and 1970s (Ed. note)
10 *Vientiane Times*. August 26-28, 2003. Passenger bus robbed.
11 **Gunn, G.C. 1986**. Shamans and rebels: the Batchai (Meo) rebellion of Northern Laos and North-West Vietnam (1918-21). *Journal of Siam Society*, 73:42-59.
12 **Gunn, G.C. 1990.** *Rebellion in Laos: Peasant Politics in a Colonial Backwater*. Boulder, USA: Westview Press.
13 *Khao San Pathet Lao*. January 1, 2003. Huaphan to slash poverty by half in 2003.
14 *Vientiane Times*. October 24-27, 2003. Opium growth to be halved.
15 *Vientiane Times*. June 13-16, 2003. Three foreigners arrested in Laos.
16 *Vientiane Times*. July 11-14, 2003. Foreign journalists walk free.
17 *Vientiane Times*. July 22-24, 2003. Signing of Nam Theun 2 agreement postponed. October 3-6, 2003. EDF to stay with Nam Theun 2 project. November 7-10, 2003. Thailand says yes to Nam Theun 2 power.
18 *Reuters*. August 4, 2003. Vietnam eyes five hydropower plants in Laos.
    Lang, C. 2003. Laos: Vietnamese consortium plans to build six dams in Laos. *World Rainforest Bulletin*, No. 74.

BURMA

B urma is an ethnically diverse country, with the non-Burman ethnic nationalities comprising an estimated 60% of the population.
Since 1962 these ethnic groups, which are considered to be Burma's
indigenous peoples, have struggled to maintain their identities and
cultures while living under successive Burman-dominated military
regimes.

Dialogue brought to a halt

Following Daw Aung San Suu Kyi's release from house arrest in 2002,
the Nobel Peace Prize laureate and General Secretary of the National
League for Democracy (NLD) prioritized contact with ethnic groups,
who welcomed her warmly when she made a series of trips to ethnic
regions around the country. This rapprochement between Daw Suu's
NLD and ethnic opposition groups, indicating a strong desire for
political change, proved to be threatening to the ruling junta. On May
30, 2003, a date that has come to be known as Black Friday, the State
Peace and Development Council (SPDC, formerly SLORC) launched
an attack on Daw Aung San Suu Kyi, her entourage and supporters
in Depayin Township, Sagaing Division. This incident constituted
the bloodiest attack on the democracy movement in Burma since 1988,
with up to 70 people killed and 200 injured, bringing any hope for
tripartite dialogue between the SPDC, NLD and ethnic opposition
groups to a radical halt. Daw Suu and at least eighteen other NLD
members were taken into "protective custody" and, as of the end of
2003, Daw Suu remained under house arrest in Rangoon.

To suppress the wave of international concern and disapproval in
the wake of Black Friday, which included the imposition of unprecedented sanctions by the United States, on August 30 newly-appointed
Prime Minister Khin Nyunt unveiled a 7-point "road map" to democracy, which would reconvene the stalled 1993 National Convention
to draft a state Constitution to be voted on in a national referendum,
ultimately resulting in "free and fair elections." The road map, however, did not specify a timeframe, or a role for the National League for
Democracy (NLD) and/or other opposition and ethnic nationality
groups.

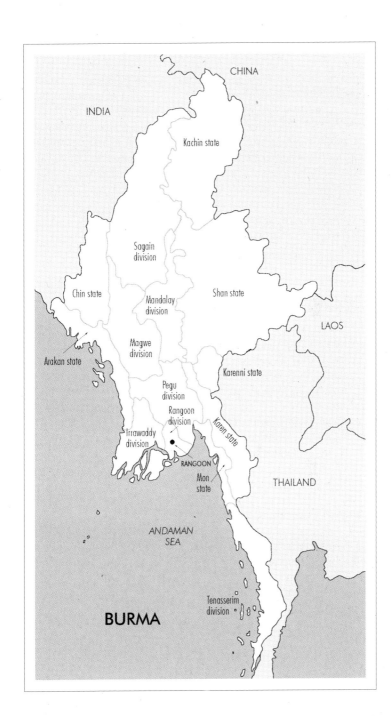

CHINA

INDIA

Kachin state

Sagain
division

Chin state

Mandalay
division

Shan state

LAOS

Magwe
division

Arakan state

Karenni state

Pegu
division

Rangoon
division

Irrawaddy
division

RANGOON

Mon
state

THAILAND

ANDAMAN
SEA

BURMA

Tenasserim
division

Militarisation

Almost two dozen armed groups were active in Burma's border regions in 2003. Fourteen ethnic armed opposition groups have signed cease-fire agreements with the SPDC since 1989 and, at the end of 2003, the Karen National Union, one of the largest armed ethnic groups, began negotiating a cease-fire. During the talks, the two sides agreed to a "gentlemen's cease-fire", yet clashes still continued between the Karen National Liberation Army and SPDC troops in Karen State. The SPDC frequently used the presence of armed and political opposition groups in ethnic areas as justification for gross human rights abuses. Crimes, including rape, robbery, looting and torture have increased in ethnic areas due to the central command's "self-sufficiency" directive.[1] The period covered in this report witnessed a military build-up in ethnic areas following Black Friday. In Mon State, five thousand tons of Russian equipment arrived for the construction of the SPDC's Russian-supported nuclear reactor, for which three hundred acres of land have been confiscated from the local people. There were also reports that North Korea was selling missiles and providing nuclear technology to the regime. The SPDC set up three new army bases to launch operations against the Shan State Army South, and increased troops along the Thai-Burma border by over 50%. The regime expanded its "Border Supervisory Companies," now renamed "Border Supervisory Battalions," consisting of immigration, police and intelligence personnel.

The regime dramatically increased forced conscription for military training and membership of the army for civilians throughout Burma. In July, the SPDC ordered all states and divisions to conduct basic military training. People were rounded up for forced conscription, and ethnic populations were co-opted into civil defense. In 2003, Burma continued to use the forced recruitment of child soldiers. According to Human Rights Watch, it is estimated that there are approximately 70,000 children in the 350,000-strong Burma Army, which makes Burma the largest user of child soldiers in the world.[2]

In September, an International Campaign to Ban Landmines (ICBL) report named Burma as one of only two countries that continued to use anti-personnel mines on a regular basis, with mines being laid most extensively in Karen State. SPDC units operating in mined areas continued to force villagers to act as porters to sweep for landmines.

Forced labour

Despite international pressure, the presence of an International Labour Organization (ILO) liaison officer and the SPDC's official 1999 ban on the use of forced labour, extensive use of forced labour continued in ethnic areas in 2003.

Earth Rights International (ERI) documented the systematic nature of the use of forced labour in eastern Burma. Orders for portering, monitoring insurgency activities, sweeping for landmines, building military camps, gathering, making, and delivering materials, and clearing roadsides were regularly issued. Forced labour was commonly accompanied by torture, sexual harassment and violence, and theft of goods. To illustrate the magnitude, the Karen Human Rights Group reported 783 orders given by the SPDC to villages in Karen State, Mon State and part of eastern Pegu Division in the period between January 2002 and February 2003.[3] Over time, forced labour erodes people's ability to provide for themselves, resulting in their being forced to flee the region to become internally displaced persons or refugees.

Displacement

Millions of people from Burma are refugees or migrants in neighboring countries, or internally displaced within Burma. Most are from ethnic areas and are fleeing civil war, forced relocation, eviction, land confiscation, political suppression, forced conscription, human rights abuses and economic crisis.

Thailand has the largest number of Burmese refugees and migrants. In 2003, there were 140,000 ethnic refugees living in camps, 2,000 refugees recognized by the UNHCR as Persons of Concern (POCs), as well as 500 political refugees, 50,000 refugees outside camps, 200,000 Shan refugees and 1,000,000 migrant workers, which includes many refugees. Migrant workers were regularly threatened with arrest and deportation if they demanded basic rights. In December, 200 migrants, who were paid half of Thailand's legal minimum wage and were striking to demand a fair wage, were arrested by Thai police and deported.

In Bangladesh, there were around 20,000 Rohingya refugees in two camps, and between 100,000 and 200,000 Rohingya refugees outside camps in south Bangladesh (often labeled as economic migrants), plus around 50 mostly Rakhine urban refugees in Dhaka, who have been granted Person of Concern status by the UNHCR. Rohingya refugees faced mass repatriation, with 704 refugees being sent back to Burma in May. Although UNHCR and the Bangladeshi government claim that the repatriation of Rohingya refugees back to Burma is voluntary, Refugees International (RI) stated that methods of coercion are used, such as inadequate food supply, beatings and threats of imprisonment. The Rohingya do not feature among the 135 "national races" identified by the Burmese government, as the Citizenship Law of 1982 renders them *de facto* stateless.[4]

In India, there were over 50,000 mostly Chin refugees from Burma, largely concentrated in the north-eastern province of Mizoram. Only 1,003 refugees had been recognized by UNHCR in New Delhi as of March 2003. Since July, more than 6,000 Chin refugees have been forcibly relocated to Burma. In November, over 800 refugees who had been holding peaceful demonstrations in front of the UNHCR office for four weeks to ask for refugee status and humanitarian assistance in New Delhi were brutally beaten by Indian police in riot gear.

In Malaysia, there were 15,000 Rohingya asylum seekers and more than 5,000 Chin refugees. All asylum seekers in Malaysia are labeled "illegal immigrants" and are subject to harsh immigration laws.

Women

State-sanctioned abuse, rape and discrimination of women continue unpunished in Burma. In January, SPDC troops gang-raped a woman only kilometers from an International Committee of the Red Cross (ICRC) delegation in Laikha, Shan State. In April, Refugees International (RI) released a report, "No Safe Place: Burma's Army and the Rape of Ethnic Women," documenting forty-three cases of rape or attempted rape of women from the Karen, Karenni, Mon, Tavoyan and Shan ethnic groups.

Burma was one of 15 countries to be placed on Tier 3, the lowest tier of the US government's Trafficking Victims Protection Act.[5] Women from ethnic communities are particularly vulnerable to being sold into the sex trade.

Women continued to face obstacles in accessing adequate health care. It was reported that the cost of birth delivery is about 450,000 kyat, which is unaffordable even on a teacher's monthly salary of about 6,000 kyat.[6]

Religious freedom

The US State Department included Burma as one of six countries on its annual list of "countries of particular concern" for severe violations of religious freedoms under the International Religious Freedom Act.

Non-Buddhist ethnic nationalities continued to face discrimination in Burma. While it is estimated that 80% of Burma's population is Buddhist, Christianity is the dominant religion among the Chin, Naga and Kachin ethnic groups, and it is also practiced widely by Karens and Karennis. Islam is the dominant religion among the Rohingyas in Arakan State. Although, in theory, freedom of religion was secured in Burma's first Constitution in 1948, since 1962 Burma's non-Buddhist religions have been associated with the ethnic nationalities and, by extension, with the armed insurgencies fighting the central government.

Christians and Muslims were subject to various forms of harassment and discrimination in 2003, making them particularly vulnerable to becoming refugees or internally displaced. Buddhist monks forcibly converted Christian children in Chin State, Christians were prohibited from engaging in meetings and missions were prohibited from running schools. Reports of the demolishing of mosques, madrassas and Muslim houses, and the distribution of anti-Muslim pamphlets in Arakan State and Sagaing Division continued.

It was reported that over one hundred Nagas were forced to convert from animism to Buddhism in Sagaing Division.

Environment

The Thai government, in cooperation with the SPDC and private Thai construction companies, revived plans to construct three hydro-electric dams on the Salween River along the Thai-Burma border. Shans, Karens and Karennis in Burma oppose the dams, which would flood an estimated 15,000 to 20,000 acres of land on both sides of the border, displacing thousands of Karenni villagers. Construction of the Tsarng Dam is already underway in Shan State, and reports state that 1,500 villagers have already been forcibly relocated. Ten villagers were killed while being forced to work on the dam project.

Global Witness highlighted forestry, which is the largest "legal" funding source for the SPDC, as a conflict trade in Burma. Along with the Philippines, Burma has the highest rate of deforestation in South-east Asia, resulting in forced logging labour and the deterioration of the natural environment and traditional cultural practices in ethnic areas.

Drugs

In order to maintain control of Shan State without reaching a political settlement with ethnic peoples, the regime is allowing numerous local ethnic armies and cease-fire organizations to produce drugs in exchange for cooperation with the state. At the same time, it ignores the involvement of its own staff in the drugs trade as a means of subsidizing its army costs.

Opium is continuing to be grown in almost every township of Shan State, with Burmese military personnel involved at all levels of opium production and trafficking. The *Shan Herald Agency for News* documented at least 93 heroin and/or methamphetamine refineries in existence in 2003, run by the regime's military allies. The Junta's token attempts at crop substitution, often with international assistance, have failed due to poor planning, coercive implementation and a total disregard for the welfare of local villagers. Under the "New Destiny" project launched in April 2002, farmers in many townships were forced to plant a new strain of rice from China, replacing the indigenous strain of Shan rice. This failed in each locality. The United Nations Office on Drugs and Crime stated in December that an epidemic of illicit amphetamine-type substances in South-east Asia might become the world's most severe drug problem. ❑

Notes and references

1 Following the results of the 1990 elections, in which Aung San Suu Kyi's party, the National League for Democracy, won an overwhelming victory (which the military junta has refused to respect), the SPDC grossly expanded the military via a policy of "self-reliance." This policy is a result of SPDC battalions being underpaid, thus making them responsible for furnishing their own basic supplies. Food, for example, is extorted from local villages and land is confiscated so that the army can establish their own plantations, usually realized the use of villagers' forced labour.

2 The Asian Regional Resource Center (Nov 2003): End the Use of Children as Soldiers in Burma.

3 www.ibiblio.org/freeburma/humanrights/khrg/archive/khrg2003/khrg0301.html

4   The Rohingya are restricted from travelling within Burma, and must carry Foreigner Identification cards.

5   The United States has imposed a tier system to evaluate governments' adherence to the Trafficking Victims Protection Act's minimum standards for the elimination of trafficking. The minimum standards include (1) Prohibiting trafficking and punishing acts of trafficking, (2) Prescribing punishment commensurate with that for grave crimes, such as forcible sexual assault, for the knowing commission of trafficking in some of its most reprehensible forms (trafficking for sexual purposes, involving rape or kidnapping, or causing a death), (3) Prescribing punishment that is sufficiently stringent to deter and that adequately reflects the offense's heinous nature for the knowing commission of any act of trafficking, and (4) Making serious and sustained efforts to eliminate trafficking. Governments that adhere to these standards are placed in Tier 1. Those countries making significant efforts are placed in Tier 2. Finally, those countries whose governments do not fully comply with the minimum standards and are not making significant efforts to bring themselves into compliance are placed in Tier 3.
    See www.state.gov/g/tip/rls/tiprpt/2003/21262.htm#tiers

6   *Democratic Voice of Burma* 14 Jan 03: The fall and fall of health service. 450,000 kyat are equivalent to 72,000 US$ - 6,000 kyat to less than 1,000 US$. (Ed. note)

NAGALIM

Naga are an indigenous people of about four million comprising more than 40 different tribes. They inhabit a contiguous homeland bound in the north by China, in the west by Assam (India), in the south by Manipur Valley and Mizoram (India) and the Chin Hills (Burma), and in the east beyond the Chindwin river and along its tributary the Uyu river (Burma). After resolutely fighting British invasion of their land and defending it against all foreign powers and intervention, the Naga declared their territory an independent sovereign republic on August 14, 1947. However, without their knowledge and consent, Naga and their land were arbitrarily divided up and passed on by the British Empire to both India and Burma. The Indo-Burma international border runs right through the Naga territory, and India further divided the Naga into four administrative states – Manipur, Assam, Arunachal Pradesh and the so-called Nagaland state. The Naga are a minority in the first three. "Nagalim" (Lim meaning Land) transcends all imposed boundaries and refers to a unified Naga homeland as one political entity.

Until the present day, India and Burma have denied the Naga the freedom to exercise their sovereign rights and to live together as a people. Gross violations of human rights through structural violence, military campaigns and economic aggression continue. Naga resistance against 56 years of occupation has taken the forms of both armed struggle and a non-violent movement.

A ceasefire between the National Socialist Council of Nagalim (NSCN) and the Government of India (GOI) came into effect on August 1, 1997 to facilitate unconditional political negotiations at the highest political level in a third country for a peaceful political settlement.

Naga leaders visit India for political talks

On January 8, 2003, 600 young Naga men and women gathered en masse waving Naga flags and singing freedom songs to welcome Chairman Isak Chishi Swu and General Secretary Th. Muivah of the NSCN at the international airport in New Delhi, India. The Collective Leadership's visit was in response to the invitation of Indian Prime Minister, Shri A.B. Vajpayee to continue "unconditional talks" made possible after the Indian government recognized "the unique history and situation of the Naga" in July 2002, and subsequently lifted the

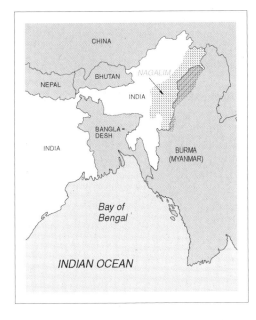

ban against NSCN and other Naga organizations as unlawful organizations.

The Delhi talks have been perceived primarily as a symbolic expression of confidence building and an affirmation to strengthen the peace process. Meetings with the Prime Minister, Deputy Prime Minister, Defense Minister and senior Indian political leaders including opposition leader Sonia Gandhi and interaction with members of the Indian civil society were positive steps in bringing about mutual understanding, while appreciating the realities and difficulties faced by both sides. The spirit of openness from the Collective Leadership to "leave no stone unturned to work out a lasting solution" has widened space for changes in attitude. The Delhi talks served as a reminder of the futility of a military solution and the imperative of seeking a political solution, with the Indian Prime Minister expressing "...determination and will to solve the problem...[the] peace process to continue and bloodshed [to be] stopped for all time..."

However, the hope for political wisdom to improve basic realities remains illusory. Activities and policies of the Indian state unfortunately continue to indicate that the response, by and large, remains rhetorical.

The peace process

Three events of the recent past are of utmost significance in the peace process: the visit of the NSCN leaders Muivah and Isak in Delhi and the lifting of the ban on NSCN by the Indian Union Government (although unfortunately not by the state governments of Manipur, Assam and Arunachal Pradesh) were mentioned above. The third development is the creation of an atmosphere far more conducive to the peace process among the Naga themselves. The most significant event was undoubtedly the disposal of Chief Minister Jamir in the Nagaland State Assembly election in February 2003. Naga mass-based and civil society organizations manifested themselves and rallied in the spirit of the 1998 stand "we want solutions, not elections" to bring an end to 10 years of Congress rule under Mr. S. C. Jamir, who has actively obstructed the peace process during the past decade and was largely responsible for the division among the Naga in Nagaland State. The newly formed Nagaland Peoples' Front forged a coalition government, the Democratic Alliance of Nagaland, with the objective of facilitating the Indo-Naga peace process for an honourable political solution. Subsequently, they formed the Coordination Committee for Peace to pursue consultations with all Naga national organizations.

Furthermore, Naga civil society organizations have continued to engage in "peoples-to-peoples" dialogue with neighbouring communities and members of Indian civil society to nurture a climate of mutual understanding. Consultations within Naga society led by the *Naga Hoho*, the all-Naga council of tribal leaders, have been sustained at different levels to sow seeds of reconciliation, to strengthen the peace process and to ensure that the discourse of self-determination is affirmed in the negotiations.

Area coverage and unification of Naga areas

During the Indian Prime Minister's three-day visit to the Naga homeland in October 2003, thousands of Naga from all over Nagalim rallied in Kohima to express to the Prime Minister their common aspirations and to demand the unification of Naga areas. Soon afterwards, in December 2003 the Nagaland state government passed a bill in the assembly for the integration of Naga areas under one administrative unit.

However, 2003 experienced the continued reluctance of the Government of India to give any commitment on the important question of ceasefire area coverage, further attempting to conveniently bring the issue of unification of Naga areas within the domain of the Indian Constitution. While such policy contradicts the very principles of "unconditional talks" it exposes India's intention to make it an issue of electoral politics. Upholding the sanctity of existing state boundaries in the Northeastern region is an issue of electoral politics in the sense that no Northeastern government (i.e. the states of Assam, Manipur, and Arunachal Pradesh) can address the issue of unification of Naga areas without seriously undermining its voter support. The result of such juggling of Naga aspirations with neighbouring communities has hardened feelings and resistance to the unification of the Naga areas. Isolation and mistrust are severing traditional ties between indigenous peoples and increasing risks of confrontation, enabling the Indian government to justify increasing the deployment of armed forces. The rights of the Naga people to their land and other issues important for negotiation are entangled in electoral power politics and constitutional matters. Issues of self-determination are thereby diverted away from the negotiating table.

Draconian legislation

The Arunachal Pradesh Control of Organized Crime Act (APCOCA) enacted by the Arunachal state government under former Chief Minister Mukut Mithi of Congress (I)[1] supposedly to tackle the growing "menace" of Naga "insurgents" was operational only in Naga Areas. Armed with extra-constitutional powers, Indian military and paramilitary forces launched "Operation Hurricane" against Naga living in the present administrative unit of Tirap and the Changlang District of Arunachal Pradesh. The new government with G. Apang as Chief Minister repealed APCOCA and called off Operation Hurricane in the latter part of 2003.

Despite the ongoing ceasefire and peace process, the Government of India continues to impose the draconian Armed Forces Special Powers Act (AFSPA); an act that gives special powers to Indian Armed Forces, including the power to shoot to kill on mere suspicion with legal immunity, thereby violating all civil and democratic norms. On grounds of the need to maintain "law and order", the Government of India refused to consider a recommendation of the Nagaland state government not to extend the Disturbed Areas Act by virtue of which AFSPA comes into force. This negates the very spirit of the peace process and raises questions about India's integrity and sincerity in relation to it. It is feared that the intention of the Indian government is not to resolve the long-standing demands of the Naga but to focus on containing them. The sustainability of the peace process is threatened.

In the name of development

The multi-million rupee economic package given by the Indian Prime Minister in October 2003 to the present Nagaland State is an indicator of a strong thrust in development and economic planning. Different rates of development within Nagaland state and Naga areas outside of this state are encouraged, and it is feared that this is an attempt to divide public opinion so as to assert state control. This policy is pursued especially in districts that form the borders of Naga contiguous areas. The construction of dams for hydro power generation, tourism, bio-diversity prospecting and exploration of oil and natural gas without people's free and informed consent and participation induce systematic transfer of non-indigenous populations to indigenous areas, causing abnormal population growth and adding to already existing tensions.

Increasing military initiatives and involvement in development through the Army Development Group (ADG) and Military Civic Action (MCA) raises ethical questions. Their activities, primarily based on psychological warfare, penetrate deep into Naga society with the objective of winning peoples' hearts, breaking their spirit for freedom and weakening the negotiation process by creating gaps between Naga negotiators and the people they represent.

India's vigorous pursuit of the "Look East policy" intended to link East and South Asia economically will remain precariously unstable as long as the policy of militarization continues and the approach to the peace process bypasses broader democratic values and principles. ❑

Note

1   Congress (I) is the political party founded by Indira Gandhi in 1978 - (I) stands for Indira - after her former party, Congress (R) lost the elections. (Ed.note)

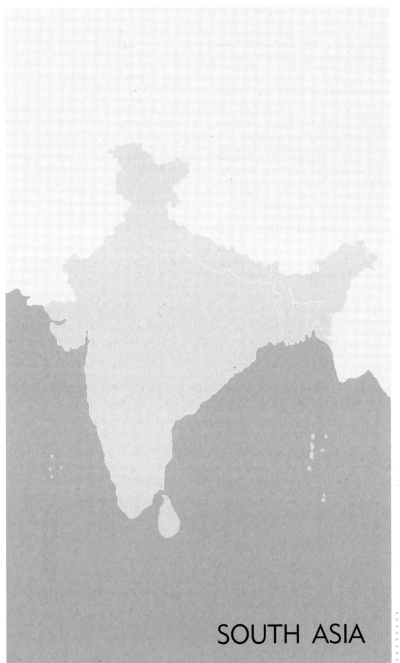

SOUTH ASIA

BANGLADESH

B angladesh (147,570 sq. km.) lies in south Asia, sharing a frontier
with India and Burma (Myanmar) to the east, west and north, and
bounded by the Bay of Bengal to the south. Out of an estimated total
population of 143.3 million (2002), Bangladesh has some 2.5 million
indigenous peoples or *Adivasis* – original inhabitants – belonging to
45 different ethnic groups, concentrated in the north and south-eastern parts of the country. However, there is no constitutional recognition of the indigenous peoples in Bangladesh except for oblique references to "backward segments of the population".

The Chittagong Hill Tracts

The Chittagong Hill Tracts (CHT) in the south-eastern corner of Bangladesh is the homeland of 11 different peoples: the Bawm, Chakma,
Chak, Khyang, Khumi, Lushai, Marma, Pankhu, Mro, Taungchangya
and Tripura. They are also called *Jummas*, for their slash and burn
form of farming, known as *jum*. Although the plains people who
looked down on the hill people originally used this term, it has been
acknowledged by the indigenous peoples as a source of national
identity and pride.

   The indigenous peoples have their own distinct identity, culture
and history. They differ from the majority Bengali people in most
aspects including physiognomy, dress, customs and religion. The
indigenous peoples are of Mongolian, Tibeto-Burman or Mon Khmer
extraction, and are principally Buddhists, with some belonging to the
Hindu and Christian faith, while most Bengalis follow Islam. Many
of the indigenous peoples have their own languages, both in written
and oral form, although many of these are in danger of extinction.

1997 Accord

In December 1997, a 25-year-long civil war ended with the government and the indigenous resistance movement, the Parbattya Chattagram Jana Samhati Samiti (PCJSS - United Peoples Party of the
Chittagong Hill Tracts) agreeing to a peace accord. This has led to
some improvement in law and order. However, tensions and conflicts
remain and the 1997 Accord has not delivered the expected peace and

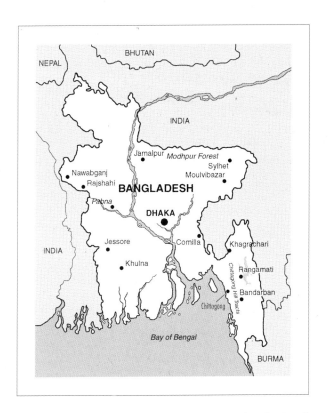

harmony.[1] To a large extent major prerequisites for the implementation of the agreement remain unfulfilled. These include:

Empowerment of the CHT institutions
The CHT Regional Council was envisaged in the 1997 Accord as an apex body, with supervisory and coordinating powers over the three hill district councils, the CHT development board, the district police force and the district civil administration. It is to be consulted regarding any proposed laws on the CHT, and has the prerogative of requesting the annulment of any law that can have a detrimental effect on the CHT. The regional council also has authority over indigenous personal law, NGOs, and some other matters. It is to have 22 members, to be indirectly elected by the Hill district councils.

An interim regional council was established in May 1999 under the leadership of the PCJSS president, J.B. Larma. It is not fully empowered, has inadequate resources and is often overlooked and ignored, as actual power remains in the hands of the civil servants. The three Hill district councils – for Bandarban, Khagrachari and Rangamati – were initially established in 1989, and were to be strengthened under the 1997 Accord. They too are nominally functional at the moment with five members selected (out of 34), and with crucial issues such as land, development, forestry and environment continuing to be administered by the civil servants. The ministry for CHT Affairs, also an Accord institution intended to coordinate work at the central level, is in place. However, the Prime Minister Begum Khaleda Zia holds the CHT portfolio in her own hands, with an indigenous deputy minister working under her direct supervision.

A land commission
The Accord also provides for a land commission to address the issue of conflicting land claims. The nine-member commission is to include the traditional authorities, representatives of the regional council and the district councils, and has the responsibility for adjudicating land claims, taking into account the customary laws of the indigenous peoples.

Most members of the land commission, including the representatives of the three Hill district councils and the regional council, as well as the traditional *rajas*, have not been formally appointed. By May 2003, more than 35,000 cases had been lodged with the commission. Almost all deal with conflicting claims between indigenous peoples and settlers.[2]

Demilitarization
The 1997 Accord includes provisions for the withdrawal of the Armed Forces from the Hill Tracts, with the exception of permanent camps tasked with border control. The CHT was turned into a military-occupied zone in 1975. The original reason the Army came to the Hill Tracts was to deal with counter-insurgency operations against the Shanti Bahini - Peace Corps, the armed wing of the PCJSS.

Despite the provisions for withdrawal, the Army continues its presence in the Hill Tracts. Its policy is currently driven by development - Operation Uttaran (Uplifting). It is engaged in economic development and infrastructure projects. It holds a position of influence and power and is actively involved in the day-to-day administration of the region. There are reported to be about 500 army camps in the CHT; of these some 35 camps have been dismantled so far, according to PCJSS reports.

Settlers burn down indigenous villages

A major concern in the Hill Tracts is the continued involvement of the armed forces in gross human rights abuses against the indigenous peoples, often in collusion with the plains settlers. In April 2003, the army and settlers burnt down indigenous houses in the Bhuiochari, Khagrachari district, when the indigenous villagers asked the settlers to stop encroaching onto their lands, and to dismantle the houses they had built. It is reported that the army encircled the village and forced the indigenous people out of their homes while the settlers looted and burnt down the houses.[3]

On 26 August 2003, Bengali settlers from a neighbouring cluster village[4] attacked, looted and burnt down 14 indigenous villages in Mahalchari, Khagarachari district. The army took no action to prevent the attack or to protect the indigenous peoples. Over 50 persons were injured, some seriously, two persons killed, and nine Jumma women raped.[5] Some Buddhist temples were also destroyed in the attack. It is estimated that over 400 houses were burned down and 2,000 people left homeless by the attack.

The PCJSS, the United Peoples Democratic Front (UPDF) and the Bangladesh Indigenous Peoples Forum have organized a number of demonstrations and rallies to protest the attack. They have demanded an inquiry into the attack, punishment of the perpetrators, and compensation for the victims. There have also been calls for a multi-ethnic police force to be re-instituted in the CHT as a building block for increased law and order – this was also agreed in the 1997 Accord.[6] Currently, the indigenous peoples live in makeshift houses in the ravaged areas, and are receiving some humanitarian assistance. The perpetrators have not been brought to justice, and although two parliamentary teams visited the site, no inquiry has been made into the attack, despite calls for one from both local and international groups.

Internecine conflict

Although the situation in the CHT has improved somewhat since the Accord, a new focus for violence has re-emerged: an internecine conflict between indigenous organizations, divided into two opposing camps of pro-Accordists (led by the PCJSS) and anti-Accordists (led by the UPDF, a more radical group). The UPDF was formed in 1998 in response to the Accord and opposes it for not meeting the demands of the indigenous peoples for full autonomy. The intra-indigenous rivalry has erupted into full-scale violence with attacks and counter-attacks taking place on a regular basis.[7]

There have been repeated attempts to resolve the differences between the two parties – they agree on enhanced autonomy for the indigenous peoples, withdrawal of the army and of the settlers – but to no avail so far. Many observers believe that the procrastination over implementation of the Peace Accord has exacerbated the differences between the PCJSS and the UPDF, and that if the Accord were to be more fully implemented, this would break the deadlock and pave the way for cooperation between the two factions.

This struggle has emerged as the most destructive of the effects of the incomplete implementation process, as it has the potential to draw attention and focus away from the crucial issue of ensuring that rights of the indigenous peoples are protected.

Political developments

The PCJSS has continued to criticize the government for the lack of progress on the Accord, and identified some 27 points that remain unimplemented.[8] A four-point movement was launched in December 2003 to mark the sixth anniversary of the Accord. Demonstrations, protest marches and road blockades have been organized in the three hill districts, to demand full implementation.

The four-point demand includes the full implementation of the Accord including the withdrawal of all army camps, police and armed police battalions from the CHT, handover of the charge of the CHT affairs ministry to a minister of indigenous origin, and the appointment of an indigenous leader as the chairperson of the CHT development board (until very recently the post was held by the chief army officer in the CHT. The present chairperson is a non-indigenous person). On 11 December 2003, the Minister in charge of the implementation committee of the CHT Accord, Rural Development and Cooperatives, Abdul Mannan Bhuiyan, met with the President of the PCJSS and Chairperson of the CHT Regional Council, Jyotirindra Bodhipriya Larma to discuss how to resolve the situation. The implementation committee held its last meeting in April 2003. No effective steps have been taken so far.

In another development, there are reports that the government has decided to review the Accord to ensure its conformity with the 1972 Constitution. Kamal Hossain, the chief architect of the 1972 Constitution and currently convenor of the Gonoforum (Peoples' Forum), has endorsed this review saying that the CHT Accord is a commitment of the constitution and any further delays in execution would be a serious injustice.

Internal displacement

There are a large number of internally displaced persons in the CHT.[9] This has been a result of various factors, mainly: (1) a large scale development project - the Kaptai hydroelectric project constructed in 1959-61 which submerged some 250 square miles, and displaced over 100,000 persons; (2) the continuing afforestation policy; (3) the settlement programme; (4) civil war and (5) militarization. Many indigenous peoples were displaced more than once as a result of these factors. In addition, over 55,000 Jummas fled the violent civil war and took shelter in India as refugees. They returned to the CHT on the basis of two agreements concluded with the government in 1992 and 1997, to find their homes and farms taken over by the settlers, and remain in temporary venues, waiting to have their lands returned to them as agreed.

The numbers of the internally displaced in the CHT are increasing. The August 2003 Mahalchari arson attack displaced 1500-2000 indigenous villagers who remain in temporary shelters. In addition, the army's acquisition of over 9,000 acres of indigenous lands to build an army cantonment in Bandarban Hill district has left around 5,000 indigenous peoples from the Mro community homeless. Another element is the government's plans for afforestation that have already displaced over 20,000 families in the Bandarban district alone, and will displace many others if it continues.[10]

Regular government food rations were stopped some six months ago. However, the plains settlers have received rations since their arrival in the CHT, and continue to do so today - an act that is described as discriminatory by the indigenous internally displaced.

Demographic manipulation

In the 1872 census[11] 98% of the CHT population were indigenous. The latest census shows a ratio of nearly 50:50. It is evident that the indigenous peoples are fast becoming a minority in their own homeland.

The government still continues to provide assistance to the settlers, including food grains estimated to amount to 28,000 tonnes of food grains per year at a cost of Taka 28 crores (US$ 4.8 million.).[12] What is of greater concern is the granting of certificates by the deputy commissioners to outsider Bengalis including the settlers as "permanent residents", thereby endorsing their presence in the CHT. There are also reports of a plan to give resident status to the 26,000 settler families in the CHT. The office of the Prime Minister issued an order for land to be identified as "khas" for the purpose of allocating it to settler families.[13] The government describes as "khas" those lands which are not recorded in the official registers as belonging to anyone, but which, in fact, are the common forest and *jum* fields of the indigenous peoples.[14]

The indigenous peoples have vehemently opposed this move and the PCJSS and the UPDF have organized marches and demonstrations to protest this further erosion of indigenous land rights. According to the prevailing legislation, endorsed by the Accord, it is the traditional indigenous authorities that have the right to issue such certificates.

Development cooperation

Current government policy in the CHT is development oriented. However, the indigenous peoples have criticized the projects and programmes being implemented in the region in the name of development as not being pro-indigenous or indigenous-driven.

The CHT has gained status as an attractive fund-raising opportunity and a large number of national NGOs have begun operations in the region. However, most of their projects and programmes largely benefit only the settler communities.

Although international development assistance ground to a halt in the CHT following the abduction of three aid workers in February 2001, a number of donors have re-initiated work in the Hill Tracts or are initiating studies and assessments to plan their interventions.[15]

The indigenous peoples' organizations are also active in this field. However, they have difficulty in obtaining funds and other resources, as the required registration with the national NGO bureau is often impossible to obtain, especially for organizations that are active in promoting the rights of the indigenous peoples. It is estimated that there are 50 international, national and local organizations working in the Hill Tracts.

Following a risk assessment report prepared in 2002, the UNDP commenced operations in the CHT and has assigned a total of US$

4.3 million for a sustainable environment management programme and US$ 3.5 million for poverty alleviation. It established an office in Rangamati, called the CHT Development Facility, in June 2003 and initiated a project on Promotion of Development and Confidence-Building in the CHT, a pilot project to provide small grants to communities for small-scale projects which could be used as building blocks towards confidence-building.

The UNDP has been severely criticized by the indigenous peoples, including the PCJSS, the Regional Council and indigenous organizations for not taking the Peace Accord and its implementation into account. It was stressed that the Accord and its implementation should be the pre-condition for any sustainable development work in the CHT. At the launch of the CHT Development Facility, the Regional Council chairperson, J.B. Larma pointed out that the UNDP had not consulted directly with the regional council or the three district councils, and had not given due recognition to the indigenous peoples of the CHT as the primary beneficiaries. This was in reference to the inclusion of a project site in Matiranga, composed primarily of settler families. Mr. Larma also pointed out that the project was not in accordance with the UNDP's own policy of engagement with indigenous peoples.[16]

This issue was taken up by indigenous peoples and their representatives at the international level and in discussions with UNDP. As a result of the concerns raised, UNDP planned to send a review team to the CHT in January 2004 to consider remedial measures including enhanced consultation mechanisms with the regional council and the Hill district councils.

Legal developments

The fundamental legislation governing the Chittagong Hill Tracts is Regulation 1 of 1900. It was originally adopted by the British, amended by successive administrations, but remains a valid law. In September 2003, the Bangladesh Jatiyo Sangsad – the national Parliament - passed the Chittagong Hill Tracts Regulation (Amendment) Act of 2003 (Act No. 38 of 2003), whereby district and sessions judge courts will be established in the three districts of the CHT. The judges are to take into account "...existing laws, customs and usages of the district concerned"[17] when trying criminal and civil matters. Previously, the civil administration also had responsibility for civil and criminal justice. The system of administration of customary law and other local laws and practices by the indigenous headmen and the chiefs will remain unchanged by the 2003 amendment.[18]

Vulnerable youth

The volatile atmosphere in the CHT, and the increasing landlessness and consequent impoverishment of the indigenous peoples has led to high unemployment, and in many cases underemployment, in particular among indigenous youth. There are reports of increasing drug abuse among unemployed youth, who face discrimination in seeking higher education and employment and become disaffected and vulnerable. There are allegations that the "the military continue to spread it [drug] and the police have chosen to ignore it. More and more indigenous adolescents are becoming involved because it offers them an escape from the current futility of their situation. This is just one of the ways in which the military continues to oppress our people after the Accord."[19]

Indigenous women

Indigenous women face many problems including displacement, unemployment and violence. They often encounter double discrimination on the basis of their race and gender. During the civil war, there were countless reports of rape, and the case of Kalpana Chakma, a young student leader abducted by the military, remains unresolved. The incidences of rape of indigenous women by settlers and/or army personnel continue to be reported e.g Mahalchari 2003, as do reports of forced marriages and religious conversion (which are often linked).

There are some positive trends - for instance the discussions in some of the indigenous groups of the need to amend customary laws that discriminate against women. However, the status and position of Jumma women need to be acknowledged and strengthened.[20] The women's groups in the CHT are taking an increasingly active role in making their voices heard and on 16 January 2004 the Hill Women's Federation plans to celebrate its 5th conference with a rally, seminar and other activities.

The government's responsibility

The indigenous peoples of the Chittagong Hill Tracts have faced many challenges in the past. The current one is to ensure a lasting peace, which is acceptable to all, and to agree to sort out any differences that may emerge through dialogue and cooperation. In its turn, it is the responsibility of the Government of Bangladesh to make an objective assessment of how best to resolve the CHT impasse in a meaningful manner, and as a first step to implement the 1997 Accord as an urgent issue. If the CHT issue is not resolved it will affect and erode national development. The government needs to take greater account of the indigenous peoples and their own demands for peace and development at their own pace; to do otherwise would be to unravel all that has been achieved, and to give in to those who oppose peace at any cost.

Garo in Modhupur Forest

In Modhupur Forest in northern Bangladesh about 25,000 Garo are facing serious violations of human rights, including killings, torture, imprisonment, rape, etc. At present they are threatened by forcible eviction from their ancestral homeland, the Modhupur Forest. The Garo's own word for the Modhupur Forest is *Habima*, meaning motherland.

The Bangladesh government decided to establish an eco-park on the Garo's ancestral homeland in 2000 without any consultation with the indigenous peoples. Project implementation started in 2003 and the present government has changed the title of the project from Eco-park to Modhupur National Park Development Project. But most project components remain the same. Critics note that rather than having "ecology" as its focus, the park has entertainment as a goal with (quoting from the project proposal) "10 picnic spots, 3 cottages, 9 lakes, 6 roads, 2 watch towers" to be built in the park. The project costs are estimated at Taka 973 million (approx. US$ 17 million).

The government does not say that they will evict the indigenous peoples. However, in 2003, the Bangladesh government started making a boundary wall around 3,000 acres of land. After the construction of the boundary wall, the indigenous peoples foresee that they will not be allowed to remain in the forest. They will be treated as illegal inhabitants and encroachers on the forest. Their movements will be restricted in the forest and they fear that they'll end up losing control of their livelihood.

Eco-park project threats the Khasi

In Moulvibazar district the indigenous Khasi and Garo face similar problems. A 1,500 acres tourist eco-park is being established on the

Adivasis' ancestral land. As in the Modhpur case, the plans have been initiated without any consent of the indigenous Garo and Khasi, who have been living in the area for centuries. The government did not even mention the villages of Khasi and Garo people in their project proposal, instead considering them almost illegal inhabitants of the forest. The eco-park was inaugurated in April 2001. Seven indigenous hill villages will be affected: 1,000 Khasi and Garo families will face forced eviction from their homelands.   ❑

Notes and references

1   See *The Indigenous World 1997-1998, 1998-1999*, and *1999-2000* for more details on the Peace Accord.
2   *Daily Star*, internet edition, May 21, 2003: Land remains hills' Achilles heel.
3   A report by the Hill Women's Federation, April 2003: *Army-Settlers burn Jumma houses in Khagrachari.*
4   Many of the plains settlers were settled in cluster villages in designated areas under close army protection and supervision.
5   See Report of the Parbattya Chattagram Jana Samhati Samiti (PCJSS): An account of Communal Attack on the Jumma Peoples in Mahalchari by the Bengali Settlers with the full backing of the Army, 10 September 2003. Also, Urgent Action: Extra judicial execution of Mr. Binod Bihari Khisa, torching of 140 Jumma houses and attack on Buddhist temple, *Hill Watch Human Rights Forum*, 18 August 2003. See also *OneWorld Net*, Sept. 2 2003: Bangladesh Hill Violence Threatens Peace. (www.oneworld.net)
6   *The Daily Star*, internet edition, 31 August 2003: Worried CHT rajas seek multi-ethnic police force.
7   *The Daily Star*, internet edition, 11 February 2004: 7 UPDF men abducted from wedding party, PCJSS cadres blamed.
8   *The Independent*, internet edition, 3 December 2003: Larma's ultimatum for army pullout.
9   For more details see Global Internal Displacement Project of the Norwegian Refugee Council, December 2003 Report: *Bangladesh: land disputes perpetuate internal displacement.* (www.idpproject.org)
10 According to gazette notifications in 1992, 1996, and 1998 the Ministry of Environment and Forests will evict approximately 200,000 indigenous peoples from their lands, as these orders will convert forests and grazing commons, homesteads and agricultural lands into industry-oriented plantations. The proposed areas amount to 7,411,286.30 acres (Bandarban: 7,28,0917.17 acres; Khagrachari: 41,907.50 acres; and Rangamati: 88,461.63 acres). These notifications remain in force despite repeated demands by the CHT Committee for the Protection of Forests and Land Rights.

11 1872 is the date of the first census conducted in the region. Since then, censuses have been conducted in Bangladesh every decade. (Ed. Note)

12 *Daily Star*, internet edition, 23 September 2003: Move on to give resident status to 26,000 Bangalee families in CHT.

13 Reference No. 11 39 00 60 of 2002-476 (550). See Report from Greater Chittagong Hill Tract Hill Youth Forum, Central Convening Committee: *A press conference in protest against the new settlement policy of present Government of Bangladesh*. Conference held at the Chittagong Press Club, Chittagong, 7 February 2003.

14 **Raja Devasish Roy. 2002.** *Land and Forest Rights in the Chittagong Hill Tracts*. Published as "Talking Points 4/02", International Centre for Integrated Mountain Development (ICIMOD), Kathmandu, Nepal.

15 See **Chandra Roy. 2003.** *The Impact of Development in the Chittagong Hill Tracts: Ways Forward*. Paper presented at the Forum for Development Cooperation with Indigenous Peoples 2003, 9-10 October 2003, Centre for Sami Studies, University of Tromsö, Norway.

16 See *Statement of the PCJSS on the UNDP project in the Chittagong Hill Tracts*, Bangladesh, July 2003.

17 **Raja Devasish Roy. 2004.** Challenges for Juridical Pluralism and Customary Laws of Indigenous Peoples: The Case of the Chittagong Hill Tracts, Bangladesh. *Defending Diversity: Case Studies*. Norway: Saami Council.

18 *Ibid.*

19 **Feeny, Thomas. 2001.** The Fragility of Peace in the Chittagong Hill Tracts, Bangladesh. *Forced Migration Review* (October).

20 **Dr. Sadeka Halim. 2003.** Insecurity of Indigenous Women: A Case from the Chittagong Hill Tracts. *Solidarity 2003: Ensure the Security of Indigenous Women*. Dhaka: Bangladesh Indigenous Peoples Forum.

NEPAL

Earning a living. Indigenous Rai boy,
Hile Bazar, Eastern Nepal.
Photo: Balkrishna Mabuhang

Nepal is in deep crisis and on the verge of failing as a state. The Maoist insurgency has spread across the country and the attacks and counter attacks have created massive insecurity among civilians whose normal lives are threatened. The deep-rooted cause of the crisis is the negligence, ignorance and impotence of the actors seated in the chairs of the government.

The social model of national unification so far has been Hinduization, which is alien to the multi-ethnic foundation of the country. The *Muliki Ain* of 1854 is a written version of the social code that had long been in practice in parts of Hinduized Nepal. With its four-fold *varna* system (grouping of people in castes that are grouped into four varna categories) the Muliki Ain codified a hierarchical social structure favouring the so-called high caste Brahmins and Chhetris.

The 1990 Constitution of Nepal guarantees the right to equality by stating that the State shall not discriminate against citizens on the basis of religion, colour, sex, caste, ethnicity or belief (Article 11.3). However, this constitutional right is negated by a clause in the Muliki Ain as amended in 1992, which states that the "traditional practices" at religious places shall not be considered as discriminatory. The country is furthermore declared a Hindu Kingdom, in spite of the country's multi-ethnic, multi-religious, and multi-lingual nature. The Act on the National Foundation for Development of Indigenous Nationalities (NFDIN)[1] recognizes 59 groups as indigenous nationalities. Of them, the national census of 2001 identifies 46 indigenous groups with the remaining 54 groups identified as caste groups including Dalits and other religious and linguistic minorities. The 1991 census identified only 26 indigenous nationalities. The indigenous population accounts for 8.2 million or 37% of the total population. There is a general problem of obtaining reliable disaggregated data

302

Biswakarma (Dalit) and indigenous Limbu children taking a break from their work as porters in conflict ridden Panchtar District, Eastern Nepal. Photo: Balkrishna Mabuhang

based on caste and ethnicity, and some indigenous activists claim that the indigenous nationalities actually constitute around 70% of the population.

The Maoist insurgency

Some analysts perceive the Maoist insurgency as an important catalyst for asserting indigenous peoples' rights – others point out that indigenous peoples are threatened and negatively affected more than most other groups by the violent conflict. Since the outbreak of the "people's war" in 1996 more than 9,000 people have been killed. Studies show that indigenous nationalities make up 33 -34 per cent of those killed by both the state (army and police) and insurgents.[2] Compared to other groups (Brahmins, Chhetris, Dalits, etc.) they are the most affected. One reason why the death toll is particular high among indigenous groups is that the Maoist cadres have recruited a large number of indigenous people, and the movement's stronghold is located in the areas of the country where indigenous peoples constitute the majority. Another underlying reason is that indigenous peoples are perceived as powerless, since they do not have much influence at the state level. Therefore the security forces hit particularly hard on these groups, and there is a wide spread attitude of *"jegare pani hune"* (whatever you like, you can do to them). The Maoists are also responsible for a large number of killings of Brahmins and Chhetris while state forces have caused fewer deaths among these groups. In the beginning, when the Maoists took action against the landlords, political leaders or rich people, their arms pointed at Brahmins and Chhetris (the highest castes), since they hold most of these possessions. However the overall picture is that the insurgency has adverse impacts on indigenous nationalities.

The insurgency is exposing some indigenous groups to particularly strong threats, since there is a tendency to see their political cause and social activism as linked with the Maoist insurgency. A pertinent example is the case of the indigenous Tharus of the Western Terai region. They experience severe harassment from the State apparatus, which with little or no evidence detains, beats, abducts or kills Tharus accused of being affiliated with the Maoist movement. Since the July 2000 abolishment of the *Kamaiya* system (i.e. Tharu serving as bonded labourers on others' land, typically that of high caste landowners) thousands of former Kamaiyas have been living in temporary settlements. These former Kamaiyas are poor and landless and the armed conflict in their area has put them in an extremely vulnerable situation. Maoists come to their settlements to recruit them; police and army personnel carry out desperate raids and gun down innocent people on mere suspicion of their involvement in the insurgency. The following cases[3] are examples of how the security forces treat the former Kamaiyas – in the name of protection of civil rights and freedom:

Two Kamaiya men, 20 year old Mohan Chaudhary, and 21 year old Kalu Chaudhary (both residents of Daiji VDC- 3 of Kanchanpur district) went to a market place across the boarder in India on December 6, 2003. On the same day a bomb went off on the Gadda Chauki road. When the two brothers returned, security forces caught them and brought them back to their home in order to identify other Kamaiyas who could be held responsible for the bomb blast. Both Kamaiyas were from the Kamaiya Bichphata Camp. The security forces that came equipped with arms and guns scared the Kamaiyas in the camp. Nobody was able to speak in front of them. Security personnel took advantage of the situation. They raped seven women of the camp. Husbands, fathers and brothers of those women were not allowed to enter their huts. Nobody was able to speak about this event. Survivors could not bring out the case for 10 days. The Freed Kamaiya Society of Kanchanpur brought the case to light as an example of how Kamaiya indigenous peoples' basic human rights have been seriously violated. Survivors put forward the case at the District Administration Office, Kanchanpur, and organized a press conference. They also met the District Administrative Officer and demanded that action be taken against the security personnel involved in the case. The district administration formed an investigation committee to find the facts. So far no action has been taken against the security personnel involved – authorities say that the victims are unable to identify the perpetrators. Security personnel equipped with arms and guns came from the State Security Camp, and violated innocent people. Is it really true that there is not enough evidence to seek justice?

Jangali Tharu, aged 35 years and a resident of Mashuria Village Development Committee-1, living at Kamaiya settlement of Andaiya, has a family of 5 members including two sons and a daughter. He held Kamaiya Identity Card No. 71, issued by the Land Reform Office.[4] He had a small hut. He went to Pahalpur in order to get employment in a brick factory. An ambush blasted at Pahalpur on November 8, 2004. On the same day, Jangali Tharu was on his way home when security personnel caught him and took him to the jungle and gunned him down saying that he was an insurgent.

Third round of peace talks

The third round of peace talks between the government and the Maoists ended in August 2003. The media reported that they had mutually agreed to discuss political issues, overall socio-economic reforms, procedures of the reforms, settlement of the armed forces and weapons, rehabilitation of the affected people and reconstruction of development infrastructure destroyed by the Maoists. The much-awaited third round of dialogue between the government and the Maoists started with the government promising massive socio-economic packages and major constitutional changes in order to accommodate the Maoist demands.

Some of the contentious issues that brought the talks to a halt were the Maoist demand for a constituent assembly, and the abolition of the institution of monarchy. The rebels labeled the government's propositions as a "hopeless offer and an attempt aimed at mere cosmetic changes in the present political system".[5] They unanimously lifted the cease-fire, when the Security forces gunned down 19 Maoists in Doramba village, Ramechhap District, on 17 August. The killings took place on the same day that a third round of peace talks between the government and representatives of the CPN (Maoist) was taking place in Dang in the Mid-western region.[6] According to human rights activists, 19 Maoists had been attending a meeting in a house in Doramba village, Ramechhap district, when the security forces arrived on the scene and opened fire. One Maoist was shot dead and 18 other individuals, including the house owner and his son were taken into custody. Human rights activists claim that the 18 were taken by the security forces to Dandakateri in Daduwa Village Development Committee, some two hours' walk away, where they were lined up and shot dead one by one. Of the 19 persons, the majority were Tamang indigenous peoples, allegedly Maoist insurgents.

National Foundation for Development of Indigenous Nationalities

The National Foundation for Development of Indigenous Nationalities (NFDIN) was established on June 26, 2003, and has a council of some 100 members. The National Foundation has been given the very broad mandate of ensuring indigenous peoples' social, economic and cultural development and uplift as well as their equal participation in the mainstream of national development. During 2003, the foundation was in the process of defining the rules and regulations that are to guide its further functioning.

The Nepal Federation of Indigenous Nationalities (NEFIN) has been recognized as the organization to recommend representatives from every indigenous nationality for the council. All the organizations that nominated their council representatives through NEFIN seem to be insensitive about gender. The Act of the Foundation provides for the nomination of 10 women from across the country, for two year terms, and with the clause that they can be members for one term only. However, male council members' tenure is 4 years, and they can be members for two terms. Indigenous women's organizations are now demanding the removal of such discriminatory clauses, so that the terms and conditions are the same for indigenous men and women.

Nepal Federation of Indigenous Nationalities

The Nepal Federation of Indigenous Nationalities (NEFIN) had its 5th National Congress from 23-25 August 2003. Addressing indigenous peoples' issues in light of the present political crisis (at a time when the cease fire was still in effect), the congress produced a resolution stressing the following points, among others:

1. *A national round-table conference with a broad participation of indigenous nationalities, Dalits, women, various religious leaders and representatives from different linguistic groups, etc. must be called to seek ways to restore a permanent and sustainable peace.*

2. *Immediate release of all indigenous people who have been arrested and accused of alleged involvement with Maoist insurgents and put in custody since the Maoist Insurgency started. Investigate unlawful killings in so-called "encounters" between the armed forces and the rebels.*

3. *The State must provide the essential peaceful environment, social security, and rehabilitation to those indigenous people who have been displaced on account of the insurgency and insurgents must respect the right of indigenous people to stay in their own residence.*

4. Since a multi-religious population inhabits the country, the State's bias towards any religion contradicts democratic pluralism. Therefore, the State must be declared secular.

5. Although indigenous nationalities account for the majority of the population in Nepal, their presence in the different aspects of the State apparatus is only nominal. Historical discrimination and exclusion against them still causes lack of representation. Therefore, a reservation or quota policy must be introduced: for education, civil service, and employment in other sectors. Affirmative action in the economic sector is also urgently required.

6. True representation of indigenous nationalities at the policymaking level is required to serve the interest of indigenous nationalities. Hence in drafting the next new constitution or amending the present one, proportional representation or special representation of indigenous nationalities should be ensured to secure a sensible representation of indigenous nationalities in the legislature, the executive, and the judiciary and other organs of the State.

7. Based on internationally developed standards on indigenous nationalities' right to self-determination, ethnic autonomy must be devised and guaranteed on the basis of historical residence, and demographic and linguistic predominance.

8. International human rights instruments address such fundamental issues for indigenous peoples as land rights, cultural rights, development rights, right to self-determination, proportional representation in the State apparatus, and federal state structure with ethnic autonomy. These issues should be taken into account seriously while exploring a political solution to the current crisis in Nepal.

9. His Majesty's Government should endorse the United Nations Draft Declaration on Indigenous Populations, the ILO Convention No. 169 and the Convention on Rights of Ethnic Minorities as soon as possible.

10. Uphold the rights of indigenous peoples to natural resources in accordance with their customary and communal rights.

11. Ensure the direct participation of indigenous nationalities in biodiversity and natural resource management and stop the creation of

wild life conservation areas, national parks and protected areas, from displacing indigenous nationalities from their original land.

12. *Free and prior informed consent must be required from indigenous nationalities prior to the development of tourist centres in order to protect them from the threat of possible adverse effects on their social and cultural livelihood as well as the cultural heritages of indigenous nationalities.*

13. *Indigenous nationalities are still considered untouchables by the Hindu varna system. In some societies, indigenous nationalities also treat Dalits as untouchables in accordance with the Hindu varna system. The 5ᵗʰ National Congress declares that Indigenous Nationalities must urgently abandon such discriminatory practices learned from the Hindu varna system and strengthen social customs and practices that are based on equality. The National Congress also commits itself to raising awareness on this issue and demanding the formulation of laws and regulations that will punish such discriminatory practices.*❏

Notes and references

1   Act No. 20 of 2002 concerning the establishment of the National Foundation for Development of Indigenous Nationalities. This act also provides an official definition of the indigenous peoples of Nepal: *"'Indigenous nationalities' means a tribe or community as mentioned in the schedule having its own mother language and traditional rites and customs, distinct cultural identity, distinct social structure and written or unwritten history"*.
2   Informal Sector Service Center (INSEC), 2001.
3   The cases are reported by the Freed Camay Society, Kanchanpur District.
4   The *kamaiya* identity card is the official recognition of a person's status as a freed *kamaiya*. Only holders of this ID can seek rehabilitation in the form of land allocations, etc. (This does not mean that the card guarantees these services – but it is a prerequisite!).
5   *Kathmandu Post*, 18 August 2003.
6   Amnesty International Press Release, AI Index: ASA 31/026/2003 (Public) News Service No. 196, Nepal: killings of 19 Maoists in Ramechhap should be investigated, 22 August 2003.

INDIA

L arge-scale development projects, mining and other industrial enterprises continue to threaten the livelihood of millions of Adivasis (indigenous peoples) of India. In the Northeast alone more than
1,000 Adivasis died during 2003, many of these as victims of conflicts
over access to natural resources after large-scale development projects
deprived Adivasis of their livelihoods. Others have fallen victims to
the heavy militarization of the area.

Millions of Adivasis deprived of their livelihood

More than 10 million forest dependent indigenous people in India
today stand threatened, evicted from their habitat and deprived
of their livelihood. These people, who have a symbiotic relationship with the forests and have earned their livelihood from the
forestlands for generations, are being harassed and hounded out.
Their houses are burnt, crops and food destroyed, women are
raped and men are shot and killed. The genesis to this barbarism
dates back to a Ministry of Environment and Forests (MoEF) cir-
cular issued by the Inspector General of Forests in May 2002, and
addressed to the chief secretaries, secretary (Forests) and principal chief conservator of forests (PCCFs) of all states and union
territories in India, outlining a "Time Bound Action Plan" for the
eviction of encroachers. According to the Forest Conservation
Act, 1980, any possession of forestland after 1980 is regarded as
encroachment. Indigenous people, who have been living on and
eking out their living on forestlands for generations, have become
encroachers simply because their ownership rights have not been
settled. Even though the legal basis of the eviction remains unclear, the Forest Department went on a rampage evicting Adivasis
from forest areas in several parts of the country (see *The Indigenous World 2003-2003*).

In the central Indian state of Madhya Pradesh, a Korku hamlet of
10 families was looted and burnt in July 2003. In Khandwa district,
an Adivasi was shot dead when he confronted the forest officials
who picked up his wife after chasing the villagers away from their
lands. The Special Reserve Protection Force (SRPF) has been deployed in the Adivasi areas of Gujarat to help the Forest Department
officials forcibly evict Adivasis from lands that they have been cul-

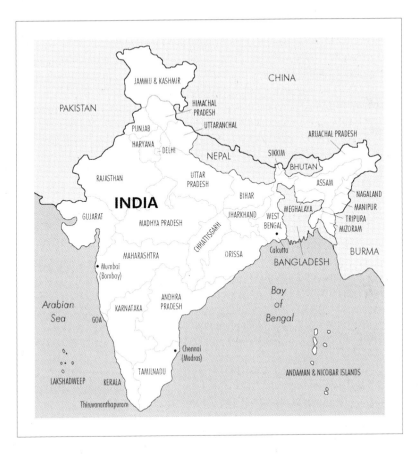

tivating for generations. The villagers are threatened, their houses looted and the men are frequently arrested and beaten up. In the Adivasi-dominated state of Chhattisgarh, the Central Reserve Police Force (CRPF) has been deployed to prevent the indigenous forest communities from going near the forests. In places like Bastar, the villages are surrounded by the CRPF. At the slightest sign of opposition, these Adivasis are branded as extremists, arrested or shot at and killed. Similar actions have been taken in the western Indian state of Rajasthan. The Forest Department team swoops down on villages, evicts and chases the villagers from their lands and destroys their houses and belongings. In December 2003, police killed two women Naxalites in Kudremukh National Park in Karnataka where the people were protesting against eviction from lands where they had been settled for the last two hundred years.

The situation has been further worsened by a marauding Central Empowered Committee (CEC), constituted by the Supreme Court and staffed with forest officials and hardcore wildlife conservationists. The court appointed the CEC to help the Court (a) examine various reports and affidavits filed by the states in response to the orders made by the court and place their recommendations before the Supreme Court, and (b) look at grievances and complaints filed by any individual to the committee against any steps taken by the government or any other authority in purported compliance with the orders passed by the Supreme Court and dispose of them or place them before the court. However the CEC has been going around the country issuing eviction orders at will.

Around 10,000 fishermen drying fish on the southern Sunderban island of Jambudwip in the Bay of Bengal have been evicted by its orders depriving almost 20,000 fishing families of their livelihood. On October 16, 2003, World Food Day, fishermen who went to the island were lathicharged (beaten with sticks) by the West Bengal police. Their equipment and food packets were destroyed and thrown into the sea. CEC was also held responsible for the massacre of the innocent, landless Adivasis who took shelter within the Muthanga Wildlife Sanctuary in the Wayanad district of Kerala (see *The Indigenous World 2002-2003*).

Both the fishermen and the forest-dependent indigenous people have filed petitions in the Supreme Court. The petitions are still being heard. In the meantime, in a coordinated move to thwart large-scale evictions, the Adivasis and other forest communities in the States of Orissa, Maharashtra, Gujarat, Rajasthan and Tamil Nadu have started filing thousands of claims concerning ownership of their lands in the office of the respective District Collectors. This process of filing claims to their lands has become a mass-movement. Around 70,000 Adivasis from the impoverished districts of Kalahandi, Bolangir and Nuapara in Orissa have declared their boycott of the forthcoming parliamentary elections if their ownership rights are not settled. The government, in a bid to tackle the growing discontent among the indigenous people before the elections, has announced its intention to settle the ownership rights of Adivasis who have been in possession of their land since before 1993. The Supreme Court has since stayed this order. The order is largely viewed with suspicion and scepticism, and the process of filing claims continues nevertheless.

Jharkhand

Khunti Declaration

The 3rd Annual Convention of the Jharkhand Jangal Bachao Andolan (JJBA) was held in Khunti in November 2003 with great enthusiasm. The convention was described as an historical event by some of the tribal elders because this kind of gathering of the tribal chiefs and elders on forest issues had not happened in the recent past. After the formation of the Jharkhand state, it was expected that the longstanding demands of the people to regain their lost ownership and management rights over forests would be taken into consideration by the State while formulating any new forest policy. Unfortunately, that did not happen. On the contrary, the government adopted a thoroughly anti- people forest policy. JJBA was formed three years ago to take up this issue and to assert popular demands to the state and the national level. The convention adopted some resolutions, which were made public as the Khunti Declaration in the open session on 29 November 2003. The following is an excerpt:

We the indigenous (Adivasis) and analogous (Moolvasi) peoples of Jharkhand gathered in Khunti, Jharkhand, India from 27th to 29th of November 2003 under the banner of the Jharkhand Jangal Bachao Andolan firmly declare the following statements: Forests are sources of our life and livelihood – the base of our society and culture. We are the rights holders of our ancestral forests, not just stakeholders. The Jharkhand government should recognize us as the only owners of our ancestral forest, land and water that were forcibly taken over from our fore parents by the British colonial state. The Forest Department has lost its credibility; it has failed miserably to protect forests and the wildlife; it should therefore, give up its claim as the owner and manager of the forests. Establishing harmony between forests and the people is the key to sustainable development of forests. We call upon the State and the civil society to recognize that through the protection and promotion of our rights and through recognizing and integrating our dynamic and holistic vision we are securing not only our future but also the future of humanity and social and environmental justice for all.

World Bank criticized by its own inspection panel

In early 2003, the World Bank Inspection Panel published a report on the Bank's Coal Sector Environmental and Social Mitigation Project

313

(CSESMP) at the East Parej coal mine in Jharkhand. The report stridently criticized the Bank for its implementation of this project, citing multiple counts of non-compliance with the Bank's own policies. The World Bank Management was to bring out its response within 6 weeks, by February 2003, but did not respond until mid-year. In its response, Bank management was soft on itself. It claimed that the World Bank "has made every effort" and "remains committed to the achievement of the objectives of the CSESMP," and "intends to continue supervising the CSESMP project until all outstanding issues have been resolved." It is difficult to reconcile the Bank commending itself for every effort, when the Inspection Panel listed 30 counts of non-compliance. There is a disturbing inconsistency here.

It is even more difficult to see how the Bank's executive directors could approve of the response as it is. The management's response contains 24 counts of "no action to be taken". Moreover, the Government of India has rejected the two main thrusts of its follow-up commitment, and the board knew this when it approved the response. These were: firstly, "to advise Government of India on apparent entitlements for subsistence allowances as per the East Parej Resettlement Action Plan, in the form of a lump sum payment made to the 121 eligible Project-affected families to the sum of US$ 300,000, to be disbursed by March 31, 2004". Secondly, they promised to set up an Independent Monitoring Panel (IMP) to follow up the various issues. Even if not rejected, this would have been of dubious value as experience in other areas has shown. IMPs have made many recommendations but they were not binding on the Bank or the borrower. IMPs recommendations were never implemented. The World Bank and the Inspection Panel remained silent spectators to this. As such, the IMP was of no benefit, and was basically an escape strategy for the Bank to exit the project.

We are left with the oft-repeated phrase "ongoing supervision and monitoring". How exactly, is the Bank going to continue to supervise and monitor? The Bank says it has learnt a number of lessons: realistic assumptions about organizational change; strengthening legislations; mechanisms for institutional coordination; critical issues to be resolved before implementation; obligations of implementing agencies to be clear; innovative approaches for income restoration to be explored; and analysis of resettlement options to be conducted. These are lessons that should have been learned *a priori*, especially as many of them were pointed out in submissions from NGOs, before the project started, and with hindsight now seem obvious. What of the Bank's claimed relations with the civil society? One would like to have seen more reference to specific actions that could be taken to improve future performance.

Follow up on POTA misuse

Human Rights organizations such as *POTA Virodhi Jan Morcha* and *People's Union for Civil Liberties* have been keeping the central and state governments on their toes with regard to the misuse of the draconian Prevention of Terrorism Act, 2002, commonly known as POTA (see *The Indigenous World 2002-2003*). The protest took the form of marches, public meetings and letters to local newspapers. The state government ignored the protests. Then the movement aligned itself with a team of eminent intellectuals and legal experts and did a review of some significant cases. The findings were published and submitted to The National Human Rights Commission, which subsequently took it to the Home Ministry which, in turn, ordered the state government to review all the POTA cases. Some 31 cases (involving 104 persons) out of 130 were found unwarranted. Then the state government was forced to withdraw the POTA charges, and it did. The sad fact remains that although POTA charges have been withdrawn from 104 persons, they have not been released. Other charges have been made against them. Most of these people have come out on bail but cases against them will continue. All this brings out the weakness of human rights organizations when it comes to facing the ruthless power of the state apparatus. Yet the struggle must go on.

Orissa

Protests against mining

On 17 January 2003, two full years after the incident took place, the judicial enquiry team submitted its report on police firing at protesters against the establishment of an aluminum refinery plant near Domba-Korala in Kashipur, Orissa. Three Adivasis died and several more were injured when the shooting took place on 16 December 2000. Several independent fact-finding missions were carried out, one of these pointed out that the police shooting was "a premeditated cold-blooded murder aimed primarily at suppressing the people's voice of protest."

The judicial enquiry team doubted the police force's stated purpose of "maintaining law and order", but justified the use of excessive force where as many as 19 rounds were fired. The team did not recommend action against anybody though they blamed the police officials. In its wisdom, the commission wanted this backward area to be "developed" stating that mining need not have adverse impacts on the environment while recommending compensation to the families of the dead and the injured.

Development projects have already displaced some 1.4 million people in the state of Orissa, mostly Adivasis. The state contains 69.7% of India's total bauxite deposits, the highest concentration being in the districts of Koraput, Kalahandi and Bolangir. In the year 1992-93, Utkal Alumina started surveying in Kashipur, alleging that it was for a railway line. Utkal Alumina is a joint venture. In 1992, INDAL, TATA, Hydro (Norway) and ALCAN (Canada) were part of the venture. Hydro and TATA have later withdrawn. HINDALCO of Birla India has replaced INDAL. Originally production was scheduled to begin by 2002, it has now been rescheduled for 2005.

The Utkal Alumina Project, estimated to cost around 1 billion US$, will extract bauxite through open cast mining. Aluminum will be exported through Visakhapatna port. Advertised as the cheapest bauxite in the world at 85 US$ a ton, this will cater predominantly to the growing demand for beer cans and other packaging, mostly in the USA, and meet the growing demands for light metal in cars on the American and Asian markets. The plant will directly affect 2,500 people in 24 villages of Kucheipadar, Hadiguda and Tikri Panchayat. But the company claims that only 147 families of 3 villages will be affected. Some 42 villages of Chandragiri, Maikanch and Kodipari panchayat will be directly affected by the open cast mining at Baphlimali. But the company claims that not a single village will be affected.

Protest against World Mining Congress

A large gathering of people representing anti-mining groups, unions and people's organizations from many states held a protest in Delhi, outside the venue of the 19th World Mining Congress and Expo 2003 on 1-2 November 2003. The Expo was organized by the Government of India to give "excellent business opportunities" for mining and other "high-priority core sectors" and to display "the most advanced technologies in mining". Large companies from around 60 countries were invited to the Expo.

The Campaign Against Plunder of Resources, formed recently in the context of the World Mining Congress, organized the campaign against the Expo. Its constituents are mainly people's organizations from various Indian states. Besides these groups, a number of Delhi-based groups played an active role in the campaign, along with a number of individual activists concerned about these issues. The Dept. of Mines and Mineral resources said that negotiations would take place shortly with companies such as Phelps Dodge, Anglo American, Alcoa of the U.S., Rio Tinto of the U.K. and other companies regarding bauxite, copper, coal, zinc, oil and diamond resources. Indian companies such as Sterlite, Reliance, and HINDALCO are also negotiating with these foreign companies. The Minister of State of Mines, Ramesh Bais, told the World Mining Congress that "a total of 157 proposals from multinational corporations for mineral exploration have been cleared specifically for reconnaissance operations in Andhra Pradesh, Gujarat, Chhattigsgarh, Madhya Pradesh, Orissa, Jharkhand, Rajasthan, Haryana, and Uttar Pradesh to attract foreign exchange, and several others are in the pipeline." Most of these areas are the homelands of Adivasis.

Kerala

Adivasis launch struggle against Coca-Cola
By December 2003 the picket outside the Coca-Cola plant in Plachimada, Kerala, had lasted over 600 days. It was on 22 April 2002 that the Malasar and Eravalar (Adivasis officially classified as "primitive tribes"), who live in this valley, launched the picket with the demand that the Coca-Cola plant be shut down because it was devastating the ground and surface water – the very source of their survival. The protestors demanded that the Coca-Cola Company be held fully responsible and liable for the destruction of livelihood resources of the people and the environment. The struggle against the unit of the Hindustan Coca-Cola Beverages Pvt. Ltd. by *Coca-Cola Virudha Janakeeya Samara Samithy* (Anti Coca-Cola Peoples Struggle Committee) was inaugurated by C.K. Janu, Chairperson of *Adivasi Gothra Mahasabha,* with a blockade by more than 1,300 people, mostly Adivasis belonging to the Eravalar and Malasar communities. The protestors were taken into custody by the police and removed.

Plachimada is predominantly an Adivasi area with over 1,000 families, mostly landless, earning a living as agricultural labourers. The Hindustan Coca-Cola Beverages Pvt. Ltd. established the Kerala unit in 1999 on a 38-acre plot (previously multi-cropped paddy lands) in Plachimada, in the Palakkad District. Some 134 permanent workers and about 150 casual laborers are employed in the factory, mostly from outside the area. On an average, about 85 lorry loads of beverage products leave the factory premises every day. Each load contains 550-600 cases with 24-300 ml bottles in each. Water is taken from 6 boreholes and 2 open wells on the factory compound, extracting some 0.8 to 1.5 million liters of water per day. The site is located a few meters away from the Moolathara barrage's main irrigation canal.

Within two years of the establishment of the Coca-Cola plant, the people around the plant began experiencing problems that they had never encountered before. The ground water receded. The effect spread to a 1.5-kilometer radius of the Coca-Cola plant. Water shortages upset the agricultural operations – the mainstay of the Adivasis. Salinity and hardness of water increased with high concentrations of calcium and magnesium that rendered water unfit for human consumption, domestic use (bathing and washing), or irrigation. Early in the factory's life the foul smelling, dried slurry was sold as fertilizer to the unsuspecting farmers. Later it was given "free" and now, with protests and objections, surreptitiously dumped on the roadsides and on fields at night.

The struggle

On 26 April 2002 a false case was filed by Hindustan Coca-Cola Beverages Pvt. Ltd in the High Court against the activists and leaders of the *Coca-Cola Virudha Janakeeya Samara Samithy* such as Venugopal Vilayodi and Veloor Swaminathan. They demanded that the picket line be dismantled, people be prevented from voicing their dissent and the plant be provided police protection. The *Samara Samithy* filed a counter-case in the High Court. The court conceded the right of people to protest peacefully and ordered the police to provide protection to the plant as well as the protesters. Since then heavy police protection has been provided to the plant, while police intimidation of the protesters persists to create a violent situation.

The first two months, the struggle faced hostility and threats from the combined strength of the mainstream political parties and the local panchayat (local elected administration). By and large, the media ignored the struggle or gave more credence to the Company's case. These factions supported Coca-Cola's campaign that the protests were "politically motivated", suggesting indirectly that extremist elements were behind this so that the State could be provided the scope and justification to crush the peaceful struggle in a violent manner. The bogey of "development" and threat of unemployment of the Coca-

Cola workers if production were affected, were raised. Coca-Cola's environmentally friendly and socially responsible approaches were also harped upon. Despite physical threats, the struggle persisted with Adivasi women, the main victims, forming the backbone of the struggle. The struggle soon acquired support from diverse sections – from the Gandhians to the radical left revolutionaries to the environmentalists from across the state, who organized agitations in support of the struggle and constituted solidarity committees. Hundreds of protesters and their supporters have been arrested on various occasions and false cases foisted on them. Support campaigns soon emerged from different parts of the country as well as internationally. Similar protests against Coca-Cola plants in other parts of the country were also reported. The media could no longer ignore the struggle despite Coca-Cola's arm-twisting. Coca-Cola finally acknowledged that there indeed was a problem with water but that they were not responsible. They offered drinking water and started rainwater-harvesting programmes within the plant's premises as well as outside.

The struggle gained popularity and support from a wide range of people in the state. The main opposition party, the Communist Party of India (Marxist), organized protests against Coca-Cola, Congress (the ruling party) and the government, undermining the local party leaders who were supporting Coca-Cola. The local leader of the Janatha Dal party - who controlled the panchayat – had to fall in line lest he lost face. Most of the parties (except the ruling party in the state, Congress) now vie with each other in declaring their opposition to Coca-Cola's water extraction. In addition, the critical days of the U.S. invasion of Iraq led to a call for a boycott of U.S. products that caught the popular imagination in the state. Coca-Cola symbolizes U.S. imperialism in the popular mind.

As early as 4 March 2002, a private laboratory had tested the water and concluded that the water contained very high levels of hardness and salinity that would render water from this source unfit for human consumption, domestic use or irrigation. This was later corroborated by the government's Primary Health Center on the basis of an analysis carried out by the government's Regional Analytical Laboratory. They concluded that the water is not potable around the Coca-Cola Factory and asked the panchayat on 13 May 2003 to ensure that the public be informed about this. In July 2003 the British Broadcasting Company (BBC) released a damning report about finding carcinogens in Coca-Cola plant waste, based on testing done in the laboratory of the University of Exeter. Dangerous levels of toxic metals and the known carcinogens, cadmium and lead, were found in the "product" passed on to local farmers by the Coca-Cola plant as "fertilizer". Some other heavy metals, including nickel, chromium and zinc, were also present at levels significantly above those expected from background, uncontaminated soils. The BBC report was subsequently confirmed by the Kerala Pollution Control Board, the official pollution monitoring authority, on 8 August 2003, which in fact reported a figure that was more than double that reported by the BBC and four times the prescribed norm by law. The Control Board then ordered the company to stop supplying the waste to others and to recover all the waste transported outside and to store it safely on the plant site. The same board, in an attempt to placate Coca-Cola, subsequently carried out one more tests, which reported negligible traces of carcinogens, but which the government itself had to reject as being conducted in an unscientific and careless manner.

The Perumatty panchayat, where Plachimada is located, cancelled the license issued to the Coca-Cola Company on 7 April 2003. This was challenged by the company, and the High Court asked the government to take a decision. The government upheld the decision of the panchayat to cancel the license on 12 June. On 16 December the High Court directed Coca-Cola to close all the boreholes and to stop extracting ground water beyond what was required for irrigating 38 acres of land. Further, the government was asked to carry out elaborate investigations into all allegations related to water and contamination of water and land. The government ordered the Coca-Cola factory to stop extracting any more water till mid-June when the monsoon is expected to break, in view of the precarious drought condition now. Production has ceased for the time being. The State and the Court continue their dilatory tactics that favour Coca-Cola.

The struggle of the Adivasis of Plachimada continues, as the situation remains the same. This struggle has become well known as a symbol of the struggle against imperialist globalization.

Northeast

The year 2003 was a distressing one for most indigenous peoples in Northeast India. Inter-ethnic clashes, threat of loss of livelihood due to development projects and military confrontation with Indian security forces saw more than a 1,000 die and many more displaced from their homes. The violence can be attributed in part to the increasing militarization of ethno-nationalist political movements and partly to the growing impoverishment of the different sectors of the economy in the region. Although a cease-fire is in effect in Nagalim, many other areas of the region remain in a state of emergency.

The Indian government's approach to resolving the conflicts has traditionally been a military response. In 2003, the government attempted to resolve some of the disputes by using administrative and political arrangements that attempted to devolve more powers to the indigenous peoples. However, these efforts have delivered very little except more conflict. One of its sources is the administrative measure that (presumably) exists to restore a sense of parity among indigenous peoples of the region. The structure for addressing indigenous peoples' issues in Northeast India relies on colonial regulations, which were incorporated in the Sixth Schedule of the Indian Constitution.[1] The Sixth Schedule is supposed to provide judicial, legislative and executive self-rule through autonomous district councils. However, these councils have not been able protect the lands and culture sof the indigenous peoples and instead have become contentious instruments of governance themselves. In theory the Sixth Schedule recognises community ownership of land and forests, but in reality the administration is oriented toward individual ownership. It treats the village chief as the owner and makes land transfer by him somewhat easy. That creates a contradiction and slowly moves the communities towards individual ownership and class formation with some persons acquiring individual titles and others being deprived of their share.

Contest over territory and resources

The fact that the Sixth Schedule does not resolve issues of custodianship over resources and justice was highlighted in three cases during the year in the state of Assam. In April, two indigenous groups - the Dimasa and Hmar - residing in the autonomous district of North Cachar Hills, carried out a series of attacks that involved armed militia owing allegiance to both groups. Growing impoverishment and contests over territory were cited as the reasons for the clashes. Similarly, in the other autonomous district in Assam, Karbi Anglong, the United People's Democratic Solidarity (UPDS), an armed opposition group seeking to redress the loss of land and resources of the Karbi people, issued a "quit" notice to other ethnic groups in the district. In the past, UPDS had also targeted Hindi-speaking settlers, who they believed had taken over much of the land in the foothills. The granting of Sixth Schedule status to the ethnic Boro community precipitated the militia's reaction. Later in the year, the Karbi armed group was alleged to have condoned the exodus of Pnar Khasi farmers from a disputed block in the district. This exodus set off a series of retaliations against Karbi students and labourers in the neighbouring state of Meghalaya, where the ethnic Khasi dominate. The Kuki in the Karbi Anglong district also came under attack. They were displaced by the Kuki-Naga conflict in neighbouring Manipur in the 1990s and occupied common land belonging to the Karbi tribe. With many immigrants from the Hindi-speaking region occupying their land, a section of the Karbi armed opposition groups began to defend their right over land and the Kuki were among its targets.

Similarly, the formation of the Boro Territorial Council (BTC) - touted as the government's showpiece for conflict resolution - created an unprecedented protest. The administration and a part of the Boro community, especially the armed militia, Boro Liberation Tiger Force, welcomed the BTC. Other ethnic groups who were left out of the political manoeuvring created a forum and decried the granting of special status to a section of the populace who, they claimed, were not a majority in the area. This sparked off conflicts mainly between sectarian political groups owing allegiance to the pro-BTC political forces on one hand, and the indentured tea plantation workers (Adivasis from central and eastern India) on the other. In June 2003, the police shot at least eight Adivasis in Darrang district as they were calling a strike against the formation of the BTC.

The end of the year also saw strikes by indigenous people in the Luit (Brahmaputra) valley against Hindi-speaking settlers and migrants. The violence was sparked by a dispute regarding jobs in the railways but has a more insidious aspect to it. Hindi-speaking settlers have been among the latest group to move to the region. Unlike the peasant-immigrants of the 1960s and 1970s, the Hindi-speaking settlers are perceived to be very close to the structures of power. The fact that they are from the same ethnic background as many key government officials involved in the counter-insurgency programme, seemed to have added fuel to the vicious targeting of settlers.

Dams and displacement

In addition to militarized violence, the sanctioning of several huge hydro-projects in the region has added to the insecurity of indigenous agriculturalists. In western Assam, the Pagladiya dam threatens to displace, by official count, more than 20,000 individuals from their farms. The people threatened with displacement, 90% of them Boro tribals, claim that the number is much higher. It will also deprive thousands more of their land without being physically displaced. Those protesting against the construction of the dam have struggled with government apathy on issues of resettlement and rehabilitation. The affected people have received a further jolt by the Government of India's proposal to link major rivers in the country. Environmentalists and human rights activists have criticized the project for its lack of consideration for the damage it would cause to the fragile ecosystems in the region.

The Hmar-Dimasa conflict in Assam is also linked to one such project. The Hmars, threatened with displacement by the Tipaimukh dam in the neighbouring Manipur were pushed into the North Cachar Hills in Assam in search of land. This dam will submerge 275.5 sq. km of land, most of it belonging to the Hmar and Zeliangrong tribes. By official count it will displace 1,461 Hmar families. The real number seems to be much higher because the Hmar live in a community ownership culture not recognized by the law. As a result, a large number of them whose families have lived for hundreds of years on community land, are not even recognized as displaced persons. They will get neither compensation nor resettlement and will have to go elsewhere in search of land.

Threatened displacement of the indigenous tribal communities in Arunachal Pradesh has the potential to cause new conflicts. For example, by official count, the Lower Subansiri dam will displace only 38 families. In practice several thousand families will be deprived of their livelihood but will not be included among the displaced because they live on community land and Arunachal Pradesh is not included in the Sixth Schedule. Many more will be deprived of their community land without being physically displaced. However, they find it difficult to resist their displacement because the region is sparsely populated.

Peace initiatives

There has not been any major ethnic conflict in Manipur though a solution has not yet been found to the simmering tension between the Naga and the Meitei communities. However, civil society groups of the Naga as well as their counterparts in the Imphal Valley have been making an effort to bring about better understanding between these two communities. The peace efforts made by the Catholic and Baptist churches working with the leaders of the Dimasa and Hmar tribes also extended to the Hmar communities in Manipur. There have been several efforts to make peace with the Khasi and Garo armed opposition groups in Meghalaya with the lead being taken by the Baptist and Catholic churches. However, counter-insurgency measures continue in this state and often hamper the peace efforts.

Thus, amid conflicts there is some hope of peace facilitated mainly by the civil society. However, these efforts cannot succeed unless the state is ready to address the justice issues linked to the livelihood and culture of the indigenous peoples of the Northeast. ❑

Note

1 The Sixth Schedule of the Constitution of India contains provisions as to the administration of tribal areas in some of the states in the Northeast (Assam, Meghalaya, Tripura and Mizoram), and specifies which areas are tribal areas. (Ed. note)

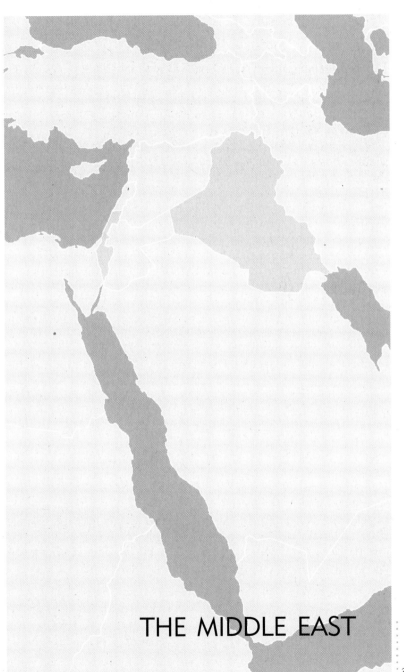

THE MIDDLE EAST

THE MARSH DWELLERS OF IRAQ

The Mesopotamian Marshes are located in the triangle between Amara, Nassriya and Basrah and represent a unique aspect of our global heritage and resources.[1] They play a key role in the intercontinental flyway of migratory birds, they support endangered species and sustain the fisheries of the Persian Gulf.

Their recent historical extent varied between 20,000 and 30,000 square kilometres. The legendary Epic of Gilgamesh was enacted on the shores of the marshes.[2] World-renowned archaeological sites on the fringes of the marshes include Ur, Uruk, Eridu, Larsa, Lagash and Nina. The dwellers[3] of the marshes have lived in harmony with the environment in a culture uninterrupted since the time of the ancient Sumerians. They traditionally constructed artificial islands, made of layers of reed and mud, on which they constructed their homes using woven reeds. They fed the sprouting reeds to their water buffaloes and they used the dung of the water buffalo for fuel. They depended on fishing and hunting, and they planted rice and tended date palms along the edges of the marshes. Cuneiform tablets document essentially the same way of life since 3,000 BC.

Following the end of the Gulf War in 1991, the people of Iraq revolted against the regime. The Marsh Dwellers were important figures in the uprising against Saddam Hussein's regime and the marshes offered a safe haven for the resistance. To end the rebellion and control the region, the Iraqi regime instituted a program for the systematic desiccation of the marshes through the combined actions of upstream damming and downstream drainage projects. Thought to have numbered some 250,000 in 1991, many of the Marsh Dwellers died during this time. Others remained in the dry remnants of the marshes, mostly along the fringes of the Tigris and Euphrates Rivers; others again were internally displaced. By the beginning of 2004, estimated populations were: 80,000 Marsh Dwellers within the marshlands, 50,000 internally-displaced in the Basrah governate, and 20,000 in Iranian refugee camps, with additional internally displaced persons across the country and other refugees scattered across the world.

Restoring the marshes

With the fall of the former Iraqi regime, the Marsh Dwellers immediately began to request the return of water flow, and the local water

authorities complied. Since May 2003, the inundated areas of the marshlands have doubled in size. Some of these areas have become re-vegetated with reeds and aquatic wildlife is returning; other re-flooded areas remain barren. Studies are ongoing to resolve this issue. In the re-flooded areas, Marsh Dwellers are returning. They are apparently migrating outwards from the remaining population centres, and from farming communities further north. In some instances, they are returning to their own land, in others, they are returning to a completely different area because their historic land remains dry.

Problems and hopes

Serious problems remain. There are no schools, no clinics, no clean water and no sanitation. Most of the Marsh Dwellers are living at

Guesthouse constructed in summer 2003 - (on the left) Inside of new guesthouse.
Photo: Eden Again (Azzam Alwash, 2003)

subsistence level or below; there are few economic opportunities in the reviving marshes at this time. The land is littered with the military waste of four wars. Areas are being re-flooded at the request of local inhabitants with no systematic planning. The result is a patchwork of small, disconnected marshes that cannot function effectively and may be doomed to failure. The ecosystem of the re-flooded areas is being over-harvested by the returning Marsh Dwellers. Since there will not be enough water to restore all of the former marshlands, how will the water be equitably distributed amongst the competing interests? Land ownership could also become a significant issue. The Marsh Dwellers traditionally held the land communally. Later, sheikhs were given title over their tribal territories. In the 1990s, members of the former Iraqi regime were granted deeds to large areas of the dried marshlands. Beyond tribal and family affiliations, there are no organized indigenous groups. The Marsh Dwellers themselves yearn for their traditional lifestyle amid blue water and green reeds, yet they also want cell phones and the internet on their floating reed platforms. All of these competing needs have to be resolved.

But there is also cause for great optimism. Unlike those of many drained wetlands, the inhabitants of the Mesopotamian Marshes want their natural ecosystem restored. Contrary to information from the former Iraqi regime, there is enough water available to restore much of the wetlands. Other countries in the region, including Kuwait and Iran, are

Women bringing home supplies. Photo: Eden Again (Azzam Alwash, 2003)

expressing interest in cooperation. There is strong international support; the Italian Ministry of the Environment and Territory and the U.S. Agency for International Development have each pledged several million dollars towards this effort. And with the healing of the ecosystem, we hope that the cultural life of the marshlands will also find new life.[4] ❏

Notes

1   See UNEP Annual Report 2001.
2   The Epic of Gilgamesh is believed to be the oldest written story on Earth. It comes to us from Ancient Sumeria, and was originally written on 12 clay tablets in cuneiform script. It is about the adventures of the historical King of Uruk (somewhere between 2750 and 2500 BC).
3   The Marsh Dwellers are sometimes referred to interchangeably as "Ma'dan" or "Marsh Arab." The term "Marsh Arab" originally referred to the group of Bedouins who moved into the marshes sometime between 200 and 2000 years ago from the Arabian peninsula; the term "Ma'dan" may refer to a Marsh Dweller or may be used to mean "rustic" or "boor." There are also differences between tribes of the different marshes. "Marsh Dwellers" is used herein to be inclusive of all who live in the marshes. See **Salim, S.M. 1962.** *Marsh Dwellers of the Euphrates Delta*. London: University of London, Athlone Press).
4   For more information on the Marshes:
     http://www.iraqfoundation.org and www.edenagain.org

ISRAEL

As 2003 came to an end, the 77,000 Bedouins living in "unrecognized villages" in the Negev Desert of Israel, could look back on a year of increased harassment and human rights abuses as the Israeli authorities continued their policy of house and crop destruction, and took steps to concentrate them into townships.

The Sharon Negev Development Plan

An estimated 130,000 Bedouins live in the Negev.[1] They all have Israeli citizenship. Some 55,000 reside in seven recognized "townships" listed among the poorest in Israel; the remaining part live in 49 "unrecognized villages". These villages lie either on land the Bedouins inhabited before 1948, or on land they were transferred to and concentrated in the Sayig Zone (reservation). Yet, these villages do not exist officially. This means, among other things that they don't appear on maps and that all constructed structures are considered to be illegal and therefore susceptible to demolition.[2]

Now, the very existence of these villages is threatened. In early 2003, the Israel government approved the Sharon Negev Development Plan with a budget of US$ 250 million and a time frame of six years. The objective is to concentrate the residents of the unrecognized villages into townships. This will allow the Israeli government to take over the land the Bedouins are currently using and convert it into 17 new Jewish settlements and 30 one-family farms.

The Negev plan is part of the government's Judaization policy, which aims at "redeeming" vast tracts of Bedouin and Palestinian-held land in the two most densely populated Arab areas inside Israel – the Galilee in the north and the Negev in the south. According to Adalah, a Palestinian Israeli NGO providing legal defence to the Arab minority, Arab municipalities in the Galilee control just 16 % of the land despite making up 72 % of the population. In the Negev, Arab councils control less than 2 % of the land despite comprising 25 % of the population. In what may turn out to be the largest settlement effort inside the Green Line in the last 25 years, the Prime Minister's Office is planning to establish some 30 new settlements, most in the Galilee and the Negev. These new settlements are conceived of as assisting

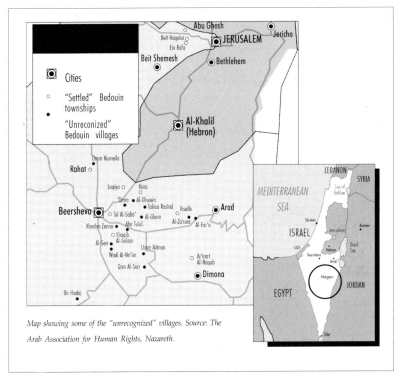

Map showing some of the "unrecognized" villages. Source: The Arab Association for Human Rights, Nazareth.

in the distribution of the Jewish population away from the center, in preserving state lands and in providing protection for the borders. Part of the project also includes the expansion of the project of settlement by individuals who intend to set up farming areas, called *Havat Habodedim*. As Uzi Kern, the adviser to Prime Minister Ariel Sharon on settlement stated, this will involve "unique individuals" who will be in charge of large tracks of land and serve as a local security guard.[3]

House demolitions

House demolitions were stepped up in 2002, and continued in 2003. Figures vary but according to Adalah, the authorities demolished 55 structures in the Negev: 36 homes, 14 shops, 3 farms, a water reservoir, and a mosque.

The mosque that was demolished in early February in Tel al-Milah set a precedent - this was the first time a holy site was bulldozed by the Israeli authorities. A team of lawyers from Beer Sheva successfully obtained a high-court ruling rendering demolition of mosques illegal,

but five months later - on 13 July - the Israeli Land Authority nevertheless issued a demolition order for a mosque and four houses in the
village of Attira (in the Yatir Forest). Due to presence of activists in the
mosque and in the village, Attira's buildings were not demolished on
the scheduled day, but in nearby Hura, Lakiya, Zilafi, and Rahat (i.e in
both recognized and unrecognized villages) homes were demolished.

The mosque and the homes of Attira remain slated for demolition.
As is the case throughout the Negev, the buildings in Attira are subject
to demolition because they have been "illegally" constructed. Although
the Bedouin were relocated to this land tract by the government in the
early 1950s, the residents have no legal way to build, as the government
still does not officially recognize their ownership of the land. It appears
that Attira's demolition orders relate to the government-approved
plans to build a new Jewish settlement in Yatir, a highly political
area, adjacent to one of 30 new single-family farms.

In July 2003, Bedouin citizens living in three unrecognized villages in the
Negev received warning notices, stating that they were living in illegal
buildings built on land owned by the state. The notices affect at least 1,500
people, who are living in the unrecognized villages of al-Dahiya, al-
Misaadiya, and 'Ateir. Both al-Dahiya and al-Misaadiya have existed since
before the creation of the state of Israel in 1948, but are not recognized by the
state. 'Ateir is a village created by the state in 1956 when its inhabitants were
internally transferred from their original land west of Rahat.

In September, the Jewish newspaper *Ma'ariv*[4] reported that the government of Israel planned to start a "governmental campaign to demolish
hundreds of Arab-owned houses" under the pretext of unlicensed building. The newspaper indicated that the Negev would be the main aim in
this campaign, in addition to Arab villages in the Galilee and the Triangle. In October five families from Alganmi in Umm Matnan received
orders to demolish their houses. Failure to do so is punishable by a large
fine, the non-payment of which is punishable by imprisonment.

Crops destroyed by toxic fumigation

Crop destruction was carried out twice in early 2003. On 3 March,
without prior warning, two airplanes belonging to the Israel Lands
Administration (ILA), accompanied by a large number of police and
the Green Patrol (a division of the military police dealing with the
Negev), sprayed toxic chemicals such as Roundup on more than
2,000 dunams (500 acres) of crops belonging to the residents of
Abda, an unrecognized village in the Negev. According to the Re-

gional Council of the Unrecognized Villages in the Negev (RCUV) elderly people and children who were in the fields were also sprayed. The children had to be evacuated to the closest clinic at Matsba Ranoun (a nearby Jewish locality), but the doctor refused to receive them until RCUV Vice President contacted the Ministry of Health and Kubat Houlim (the health insurance company).

On 2 April another attack occurred with airplanes spraying the cultivated land of six villages - some 5,500 dunams. A few days later, thousands of Bedouin citizens from the Negev rallied in the streets of Beer Sheva to protest. Hundreds of policemen accompanied by airplanes and cars to spray water, used force against the demonstrators to keep them away from the main street. Studies published in recent years have revealed a correlation between Roundup and elevated levels of congenital defects (among Minnesota farmers), as well as impaired fertility in livestock.[5]

The case of Wadi el Na'am

In September, the El Azzazme Bedouins' case on the issue of their proposed transfer and resettlement was heard by the Supreme Court. The case concerns two groups of Bedouins from the same tribe living in two separate areas, one in Wadi el Na'am, a village, and the other near the Jewish development town of Yerocham. The case has dragged on since 1998, when the Bedouins first received an evacuation order, and this was its third appeal. The ruling at the district court in Beer Sheva three years ago was in favour of the State - the El Azzazme Bedouin were told they must leave immediately, "without leaving a trace of their existence," and go to live in Segev Shalom, a government-built township.

The Bedouins appealed the case but not because they have any particular attachment to Wadi el Na'am, which was founded in 1953 when the Israeli government relocated them from their original village, Halasa. Today Wadi el Na'am with 4,000 inhabitants is one of the largest unrecognized villages but is not connected to water, electricity, sewage, or any other state infrastructure. Furthermore, it is adjacent to the Ramat Hovav industrial zone where Israel's most polluting industries are concentrated, and a hazardous chemical material disposal site exposes the population to extreme health risks on a daily basis. So while the villagers would not mind moving to another location, they want to preserve their traditional agrarian and pastoral way of life and resist being uprooted and transferred into a structurally neglected city that also lies in the immediate vicinity of Ramat Hovav and has rampant unemployment and disproportionately high rates of crime and drug abuse.

At the hearing in September, the land authority presented its standing offer that includes a move to the Segev Shalom or a new township to be established as part of Sharon's Development Plan, "Bir – Chayil." They stressed that the Bedouins would not be removed forcibly in the near future provided they abide by two stipulations: the first that they move away from areas retroactively zoned as "closed military zones" and the second, that they refrain from any and all "illegal building".

The Bedouin Rights' lawyers spoke of the ineffectiveness of the protracted negotiations with the land authority. They were afraid if the case was dismissed and they no longer had the protection of the Supreme Court, then the El Azzazme Bedouins would be forcibly expelled by the police without having reached an agreement. They appealed for the judge to appoint a mediator and allow the sides more time to arrive at an agreement. After considerable deliberation the judges decided to postpone their ruling indefinitely. After promising to give thought to the idea of a mediator, the session was adjourned.

So far nothing further has happened. By the end of the year, people were still living in Wadi Na'am and thanks to the support of an NGO coalition headed by Bustan L'Shalom and the active involvement of the residents and volunteers, many of them Israeli, a fully equipped medical clinic was under construction.

Hate speech

The implementation of house and crop demolitions and the resettlement policy have been accompanied by an inflammatory public campaign against the Bedouins, raising the spectre of "a Bedouin effort to take over the Negev" and "create a linkage between the West Bank and Gaza Strip which would cut Israel in two." The "unrecognized" Bedouin villages are presented as pawns in this program of "a creeping Palestinian annexation of the Negev", and therefore, destroying them and concentrating the Bedouins in small areas is conceived as "self defence" and defence of "national security". Further elements in this campaign are assertions of high Bedouin involvement in crime (e.g. extortion, burglaries and drug-trafficking). Anti-Bedouin propaganda also includes a highly prejudiced presentation of the practice of polygamous marriages still prevalent among some of the Bedouins.

The campaign is conducted by such people as Tzahi Hanegbi, Minister for Internal Security, who has "instructed the police to give priority to Bedouin crime in the Negev" and Prof. Arnon Sofer of Haifa University who is doing detailed research about "the demographic threat" posed to Israel by Bedouins and other Arabs. Newspapers such as *Ma'ariv* sometimes give extensive space to such allegations.[6]

Health report

Physicians for Human Rights - Israel (PHR-Israel)[7] and the Regional Council for the Unrecognized Villages in the Negev (RCUV) have released a new report entitled: "No Man's Land - Health in the Unrecognized Villages in the Negev".[8] The report addresses the state of health and the realization of the right to health in 46 unrecognized Arab-Bedouin villages in the Negev.

The report gives an overview of the physical, environmental and sanitary conditions in the unrecognized villages and how the current situation makes it difficult for Arab Bedouin communities to lead a healthy life and to secure such a life for their children. For example, infant mortality rates among the Arab Bedouin population are the highest in Israel. In 2000, the rate was 14.7 per 1,000 live births – compared to 3.9 per 1,000 births among the Israeli Jewish population. The elevated rate is explained by various factors, including congenital defects, premature births, infectious diseases and factors defined as "other" or "unknown", which account for 14% of fatalities.

Summing up, the report concludes that

> *Since its establishment, the State of Israel has denied the basic right to health to a significant group of its citizens, and, in so doing, has tarnished its own standing. The limited services provided for the residents of the unrecognized villages are the result of petitions to the High Court of Justice. The residents' claims are usually accepted by the court, since the state's policies are clearly inconsonant with the principles it has set itself – equality, equitable distribution and non-discrimination among its citizens.*

Declaration by CESCR

In a concluding report published in 1998 on the implementation of the Covenant on Economic, Social and Cultural Rights in Israel, CESCR

- the UN committee responsible for the implementation of the covenant - noted its regret that the plan for the development of the Negev envisaged a future in which little room would be left for the Arab citizens of Israel, whose needs were not addressed.[9]

Five years later, in a report published in 2003, the committee had the following observations:

> *The Committee continues to be concerned about the situation of Bedouins residing in Israel, and in particular those living in villages that are still unrecognized... the quality of living and housing conditions of the Bedouins continue to be significantly lower, with limited or no access to water, electricity and sanitation. Moreover, Bedouins continue to be subjected on a regular basis to land confiscations, house demolitions, fines for building "illegally", destruction of agricultural crops, fields and trees, and systematic harassment and persecution by the Green Patrol, in order to force them to resettle in "townships". The Committee is also concerned that the present compensation scheme for Bedouins who agree to resettle in "townships" is inadequate. The Committee further urges the State party to recognize all existing Bedouin villages, their property rights and their right to basic services, in particular water, and to desist from the destruction and damaging of agricultural crops and fields, including in unrecognized villages.[10]* ❑

Notes and references

1   The Bedouins constitute about 12% of the Arab Palestinian 1.2 million large minority still living in Israel.
2   See *The Indigenous World 2002-2003* for more details.
3   Zafrir Rinat. Rush order for 30 new villages inside Green Line. *Haaretz,* 20 July 2003.
4   *Ma'ariv,* 29 September 2003.
5   **Vincent F. Garry et al. 2002.** Birth defects, Season of conception and sex of children born to pesticide applications living in the Red River Valley of Minnesota, USA. *Environmental Health Perspective Supplement* 110(3): 441-449.
6   See for instance *Ma'ariv,* 3 July 2003.
7   Physicians for Human Rights-Israel (PHR-Israel) is a non-partisan non-profit organization founded in 1988.
8   The report (English version) may be downloaded from: http://www.phr.org.il/Phr/downloads/dl_155.doc
9   *Concluding Observations of the CESCR: Israel,* 4 Dec. 1998, Art. 27.
10 *Concluding Observations of the CESCR: Israel,* 23 May 2003, Art. 43. http://www.unhchr.ch/tbs/doc.nsf/

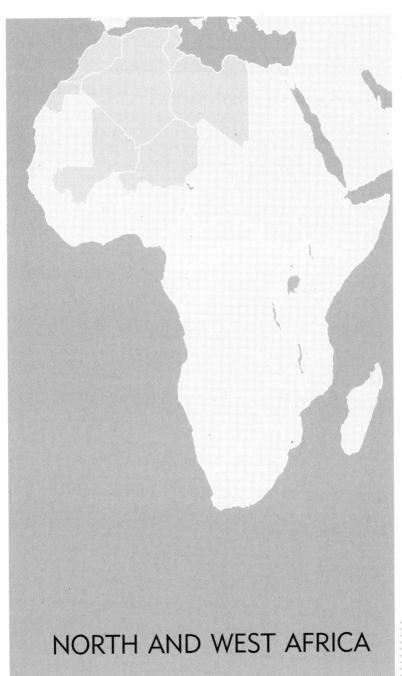

NORTH AND WEST AFRICA

MOROCCO

Crucial developments and terrorist attacks

I mportant developments and events have taken place in Morocco in 2003, which will have major repercussions on the lives of indigenous peoples in all of North Africa. Among these developments and events are the official adoption of the old Amazigh characters for the teaching of the Amazigh language and its integration - for the first time - in the educational system; the adoption of a new family law and the creation of a higher committee for information aiming at liberalizing this sector. Furthermore an "Equity and Reconciliation Committee" has been created with the aim of shedding light on disappearences and arbitrary arrests and doing justice to those who disappeared and those who were arrested arbitrarily during the post-independence period. Morocco also witnessed serious events that endangered the safety and security of its citizens and that constitute a violation of human rights. These are the terrorist attacks on May 16, 2003 and the adoption of the law against terrorism that was followed by many trials, the most important being those involving a number of journalists who were victims of harsh judgements that were criticized by defense lawyers for not fulfilling the conditions of a fair trial.

Teaching the Amazigh language

A national willingness to rehabilitate the Amazigh (Berber) culture and civilization through the unanimous recognition of the Amazigh identity manifested itself in the creation of the Royal Amazigh Culture Institute in 2002. In January 2003, the ancient Amazigh writing system, known as Tifinagh (and still used by the Tuaregs), was finally adopted to be used to teach the Tamazight language in schools. In this connection, the Royal Amazigh Culture Institute entered into partnership with the Ministry of National Education to provide the teaching of Tamazight language in about 317 primary schools as a starting point for the generalization of Tamazight language in all Moroccan schools by the year 2010. This gave little time for working on the standardization of Tifinagh (three distinct dialects are currently spoken in Morocco), preparing text books and training teachers, but thanks to the efforts made by the Institute, teaching in Tamazight was introduced at schools starting in September 2003.

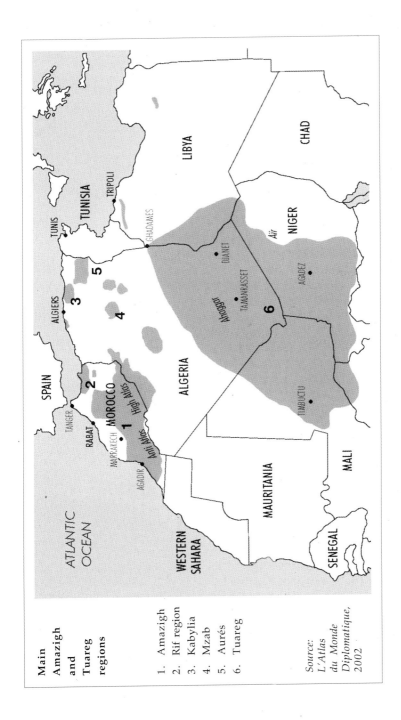

Main
Amazigh
and
Tuareg
regions

1. Amazigh
2. Rif region
3. Kabylia
4. Mzab
5. Aurés
6. Tuareg

Source:
L'Atlas
du Monde
Diplomatique,
2002

339

Terrorist attacks and anti-terror legislation

On May 16, 2003 several bomb attacks were perpetrated in different parts of Casablanca, resulting in many casualties and leaving the country in a state of shock. The attacks were later claimed by the international terrorist organization al-Qaeda through a group called "*Salafia Jihadia*". In the Moroccan Parliament there were varied opinions about the proposed anti-terrorist law, but the scale of the terrorist attacks hastened its adoption and undermined the Islamic organizations that shouldered the moral responsibility for the terrorist events. The coalescence of the Moroccan people against terrorism was swift and unwavering. The Amazigh movement was also ideologically resolute in its fight against this terrorism.

Journalists arrested

Subsequent to the adoption of the law against terrorism, many journalists were arrested and convicted in trials that the defence and human rights associations considered void of the principles of fair trial.

In fact, at the end of May, the journalist Ali Lamrabetwas prosecuted for lack of respect for the King and the royal regime and for threatening national unity and sentenced to three years imprisonment. Another journalist, Mustafa Ell Alaoui, was arrested on June 5, 2003 and was sentenced to one year non-enforceable imprisonment. Other imprisonment judgements were passed against Mustafa Kachini (two years), Miloud Boutriki and Abdelaziz Jallouli (one and a half years) and Mohamed El Hard (three years of enforceable imprisonment). The trial of these journalists created much public criticism, and they were all released following a royal pardon at the beginning of January 2004. The amnesty abolished all judgments against the journalists condemned during trials that did not fulfill the conditions of a fair trial.

Adoption of new family law

Through its parties and bodies, the Islamic movement has for many years formed a strong opposition against the integration of women in development, and has opposed all political currents that tried to amend the law in favour of more equality between men and women.

The Amazigh movement and the women's movement were among those calling for full equality between the two sexes.

The public rejection of the Islamic parties, whose political impact declined in parliament as well as in the public due to the terrorist attacks, prompted the King to take the initiative to state the basic principles on which gender equality should be based in his address at the opening session of Parliament on October 3, 2003. This encouraged the government and the Parliament to introduce and adopt the new family draft law characterized by major progress in the establishment of equal civil rights for men and women. The new law introduces a number of new rights for women: they are now considered as adults and full members of society, no longer submitted to the guardianship of a male; and the concept of a male head of family disappears, entrusting instead the care of the family to both the husband and the wife. Repudiation as a means of divorce has not disappeared but can now also be practised by the wife, and the husband faces a number of (economic) obligations if he wants to repudiate his wife. The legal age of marriage for a girl increases from 15 to 18 years, and she now has the right to marry without being represented by a matrimonial tutor. It was previously the father, brother or the judge who were entitled to give the woman away in marriage. Finally, polygamy is tolerated only when the husband fulfills a number of conditions that are difficult to meet.

Creation of the Equity and Reconciliation Committee

The Arbitration Committee which was set up to assess compensation for detention victims and the families of reported missing persons from the 1960s to 1999 ended its mission leaving the problem unresolved. This motivated the families of the victims and human rights associations supporting them to call for the establishment of a victims' rights committee. In this connection, a new body was created by King Mohammed VI, named the Equity and Reconciliation Committee whose goal is to find the truth about the fate of a number of disappeared people and compensate the victims and their families. This committee is made up of a number of human rights bodies and former detainees. The deadline for the registration of cases to benefit from compensation was set for January 12 to February 12, 2004. ❏

ALGERIA

The Amazigh (Berber) people are the first people of North Africa and the Sahel. In Algeria, between 20% and 30% of Algerians – six to eight million people – speak the Amazigh language of Tamazight.[1] Tamazight speakers today live in disparate areas of Algeria, with significant concentrations around Kabylia, Aurès, Mzab and in Tuareg country. Other much smaller areas, such as Chenoua (Tipaza region, to the east of Algiers) or the Ksours (south Oran) continue to survive in a quite frankly hostile environment.

Each Tamazight-speaking region has developed in its own way. Kabylia, geographically close to the capital, benefited very early on from the contributions of French schools. A mountainous and poor region, it was - and to a lesser extent still is - a reservoir of emigration to Europe, particularly France. Rebellious and demanding, Kabylia was and remains a hotbed of political dissent.

The area of Aurès is also mountainous and poor. Leading a pastoral life, the Chaoui (Auresians) have emigrated little. Despite a certain Arabization, the young people have, since the 1980s, become increasingly aware of their Amazigh identity and have created their own movement, the MCA (*Mouvement Culturel Amazigh* – the Amazigh Cultural Movement).

Mzab is characterised by Ibadism, a fundamentalist Islamic sect. This has historically created an inward-looking region, all the more so as there exists a complete intolerance to these people on the part of other Muslims. It was only from the 1980s onwards that the young people of Mzab began to show a cautious interest in Amazigh issues. As for Tuareg country, 2,000 km from Algiers, this is very far from the centres of political decision-making. Nomads, these "blue men" generally have little schooling and, consequently, have lost none of their traditions. Their dialect is considered a linguistic reservoir from which a prescriptive Amazigh language could be built. A small elite has, for some time, formed part of the Berber protest movement of northern Algeria.

Arabization policy in Algeria

The vicissitudes of history have meant that the Amazigh language has now been reduced to the level of dominated language. A centralist state, Algeria has long believed that Tamazight could be a factor in undermining national unity and destabilising the established institutions. The Arab language was universalized and Arabization campaigns run for many years. Tamazight became confined to home use, and was perceived as a method of communication among the uncivilised, thus creating a deep sense of "linguistic insecurity" among its speakers. But in spite of all this, the Amazigh language has lost none of its vitality. On the contrary, the effect of all the state's efforts to "de-Berberise" Algeria has been none other than to strengthen the struggle to maintain an Amazigh identity.

The protest movement and the Amazigh spring

Initial awareness of identity and language dates back to the start of the last century, and local francophone authors. Subsequently, since the 1940s, the rhetoric of protest - in terms of the right to language and identity - has become explicit. Put on hold during the war of liberation, the demands (both political and cultural) were taken up once more after independence. Initially cultural, with permitted courses in Tamazight given by Mouloud Mammeri (writer and university lecturer of Kabyl origin, considered to be the spiritual father of the Berber cultural movement), the protest rapidly became political, particularly with the activists from the *Front des Forces Socialistes* (Socialist Forces Front) who, around Dr Sadi – the current President of the RCD, the *Rassemblement pour la Culture et la Démocratie* (Gathering for Culture and Democracy) – led the events at Tizi-Ouzou (Kabylia) in 1980, known as the *Amazigh spring*.

Mouloud Mammeri, invited by the university community of Tizi-Ouzou to a conference on ancient Kabyl poetry, was prohibited from speaking by the local political authorities. This led to street demonstrations, which rapidly took on the air of an uprising. The state was nowhere to be seen for two weeks, until it brutally intervened with the storming of the university and hospital. The toll of this repression was hundreds wounded and many arrests. Far from pacifying Kabylia, this led to a pre-secessionist movement that forced the Governor to free those arrested in an effort to reduce tensions.

The protest, however, began to expand and awareness grew. The Berber Cultural Movement (*Mouvement Culturel Berbère* - MCB) appeared, with its main demands: democracy and freedom of speech; the teaching of popular languages - Tamazight and the local Arab dialect; and, subsequently, national and official language status to be given to Tamazight.

The introduction of multi-party politics (1989) gave rise to many hopes but these were soon to be dashed. In 1990, the MCB organised a peaceful march that attracted more than a million people to Algiers. The result: two Tamazight language-teaching departments were opened in Kabylia. These two university structures had the distinction of teaching the first Master's degree in the Amazigh language. Then silence once more. In 1994, the organisation called for a "satchel strike" to demand the teaching of Tamazight. Once more the authorities gave way. This student strike enabled the establishment, albeit cautiously, of a High Commission for Amazigh Identity (*Haut Commissariat à l'Amazighité* - HCA), an institution reporting to the Presidency of the Republic and responsible, in theory, for promoting, establishing and spreading the teaching of the Berber language. In fact, it was an "integrationist/co-opting" institution that was to act only half-heartedly, significant resources never being made available to its staff. Eight years on, its impact remains very limited. The human, material and financial resources allocated to it enable no more than a few scientific symposia or cultural events to be organised.

The status of Tamazight teaching has, nonetheless, changed. Departments have become whole institutes and the first "wave" of graduates are already in post. There is a need, nonetheless, to put this success into perspective, for the number of students is continually in decline due to strong pressure from the authorities (demand for paternal authorisation, refusal to teach Tamazight on the part of some establishment heads, etc.).

The Black Spring and the status of national language

The murder of a young secondary school student in a village in Tizi-Ouzou (upper Kabylia) at the hands of a police officer in April 2001, within the police station itself, was to cause turmoil in this region, ending in bloodshed: 123 young people dead under police fire and hundreds more disabled for life. Children scarcely in their teens were shot in the back with exploding bullets (doctors' certificates, photographs, video footage, written and recorded statements all support this).

Following these events, the social Aârch movement (confederation of tribes) organized into a structure. Every village and all of Kabylia's districts appointed delegates to represent them in decision-making. In addition to the almost daily demonstrations organised locally, it was decided to march to Algiers. This march attracted between 500,000 and one million people (depending on the source). Once more, the state resorted to repression. But the many arrests could not stop the enthusiasm of the young Kabyls. Quite the opposite, the social movement grew and solidarity committees sprang up in Aurès and in Algérois.

Given the extent of the movement, the Algerian government ratified the President of the Republic's decision to grant the Berber language national language status (2002).[2] The aim of this purely symbolic status was to calm the people down. But it was too late; too much blood had already been spilt. This achievement, which might have been heralded as a great success in other times, went unnoticed: too high a price had already been paid.

Nevertheless, Tamazight remains the poor relative in Algerian linguistic policy. No special budget has been granted to right this historic wrong in any way. The teaching that is provided on certain courses, and only in Kabylia (hotbed of protest), remains ineffectual as it is still not allocated a mark that could improve a pupil's annual average. Not to mention the continual attempts to divide the sparse teaching body and pupils over the choice of transcription (Arab, Tifinagh or Latin) when the Amazigh-speaking community has already opted in favour of the Latin alphabet, chosen for its universality.[3]

The Algerian Constitution and the Amazigh issue

It was not until 1996, and the second revision of the 1976 Constitution, that the term Amazigh appeared in the constitution for the first time. Algerian identity – thus far based on Arab-Islamic ideology – was reviewed and corrected, since it states (in the preamble in bold type) that its fundamental components are Islamic, Arab and Amazigh. It should be noted, nonetheless, that no law includes this latter component within the body of its text.

2003, a year of extremes

The year 2003 was both the year of the greatest repression of the civilian population and also that of the greatest progress for Amazigh identity.

The Aârch movement's determination forced the authorities to agree to negotiations with its delegates on the basis of a platform of demands that would scarcely have been conceivable under different circumstances. Apart from the MCB's usual demands (Tamazight as a national and official language), the withdrawal of the police from Kabylia was explicitly requested. This request has now been partially satisfied since numerous units have, for the moment, been withdrawn from their police barracks. Pressure on the authorities has also resulted in the release of detainees.

2003 was a pre-election year (presidential elections in spring 2004), which explains the state's current and uncustomary desire to reach a negotiated solution. Everything is being done to speed up the process and some Aârch delegates are already supporting the plan of the Prime Minister, appointed by the President of the Republic to handle the "Kabylia dossier".

Other delegates, however, insist that the movement's platform should be adopted as it is, including the demand that some of the deputies and mayors elected in 2002 be removed from their respective posts. The Aârch platform calls them the "unduly elected" because they were elected with less than 10 votes as the result of the Aârch movement's successful call for a boycott of the legislative and local elections in Kabylia. However, the authorities seem uwilling to agree to this demand.

The movement is therefore at a crossroads. The schism between those willing to accept dialogue and those who do not, seems to have considerably weakened it and the authorities will, most likely, exploit this situation.

It is possible that the government and the President, who need social peace in Kabylia (the events risk spreading to other parts of the country), may go so far as to accept the delegates' grievances (including those of the hardliners). Another possibility, however, is that everything will be done to bring about a situation in Kabylia in the weeks leading up to the elections with the aim of incapacitating an electorate hostile to the current President of the Republic.

2003 also heralded the organisation of the third MCB seminar, in July, during which the Berber Cultural Movement (still not a legal entity) established its ideological platform and took the decision to move towards its first congress. Although the third seminar took place in Kabylia for practical reasons (it was the only place where its organisation would not cause substantial problems), it should be noted that large delegations from Aurès, Mzab and Chenoua also took part. A message was also sent from the Tuareg, who were not able to attend.

Conclusion

From all this, it seems that any resolution of the Amazigh issue would be a complex endeavour, given the political context of Algeria. Achievements are still the result of bitter struggles, and are never irreversible.

However much the status of national language (article 3b of the Constitution) is respected by the authorities, the Tamazight language will never truly flourish unless it obtains the status of official language, at the very least in those areas of the country where there exists a strong social demand for this. The answer to the problems of identity, culture and language in Algeria lies rather in changing the nature of the state towards more regional autonomy. This would make it possible to pacify a tense situation and avoid it drifting out of control, something which the people and the Berber Cultural Movement have thus far been able to avoid. ❏

Notes

1 This is an approximate figure, given that there has been no linguistic census since 1966. That census did note the Berber component but was marred by numerous irregularities.
2 Article 3b of the Constitution.
3 The recent choice of the Tifinagh alphabet by the Imazighen in Morocco has had no impact in Algeria. This choice is perceived as a desire on the part of the Moroccan monarchy to compromise between the "Arabisers" and the "Gallicisers". According to MCB, it would be difficult given the archaic nature of Tifinagh (consonantal and without cursive script) to develop the language in the right direction.

For more information on the MCB visit their Web site:
http://www.mcb-algerie.org

THE TUAREG PEOPLE

L ast year's edition (*Indigenous World 2002-2003*) stressed two potentially problematic issues for most of the Tuareg populations in
the Sahara-Sahel regions of northern Niger, northern Mali and southern Algeria. The first of these was the need for a full evaluation of the
refugee resettlement programme, especially the extent to which initial
grievances and the fundamental causes of the revolts of the 1990s have
been resolved. The second was the prevailing insecurity throughout
most of this region. The first has still not been addressed adequately,
while the second has deteriorated seriously during the course of 2003.
Indeed, the major problem now facing this entire region is that mount-
ing insecurity is increasing peoples' perceptions and fears that the
issues which underlay the Tuareg revolts of the 1990s in Mali and
Niger may re-emerge.

The deterioration of security

The background to the deteriorating security in Tuareg regions was
described in last year's edition. The main factors at that time were: (1)
the spill-over of Algeria's Islamist struggle, in the form of outlaws,
such as Mokhtar ben Mokhtar, and members of the militant Islamic
fundamentalist groups, notably the Salafist Group for Call and Combat (*Groupe Salafiste pour la Prédication et le Combat* - GSPC), setting up
bases in the northern zones of Niger and Mali; (2) The increase in
smuggling of illegal goods across the Sahara, notably cigarettes, hard
drugs, arms and the trafficking of illegal migrants to Europe. In the case
of trafficking people, the major gateway to the Sahara, North Africa and
Europe was Gao in Mali. However, in the course of the last year another
network, described by local Tuareg as the "Mafiosi", has opened up from
Niamey to Agades in Niger. Although Tuareg are probably only mini-
mally involved in these activities, their increasing concentration in Tuareg regions has played a major part in their destabilisation. In the course
of the last year, a third cause of insecurity and regional destabilisation
has come to the fore. This is the rise of an alleged terrorist, now dubbed
"al-Qaeda", presence in the region and the associated "counter-terrorist"
activities by the United States and their regional military allies.

The alleged presence of al-Qaeda networks in this part of Africa
stemmed from America's invasion of Afghanistan. As U.S. Air Force

Maj. Gen. Jeff Kohler, Director of Plans and Policy division for Supreme Allied Command, Europe (EUCOM), recently admitted: "As terrorist cells were uprooted from Afghanistan and elsewhere by U.S. Central Command, ...they shifted to... the wide-open, relatively desolate areas of Africa, ... an easy back door into Europe through Algeria, Morocco and Tunisia."[1] The soft under-belly of this "back-door" to Europe is the vast expanse of Sahara and Sahel that runs from Mauritania in the west, through northern Mali and Niger, southern Algeria, eastwards through Chad and into Darfur. This area, which encompasses most of the Tuareg's traditional domains of Mali, Niger and southern Algeria, is now the focus of a $100 million "anti-terror" initiative. The United States is now equipping and training troops in Mali, Chad, Mauritania and Niger as part of a Pan Sahel Initiative (PSI), to protect their countries from "terrorists". The PSI rolled into action on 10 January 2004 with the disembarkation in Nouakchott of an "anti-terror team" of 500 U.S. troops and the deployment of 400 U.S. Rangers into the Chad-Niger border region the following week. This brings the number of U.S. military personnel in the region to at least 1,000.

The image of Tuareg lands as a "terrorist" zone

The precise number of alleged "terrorists" or "Taliban elements" that moved from Afghanistan to this part of Africa is unknown. Tuareg seem inclined to place the number in dozens rather than hundreds. These elements have intermingled with pre-existing smuggling and trafficking networks, as well as local outlaws and elements of Algeria's militant fundamentalist groups, notably the GSPC. The picture that the Bush administration has created in the last few months is of a region being overrun by "terrorists", "bad people", and al-Qaeda subsidiaries. While this picture is certainly not without foundation, the "sexed up" language has done much to legitimise the U.S. military presence in the Sahel and its acquisition of base rights across the continent. The importance of this region to the United States is that it lies between American strategic oil interests in West and North Africa and hence provides a potential threat to them.

This image of Tuareg lands becoming a terrorist zone was enhanced further by the kidnapping of 32 European tourists in southern Algeria in February-March 2003. One group of hostages was freed in May after an assault by the Algerian military; the second group was taken to northern Mali where their release was negotiated in late

August. The abduction, blamed first on the Algerian outlaw, Mokhtar ben Mokhtar, and then on members of the GSPC under the leadership of Abderazzak Lamari (Amari Saifi), known as El Para, received global media attention. The abduction had two main consequences for the region. One was that it decimated tourism to the Central Sahara and thus denied Tuareg one of their main livelihoods. The other was that it proved to the Americans and their allies in the "war on terror" that GSPC "terrorists" operated across the Sahara, thus linking al-Qaeda operatives in the Sahel with those in North Africa and from there into Europe.

The veracity of this "official" version of events is doubted by those who believe that the abduction was instigated by elements within the Algerian military establishment, perhaps even with the condonation of the United States. One commentator,[2] in outlining this alternative view, pointed out that the abduction was convenient to both Algeria and the United States: by demonstrating the existence of "terrorist" activities in southern Algeria and an al-Qaeda network across the Sahara, the hostage crisis has given further legitimacy to America's prosecution of its "war on terror" and its acquisition of base rights in this part of Africa, while for Algeria the incident has almost certainly accelerated the provision of the weapon systems that it has been seeking from the United States.[3]

Some 62 members of the GSPC accompanied the hostages into northern Mali, where it was agreed that they could remain as long as they didn't bother the local population. However, their existence in northern Mali merely exacerbated the security situation in the region and in December the Algerian military, supported by American spy satellites and other surveillance equipment, moved on to an "anti-terrorist" offensive. The military's control of all news from the area, combined with rumour and official disinformation, makes it difficult to know how many "terrorists" have been killed by Algerian and Malian forces along the Mali-Algerian border region since the offensive began. While the military have confirmed that at least four "terrorists" have been killed, unconfirmed reports suggest that the number may be more than 30. The Algerian army also reports the capture of substantial quantities of arms, allegedly bought with the ransom money that is said to have been paid to the kidnappers.

Deterioration of governance in southern Algeria

While the Americans will be delighted by the apparent military suc-cess of their new ally, coinciding as it does with their own Pan Sahel

Initiative, they are unlikely to be so enamoured by the nature of civilian government in southern Algeria, particularly in the Tamanrasset *wilaya*, where the security situation deteriorated during the latter part of 2003 as a result of the regional administration's bad governance and association with smuggling, banditry and the harassment of local Tuareg.

The question of "good" or "bad" governance in Algeria tends to be located at the local level in the qualities and performance of the *wali*.[4] The problems associated with the present *wali* of Tamanrasset were outlined in last year's edition. When it became clear to local people that the central government had no intention of heeding their appeals to replace him, many began to believe that he was being "protected" by a faction in government or that he had been sent to the region with a specific but unknown agenda. Some even believed that it was to provoke local disturbances and to destabilise the region, especially as a persistent feature of his rule was to impede the tourism industry, which is the local Tuareg population's main commercial activity. A more disturbing picture emerged in December 2003 when local Tuareg discovered that senior members of the regional administration, including members of the security and tourism directorates, were associated with cross-border smuggling and banditry. Events took an even more serious turn when the police and other state officials began to harass those Tuareg who had been responsible for reporting acts of corruption and maladministration by regional officials to the central government in Algiers. President Bouteflika, whose office has been briefed on the situation, was scheduled to pay a two-day visit to Tamanrasset in mid-February (2004). Failure to remove the *wali* and clean-up local government is likely to result in increased disquiet and political tension in the region.

Warning signals from Mali and Niger

Warning signals are also beginning to be manifest in the PSI (Pan Sahel Initiative) region. America's description of the region as "uncontrolled", "ungoverned", full of "bad people" and "a base for al-Qaeda", is unlikely to endear them to local people. In northern Mali, people are beginning to ask why their lands are being "invaded" - by both "terrorists" and Americans. They want to know why the Americans have come to their land and what they want from them. Irrational as it might seem, there are those who are beginning to fear that the U.S. presence may lead to the withdrawal of aid, their further marginalisation and the return of the conditions that led to the army massacres of the previous decade.

The Tuareg regions of northern Niger are equally tense, especially following the recent uncharacteristic "mafia-style" killing (four bullets in the head and two in the stomach) of Adam Amangue (Anamegi), a young member of the ruling MNSD-Nassara (National Movement for a Developing Society-Nassara) at the village of Tchighazérine (25 miles northwest of Agades). In February 2004 the Tuareg community was shocked even further by the dismissal from ministerial office and subsequent arrest of the most prominent Tuareg Minister (for tourism) in the government, Rhissa ag Boula, for complicity in the murder. Ag Boula, who played a leading role in the Tuareg rebellion in northern Niger from 1980 to 1995, has denied any involvement in the killing. It is possible that the killing was related to the hold-up, robbery and kidnapping of a tourist group near Timia (Aïr) a few days earlier, or the recent emergence of the "mafia-type" network in Niamey and Agades involved in trafficking people across the Sahara,[5] or perhaps even the up-coming elections. It almost certainly has nothing to do with the arrival of Americans in the Sahel.

Nevertheless, the danger for the Americans in their Pan Sahel intervention is that such expressions of anxiety become associated with their arrival in the region. That will be particularly uncomfortable for an American administration that is extending itself militarily across this fundamentally hostile and complex region.

Developments in regional self-government in Mali and Niger

While the quality of governance in the Tuareg regions of southern Algeria, notably Tamanrasset, has deteriorated in the last few years, especially in 2003, the converse is probably true for most Tuareg regions of Niger and Mali. Although many of the old complaints against national government, notably the withholding and abuse of aid, are still rife, the increased regional self-government of predominantly Tuareg areas is now well developed. This has been aided by the use of the internet, with most local agencies and regional (municipal) governments now creating their own Web sites. A particularly good example is that of the Kidal (Adrar-n-Iforas) region in Mali,[6] which provides clear information on the composition and contact details of most local government bodies. While this increase in local regional autonomy may have led to an improvement in the quality of local governance in Tuareg regions, it may also be seen as the price that the central governments had to pay for ending the rebellions. It is also a reflection of their continued marginalisation and what many would argue is the further weakening and withdrawal of already weak states. This "marginalised autonomy" must also be seen within the general contexts of the deteriorating security situation in these areas and the fact that many of the issues, which underlay the rebellions, have scarcely been addressed.

Indigenous rights and Islamo-Arabism in Algeria

The governments of Algeria, Niger and Mali have all received widespread admonishment in recent years for their abuse of both human and indigenous rights. In Algeria, the latter have centred on the situation of the indigenous *Amazigh* peoples. While much has been said and written about *Amazigh* peoples in the north of Algeria, especially the Kabyles, little has been said about the situation amongst the Tuareg in the country's south. In 2003, research was undertaken to look at how far the Algerian government was in compliance (assuming that both instruments were in force) with the ILO Convention No 169 on Indigenous and Tribal Peoples and the Draft UN Declaration on the Rights of Indigenous Peoples (in its present state).[7] The findings revealed what many people might regard as a surprisingly high degree of compliancy. It should be noted, however, that this research was undertaken and published before the marked deterioration of governance in the Tamanrasset *wilaya* mentioned above.

At the social level, a major influence in all Tuareg societies, especially southern Algeria, is the pervasive impact of the processes of "Arabisation" and "Islamisation". Research published in 2003[8] has shown how these two processes, alongside that of "sedentarisation" and other aspects of "modernisation", have resulted in a considerable degradation of the position and roles of women in society, while posing serious threats to their health and general well-being.

Keenan's research,[9] published in 2003, has shown that women, in colloquial parlance, have suffered a "double whammy". The decline in the relevance of descent, especially the significance of the matriline, has undermined women's pre-eminent position in society, while sedentarisation has had a profound effect on their social roles. Working behind a reed, mud brick or stone wall, instead of the hearth of an open tent, has set women physically more apart than was the case in the encampment, and thus added to the air of seclusion that is in keeping with the increased Arabisation and Islamisation that have accompanied the process of sedentarisation.

The growth of Tamanrasset, the regional capital, from about 4,000 in the 1970s to 40,000 at the end of the 1980s and an estimated 150,000 today, has had a profound impact on Tuareg society. Once seen as external to their socio-cultural domain, young Tuareg men, attracted by the modernity that Tamanrasset offers, have pulled down the cultural drawbridge. Arabism, the contradictions inherent in the national strands of secularisation and Islamisation, the Internet, the cell phone, state controlled television and other such powerful symbols of modernity are being transplanted into the heart of Tuareg society. For the most part, this transplanting is without discernment or comprehension, reducing the virtues of both Arabic and Islamic cultures to little more than a parody of an Islamo-Arabism which advocates the seclusion of women and polygyny. Many older Tuareg, observing these lifestyle changes, have described the associated general behaviour as "debauched" and "depraved".

The most immediately noticeable changes in social behaviour in regard to marriage and the general position of women are as follows:

- Girls are marrying at a much earlier age. In "traditional" times girls usually married in their early 20s. They are now marrying much earlier, frequently as soon as they are nubile around the age of 14 or even younger.
- Many of these young girls are marrying men much older than themselves. Tuareg say this is a symptom of the increasing Arabisation of their society.
- An increasing number of marriages are arranged years in advance.
- An increasing number of marriages are ending in divorce.

Tuareg explain the last as a consequence of the two previous points. A second reason is that girls get married with the intention of getting divorced as soon as possible, and especially before having a child, so that they can free themselves from the increasingly restrictive and onerous pressures of the family, in both Islamo-Arabic cultural practice and associated legal statutes, and thus acquire some measure of independence and control over their own lives. There is also a noticeable trend amongst old women to divorce their aging husbands so that they will not have to endure the seclusion, required by Islamic law and the "family code", of four months and 10 days following the death of the husband. Further reasons are more complex and include general decline in respect for women associated with sedentarisation, Arabisation, the decline in importance of the matriline; the absence of traditional authority structures and the manipulation and abuse by men of Islamic divorce procedures.

In their ignorance of the law, women believe and fear that the new Islamo-Arabic order gives men the right to discard them and take another wife as and when they want. Several women confirmed that one reason why they are so frequently pregnant, when forms of birth control are readily available, is to demonstrate that they are still young and fertile and thus attractive to their husbands. In traditional times, women rarely had more than four children, with births usually being fairly well spaced. Although there are other reasons for the increased birth rate, notably a more assured food supply and better medical facilities, the reason frequently given by women themselves for the current high birth rate is the belief that proof of fertility, and hence youth, is their safeguard against being cast aside. The implications for women's health are serious.

The research also identified a higher rate of infant mortality today than in earlier times. A summary survey amongst one Tuareg group living close to Tamanrasset revealed that 52 of the 301 children (17%) born in the last 10 years had died in infancy. Infant mortality, as well as the noticeable difficulties many women now have in conceiving, would appear to be correlated to an increase in sexually transmitted diseases.

Older women especially feel excluded from the juridical and political process. They consider that the abolition of the traditional political system has left them with no means of appeal. They believe that the traditional system of political authority would not have allowed either the "debauched" behaviour mentioned above or the current abuse of women's marital rights. Although protected in theory by the state and the courts from such abuse, they see the courts as largely inaccessible. A particularly interesting response is that a growing number of women are deciding to live independently of men and are re-establishing themselves in the nomadic milieu in all-female communities, usually of three generations (i.e. grandmother, daughter and children).

Conclusion

The year 2003 began in a state of broad optimism with good rains and pasture in most Tuareg areas and the promise, in spite of the threat of war in Iraq, of a continued resurgence in tourism. The prospects for 2004, in the wake of the hostage crisis, increased insecurity, the Algerian-U.S. led anti-terrorist offensives, the decimation of tourism and Algeria's harassment of local Tuareg, are distinctly depressed, and with the possibility of the entire region being declared an "international crisis zone". The great misfortune for the Tuareg is that their traditional domain falls within the sphere of America's imperial grand design.❏

Notes

1   *Stars & Stripes* 15 January 2004 (European edition, 11 January 2004).
2   **Barth, M. 2003**. Sand Castles in the Sahara. 2003. US Military Basing in Algeria, *Review of African Political Economy*, 98, pp. 679-685.
3   For a review of Barth's article and an account of U.S. policy, terrorism and insecurity in this region, see: **Keenan, J. 2004**. Americans & "Bad People" in the Sahara-Sahel, *Review of African Political Economy*, No. 99, pp. 643-651.
4   A *wali* is the governor of an administrative region (*wilaya*), equivalent to a French *préfet*.
5   People-trafficking across the Sahara, mostly from West African countries to the North African coast and then to Europe, has become a huge clandestine business. Many die *en route*. In 2003 more than 17,000 illegal migrants were intercepted while attempting to enter Spain by sea. The main gateways to the Sahara for this traffic are Gao (Mali) and Agades (Niger).
6   See www.kidal.info/index.php
7   **Keenan, J., 2003**. Indigenous rights and a future politic amongst Algeria's Tuareg after forty years of independence. *Journal of North African Studies*. (Special Issue), Vol. 8 numbers 3-4, pp. 1-26. Also in: **Keenan, J. 2003**. *The Lesser Gods of the Sahara. Social Change and Contested Terrain amongst the Tuareg of Algeria*. Frank Cass, (Routledge 2004), pp. 1-26.
8   **Keenan, J., 2003**.The end of the Matriline? The changing roles of women and descent amongst the Algerian Tuareg. *Journal of North African Studies* (Special Issue), Vol. 8 numbers 3-4, 121-162. Also in: **Keenan, J. 2003**. *The Lesser Gods of the Sahara. Social Change and Contested Terrain amongst the Tuareg of Algeria*. Frank Cass, (Routledge 2004), pp. 121-162.
9   *Ibid.*

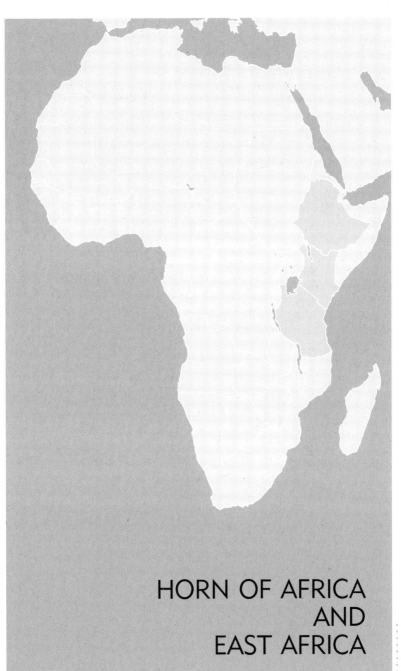

HORN OF AFRICA
AND
EAST AFRICA

ETHIOPIA

Most of the pastoral communities of Ethiopia live in the peripheral regions of the country while a minority of them live in regions of the hinterland. They constitute close to 12% of the country's population but inhabit 61% of the country's landmass, which in the main is arid and semi-arid and characterized by a harsh environment. The main pastoral ethnic groups are the Somali of Eastern Ethiopia, the Afar in the east and northeast and the Oromo of Borana in the south bordering Kenya where their kin live in northern Kenya. The other smaller pastoral communities are the Nuer of western Ethiopia whose kin live in Sudan, the Ommotic communities such as the Hamer, Arbore and Dassanetch in southern Ethiopia and the Kereyu Oromo in eastern Ethiopia.

The dynamics of change within pastoralist communities are so slow that for most of them livestock production is still the main stay of their livelihood and they still practice transhumance (seasonal movement of livestock to different grazing areas). Very few groups have become agro-pastoral combining both livestock and crop cultivation as their means of livelihood. As a result, pastoralists are believed to own most of the cattle in the country: 40% of the cattle, 75% of the sheep and 100% of the camels. Some of the biggest rivers of the country such as the Awash, Genale, Wabi Shebelle, Omo, Baro, Abay (Blue Nile) and Akobo flow through pastoral regions. Most of the national parks are situated in the pastoral regions. The pastoral regions are also believed to have other natural resources. Despite such actual and potential economic resources, they live in abject poverty and are exposed to periodic famines. Pastoral communities have been neglected for centuries and thus constitute the single largest marginalized community politically and socially.

Despite the political changes after military rule came to an end (1991), the marginalization of pastoralists has persisted. Following a rigorous advocacy campaign on pastoral rights for the last decade carried out largely by the Pastoralist Forum Ethiopia (PFE), the government has started to take the first positive steps to recognize and meet the needs of Ethiopia's indigenous pastoralists.

Developments in 2003

The year 2003 saw the outbreak of the third major famine in three decades involving some 15 million people. The most affected commu-

1. Gambella National Park   2. Omo National Park   3. Awash National Park

nities are the pastoral ones, such as the Afar who have lost most of their cattle and an unknown number of people. Other pastoral peoples such as the Somali and Southern Oromiya are also highly affected. PFE organized a roundtable on drought and famine in pastoral regions to enable the voices of pastoral elders and experts to be heard. Invariably, pastoral elders put the blame squarely on the government for completely forgetting them and for not doing what it is supposed to do as a government.

Although this was the first major drought to happen in many years, there were indications that rainfall patterns have changed and that small-scale droughts causing large-scale food shortages have taken place almost every two years since the late 1980s. These series of droughts caused large-scale destruction of cattle and property. In the years 1999-2000 Borana and Somali pastoralists lost close to 80% of their cattle due to drought. The consequences of such a loss is devastating as livestock production is the mainstay of pastoralists. With such recurrent losses and continued drought, pastoral livelihood systems are constantly at risk and pastoralists are vulnerable to impoverishment and famine. The conference spelt out this danger and passed recommendations asking the government to come up with a comprehensive pastoral development policy.

On the ground, large-scale famine relief activity - particularly in Afar - was coordinated by Oxfam (UK), and saved many lives. Despite the enormous loss of lives and cattle and the consequent precarious life that pastoral communities lead, a viable and pastoral-friendly development policy on the part of the government is still lacking. The government's policy objective as far as pastoralists are concerned is to get them into settlements. However all pastoral communities and pastoral development experts argue against settlement as the solution to fight pastoral poverty and under-development. As one pastoral elder from Borana put it at a PFE conference in 2001, settlement is the fastest way to make pastoralists perish.

Changes in government policies

Though the government has recognized the necessity of pastoral development and set up pastoral commissions in a few regions, it seems to be unclear about what pastoral development is and what it constitutes. The NGO sector, which is clear on pastoral development interventions, is not consulted at all, reflecting the persistence of the government's perception of itself as the sole actor in the development process. Consequently, the government is still preoccupied with the notion of settling pastoralists both as a precondition for their development and as an objective of its poverty reduction strategy. As such, issues and development initiatives aimed at diversification of pastoral livelihood systems have not yet been considered by policy-makers.

The government has come out with new initiatives both at federal and regional levels without changing its overall strategy of settlement. The federal government has developed a "Pastoral Oriented Education System" and is trying it in areas such as Afar. Though the substance of this system is not very well known, it has at least one component which was advocated by NGOs for a long time, namely mobile schools. This is indeed a substantial advance on the part of the government. However, problems remain with the modalities of its implementation, even as a pilot programme, as the government has no comprehensive or well thought out pastoral development strategy. The second problem is the issue of capacity, as the government has had no direct experience in pastoral development at the grassroots level. It is highly doubtful if the pilot programme will bear fruit, as the government has no intention of cooperating with those working at the grass-roots level, namely NGOs.

On the other hand, the World Bank has come up with a new pastoral initiative called the "Pastoral Community Development Project" involving millions of dollars. This project is going to be implemented with the government as the lead agency. Despite the request by the Bank to involve NGOs in the implementation of this project, the government refused. Instead, the Bank raised a sum of $ 2 million from the Japanese government that would be solely managed by the NGOs for the purpose of community development. PFE was selected as the lead contractual agency to disperse the fund for NGOs.

At the regional level, regional governments such as those of the Oromiya, Afar and the Southern Peoples, have also developed what they call "integrated pastoral development programmes" based on a strategy of settling pastoralists.

The Pastoralist Day

One unique experience in Ethiopia is the celebration of the annual Pastoralist Day on January 25. Started by the Pastoralist Concern Association of Ethiopia, a local NGO, and pastoralists from Filtu, Ogaden (Somali region, Ethiopia), the Pastoralist Day is marked colourfully. This year, the fifth Pastoralist Day was celebrated in one of the remotest areas of the country, a place called Turmi in southern Ethiopia. The day brought together elders, youth and local government representatives from various pastoral regions. This was complemented by media coverage in the capital to make the plight of pastoral communities known. During this half-day celebration, national ethnic costumes of the various pastoral communities were displayed and it was a source of inspiration for pastoralists themselves to discover the variety of the pastoral communities in the country. For many pastoral elders, the Pastoralist Day was the first occasion for them to meet members of other pastoral communities from various corners of the country. This was followed by ethnic folklore dances by the various communities displaying the richness and diversity of pastoral cultures. Apart from the national celebrations, the Pastoralist Day was also marked at local level in a number of pastoral regions and the media covered the events.

The Pastoralist Day is an important strategic tool for the PFE targeting both society and policy-makers. Ethiopian society is largely unaware of the plight of pastoralists and the fact that policy-makers neglect them - and how that impacts on poverty. A negative perception of pastoralists has existed for centuries and has its roots in the religious wars between Muslims and Christians of the 15th and 16th centuries. The traditional Ethiopian polity is dominated by Christians and two ethnic groups and has marginalized Muslims and other ethnic groups. The European scramble for Africa exacerbated this situation when Menelik, the Ethiopian emperor at the time, responded by expanding his empire. That particular expansion brought about serious ethnic inequality and the expropriation of land from newly conquered peoples and the political domination by the Amhara and Tigrayan ethnic groups. The negative stereotypes about pastoralists being unruly and uncivilized have this historical basis. As such, it isn't that easy for Ethiopian society to recognize the marginalization of pastoral communities, though a significant advance has been made in this respect due to the advocacy work by PFE. The Pastoralist Day is one of those occasions where the PFE appeals to the public to listen to the plight of pastoral communities. The Pastoralist Day is also one of those days when policy-makers are reminded of the plight of pastoralists and that they deserve an appropriate development policy and a strategy to accomplish it.

The Pastoralist Day is now being replicated to other countries, Kenya being the first to do it. NGOs in Kenya devoted the first week of December to pastoralists. The first Week of Pastoralists was marked with colourful celebrations, which combined seminars, traditional pastoral costume shows and other activities. It is expected that the week will be marked every year.

The Pastoral Standing Commission

This year, a Pastoral Standing Commission comprising 20 deputies was formed in Ethiopia's federal parliament with Abdul Karim Guleid as its chairperson. The idea of forming a pastoral parliamentary group initiated by the Pastoralist Forum Ethiopia (PFE) had been floated for sometime before its realization. The Pastoral Commission is cooperating with PFE in a bid to advance the cause of pastoral communities. The formation of the standing commission is one huge advance in the pastoral advocacy work. With the help of Minority Rights Group International (London), a regional meeting was held in Kampala that led to the establishment of an inter-parliamentary network of pastoral parliamentary groups in Ethiopia, Kenya and Uganda. This group is expected to play a positive role in advocating via the regional inter-governmental body known as the Intergovernmental Authority on Development (IGAD)[1] and the African Union. PFE is instrumental in facilitating the establishment of this regional body. PFE is at the moment working towards the formation of a pastoral NGO network at the Eastern Africa sub-regional level (the Horn of Africa and East Africa) involving national pastoral NGO networks and others not included in the national networks.

National conference on pastoral development

The third annual national conference on pastoral development organized by PFE was held on 23-24 December on the theme *Pastoralism and Sustainable Development*. The objective of the conference was to take the discourse on pastoralism beyond the immediate concerns of drought and famine and dwell on strategic issues of social development in the context of pastoral development. Important strategic directions for pastoral development were pointed out and recommended to policy-makers. The issues dwelt upon were: development strategies, capital accumulation, livestock marketing mechanisms, micro-finance, conflict management and international instruments.

Gender forum in Afar

Panos Ethiopia, which is hosting PFE, has recently expanded its gender project to five administrative regions that include Afar. The main activity is the gender forum, which involves a bi-monthly forum targeting development practitioners, gender coordinators of government institutions and NGOs, students and teachers of higher learning, religious leaders and law enforcement agencies. The objective of the forum is to reflect on gender issues particularly those that deserve policy and law enforcement. That includes deconstructing the dominant ideas behind violence against women. Violence against women in pastoral regions, particularly those based on harmful traditional practices, is rampant. Although advocating for pastoral rights is one thing, violence against women cannot be tolerated.

Violence against women in Afar takes the form of female genital mutilation (FGM), child marriage and other forms of violence related to marriage. Apart from violence, the general position that women occupy in Afar society can be described as pathetic. Women are not equal to men. They can't own property and they have no right to divorce, to inherit nor do they have access to resources. The position that women occupy in the Afar society has a lot to do with the prevalence of poverty. It is hardly possible to overcome poverty without attaining equality between the two sexes. The gender forum in Afar will be addressing these structural problems and providing tools for analysis for development practitioners, and gender project coordinators in particular. By addressing policy issues it also advocates for the introduction of new gender sensitive policies and the enforcement of existing laws that respect the rights of women such as the ones in the country's constitution. Similar concerns of pastoral women will also be addressed at two more regional forums, namely in Oromiya and Southern region, where a substantial pastoral population also lives. These are indeed extremely difficult, if not risky, undertakings in a country where policy advocacy work is considered opposition political activity. Recently, the regional parliament of the Oromiya administrative region passed a new family law, during which the issue of polygamy was fiercely debated. Unfortunately, the regional parliament passed a family law that does not make polygamy illegal. This amounts to a *de facto* legalization of the practice of polygamy. NGOs and other civil society organizations signed a petition demanding that polygamy be illegal. The response of the Oromiya regional government was to send hostile letters to those who signed the petition - letters which they took as intimidation and threats.   ❏

SPECIAL REPORT FROM GAMBELLA

IWGIA has received reports about massacres committed against the Anuak people in the Gambella region of Western Ethiopia in December 2003. The Anuak minority number over 100,000 people in Ethiopia and Sudan. According to reports from the region more than 400 people have been killed with over 200 more injured and some 85 people unaccounted for. Since December 2003, sporadic murders and widespread rapes have continued.[2] The pretext for the massacres was the ambush of a vehicle on December 13 by an unidentified gang who killed its eight passengers, who were U.N. and Ethiopian government refugee camp officials. There is no evidence that the killers were Anuak. However, government troops responded by killing hundreds of Anuak civilians in Gambella and surrounding areas and burning down their homes. Local people from highland areas are also reported to have taken part in the killings and other atrocities.[3] The organization Genocide Watch has checked these reports with eyewitnesses in Gambella as well as with the United States State Department and the United Nations, who have confirmed that the massacres were committed by Ethiopian government forces. Between 3,000 and 5,000 Anuak refugees are reported to have fled into Sudan from the massacres in Ethiopia.[4]

Grave human rights abuses are being reported from Gambella. These include dehumanising treatment of victim's bodies and the existence of mass graves, mass rape of women, control of information and restricted access to the region, and the targeting of the educated and community leaders who could lead resistance efforts. These factors are consistent with those identified by groups including the International Campaign to End Genocide (ICEG) as indicators of potential "genocidal intent" based on situations such as the Rwandan massacres in 1994.[5] Reports of an earlier massacre of Anuak in July 2002 failed to reach the international media until January 2003. The recent reports on massacres against the Anuak people have fuelled concern among international observers. The UNHCR pulled nonessential staff out of the region following the December incidents and the United States Department of State has protested the massacres at the highest level of the Ethiopian government.[6] ❏

Notes

1   IGAD (Intergovernmental Authority on Development) is a regional body formed by Ethiopia, Djibuti, Eritrea, Kenya, Somalia, Sudan and Uganda. (Ed. note)
2   Genocide Watch and Survivors Rights International. January 2004. *"Today is the Day of Killing Anuaks". Crimes against Humanity, Acts of Genocide and Ongoing Atrocities against the Anuak People of Southwestern Ethiopia.*
3   *Ibid.*
4   Survivors' Rights International *"Genocide Watch: The Anuak of Ethiopia"* 23 January 2004
5   Minority Rights Group, 13/01/2004. www.minorityrights.org
6   Minority Rights Group, 13/01/2004. www.minorityrights.org

KENYA

In Kenya, the peoples who identify with the indigenous peoples' movement are mainly hunter-gatherers and pastoralists. The total population is not known, but pastoralists alone (who comprise many different linguistic and cultural groups) are estimated to be approximately 25% of the population of 28 million people. They are mainly found in the drier northern and southern parts of the country, usually referred to as arid and semi-arid lands. There are also a number of hunter-gatherer communities mainly in the more forested areas of the country, in the central areas and small pockets in the north-eastern zone. Most of them share the languages of the more numerous neighbouring groups.

Because political representation is decided on the basis of numbers and indigenous peoples are relatively few in comparison to the more numerous farming communities, they are inadequately represented, particularly at the national level. On the local level, there are indigenous communities that have no political representation either at the council level or at the level of chiefs. Because politics to a large extent determines the economic situation in most developing nations, the weak political situation reflects an equally poor overall socio-economic situation. The infrastructure in areas occupied by indigenous peoples is generally poor and the services provided are always inadequate. This makes for poorer health, fewer educational institutions, fewer trained teachers and thus lower levels of literacy and poorer communication networks, hence inadequate levels of information, etc. Lack of information, in turn, results in inadequate interaction in the political sphere and therefore a lower level of participation in the affairs of the state, leading to little improvement in the socio-economic status of indigenous peoples.

The political and legislative context

The 2002 national election victory by the National Rainbow Coalition (NARC) was the highlight of the early part of 2003. The NARC was a coalition formed between opposition political parties (as a marriage of convenience) in order to defeat the former ruling party, the Kenya African National Union (KANU). Since only one party had ruled the country since independence in 1963, experience with coalitions was non-existent. As a result most of 2003 was occupied in disagreements

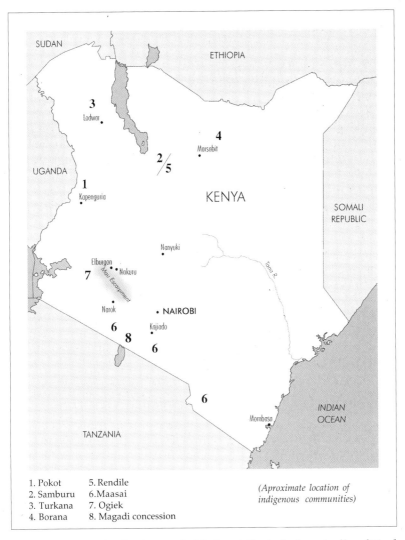

SUDAN

ETHIOPIA

3
Lodwar

4
Marsabit

2/5

UGANDA

1
Kapenguria

KENYA

SOMALI
REPUBLIC

Nanyuki

Elburgon
7   •Nakuru
Mau Escarpment

Tana R.

Narok

• NAIROBI

6
8   Kajiado

6

6

INDIAN
OCEAN

Mombasa

TANZANIA

1. Pokot	5. Rendile
2. Samburu	6. Maasai
3. Turkana	7. Ogiek
4. Borana	8. Magadi concession

(Aproximate location of indigenous communities)

relating to power sharing and this has affected almost all political discussions and actions throughout the year.

Disagreements within the ruling coalition started soon after the new government was sworn in and centred on misunderstandings on power sharing arrangements outlined in the Memorandum of Understanding (MOU), signed between the constituent parties of the coalition. By the end of the year, the disagreements between the two main parties of the coalition, notably the National Alliance Party (NAK) and the Liberal Democratic Party (LDP) had not been resolved. As a result, Kenya has a rather fragile coalition government.

Indigenous vote influenced by fear

The victory of NARC in the elections was accompanied by high expectations for better governance, transparency, reduced corruption, and better overall standards of living, in line with the election pledges made during the campaign period. These expectations were shared by most indigenous peoples. One important expectation was that there would be equitable distribution of development benefits. This is understood to mean the extension of infrastructure and social services to parts of the country that had hitherto been neglected.

But since KANU had ruled for so long, a common belief, and one shared by most indigenous communities, was that KANU would always win elections. And should this happen, it would be politically safe to vote for it since there might be reprisal against those voting against it. Opposition against the government of the day had never been tolerated before, although reprisals and collective punishment had only been experienced by indigenous communities in isolated parts of the country. Consequently, KANU won in indigenous peoples' areas although, unlike in past elections, it did not get as many votes as they usually do.

Constitution-making process continues

Matters relating to the writing of a new constitution continued for a third year running, and one of the highest expectations since the new government came into power was a new constitution within the first 100 days of its ascending to power.

During 2002, views from the public were collected, to be discussed and debated by a constitutional conference of 629 delegates. These delegates include 29 review commissioners (who are ex-officio members without the right to vote), all Members of Parliament (MPs) and three district representatives from each district, who must include at least one woman. In addition, religious organizations have 35 representatives, professional bodies 15, women's organizations 24, NGOs 23, trade unions 16, and other interest groups 13. At least one third of the civil society representatives are women.

As discussions on the constitution continued, there was concern that key members of the Kibaki administration were no longer keen on the review process and were out to scuttle it. The Commission chairman, voiced concern over an apparent lack of interest and manifest hostility to the process by people thought to be closest to the President.

The murder of the Devolution Committee chairman, further drove a wedge between the government and a section of the delegates who suspected complicity by individuals close to the government.

The third phase of the National Constitutional Conference which had been scheduled to start in November 2003, was again pushed to the following year. This was greeted with outrage, even as the President gave the government's commitment to the process. It was agreed that the final phase of the conference was to continue in January 2004 and a new constitution would be ready by June. However, by the end of 2003, the second phase of the Constitutional Conference was still going on and since disagreement marked every stage of discussion, there was little faith in the government's commitment to completing the process.

Contentious issues

Some contentious issues for indigenous peoples emerged during the Constitutional Conference. Of particular concern were the clauses that suggest devolution of power to regions and the reduction of the powers of the President. Indigenous peoples had been quite vocal all along in their support of devolution of power away from central government. This is partly because it would grant them greater control of land and natural resources that are presently expropriated by the central government. It would also create a measure of political autonomy or self-governance.

Two other important items discussed during the constitutional review conferences that were of interest to indigenous peoples and minorities were affirmative action measures for women and minority groups.

Ratification of the international convention on the rights of the child was also given a lot of publicity, and this has led to the application of the law in the protection of girl-children against female genital mutilation. This is a common practice among many indigenous communities, most of whom are ambivalent about this law and its ramifications for various reasons.

Indigenous peoples, along with peoples who called themselves minorities (including pastoralists and hunter-gatherers as well as Muslims and coastal peoples), lobbied together for issues in which they had similar interests during the constitutional review process. The terms *indigenous people, pastoralists* and *minorities* are used to refer to these peoples in the draft constitution.

Tackling corruption

While the constitutional review was staggering along, the government also addressed the issue of corruption, which was another election pledge and one that was attractive to all peoples. This was done by setting up the Goldenberg Commission of Inquiry to investigate government bribery and the Ringera Commission to investigate corruption in the Judiciary.

The Goldenberg Commission was to investigate the loss of revenue through high-level corruption, involving highly placed government officials who granted export compensation through the Central Bank to big businesses for non-existent gold and diamond exports. The scam was started in the early 1990s and came to be known as the Goldenberg Scandal.

On the Judiciary, the Commission recommended the sacking of 18 of the 36 High Court judges along with five judges of the Court of Appeal. In their place, 11 judges were appointed to the two courts.

While there was general consensus that reforms were necessary because the integrity of the judiciary had been seriously tainted, there was no agreement on how the cleanup should take place. Two tribunals were appointed to investigate the allegations levelled against the judges and these were supposed to determine the cases by December. In the meantime, some of the judges were given notice to vacate government houses while their cases were pending. In the process a number of the judges opted to resign or retire, citing witch-hunting, while those who were convinced of their innocence have decided to face the tribunals. By the end of the year, however, no tribunal had delivered any verdict.

The Standing Committee on Human Rights was re-named Kenya Commission on Human Rights and expanded to include more commissioners from different parts of the republic. Also toward the end of the year, a commission, headed by the Vice President, was set up to examine and advise government on matters relating to setting up an economic and social council.

Government initiatives on arid lands and forests

On development specifically focusing on indigenous people, the government reported that it was going to get a loan of 2.8 billion Kenyan shillings (KES) – some 36,5 million US $ - from the African Development Bank to develop arid areas. The six-year development programme, to start in July 2004, would benefit 21 arid and semi-arid districts that are occupied mainly by indigenous peoples.

On the environment, the government made a move to repossess all illegally acquired forest land. The Ministry of Lands is working on a massive afforestation and reforestation programme to be put into effect before the end of the year and the Ministry is to work closely with the Saudi government to combat desertification. At the same time, land that had been allocated to private developers in Nairobi will be repossessed. Many indigenous peoples wish this would apply to the whole country.

Lions encroach on indigenous lands

Marauding lions have killed quite a number of Maasai livestock in Kitengela area of Ngong division, located just south east of Nairobi, but outside the Nairobi National Park. This angered the local Maasai herdsmen who threatened to hunt down the lions and kill them. The Minister for Environment and Natural Resources issued a strong warning that they risked being arrested if they killed the lions. The herdsmen stated collectively, through the public media, that they would continue to kill lions whenever they kill livestock. By the time the standoff was over, 11 lions had been killed. The herdsmen are members of an association called the Kitengela Ilparakuo Landowners' Association which has lost many livestock in this manner. But the Minister, being new in the job, was unaware of the sacrifices pastoralists make to wildlife conservation and how confrontation might worsen the situation. No sooner had he given the warning than he adopted a more reconciliatory tone and no one was arrested. Instead, despite the policy of non-compensation for loss of property to wildlife, some money was paid out to cover the loss of livestock incurred by the herdsmen. However, this was a special and impromptu arrangement to fend off the crisis. The government has indicated that it will re-examine the possibility of reinstating the compensation policy. Until that time, conflict persists.

Indigenous peoples' protest rallies

In another area, the Maasai community in Naivasha made an appeal to the government to repossess land at the African Development Corporation (ADC) Ndabibi farm, which had been allocated to influential people in 1996. The community, through its spokesman, who is also the chairman of the Enaiborr-ajijik location, demanded the land be redistributed to them as former owners and as "squatters". They claim the land was initially meant for the resettlement of squatters but they were replaced by people who were not members of the community. They had pitched tents at the farm with their families and more than 5,000 heads of cattle.

In an adjacent area, members of Olkaria Maasai claimed that their cattle were dying and the health of the community had deteriorated due to poor nutrition. This was happening because most of the land originally belonging to the Olkaria Maasai is under the control of Kenya Wildlife Service (KWS), which established the Hell's Gate National Park. People residing next to the Park are subjected to regulations that the residents feel curtail their freedom of movement. The colonial and post-independence governments assumed the forests were not occupied and gazetted them as public land. This marked the genesis of the land dispute involving local communities. The land was later excised and allocated to private individuals for cultivation of cash crops such as tea, pyrethrum and flowers.

Other protest rallies organized by the Maasai of Naivasha included demands for employment at the hydro-electric power plant, which is in their area but only employs outsiders. The protest led to the brief shutdown of the plant during negotiations. It is unclear how many jobs the residents ended up with following negotiation, but talks have been initiated.

Then in Magadi area, south of Nairobi, the Maasai also protested that the 99-year leases signed with the colonial administration and which were coming to the end in 2023 should not be renewed. However, before the lease was to expire, the company requested a renewal of the lease for a further 99 years without the consent of the community. The case against the renewal is pending in court by the end of 2003.

Ogiek hunter-gatherers seek compensation

Representatives of the Ogiek community filed a case in the High Court claiming that the law had been contravened since the eviction of about 5000 members of their community from Tinet forest. Representatives of the community said the resettlement issue was dragging while members were suffering, following their eviction from south west Mau forest. They applied to the High Court as a matter of urgency for two declarations, namely, their rights to protection under the law not to be discriminated against and to reside in any part of Kenya, and secondly, their right to life which had been violated by the forcible eviction from Tinet forest. The community also sought compensation from the government.

During the 22nd session of the Governing Council, of the United Nations Environment Programme (UNEP), members of minority communities in Kenya organised a parallel civil society forum to demand land rights. The focus of the Governing Council was on environment and biodiversity. Representatives of the Ogiek, Olkaria Maasai and other small pastoralist communities in Kenya presented their cases. Prior to the symposium ,the Centre for Minority Rights Development (CEMIRIDE) also launched its study titled "Kenya's castaways: the Ogiek and National Development process."

The study indicates that the loss of ancestral lands of the Ogiek had resulted in poverty, illiteracy and poor health. It recommends that the new constitution recognise the existence of indigenous groups. It also calls on the government to ratify and implement the International Labour Organisation (ILO) Convention No. 169 on indigenous peoples. It urges that all exemptions from the logging ban in Ogiek-inhabited areas be ended.

Further, the report shows that where there are adjacent farms, some of the fertilisers used on the farms have poisoned bees, reducing honey production, an important traditional economic activity among hunter-gatherers. Logging has also destroyed the forest cover in the inhabited areas. Some of the trees and herbs have great medicinal value making the forests "pharmacies" for the community. The trees and fresh waters that surrounded homesteads are no more.

The government has been urged to resettle members of the Ogiek community as a matter of urgency. The community implicated three members of parliament with the grabbing of over 450 acres of the forest for tea cultivation. It is reported that the case was finally determined in the favour of the Ogiek, however the details are not available at present.

Education

The government underlined its commitment to free primary education by releasing KES 519 million to schools. From the initial allocation,

In order to raise community awareness on how to avoid further land loss among the Maasai, organizations like SIMOO use theatre performances.
Photo: Marianne Wiben Jensen

Destruction of the Mau Forest where the Ogiek people have traditionally been living. Photo: Marianne Wiben Jensen

The Ogiek communities are contributing to re-plant parts of the Mau Forest Photo: Marianne Wiben Jensen

each of the country's more than 17,000 primary schools will receive KES 28,871 to buy the teaching aids. Although there has been no head count of the children enrolled during the first term of the year, it is projected that first class intake would range between 1.5 million to two million, up from the usual one million. As of last year, it was estimated that there were three million eligible children who were not receiving schooling most of them drop-outs who had left because they could not afford levies or were forced out for social and cultural reasons.

A few indigenous adults and youth (commonly known as *morans*) took advantage of free universal education to join educational institutions in spite of the derision of many. However, overall, since the cost of schooling has not changed much (since uniforms, boarding facilities, some books, examination fees, etc. are not free), few indigenous children are likely to benefit from the free primary education.

Gender issues

Women have taken nine of the 12 positions given to the three qualifying parties - the NARC, KANU and Ford People. However there were accusations that the government sought to empower women through parliamentary representation by simply seeking out well-connected women. It was preferred that the choices reflect some special interests such as religious, racial and cultural groups which had been overlooked. Pastoralist, Asian and Muslim women felt left out. Overall, although the present government has made women more visible politically than at any other time in the history of the country (three women ministers to the cabinet, three assistant ministers, three judges of the High Court, etc.), most gender activists were not impressed by the way the selections were made. ❏

TANZANIA

I ndigenous Peoples in Tanzania continued to experience different impoverishing forces in the year 2003. Their livelihoods increasingly came under pressure from different circles, causing greater livelihood insecurity and frequent food insecurities. While the national economy continued to grow at the rate of between 5.8% and 6.5%, such growth is not realized in the rural areas in general and the situation in the territories of indigenous peoples in particular is getting worse.

Privatisation in Tanzania

Market economics continued to penetrate further into all segments of Tanzanian society. Public sector reforms have been implemented and several public utilities are being privatised. Globalization and liberalization policies are expected to bring about improved efficiency and increased capacity of producers to allocate and utilize resources optimally. This, in turn, is supposed to create economic and financial opportunities, offer new employment opportunities, bring in new skills, capital, and technology, increase government revenues through taxes and reduce public expenditure.

Structural Adjustment Programmes (SAPS) and different forms of market liberalization have necessitated the formulation of pro-market policies in land, agriculture, livestock, mining, tourism, and wildlife management. The National Land Policy (1995), Land Act (1999) and the Village Land Act (1999) give land a market value, with foreign capital and foreign investment being given emphasis as they are seen as the engine of economic growth.

Different public utilities, among others the National Bank of Commerce (NBC), the National Insurance Corporation (NIC), and the Tanzania Electricity Corporation (TANESCO) have been privatized. Other important institutions such as the veterinary services and National Ranches Corporation (NARCO) are in the process of being privatized and this privatization process has had a negative impact on indigenous peoples.

Greater involvement of the private sector in economic policy and management is re-structuring the economy and has widened the gap between the rich and the poor. These changes have had negative impacts on the livelihoods of the indigenous peoples.

The privatization policy has recently been re-directed to the livestock industry, with rangelands being targeted for commercial ranching. The emphasis is on profit, and it is proposed that the model adopted by Botswana should be emulated in Tanzania, since this is seen as a success story in Africa.

The initiative is intended to maximize livestock sales. It is said that Botswana[1] has a livestock population of about 3 million, that brings to the economy significant foreign earnings (estimated to be in the region of US$ 600 million per annum) compared to Tanzania that has a much bigger livestock population (estimated to be 17 million heads of cattle) and that brings only a small amount of money (estimated to be US$ 6 million a year) into the country. Commercialization of rangelands poses a serious threat of displacing indigenous livestock keepers and depleting indigenous breeds of livestock as the sector moves towards mono-cropping and promotion of exotic breeds.

Already, nearly 13 NARCO ranches of about 70,000 hectares each have been identified for subdivision into smaller portions of about 4,000 acres each and sale to private companies or individuals. Teams of foreign investors from South Africa and Zimbabwe have visited Tanzania to explore the potential in the agriculture and livestock sectors. After the visit, the teams resolved to invest in Mozambique, citing the investment climate as more favorable there.

New laws have already been introduced that are intended to control livestock diseases so that beef can be exported. However, the laws are restrictive on the movement of pastoralists and their livestock, as laws stipulate that livestock must be transported to markets on lorries. In areas where neither roads nor lorries exist, people have no choice but to walk their animals to market.

Creation of the Land Bank

Another worrying development has been the initiative by the Tanzania Investment Centre (TIC) to create a land bank. Letters were written to all regional commissioners who in turn wrote to all village executives, asking them to provide information related to all village lands. The letters specifically asked village executive secretaries to provide information on the total acreage of land that could be included in the TIC Land Bank for investment purposes. Foreign investors coming to Tanzania will have a one-stop centre through the Land Bank where all investment issues are addressed.

Amendments have been made to the land acts and it is now possible to sell and buy "bare" lands.[2] This development poses threats to many lands belonging to indigenous peoples, such as pastoral

378

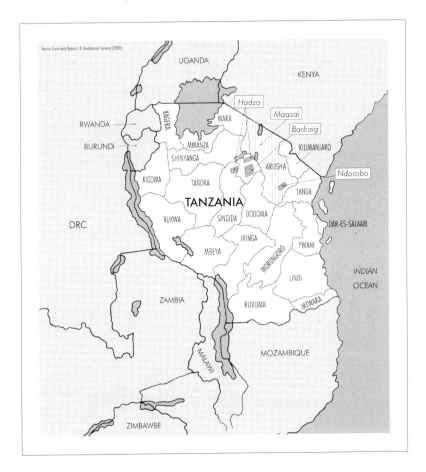

lands and lands used by hunter-gatherers, as these are often seen as un-developed and un-used lands. While the act reinforces the concept of "willing seller, willing buyer", it threatens security of tenure for different subsistence groups in the country.

The situation of the indigenous peoples

The situation of indigenous peoples continued to deteriorate with hunter-gather communities suffering even further by losing access to hunting resources, berries and roots. Pastoralists in both traditional territories and new lands continued to lose lands, stock routes, water resources and minerals.

Hadzabe and Akiye (Ndorobo) hunter-gatherers

The foraging Hadza and Akiye indigenous peoples live, surrounded by encroaching pastoralists, agriculturalists and conservationists.

The Hadzabe and Akiye experienced serious food shortages in 2003. This has been caused partly by drought, but also by the legislation that banned subsistence as a livelihood system. The Akiye (or Ndorobo[3] in the Maasai language) communities such as Napilukunya village in Kiteto District experienced what they consider the most serious food shortage in living memory. According to them, shifting cultivation has cleared all of the bush and destroyed most of the wild berries and roots that are critical for their survival. Clearing bush for farming also destroyed various plants and flowers that wild bees depend on for producing honey.

Besides the encroachment on their territories by farmers and pastoralists, hunting and gathering of wild berries, that mediated their livelihoods, are becoming increasingly difficult because of different wildlife policies that allocate hunting blocks within the areas belonging to indigenous peoples. Consequently, the ability of hunter-gatherers to obtain food is increasingly constrained, and this is creating uncertainty and serious food insecurity.

The Maasai

The indigenous pastoral Maasai experienced threats to their key resources. Land alienation continued as crop farming, wildlife management, mining and infrastructure projects continued to expand in 2003.

Different ways of utilizing wildlife resources for money remained a key threat to the livelihoods of the Maasai in Tanzania. The Maasai along the border with Kenya had disputes with companies that were allocated hunting blocks in northern Tanzania. Although hunting should not prevent residents from grazing and watering their animals, the practice has been that people are not supposed to graze in certain areas during the hunting season to avoid chasing away wild animals.

The Maasai in the Ngorongoro Conservation Area (NCA) continue to experience threats of eviction from the NCA. While they live and graze in the conservation area, their socio-economic development is constrained by conservation policies that place wildlife interests before those of the local communities.

In central Maasailand (areas around Monduli) land used by the army for military training restricted access to critical resources for the pastoralists from the villages of Meserani, Arkatani, Mti-mmoja, Loosimingori, Mmbuyuni and Makuyuni during the drought of 2003. Some cases were reported where pastoralists lost animals because of shells and artillery.

In Simanjiro district, the Maasai experienced expansion of large-scale farms, wildlife management groups and mining companies. Also, conflicts over water resources were reported in areas in the eastern part of the district.

Land use conflicts intensified in Kiteto District. Violent conflicts were reported in the villages in the southern parts of the district where migrant farmers have moved in large numbers.

Resource-based conflicts in Mbeya, Iringa and Morogoro triggered strong sentiments against pastoralists, and migration strategies are seen as sources of such conflicts. Various political statements from different circles state that pastoralists should be settled down permanently since movements of people and livestock are environmentally destructive, prone to conflicts and hamper disease control.

The Barbaig

Hanang, the traditional district of the indigenous Barbaig people, continued to receive small-scale farmers who moved in from the neighboring districts of Babati and Mbulu, forcing the pastoralists to migrate south in search of pasture and water for their livestock. Prime Barbaig pastures became permanent settlements for small-scale farmers from different parts of Manyara region. In 2003, Barbaig and their livestock moved further on to Dodoma, Iringa and Morogoro. Some migrated further into Singida, Shinyanga, Rukwa and Mbeya regions. The Barbaig have not found a place they could call home in those areas as they were always considered intruders who have no respect for other people's property or cultures. Perceived by mainstream groups as footloose herders, the Barbaig are constantly discriminated against and exploited by different groups. Before 2003, different local authorities saw them as a source of revenue for district councils since they paid both production and sale taxes. Since July 2003, when the central government abolished nuisance taxes that included livestock levies, various local authorities complained that the Barbaig and other pastoralists were a strain to their economies.

Land use conflicts between farmers and agricultural pastoralists are a recurrent feature and they are intensifying. The mainstream media is biased against pastoralists in its coverage of issues related to conflicts. It often reports pastoralists as the aggressors and the pastoralists' views are seldom put across. There have been calls from mainstream groups to send pastoralist Barbaig and Maasai back to where they came from: their traditional territories. However most of these are now being used by others for wheat and other grain production or fall under protected areas.

Hundreds of thousands of acres that were once owned by NAF-CO[4] for wheat schemes are being prepared for privatization. NAFCO, like many other para-statal organizations, failed miserably in its performance. In spite of heavy capital input from the Canadian International Development Agency (CIDA) and heavily mechanized farming methods, wheat production was always too low to justify the levels of investment. The level of environmental destruction is recorded as being one of the highest in the country and the costs in terms of human suffering for the indigenous Barbaig have reached intolerable levels. Sources say that talks on selling the Hanang wheat farms in Basuto to a private investor started recently, and like many other privatized public utilities, the deal has not involved any consultations with the Barbaig community, who are the true owners of the land. Worse still, there is no discussion about restoring the land to the indigenous Barbaig for their own use as pastures. Loss of huge tracts of pastures also meant alienation of holy sites for the Barbaig. This alienation of holy sites, ancestral graves and sites of cultural significance for the Barbaig had deep spiritual and cultural significance for the community.

Resource alienation and shrinking resource bases

All indigenous peoples in Tanzania continued to experience losses of their production bases and the remaining lands are becoming increasingly too small to allow indigenous patterns of resource utilization to be practiced. This restriction of indigenous patterns of resource utilization and management is further constraining indigenous coping strategies.

Hunting companies were a major threat to the livelihoods of the hunter-gatherer communities. While the Maasai have already lost critical resources to wildlife conservation,[5] large and small-scale farming, mining companies and infrastructure development, there are threats to alienate areas around Lake Natron and Kimotok as part of the Ramsar[6] sites and the wetlands protection programme respectively.

Access, coverage and quality of social services

Social service facilities such as schools, health facilities and other services are few and far apart in the areas of indigenous peoples. Illiteracy levels are very high among the Akiye, Hadza, Barbaig and the Maasai. The Akiye and the Hadza do not have a single primary school in their areas. The Barbaig had primary schools in Hanang but they were used mostly by children from other communities. The Maasai are better off than the other three groups in terms of the number of schools and other social services available in their area. However, the schools in their areas are poorly equipped and poorly staffed, and often performance of pupils in the national examinations is very poor. Other social services such as health care facilities, veterinary services and water supply schemes are also either non-existent or few and of poor quality.

Indigenous peoples' organizations

As a result of the marginalization of indigenous peoples, civil society organizations have emerged that work to promote the rights of indigenous peoples in Tanzania. These include two umbrella organizations PINGOS[7] and TAPHGO[8] as well as numerous community-based organizations (CBOs) that work with pastoralist Barbaig and Maasai.

A number of NGOs and CBOs emerged in the 1990s in response to various forms of deprivation, land loss and marginalization and organized their work around indigenous peoples' rights to land and to participation in development and in political processes. Some of these organizations have remained CBOs or people's organizations, which are mainly loosely organized grassroots movements and have remained people-centred. They are mostly initiated and run by activists through articulation of felt needs of the pastoralist communities. They are often characterized by the spirit of self-help and voluntary work. Although their levels of organization often have remained low, their levels of popular participation is often very high, and this has served as an instrument for sustainability.

The indigenous Maasai peoples have several NGOs and CBOs that include: Inyuat e Moipo, KINNAPA, KIPOC, LADO, Ilaramatak lo olkonerei, CORDS, Inyuat e Maa, Pastoralists Women's Council, OIDA and Ngopadeo.

The indigenous Barbaig peoples have three CBOs: EKABA, Bulgada and KIPOC Barbaig. There are other emerging CBOs and potential NGOs[9] among the Barbaig, but they are yet to be registered formally.

The Hadzabe do not have any NGOs or CBOs of their own. However, a movement has started among the Hadza and the registration of the Hadza Survival Council of Tanzania has now reached an advanced stage. The Akiye (Ndorobo) do not have any NGO or CBO of their own but the Ndorobo Safari Company (Ltd) has been doing some work with them.

Development cooperation, aid and indigenous peoples

Some bilateral donor organizations have started working with indigenous communities in the country. In 1998, DANIDA (Danish International Development Assistance), in collaboration with civil organizations working with the Maasai of Ngorongoro initiated the ERETO – Ngorongoro Pastoralist Project. The first phase of the ERETO project was initiated in the Ngorongoro Conservation Area (NCA) as a project to (1) improve access to water for both people and livestock; (2) provide veterinary services; and (3) restock resource poor pastoral households within the NCA. The ERETO project succeeded in restocking pastoral households based on traditional re-stocking methods, supplied water for people and livestock as well as veterinary services. It further raised rights awareness among the target population. A total of 3,400 households were restocked and female heads of households played a key role in the process of restocking.

The restocking component of the first phase of the ERETO project has been an effective poverty alleviation strategy. As a strategy, it reversed the trend of marginalization as the restocked households were restored back into pastoralism, which to them is much more than just an economic system – it is also a heritage, a form of spirituality and a determinant of identity.

Livestock numbers have now increased in the NCA but this has had no negative impact on the environment. Prior to ERETO project, the few watering points in the conservation area necessitated the concentration of people and livestock around those points, which had a negative environmental impact. However, with the construction/ rehabilitation of more watering points, this is no longer an issue as animals and people are now more evenly distributed in a wider area. The ERETO project has also contributed to the protection of wildlife in the NCA, as poverty levels had reached a point where the Maasai were almost forced to start eating game meat.

The first phase of the ERETO project has had a significant impact in the areas of supporting the indigenous peoples' primary production and livelihood systems, poverty reduction among the resource poor pastoralists and environmental protection. However, this phase did not link up to national policy dialogue processes on pastoralism due to the legal isolation of NCA Authority, but the second phase of the ERETO project intends to address the policy dialogue and has great potential and opportunity to do so.

Other development actors working with indigenous peoples' organizations include: Ireland Aid, Oxfam GB and Oxfam Ireland, CUSO, SIDA, CORDAID, NOVIB, MS-Tanzania, IWGIA, Trocaire and TRIAS. These organizations are supporting different development initiatives undertaken by pastoralists in Northern Tanzania. Most of them work with the pastoralist Maasai whose NGOs and CBOs are more organized and stronger than those of the other communities.

Policy formulation

While the existence of indigenous peoples is contested and indeed denied altogether in some policy circles, it is accepted informally that communities such as the Hadza, the Ndorobo Akiye, the Barbaig and the Maasai are indigenous, and representatives from these communities have been participating in different fora of indigenous peoples and in policy advocacy fora.

Through the two umbrella organizations (TAPHGO and PINGOs) and other networks, representatives of indigenous peoples participated in fora that discussed policies, strategies and national programmes.

Broad consultations were held to discuss and review the Poverty Reduction Strategy (PRS), which is being reviewed nationally, and pastoralists provided their own perspectives: pastoral perceptions of poverty and the strategic choices they prefer to be adopted nationally. The participation of hunter-gatherers in such processes was minimal.

Indigenous peoples have also begun to get involved in different programmes at the national level that relate to the PRS. Different pastoralists groups are undertaking consultations with the Ministry of Agriculture, especially the Agricultural Sector Development programme. This is a very important programme that touches on land, water resources, rangelands and livestock. In such agricultural programmes (where the analysis is done by farmers), pastoralism is perceived negatively and seen as a problem. The government thus gets a one-sided story from farmers that presents pastoralism as environmentally destructive and that depict pastoralists as respecting neither farmers nor their crops.

Pastoralists are engaged in these policy processes in order to present pastoralism as a viable economic system, benefit from the programme themselves, and prevent agricultural investment from displacing pastoralism. Sector programmes have intrinsic limitations, as issues such as indigenous peoples pastoral and hunter-gather livelihoods cannot be squeezed into one particular sector. This is one of the challenges that sectoral models of development need to address adequately.

TAPHGO plans to organize study tours to Kenya and Botswana in 2004 to study models of ranching in those two countries. Findings will be shared with stakeholders in two separate workshops. Participants in the first workshop will include parliamentarians from constituencies where indigenous peoples live, district commissioners from indigenous peoples' communities, people from government funding agencies and NGOs. Participants in the second workshop will include traditional leaders from indigenous pastoralist communities and the aim will be to discuss findings from the study visits and strategize on how to get involved in the formulation of the livestock development policy that is currently being formulated. ❑

Notes and References

1 Botswana sells its meat (an estimated 20,000 metric tonnes per year) to the European Union.
2 Bare land is land without "visible" developments such as fixed structures and crop production.
3 Ndorobo is a Maasai word that means someone without livestock and hence being dependent on hunting and gathering.
4 National Agricultural and Food Corporation.
5 Some of the protected areas curved out of Maasailand include Serengeti (Siringet), Manyara, Tarangire, and Nkordoto National Parks. Although Ngorongoro is supposed to be shared between people and wildlife, people have clearly lost out at the expense of conservation.
6 Ramsar, a city in Iran, is the common name for the convention on Wetlands of International Importance especially as waterfowl habitat.
7 PINGOS stands for Pastoralist Indigenous NGOs.
8 Tanzania Pastoralists' & Hunter-gatherers' Organisation.
9 DILEDA; NUMUCHU, HANANG Agricultural and Livestock Organisation, RAGUNDEGA; SINAGI AND GEJARU are some of the newly formed Barbaig NGOs that await registration.

African Commission on Human & People's Rights. 2003. *Report of the Working Group on Indigenous Populations/Communities in Africa*. Adopted during the 34th Ordinary Session of the Commission in Banjul, Gambia. Unpublished.

IWGIA. 2003. *The Indigenous World 2002-2003.* Copenhagen: IWGIA.
Organisation of African Union. 1983. *African Charter on Human and Peoples'*
 Rights
United Republic of Tanzania:
    1977. Constitution of the United Republic of Tanzania.
    2001. Agricultural Sector Development Strategy.
    2002. Agricultural Sector Programme Support, Phase II.
    2003. ERETO 2 Ngorongoro Pastoralists Project 2nd Phase.
    Final project document.

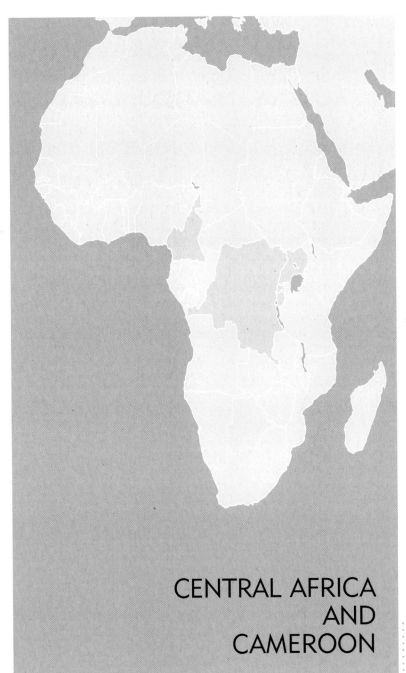

CENTRAL AFRICA
AND
CAMEROON

THE GREAT LAKES REGION

Political overview

Violent conflicts have ravaged the Great Lakes region of Central Africa since the genocide in Rwanda in 1994, in which over 800,000 Tutsi, Twa and moderate Hutus were killed in three months, and whose effects spilled over into neighbouring countries. The International Rescue Committee estimated that the conflict caused 3.3 million deaths in Democratic Republic of Congo (DRC) between August 1998 and November 2002. Gross human rights violations, including murder, summary executions, torture, rape, pillage and cannibalism, have been perpetrated by many different factions.

During 2003 there were welcome increases in political will and practical action to move towards peace by governments and the UN. The emergence of power-sharing governments in Burundi and DRC helped to focus on political solutions to resolving conflicts about control of resources and influence and has weakened the raison d'être of armed militias and factions that have been, and still are, terrorising local populations. Uganda is also involved in this process, through its links with the Rwanda military, and its influence and direct participation in the conflict in the northeast, especially in the Semilki valley and near Bunia, where new oil exploration is now underway.

By April, **Uganda** began withdrawing its 2000 troops that were still in Ituri District (DRC), despite previous accords requiring their withdrawal. Refugees continued to seek refuge from the fighting by flooding into western Uganda's Bundibugyo area. Uganda re-established diplomatic relations with DRC in October. In December the repatriation of former fighters from rebel movements opposed to the Ugandan government was hailed as a "breakthrough in the normalisation of relations between Uganda and Congo".

Although **Rwanda** itself has remained relatively stable since the genocide in 1994, it has justified its continued involvement in the war in DRC on the grounds of having to protect its borders from Hutu insurgents who took refuge in DRC's forests after the genocide in Rwanda, and continued to attack Rwanda. Despite having ostensibly withdrawn its troops from DRC, several reports during 2003 indicated continued Rwandan involvement in conflict areas. Towards the end of the year, the DRC government pledged to root out Rwandan Hutu

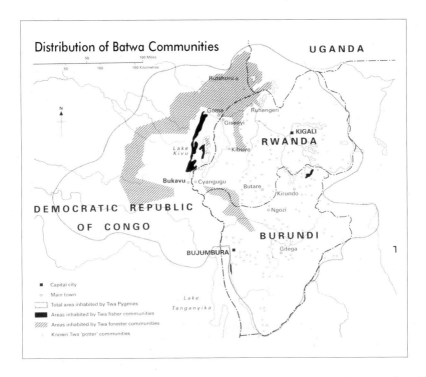

Distribution of Batwa Communities

UGANDA

RWANDA

KIGALI

DEMOCRATIC REPUBLIC OF CONGO

BURUNDI

BUJUMBURA

Gitega

Lake Kivu

Bukavu

Cyangugu

Butare

Kirundo

Ngozi

Goma

Gisenyi

Ruhengeri

Kibuye

Rushuru

Lake Tanganyika

■ Capital city
◦ Main town
Total area inhabited by Twa Pygmies
Areas inhabited by Twa fisher communities
Areas inhabited by Twa forester communities
Known Twa 'potter' communities

rebels in eastern DRC in a bid to normalise relations with Rwanda. Shortly afterwards, the commander of the Hutu combatant group FDLR (*Forces Démocratiques de Libération du Rwanda*) surrendered voluntarily to the Rwandan government after nine years in DRC leading some 15-20,000 guerrillas. This encouraged more former combatants to present themselves to the Rwandan authorities for reintegration; however thousands more are still roaming the Congolese jungle and attacking the local populations in DRC and Burundi.

Presidential elections returned Paul Kagame as President, with 95% of the vote. While this result probably reflects to a considerable degree the Rwandan peoples' wish for continued political stability, some outside agencies considered that the election process had been marred by intimidation and harassment of supporters of opposition candidates by the ruling Rwanda Patriotic Front (RPF). Parliamentary elections followed the presidential elections. However, the main opposition party, the *Mouvement Démocratique Républicain* (MDR), had been banned by the government in May. The RPF won a landslide victory with 74% of the vote. Over half of the new MPs are women. The new government marks the end of a 9-year transitional period since the genocide in 1994.

In January 2003 the government released more than 19,000 of the 130,000 prisoners held on genocide charges, to relieve congestion in the prisons prior to their trial by *gacaca* jurisdictions. These traditional "courts" consist of 19 people of integrity (*inyangamugayo*) chosen by the communities. Their function is to establish the truth of what happened at the actual location of the crime, draw up a list of victims and identify the guilty. Some 5,770 of the released prisoners were later re-arrested after fresh allegations were made against them by Ibuka, the organisation representing genocide survivors.

In **Burundi**, a ceasefire agreed in December 2002 between government and rebels remained unimplemented for most of the year as two rebel factions, the CNDD-FDD (*Conseil national pour la défense de la démocratie-Forces pour la défense de la démocratie*) and FNL (*Forces Nationales de Libération*) continued to fight government forces. Insecurity increased as 1st May approached when Pierre Buyoya, a Tutsi, handed over the presidency to the Hutu Vice President, Domitien Ndayizeye in accordance with the Arusha peace accord signed in 2000. However, in October the situation improved when the CNDD-FDD signed a ceasefire agreement with the government, giving the former a role in the armed forces, the police and intelligence services.

With CNDD-FDD in government, one faction of the remaining rebel group, FNL, transformed itself into a political party in December. However, another FNL faction, led by Agathon Rwasa, continued to fight government forces around the capital Bujumbura and by January 2004 talks with the government had still not resulted in any ceasefire agreement.

In the **Democratic Republic of Congo (DRC)** the process of political unification continued in 2003. By December 2002, most foreign troops had withdrawn from DRC, and a comprehensive peace agreement was signed. A new constitution was adopted in April 2003, and a two-year, transitional power-sharing government was inaugurated in August 2003, composed of representatives of the outgoing government, the pro-government Mayi-Mayi militia, armed rebel movements, the unarmed political opposition and civil society. A national army was established, unifying the forces of the former Kinshasa government and those of the various rebel movements.

Despite these political developments, the new government still does not have proper control of areas previously under rebel administration and the needs of the population remain very high. During 2003, violence continued in eastern DRC, especially north & south Kivu, and Ituri district in the northeast where rival militias (some backed by Rwanda and Uganda) vied for control of mineral resources and continued to aggravate conflicts over land between local Lendu and Hema ethnic groups. Human Rights Watch estimated that since 1999 more than 50,000 people have died in Ituri, and over 500,000 people have been displaced. By early 2003, many humanitarian agencies were issuing warnings of genocide. Reports of rape, child rape, abduction, torture, summary executions and cannibalism were investigated and confirmed by the UN mission in DRC. The deployment of strengthened peace enforcement troops led by the EU and by the UN helped to reduce local fighting, but massacres still continued.

International condemnation of the atrocities and violence increased: the UN special rapporteur on human rights in DRC, Iulia Motoc, reported that the genocide, crimes against humanity and war crimes served to "create a frightening picture of one of the most serious human rights situations in the world", and that "the rights of indigenous peoples, such as the Pygmies, must also be respected". The International Criminal Court (ICC) selected Ituri as "the most urgent situation" under its jurisdiction to be addressed and began analysing the available information and seeking additional information on crimes committed.

In October the UN Panel of Experts on the Illegal Exploitation of Natural Resources and other forms of Wealth of the DRC released its final report, listing names of individuals, companies and governments involved in the plunder of gems and minerals. A coalition of NGOs called on the UN Security Council to insist that member states launch immediate investigations into the involvement of multinational corporations, including companies based in western countries, accused of profiteering from war in DRC. ❑

Indigenous peoples' situation

UGANDA

D ue to increasing competition for land from immigrants and the impact of some conservation projects which have taken over their remaining traditional lands since the early 1990s, several thousand indigenous Batwa people in South West Uganda have become landless and lost access to their traditional semi-nomadic hunting and gathering lifestyle. Most Batwa's livelihoods have always been linked to forests, and as forests have disappeared or been taken away for conservation, their livelihoods have become extremely insecure. Now many face extreme poverty. Their continuing social marginalisation, lack of access to adequate compensation for their lost forest access, low literacy rates, lack of access to social services, and chronic poverty has led to a serious threat to Batwa livelihoods and to the survival of their culture. So far government, donors and NGOs have failed to address Batwa needs or deliver fully their promises to address their poverty. Batwa have therefore decided to work to promote the acquisition of land for themselves while also securing education, training, and income generation opportunities for Batwa communities. Supported by a national Twa NGO, the United Organisation for Batwa Development in Uganda (UOBDU), Batwa from across southwest Uganda have held a series of community consultations over the past three years to discuss the impacts of the Mgahinga and Bwindi National Parks on their livelihoods and their human rights. Extensive regional-level meetings have also been held between Batwa representatives, and government, development and conservation agencies working all over southwest Uganda. During these meetings Twa also raised their landlessness, still severely neglected by programmes set up to mitigate the parks' impacts on local people. In February 2003, UOBDU began extensive community consultations with Batwa to develop, and then validate its first formal workplan. In early 2004 this work programme will be presented to donors and NGOs in Kisoro, Uganda, where UOBDU's office is based. This consultative process will be the culmination of three years effort by Batwa and their support organizations to build Batwa self-sufficiency and promote their rights, a process that has resulted in widespread donor and government acceptance of Batwa's special needs; recognition that is linked to UOBDU's success and strengthening credibility in southwest Uganda. ❑

RWANDA

In the run-up to the elections, the political climate became tense due to the authorities' use of supposed threats to national unity to clamp down on so-called "divisionists". Several prominent people fled the country, were arrested or "disappeared". The Twa's ongoing campaign for recognition of their rights was viewed with increasing suspicion, and Twa activists were warned that they were under scrutiny. One of the national Twa organisation CAURWA's legal advisors, Lt. Col. Augustin Cyiza, "disappeared". According to a Human Rights Watch report documenting the government's tightening of control prior to the elections, this was because he was considered a political opponent. He is thought to be dead or in military detention.

Despite these constraints, CAURWA stepped up its advocacy and sustainable livelihoods work, and pressed the government for affirmative action to improve the livelihoods of the country's Twa population.

CAURWA is actively engaging with the government on justice and environment issues, has a Twa observer monitoring the traditional *gacaca* courts set up to try those accused of genocide-related crimes, and produced a briefing paper to lobby the government to recognise Twa land rights. CAURWA is currently dealing with 20 cases in which Twa lands have been expropriated by neighbours or by local authorities, and four cases of unprovoked killings of Twa individuals, including a Twa prisoner who was ordered to retrieve a lost mobile phone from a latrine, and subsequently drowned there.

Prior to the amendment of the constitution, CAURWA lobbied the government to recognise Twa land rights, guarantee their access to education and increase Twa participation in public life. The constitution, approved by referendum in May, contains provision for eight representatives of "historically marginalised communities" to sit in the Senate. However, Twa hopes for political representation through this means are fading, as the four representatives nominated by the President so far do not include any Twa. In the run-up to the elections CAURWA sent an open letter to the four presidential candidates that was published in the official press, asking them to take account of Twa concerns if they got elected. This letter was widely applauded by civil society groups.

CAURWA is supporting over 70 Twa associations to increase their food security and income from farming, small animal husbandry, tile making and sewing. A main focus is the validation of Twa culture through the promotion of their traditional pottery and dance, and the development of a Fair Trade commercial enterprise selling Twa pottery. CAURWA supports 60 secondary school children and has pioneered the use of the REFLECT methodology in its 12 adult literacy circles. In collaboration with the statistics office of the Ministry of Finance, CAURWA and a team of Twa data collectors carried out a nationwide social survey of Twa communities. The report, due in 2004, will provide valuable data for advocacy and strategic interventions to promote Twa rights and improve their living conditions.

A meeting of the Central African members of the International Alliance of Indigenous and Tribal Peoples of the Tropical Forests was organised by the Twa group APB (the regional coordinator of the Alliance) in Kigali in September with assistance from Forest Peoples Programme. Participants were briefed on donor policies, exchanged information on how these policies affected their peoples, and reviewed the functioning of the Alliance in Central Africa. Participants called on their governments to ratify ILO Convention No.169. ❑

BURUNDI

The situation for Twa in Burundi remained bleak, as rebel attacks continued and the fragile political system made little progress in rebuilding the country and addressing the population's severe economic and social problems. The UN special rapporteur on human rights in Burundi, Marie-Therese Keita-Bocoum, recognised the widespread marginalisation of the Twa in the region, and urged humanitarian agencies to protect human rights especially of women and the Twa people. Conflicts over land are likely to increase as thousands of refugees return following the agreement between the government and the CNDD-FDD rebel group. Twa communities, lacking political or economic power, are likely to be further marginalised in this process.

A conference on social integration organised in December by UNI-PROBA, and funded by Minority Rights Group, brought together Twa from the four countries of the Great Lakes region. Participants called on their governments to urgently implement measures guaranteeing their people greater access to land and education.

The Gitega-based organisation UCEDD continued its work to support Twa communities in agriculture, provided training in trauma healing and prevention of HIV/AIDS and supported more than 2000 primary school children. ❑

DRC

During 2003 indigenous organisations and support NGOs repeatedly condemned the continuing violence that is taking its toll of "Pygmy" communities, through murder, rape, summary executions, forced abductions, looting and most horrifically, cannibalism.[1] In January 2003, Mbuti people visiting Kinshasa provided eye-witness accounts of cannibalism in Ituri district by MLC (Ugandan-backed rebels) soldiers. One witness, Nzoki Amzati, said, "I was returning from the field and had time to hide in the brush, from where I saw members of my family being killed and eaten by soldiers of [MLC leader] Jean-Pierre Bemba. ... I saw soldiers tear out the heart of a child and then eat it after having roasted it over a fire," he added. An investigation by the UN Mission to the DRC (MONUC) confirmed the allegations. Twa organisations from Kivu travelled to Ituri to document and publicise the atrocities and give support, and the organisation AAPDMAC presented a statement denouncing the cannibalism at the UN's Permanent Forum on Indigenous Issues. Indigenous groups secured a commitment from the DRC State Prosecutor to investigate the allegations, and several human rights NGOs and activists planned missions to the region to collect evidence for presentation to the Prosecutor at the International Criminal Court.

The political unification of the country and official cessation of hostilities did not halt the violence in the northeast and east of the country. At the end of the year, Twa groups in Bukavu and Kalehe reported Interahmwe attacks at Bunyakiri and Kalungu/Bushushu, resulting in killings, forced abductions and burning of Twa villages. Desperate Twa sought assistance from local Twa organisations, which issued an urgent appeal to relief agencies for help.

Twa organisations in eastern DRC continued their advocacy and education work, as well as trying to deal with the urgent welfare needs of Twa communities. UEFA, a Twa women's organisation, worked with Twa victims of sexual violence to document their cases, provide counselling and small-scale income generating activities. Indigenous representatives participated in a workshop in Kinshasa on DRC's new forest law, organised by the Rainforest Foundation to enable civil society organisations to challenge provisions in the law that affect local community rights. the local support NGO, CAMV, produced booklets in local languages to inform Pygmy communities about their land rights and women's rights, ran workshops on indigenous rights and techniques of trauma counselling for Pygmy peoples, and documented human rights abuses against Pygmies in north and south Kivu, including forced labour, arbitrary arrest, looting, sexual violence and killings. A preparatory workshop for DRC indigenous activists attending the World Parks Congress in Durban, coordinated by CAMV, produced a draft position paper for the Congress. The local indigenous NGO, PIDP (*Programme d'Intégration et de Développement du Peuple Pygmée au Kivu*) organised a workshop to produce an indigenous shadow report to accompany the DRC State Report to the African Commission of Human and Peoples Rights. As a result of PIDP's report, Commissioners questioned the DRC representative closely on his government's neglect of the human rights situation of indigenous peoples in DRC. PIDP carried out a strategic planning exercise that identified education, literacy, human rights, income generation, health and institutional capacity as its priority areas over the next three years. The Kalehe-based group, ADELIPO, carried out a research study of the socio-economic situation of Twa communities expelled from the Kahuzi-Biega National Park in South Kivu, and their continuing dependence on the resources of the park.

At the national level, several indigenous organisations are emerging, including a national network, LINACOPY. The Kinshasa-based *Centre international de défense des droits des Batwa* (CIDB) held seminars in DRC and Republic of Congo to train Twa trainers in defending indigenous rights, organised celebrations for the International Day of Indigenous Peoples in Kinshasa, and has started raising awareness of indigenous communities about ILO Convention No. 169 and other indigenous rights instruments. CIDB produced a report documenting violations of rights of Pygmy women and children, land rights, and acts of violence and discrimination against Pygmy individuals, focussing on the northeast and northwest parts of the country. *L'Union pour le développement des minorités Ekonda* (UDME) working in Kinshasa, Bandundu and Equateur provinces, documented the situation of Pygmies who have migrated to Kinshasa. Half of the group interviewed reported no problems of discrimination by their neighbours; however, educational levels were very low and most survived from begging and handouts. ❑

Workshop on tropical forest management

In March the International Union for the Conservation of Nature (IUCN), assisted by the Rwandan Twa organisation, CAURWA, organised a workshop in Kigali for indigenous peoples of Central Africa. The workshop was held under the auspices of CEFDHAC (Conference on Tropical Forest Ecosystems in Central Africa), an interministerial process aimed at developing a harmonised approach to sustainable forest management in the region. The workshop aim was to strengthen the involvement of indigenous and local peoples in sustainable management of Central African Forests, as well as discussing indigenous peoples' traditional knowledge in the management of forest resources, and encouraging dialogue between governments and indigenous peoples concerning recognition of their rights and citizenship. Indigenous participants called for increased participation in management of protected areas, increased benefit sharing and support for regional indigenous networking. Conference participants also criticised the Rwandan government for its inaction in tackling the problems faced by disadvantaged populations.

Twa women

A report on the situation of Twa women in the region, within the context of international human rights law and national policies, concluded that Twa women were doubly marginalised, as indigenous people and as women. The report highlighted lack of secure land rights as the central issue for Twa women and their communities, contributing to their marginalisation and impoverishment and threatening their cultural survival.[2] ❏

CAMEROON

Cameroon remains one of the more stable countries in Central Africa, in spite of its continuing reputation for corruption and mismanagement of its natural resource base, especially in the southern forest zone - the home to up to 60,000 indigenous forest peoples.

Political overview

The Cameroon government is continuing to be encouraged by bilateral donors to work towards improved management of its bureaucracy, especially those ministries responsible for the allocation and management of natural resource rights. However recent reports by the independent forest monitor demonstrate the apparent lack of will by government to address the numerous violations of the forestry code by local and international timber companies. In spite of the 1994 forestry law, which stipulates community involvement in the management of their lands, the continuing alienation of communities from decisions affecting the lands close to rural communities fosters persistent mistrust of central government authorities. It also leads to increasing competition for local lands between communities who are, in turn, also affected by timber exploitation from outside. Debates over the distribution of forestry revenues between central and local government authorities are a central feature of domestic discussions over how to promote increased transparency in this sector, and a fairer distribution of forest revenues to local communities.

The indigenous peoples of Cameroon

The extreme poverty of the rural poor across southern Cameroon and the lack of investment in basic social services, coupled with growing rural populations and continuous growth of a national "bushmeat" trading network, is leading to growing pressure on the rights of Cameroon's indigenous forest communities, such as Bakola, Bagyeli and Baka. The Cameroon government aims to protect 30% of its land from exploitation, and over the past decade international conservation organisations have been very active in supporting the Ministry of Environment and Forests (MINEF) to build up the network of national parks and reserves. Unfortunately, local communities were rarely

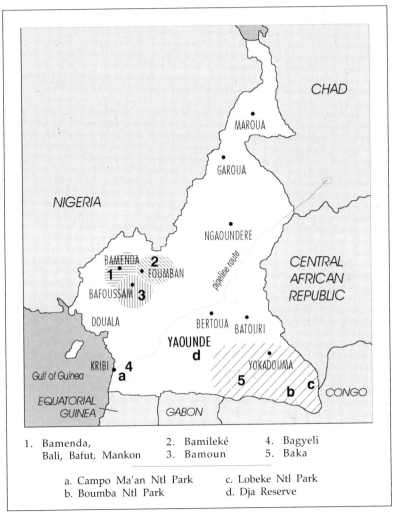

1. Bamenda,   2. Bamileké   4. Bagyeli
    Bali, Bafut, Mankon   3. Bamoun   5. Baka

     a. Campo Ma'an Ntl Park   c. Lobeke Ntl Park
     b. Boumba Ntl Park   d. Dja Reserve

consulted about these plans, and when they were, indigenous hunting and gathering communities were almost never involved – this has been extensively documented since 2001.[3] The result is that Baka and Bagyeli have little say in the management of their lands, and in many cases are losing access to forests that they have inhabited for centuries. Their culture and continuing dependence upon these forests to secure their livelihoods, combined with their lack of access to lands to cultivate or a decent wage to do so for others and their social marginalisation, means that most still have little access to formal schooling, or basic health services, and virtually no influence with government agencies or other civil society institutions.

With increased support from local and international NGOs over the past few years, Baka, Bagyeli and Bakola have become more engaged with government and donors, and this is helping indigenous men and women establish their own community associations to secure their rights, and start new initiatives. Since 2002 Bagyeli and Bakola from the zone traversed by the Chad-Cameroon oil-pipeline have been receiving support from a number of international organisations to secure increased participation in civil society, and their forest rights and, hopefully, their communities' eventual participation in the design and implementation of the much-promised Indigenous Peoples Plan (IPP) required through World Bank funding for this project. This year a report by the Inspection Panel of the World Bank identified serious delays to the development of a transparent and workable IPP by the Foundation for Environment and Development in Cameroon (FEDEC), a foundation set up by the oil consortium to fund the IPP and environmental offset. The result of efforts so far is a virtually non-existent IPP ("a work in progress", according to the inspection panel) after three years, which is shocking, given that the pipeline is already built and operating, almost a year ahead of schedule.

Baka and Bagyeli all over the southern forest zone continue to build the capacities of their own support organisations and their negotiation skills, to secure identity cards, to gain access to legal advice, to create their own land use maps, and to develop alternative sources of income. However their incomes, institutional capacities, and confidence remain very low and long-term support from government and donors to promote their rights is still difficult to obtain. In spite of this, since 2001 Bagyeli and Bakola from the southwest have begun to engage directly with donors such as the World Bank over the project's impacts on their rights. Baka from the south and southeast have their own young NGOs, and some indigenous communities are establishing their own community associations. Baka and Bagyeli are also building up their links with international and national conservation authorities, which are beginning to accept openly that their rights have been neglected in previous conservation plans. Baka and Bagyeli representatives are also participating in local consultative processes over international standards such as upcoming reviews in Cameroon of ILO Convention No.169. ❑

Notes and references

1   See IWGIA *The Indigenous World 2002-2003* for a more detailed report.
2   **Jackson, D. 2003**. *Twa Women, Twa Rights in the Great Lakes Region.* London: Minority Rights Group.
3   **Nelson, J. and L. Hossack (eds). 2003**. *Indigenous Peoples and Protected Areas in Africa: from principles to practice.* Moreton-in-Marsh: Forest Peoples Programme. See www.forestpeoples.org.

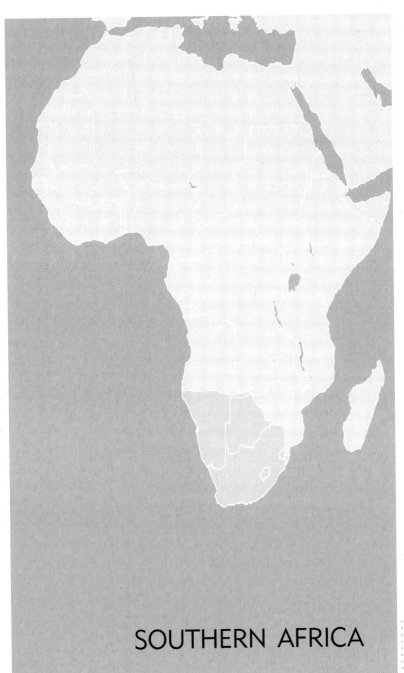

SOUTHERN AFRICA

ANGOLA

For almost 27 years, the civil war in Angola made it impossible to follow the situation of the small San minority living in the southern part of the country. In 2003, Trócaire Angola and WIMSA[1] were able to commission two consultants to visit the area for the first time. Assisted by two OCADEC[2] development workers, the consultants travelled extensively throughout the provinces of Huíla, Cunene and Cuando Cubango . Their purpose was to assess the situation and the needs of the San in order to establish a basis for further assistance and development planning. The following information is based on their report.[3]

San communities in Angola

The San of Angola constitute a small ethnic minority living in small, dispersed groups in the south of the country. They are the oldest inhabitants of the territory of Angola and have lived as hunter-gatherers there as in other parts of southern Africa.

The assessment team visited 43 San communities and collected information about a further 29 San groups. Contact was made with a total of 2,014 San people. Reliable information suggests that at least 3400 San people live in southern Angola, mainly in small groups. All of those contacted identified themselves as !Kung[4] speakers.

The size of the San communities visited ranges from small family groups of 6-10 people to larger villages of up to 230 people. Most settlements have a total population of 25-40. Some groups are settled more permanently while others are more mobile. Not all groups are composed of people who have lived together for a long time. Some consist of people from different places who all have a different history of displacement. In other groups the majority of people have lived in the same place for generations or have a shared history of displacement.

The large number of San groups that live in relatively fixed settlements have small fields and homes made of wood with thatch roofing. They usually work for their Bantu neighbours and go out to hunt and to search for "bushfood" such as tubers, nuts, wild melons, etc. Permanent settlements are frequently found near streams or natural water sources.

Other groups move frequently within a specific area depending on where there are bushfoods to harvest. Settlement patterns are influ-

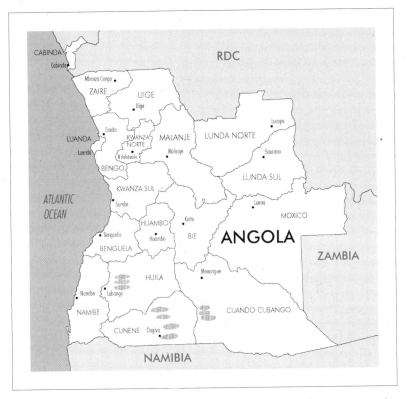

enced by the degree of access a community has to what was once its ancestral land or *n!ore*. Groups that move around less are those that have nowhere to move to; their *n!oresi* are now inhabited by other people with large fields and cattle.

Land issues

The San in Angola live as minority groups in areas of mixed settlement on land that was once their ancestral land. Their settlement patterns are unstable. Some San communities have recently returned to their places of origin, while others are thinking of moving to a former place of settlement within what they perceive to be their n!ore or ancestral land.

However, none of the communities visited enjoy exclusive use of the land on which they are settled. All live in close proximity to Bantu cultivators and pastoralists who usually cultivate larger areas of land, own cattle and produce a certain amount of surplus food, which they store. Residents and returnees all said that the local Bantu *sobas* (leaders) and local administration officials recognise their land rights. However, this entails recognition of only very limited rights. The San or their leaders do not exercise control over or have jurisdiction over "their land", thus they have no power to allocate land. The control of land resources and all social authority rests with the Bantu *sobas*. In most cases the land rights of the San groups are limited to their presence being tolerated on terms and conditions almost entirely beyond their control.

Angola's existing land law protects peoples' land rights on the basis of occupancy rights but it has not been applied consistently, and due to a very weak judiciary and legal system, land rights and the land law are very confusing and fluid in Angola.

Returning to land once occupied, repossessing land previously owned or acquiring new land is currently a crucial concern for many rural Angolans. There are reportedly four million internally displaced people – as well as many refugees – who are in the process of returning to their places of origin, and it is expected that many of them will face a challenge getting back what was once their land but may now be occupied by others. Angola also currently has millions of people trying to secure assets to improve their quality of life. A growing class of Angolans with access to resources and power is focused on accumulating assets and creating wealth. After oil and diamonds, land is now the focus of such ambition and activity.

In recent months, Angolan legislators, civil society organisations and interested stakeholders have been discussing a controversial new Land Bill, and technical commissions have been established to consider submissions on the proposed new law. This much-criticised bill contradicts the principle of acquired rights and does not recognise land rights on the basis of occupancy. It strongly favours business interests, contradicts provisions of the Constitution of Angola that protect the land rights of rural communities and women, and does not clearly define who the representatives of rural communities may be. It also does not clarify the roles of customary law and traditional leaders in the allocation of land, and contains no provisions on natural resource management.

The San communities' position is weak in this situation - not only because they in some cases have shared the land with Bantu groups over generations, and risk that these groups will claim such land as their ancestral land, but also because recognition of land rights is closely associated with recognition of political authority and community leaders. While most of the San groups visited have people designated as "leaders", almost all said that their group falls under the jurisdiction of the local Bantu *soba* and this is the person to whom the groups turns to resolve serious disputes. In a number of cases people said their San leaders had been appointed by the Bantu *sobas*. The overall impression the team gained is that there is no shared decision-making: power lies solely in the hands of the Bantu *sobas* and San leaders are called to meetings only to receive orders or instructions for their communities.

Food insecurity

All the San communities said that hunger has been a major problem, and most said they currently face a shortage of food. For their survival almost all depend to a large extent on food they receive in exchange for working in the fields of Bantu neighbours. Additional food is acquired by gathering bushfoods, collecting honey and hunting.

Some communities also cultivate small fields. A small minority had no fields of their own. Big differences were found between communities in terms of how seriously and extensively they were cultivating their own fields. Many factors influence the cultivation situation, including availability of seed, agricultural implements and cattle for ploughing, soil fertility or barrenness, rainfall, and the habit of cultivation. A number of the communities possess a few chickens and goats, but only three have cattle owners or own a few heads of "community cattle". The majority of the San communities were found to have very little food security and some were found to be food insecure.

The health situation

Health in all the communities visited is critical, with a lack of services and medicines placing people at risk of serious illness and even death. Though the communities have survived these conditions for a considerable length of time, the reported high morbidity and infant mortality rates are raising concern. The three main categories of disease to which Angolan San are prone are malaria, respiratory and diarrhoeal diseases. Poor conditions of local health and medical services are a serious problem in vulnerable communities throughout rural Angola. However, all the communities reported that they use San traditional medicine and many practise the San healing or trance dance.

Education and culture

Very few of the San adults are literate and hardly any of the children attend school, mainly due to maltreatment by other children and a lack of funds for materials, uniforms and fees. The team established that among all the groups interviewed there are fewer than 20 persons in total with some degree of literacy. Grade 4 is the highest level of formal schooling attained.

All communities value the !Kung language, but practise !Kung culture to varying degrees, storytelling being a common practice. The team noted that a number of communities had adopted cultural practices of their Bantu neighbours such as their songs, puberty rites and initiation rites.

The communities are relatively egalitarian in that everyone is equally poor and community members of all ages and both genders are very dependent on each other for their survival. Finding food is everyone's responsibility – men and women, youth and children. The men do all the hunting, build homes, look for firewood, collect honey and, if necessary, help the women and children with their tasks of fetching water and gathering bushfood. Men, women and older children work in the fields of neighbours in exchange for food. It was the team's impression that there is flexibility in the division of labour, and the opinions and ideas of women are normally taken into account in making decisions. It appears that men habitually represent the San communities to outsiders, thereby creating the impression that they are "in charge". One reason for this is that more men than women speak other languages than !Kung.

Exploitation and discrimination of San

San communities throughout southern Angola experience social exclusion, discrimination and economic exploitation. Their human rights are routinely disrespected and violated. Greatly reduced access to land and natural resources and insecure and very limited land rights have led to an erosion of the former San hunter-gatherer lifestyle and livelihood so that today the overwhelming majority of Angola San live in uneasy relationships of servitude and dependency with their Bantu neighbours. All the visited communities expressed very strong feelings of anger and pain due to discrimination on the basis of ethnicity and cultural characteristics. They say that they are not treated in the same way as others only because they are

San population in South Africa			
Country	Size of Country	Population (July 2003 estimate)	Number of San
Angola	1,246,700	10,766,471	3,500
Botswana	581,730	1,537,267	47,675
Namibia	824,290	1,927,447	32,000
South Africa	1,221,040	42,768,678	7,500
Zambia	752,610	10,307,333	300
Zimbabwe	390,580	12,576,742	2,500
TOTAL	5,016,950	79,873,938	93,475

Data obtained from: James Suzman, (2001) An Introduction to the Regional Assessment of the Status of San in Southern Africa, Windhoek, Namibia: Legal Assistance Center; the Working Group of Indigenous Minorities in Southern Africa (WIMSA); Chennels-Albertyn, South Africa; and the Southern African Development Community (SADC), The World Factbook (2003). Compiled by Robert K. Hitchcock.

San: their rights to "their" land and the sanctity of their homes is not respected; they are not paid as much as others are paid; and they are commonly regarded not as human beings but as "lower beings" with fewer rights.

San of all ages reported that they are frequently abused, insulted and treated disrespectfully by non-San. The team witnessed numerous incidences of San being spoken to in a rough manner or being ignored or treated as if they had no opinions to offer or were incapable of expressing an opinion. San children who had attended school reported experiences of discrimination there.

The following statement by a literate Kwanyama farmer interviewed in the Cunene Province encapsulates a not uncommon view of the San held by members of Bantu groups with whom they live. "They are animals. They are our slaves. They depend on us for their life."

"The first are last"

The San are known to be the first inhabitants of southern Africa and of Angola. But today their situation can be assessed as one where "the first are last". However, the San do not accept this fate. Many of them know that they have equal rights under Angola law, and ask that these rights be respected and that they be given the same opportunities as all other Angolans.

All the San interviewed wish to be freed from dependency and exploitation, and the overwhelming majority wish to work and produce food for themselves. All the communities want help to improve their food security by cultivating land. Time and again the team heard these words "We are ready to work. We need seeds and tools. We want to be equal to all other Angolans". ❑

Notes and references

1   Trócaire Angola: Irish Catholic Agency for World Development (Angola). WIMSA: Working Group of Indigenous Minorities in Southern Africa.
2   OCADEC: Organizaçao Crista de Apoio ao Desenvolvimento Comunitário (Christian Organisation Supporting Community Development).
3   **Pakleppa, Richard and Americo Kwononoka. 2003.** *Where the first are last – San Communities fighting for survival in southern Angola.* Windhoek: Trócaire Angola and WIMSA, in collaboration with OCADEC.
    See also: www.wimsareg.org
4   Also known as !Xun, which is the term now most commonly used elsewhere in southern Africa.

NAMIBIA

In 2001, the Government of Namibia's Emergency Management Unit (EMU) estimated that between 17,000 and 22,000 of the country's approximate 34,000 San were dependent on food aid.[1] In the Nyae Nyae region of northeastern Namibia, populated primarily by Ju | '-hoansi San, there was hunger in 2002-2003. In 2003, the Namibian government supplied mealie meal in order to offset nutritional problems. The mealie meal has helped alleviate the hunger but some people have experienced difficulties and have asked that additional commodities be provided (e.g. pulses, oil).

Another concern of the Ju | 'hoansi San in the Nyae Nyae region was regarding the impact of wild animals, notably elephants, on their water points and gardens. The large numbers of elephants in the Nyae Nyae region was reportedly wreaking havoc on water pumps, gardens and fences around people's homes. There were calls for government and the private sector to do something about the elephants and to protect people's property.

Plans for refugee camp stalled

One of the issues facing the San and other peoples residing in northeastern Namibia over the past few years has been the possibility of establishing a large refugee resettlement facility, housing as many as 21,000 refugees in the M'Kata region of Tsumkwe District West, in the area where the Ju | 'hoansi and !Xun San reside. The proposal to move the refugee camp from Osire in central Namibia has stemmed in part from complaints by commercial farmers in that area.

In March 2003, the Representative of the United Nations High Commissioner for Refugees in Namibia met with donors who have supported refugee programs in the country. The UNHCR Representative informed the donors that there had been a change in the refugee situation in Namibia, brought about by the end of hostilities in Angola and the signing of a Peace Accord between the government of Angola and UNITA, the main opposition group involved in the armed struggle in that country.[2]

Most of the 21,000-plus refugees in the main UNHCR refugee camp at Osire and in the smaller camp at Kasava said in interviews carried out in February 2003 that they wished to be repatriated to their former homes in Angola. The repatriation of Angolan refugees was initiated in June 2003. It is anticipated that this process will serve to reduce the pressure to establish a new refugee camp in Tsumkwe District. But, as of January 2004, the Namibian government had yet to officially rescind its plans to establish a new refugee camp in Tsumkwe District.

Challenges continue to face the San with respect to land and resource rights in Namibia. There have been thousands of people dispossessed over the past few years as labor laws have come into effect, and people on commercial ranches and farms have begun to reduce the numbers of workers and their families. It is estimated, for example, that several thousand people lost their residency rights in the Gobabis Farms region of eastern Namibia. Large numbers of dispossessed San are now found in places such as Gobabis , attempting to eke out an existence doing odd jobs and seeking help from their neighbors.[3]

The new N‡a Jaqna conservancy

There are some potential bright spots, however. One innovation in Namibian development is the concept of the conservancy. A conservancy is an area of communal land where communities have some control over natural resource management and utilization. This is achieved through a statutory body that is officially recognized by the government - a conservancy committee.

Since 1996, the Working Group of Indigenous Minorities in Southern Africa (WIMSA) - a regional NGO networking San communities and organisations - has been working with the San community of Tsumkwe West to establish a community-based tourism project, co-ordinating training programs for traditional leaders and by assisting the community with preparations to form a conservancy in the area. The formation of a conservancy was to give the community the right to jointly manage, use and benefit from wildlife in the area. An application to register a conservancy in the area was submitted in 1998 but it was only in July 2003 that the government finally gazetted the N‡a Jaqna Conservancy. The official inauguration, jointly organised by the Ministry of Environment and Tourism and WIMSA, took place on 16 December 2003. Around 400 adult community members from all over Tsumkwe District West witnessed this joyous event.[4]

Another positive step is the envisaged overall co-operation between the management of the N‡a Jaqna Conservancy in Tsumkwe District West and the experienced management of the Nyae Nyae

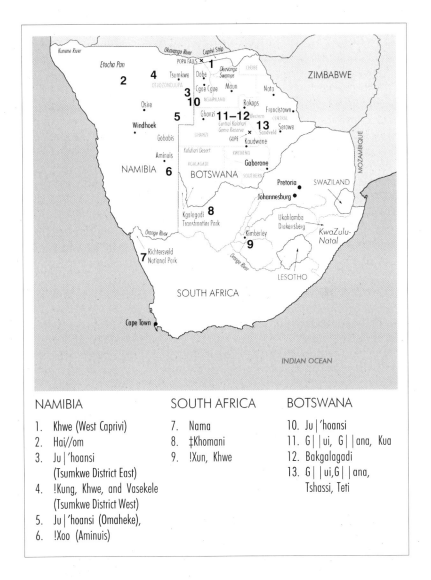

NAMIBIA

1. Khwe (West Caprivi)
2. Hai//om
3. Ju|'hoansi
   (Tsumkwe District East)
4. !Kung, Khwe, and Vasekele
   (Tsumkwe District West)
5. Ju|'hoansi (Omaheke),
6. !Xoo (Aminuis)

SOUTH AFRICA

7. Nama
8. ‡Khomani
9. !Xun, Khwe

BOTSWANA

10. Ju|'hoansi
11. G||ui, G||ana, Kua
12. Bakgalagadi
13. G||ui,G||ana,
    Tshassi, Teti

Conservancy. The sense of ownership of all the San members of the N‡a Jaqna Conservancy will be deepened by the detailed community-based land use and development planning currently underway. In addition, the planning exercise will provide a powerful tool to allow the conservancy membership to take control of the natural resources in the area.

However, while there have been over a dozen conservancies established on communal lands in northern Namibia, some of which are in the hands of San communities, there are threats to the long-term viability of these conservancies because of population growth, in-migration of other groups and possible changes in land tenure.

Threats in West Caprivi

In West Caprivi, the Namibian government announced in 2002 that the West Caprivi Game Reserve would be turned into a national park, the Bwabwata National Park. There will be restrictions placed on where people can live in the national park and on the kinds of activities that they can pursue there. For example, people will not be allowed to keep cattle in some parts of the new national park, and there will be limits placed on agricultural activities. The Khwe and !Xun (Vasekele) of West Caprivi are concerned that they will not receive the benefits they have been promised in the Ministry of Environment and Tourism's *Vision for Caprivi* plan and that they will potentially be excluded from decision-making in the new national park.

Another potential threat facing the Khwe, !Xun, and other San in Namibia is the proposed construction of a dam on the Okavango River, near Popa Falls. This dam could potentially have significant impacts on down-stream populations and habitats, not only in Namibia but also in the Okavango Delta region of Botswana, which supports sizeable numbers of people, including many San. At present, the plans for building this dam are on hold for economic reasons but the Namibian government hopes to go ahead with the facility at some point in the not-too-distant future. There was also talks in early 2004 of the Namibian government revisiting the controversial Epupa Falls dam scheme on the Cunene River, where Himba and other people have grazing land, sacred sites and important resources.

The governments of Angola and Botswana and various non-government organizations have protested at the Namibian government's plans for dams and other water projects on the Okavango and the Cunene Rivers in Namibia, as have organizations such as the International Rivers Network (IRN), Greenpeace and the Okavango Wildlife Society in South Africa.

"We are people who suffer"

The San feel that they are marginalized minorities who have less access to rights and resources than other groups in Namibia. They are concerned about the trend, even in community-based natural resource management in Namibia, which they see as having potential benefits but which increasingly appears to them to be overseen by other groups or individuals who reap the majority of the rewards. If current trends continue in Namibia, some San believe they will face further problems in terms of lack of access to natural resources and development programs. It is for this reason that the San of Namibia have sought the assistance and support of organizations such as WIMSA, which collaborates with them in efforts to promote San rights. Without collaborative, participatory, community-based development and education programs in Namibia and the support of government and non-government organizations such as WIMSA, the San will continue to be marginalized, dispossessed, and poverty-stricken, facing a future with little hope. ❏

References

1   Suzman, James. (Ed.) 2001. *An Assessment of the Status of the San Namibia.* Windhoek, Namibia: Legal Assistance Center.
2   United Nations High Commissioner for Refugees. 2003. What Next for Osire Refugees? *Newsletter of the United Nations in Namibia*, Issue 1, May, 2003. Windhoek, Namibia: UNHCR.
3   Sylvain, Renée. 2002. Land, Water and Truth: San Identity and Global Indigenism. *American Anthropologist* 104(4):1074 -1085.
4   Working Group of Indigenous Minorities in Southern Africa. 2003. Report on Activities April 2002 to March 2003. Windhoek, Namibia: WIMSA.

BOTSWANA

In some areas of the world where indigenous peoples have been displaced from their ancestral areas, prospects are looking up for the return of their land and resource rights. Some progress is being made, for example, in Australia, Canada, Greenland, New Zealand and South Africa. These small successes have been achieved through (1) negotiated settlements, (2) government legislation, (3) use of customary, international and national law and (4) court action. Some progress has been made in South Africa in recent years, through negotiated settlements and court action. By and large this has not been the case, however, for San residing in Botswana.

CKGR residents go to court

In Botswana, San and Bakgalagadi living in the Central Kalahari Game Reserve (CKGR) were forced to leave their ancestral lands as a result of the Botswana government's decisions regarding the status of the reserve and the rights of the people who lived there. The CKGR, the second largest game reserve in Africa, was set aside in 1961 for the purpose of protecting habitats and the people that utilized the resources and had lived in the region for generations. In 1986, the Botswana government decreed that the people of the CKGR had to move out of the reserve. This event set in motion a whole series of efforts on the part of Central Kalahari residents and support groups to try and force the Botswana government to reverse its decision. A Negotiating Team of CKGR residents and supporters was formed in 1996, which attempted to engage the Botswana government in discussions as to the future of the CKGR, to no avail.

By early 2002, nearly all of the reserve's residents, who had numbered well over a thousand in the 1980s, had been relocated by the Botswana government and District Councils to two large settlements and one smaller settlement in areas on the periphery of the reserve. There the resettled people were eking out an existence and living on government rations and what was left of the compensation payments that some of them had received. Some of them were being arrested for hunting, while others had been stopped from entering the game reserve, even in cases where they were seeking lost livestock. During 2003, some San returned to the Central Kalahari, mainly to three former settlements, where they resided and foraged for a living and

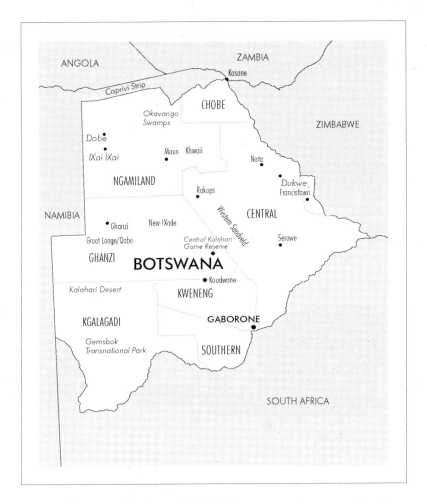

grew some crops. By the end of 2003, however, there were less than 100 San and Bakgalagadi still on the reserve.

The Botswana government officially argued that the reason for the resettlement was to ensure that local people in the Central Kalahari could benefit from development opportunities and services provided by the government. Officials also argued that, by being outside of the reserve, people could more easily participate "in the life of the nation". However, judging from interviews, many of the people living in the resettled communities felt that they were worse off after the relocation than they were before, when they lived inside the Central Kalahari Game Reserve.

In February 2002, the G|wi and G||ana San and Bakgalagadi of the central Kalahari region of Botswana filed a legal case in the High Court of Botswana in an effort to force the Botswana government to reverse its decision to require residents of the Central Kalahari Game Reserve to leave the reserve and to oblige it to restore services such as the provision of water, which the people of the Central Kalahari – and their supporters – felt was a basic human right. The Botswana High Court dismissed the case on a technicality, arguing that the case had not been filed properly. An appeal was successfully made, and it is now likely that a new legal case will be heard in the High Court of Botswana in mid-2004.

Hunting rights

Another area of concern for San and Khoe in Botswana relates to subsistence hunting rights. Subsistence hunting licenses, known in Botswana as Special Game Licenses (SGLs), were abolished in 2002. Now, the only way the San can get access to wildlife for subsistence purposes is for them to establish a community-based organization (CBO) with a constitution and management board and then request the Department of Wildlife and National Parks to grant the organization rights to the wildlife in their area. This granting of rights over wildlife resources does not, however, imply that the people have land rights to the community-controlled hunting area (CCHA). Some San obtained licenses through the normal citizen hunting license system but there were reports in 2003 that even they were being denied the license when it was learned who had received them.

Land and resource tenure rights

The problem facing the San and some other rural people in Botswana is that they have not been able to obtain secure land and resource tenure rights. The reasons for this situation are complex but they are due, in part, to the fact that the Botswana government and the District Land Boards and Councils have been unwilling to grant land rights to groups who make claims on the basis of customary rights and traditional livelihoods. The efforts to lay claim to ancestral territories on the basis of "indigenousness", the notion that San peoples were "first comers" or "native to the areas in which they lived", have been rejected by the Botswana government, which does not accept the argument that the San or any other group is indigenous. The Botswana government maintains that all the country's citizens are indigenous.

In 2003, the Minister for Local Government in Botswana, Margaret Nasha, discussed the issue of land rights under the country's new land policy. She categorically rejected the idea of San having special rights different from other citizens of Botswana, and said that the San have the same rights to apply to the Land Board for land as other citizens do. The idea that the settlements developed under the Remote Area Development Program, of which there are currently 64, are in the hands of local people is inaccurate. In fact, virtually all of them have seen other people from the outside moving into them, often bringing with them their cattle and other domestic animals, or starting small shops. The San who apply for land in these places often have difficulty in obtaining business licenses, whereas other people who are not San seem to have little trouble. What this means, in effect, is that San are treated differently by Land Boards on the basis of their ethnic background, which is illegal under Botswana law.

In Botswana, the National Policy for Agricultural Development (NPAD) and the Fencing Act have the potential to dispossess even more people than the Tribal Grazing Land Policy, which the World Bank estimated displaced between 28,000 and 31,000 people during the 1980s. The total amount of land allocated to commercial ranches under TGLP was 335,000 hectares. There were commercial areas in Central, Kweneng, Ngwaketse (Southern), Kgalagadi, Ghanzi and North West Districts. Now, under NPAD, it is estimated that there will be 539 ranches, each of which will be 6 by 6 km in size (36 sq km, or 3,600 hectares). Most of the ranches (over 90%) that will cause dispossession will be in the Sandveld region of Western Central District and the Botletle River region.

Judging from comments made in consultations and interviews with the media, San in Botswana are not asking for special rights – they simply want to be treated like other citizens of Botswana. It is not just San who have lost access to land in national parks, game reserves, national monuments or commercial ranching areas but other people as well. The difference is that San, when they apply for water rights or for grazing rights, do not usually get these rights allocated to them by the Land Boards.

Some reports (e.g. the assessment of the Remote Area Development Program of Botswana, 2003) argue that the reason San do not get land is because they do not know the correct procedures by which to apply for land. This assumption is false. San have been applying for land from Land Boards since their inception in Botswana in 1970, as can be seen, for example, in the efforts of Ju | 'hoansi San to apply for land at Dobe and |Xai |Xai in Ngamiland (North West District).

In 1999, the Trust for Okavango Cultural and Development Initiatives (TOCaDI), a San support organization, began assisting San communities in North West District to dig wells and drill boreholes and seek water rights from the Land Boards. As of mid-2003, water rights had been obtained by several of the San communities, but the agreements had not been acted upon, pending final approval by the Technical Advisory Committee (TAC) of the North West District Council. It remains to be seen whether or not the North West District Council will grant *de jure* (legal) land and water rights to the people of Ngamiland. The various San support organizations, including TOCaDI and the Working Group of Indigenous Minorities in Southern Africa, continue to push for full rights to land and resources to be granted.

The Khoe and San Conference

In 2003, there was a major conference on Khoe and San peoples held at the University of Botswana. Entitled "Research for Khoe and San Development", the conference was held at the Center for Continuing Education of the University of Botswana from 10-12 September 2003. Several conclusions were reached at the conference, including (1) the need for greater participation of San and Khoe peoples in research and development, (2) the importance of language retention and community-oriented education, (3) the significance of greater emphasis on land and resource rights for San and Khoe peoples, and (4) the need for greater empowerment efforts among San and Khoe. ❏

References

Botswana Institute for Development Policy Analysis. 2003. Review of the Remote Area Development Program. (Draft, May 26, 2003). Gaborone, Botswana: Botswana Institute for Development Policy Analysis.

Cassidy, Lin, Ken Good, Isaac Mazonde, and Roberta Rivers. 2001. *An Assessment of the Status of the San in Botswana*. Windhoek, Namibia: Legal Assistance Center.

Suzman, James. 2001. *An Introduction to the Regional Assessment of the Status of the San in Southern Africa*. Windhoek, Namibia: Legal Assistance Center.

SOUTH AFRICA

South Africa is edging towards being the first African country to formally recognise the rights of indigenous peoples - or "vulnerable indigenous peoples" as they are officially called. Indigenous civil society continues to build capacity and interact with the United Nations and other international norms and standards relating to the rights of indigenous peoples.

South Africa's population is made up of at least five major groupings. These include the Khoe and San first peoples, most of whom were obliterated during colonialism, although some communities survive, and an increasing number of assimilated descendant groups are claiming back their aboriginal heritage. Other major groups include Black Bantu-language speaking groups who migrated to South Africa from the north about 800 years ago and make up the majority population. They were disenfranchised and suffered gross human rights violations on the part of the white minority during the 40 years of apartheid rule. Apartheid laws did not recognise the presence of indigenous first peoples, who were considered to be "extinct". Other population groups include people of White European settler origin, various peoples of Asian origin, African immigrants and migrants, and people of mixed race.

Towards a new policy framework

After a five-year process of looking at constitutional accommodation through changes to the Traditional Authorities Act, the Portfolio Committee in Parliament made the important decision to separate Khoe-San issues from the general issue of (Bantu language-speaking) traditional leadership. This may look like a step backwards but is likely to benefit the indigenous peoples in the longer term. The Portfolio Committee and the Department of Provincial and Local Government (DPLG) are asking Cabinet to create a broader policy framework to accommodate indigenous peoples, which would go beyond the tricky issue of hereditary chieftaincies. DPLG, in consultation with the National Khoe-San Council, will promote a more holistic policy process involving all government departments and touching on key areas of language rights, land rights, as well as governance and traditional authorities.

One issue has been whether to include as first peoples the !Xun and Khwe communities who were brought to South Africa in 1990 by the military from Angola and Namibia and now live in Kimberley. A draft consultant's report commissioned by DPLG on traditional leadership, which includes a rough summary of community histories and issues, recommended that the Department consider advising Cabinet to recognise only the ‡Khomani San as indigenous peoples, excluding the more numerous !Xun and Khwe. The San Council, who met to discuss the draft report, however, took a firm stand stating that all San communities should be recognised as indigenous, regardless of where they were born.

Though the time frame for a new policy statement remains somewhat discreet, it is evident that the government sees the resolution of the Khoe-San issues as a priority. There has been a long-standing tension between the slow process of domestic policy development and the concern of the Department of Foreign Affairs to take a stand at UN forums on international standards. A new policy framework should clarify which department or departments are meant to drive the broader domestic policy process.

South Africa supports indigenous cause internationally

In May 2003, the Indigenous Peoples of Africa Co-ordinating Committee (IPACC) and South African indigenous activists met with South African diplomats in New York City. The South African diplomats advised the African indigenous groups to become more focused in their lobbying and to work more closely with the various African legations in New York. South Africa is playing a leadership role in the African diplomatic caucus, which puts it in a strong position to promote indigenous rights at the United Nations.

In September 2003, South Africa's diplomats took the floor at the Inter-sessional meeting on the Draft Declaration on the Rights of Indigenous Peoples and called for both an extension of the UN Working Group on Indigenous Populations' (WGIP) mandate and support from African countries for the Draft Declaration. This is the first overt statement by an African government in this particular forum.

The challenge for South Africa is that it cannot adopt any formal foreign policy positions until there is a clear domestic policy based on constitutional principles. The pursuit of domestic policy on traditional authorities has, in some ways, been a cul-de-sac delaying the emergence of a clear foreign policy. The government is used to dealing with Black agro-pastoralists with a long history of colonial and pre-colonial traditional authorities. Historically, hunter-gatherers and herding peoples have tended not to have such permanent traditional authority structures. Where there were traditional authorities, these tended to be related to the qualities of individual leaders rather than any systematic inheritance of power. This rather evident point was not factored into the first policy push towards recognising traditional authorities. The new holistic approach by the government may resolve this impasse and see the rapid emergence of a new policy, opening the door towards signing ILO Convention No. 169.

A landmark court victory

The most important event in 2003 was the landmark court victory for the Nama people of the Richtersveld. The Nama, an indigenous pastoralist Khoe people, laid claim to mineral rights in their rich but greatly exploited home territory in far north-western South Africa. The Land Claims Court rejected their claim against the parastatal mining company, Alexcor. However, they took the case to the Supreme Court of Appeal (SCA). After a difficult process of establishing their identity as first peoples, the court eventually accepted that (1) the Nama lost their land before 1913 on the basis of racial prejudice and administrative action; but (2) that even though it was before the cut off date 1913 for any land claims, the same principle of restitution should apply. The SCA agreed that rights to the land (including minerals and precious stones) were similar to common law ownership and that they constituted a "customary law interest".[1]

Lawyers from the Legal Resources Centre (LRC) drew on the argument of "aboriginal title" as understood in Canadian law. This event was not only a victory for South Africa's indigenous peoples but also opens the door to other Commonwealth courts being willing to recognise aboriginal title using South African and Canadian jurisprudence.

Intellectual property rights: latest developments

One major event in 2002 was the signing of an out-of-court settlement on the intellectual property rights of the San in relation to the commercial exploitation of !khoba (*hoodia gordonii*). In 2003, Pfizer, who held the licence to develop !khoba for the international market, pulled out of the deal on the grounds that the phyto-nutrients (or more simply stated the active ingredient) in !khoba could not viably be synthetically produced. It is likely that the Council for Scientific and Industrial Research (CSIR), the patent holders and signatories to the agreement with the San Council of South Africa, will find a new international licensee to get the product on the market. There are already illegal versions of !khoba being sold in South African retail outlets.

The San Council also negotiated a positive outcome with the KwaZulu-Natal authorities over their status as guardians of the San heritage prior to the launch of Didima Rock Art Centre in the Drakensberg. Initially, the San leadership had not been consulted on the development of the multi-million Rand[2] tourism and cultural heritage venture, taking place in the heart of the only World Heritage Site based on the San rock art of the Ukahlamba Drakensberg Mountains. This oversight was rectified and the KwaZulu-Natal authorities invited the San Council to attend and deliver a keynote address at the official opening of the rock art centre. Current initiatives include the addition of a heritage information section provided by the San themselves, conveying information about contemporary San peoples, and a commitment to securing San representation on the heritage management of the Ukahlamba Drakensberg world heritage site.

Other progress

The attention given to indigenous issues is having an impact on civil society formation in rural indigenous areas. The Nama people of the Richtersveld, fresh from their court victory, have nominated their first "Kaptein" in over a century. Gert Links, a descendant of the last traditional leader of the Nama people of that area in the 19th century, is preparing to take his claim to the new Framework Commission that has been established by Government to process applications for chieftaincies on the part of Black, Khoe and San leaders.

In preparation for the 2002 World Parks Congress, Nama, Griqua and San leaders held a workshop on their experiences with South African National Parks (SANP). The results of the workshop and case studies of four Parks on indigenous peoples' lands were published by IPACC and SASI and distributed at the Durban WPC.[3] The Interim Working Group on Indigenous Peoples and Parks (IWGPP) is likely to continue operating in 2004 in order to put pressure on SANP to standardise its social ecology programme for indigenous peoples. Parks involved include Kgalagadi Transfrontier Park, Richtersveld National Park, Augrabies Falls National Park and Knersvlakte Provincial Biosphere Reserve.

Language issues are also slowly progressing in terms of both policy and practice. There are pilot schools for Khoekhoegowab (the language spoken by the Nama people) in both the Richtersveld and Riemvasmaak, both remote rural areas on the Orange River. The National Khoe-San Consultative Council (NKCC) continues to act as a civil society forum uniting the various groups that see themselves as indigenous. This includes Griqua, Nama, San and revivalist Khoe-San groups. The NKCC poses a distinct challenge to the National Khoe-San Council created by the Government during consultations in the late 1990s and whose legitimacy and mandate are in question. ❑

Notes

1 See www.lrc.org.za for more information.
2 South African monetary unit (1 Rand = 0.14 US dollar).
3 Publication available from IPACC, see www.ipacc.org.za

PART II

INTERNATIONAL
PROCESSES

THE SPECIAL RAPPORTEUR: 2003 OVERVIEW

During 2003, the Special Rapporteur (SR) continued to gather information on the situation of the human rights of indigenous peoples; follow developments in the United Nations system; and participate in international and national-level conferences and research seminars, evaluations, training workshops and the like that deal directly with the issues of his mandate. He also undertook research into some of the major issues affecting indigenous peoples and carried out several visits to countries and indigenous communities.

In the SR's report,[1] to be presented to the 60th session of the UN Commission on Human Rights (April 2004), Mr. Stavenhagen concentrates on the obstacles, gaps and challenges faced by indigenous peoples in the realm of justice administration and the relevance of indigenous customary law in national legal systems, issues that have repeatedly been identified as being of crucial importance to full enjoyment of human rights on the part of indigenous peoples.

As stated in the report, indigenous peoples the world over are usually among the most marginalized and dispossessed sectors of society, the victims of perennial prejudice and discrimination. Even when protective legislation is available, their rights are frequently denied in practice, a pattern that is of particular concern when it occurs in the administration of justice. As has been emphasized by the SR on several occasions, a fair and effective justice system is crucial to fostering reconciliation, peace, stability and development among indigenous peoples.

According to the Special Rapporteur's report, information brought to his attention indicates that, in many countries, indigenous peoples do not enjoy equal access to the justice system and they frequently encounter discrimination of all kinds in its methods of operation. This is partly due to racism and partly the result of a failure to accept indigenous law and customs on the part of the official legal institutions of a national state. Indigenous people tend to be over-represented in criminal justice, are often denied due process and are frequently the victims of violence and physical abuse. Indigenous women and children are particularly vulnerable in this respect. In addition, numerous cases of criminalization of indigenous social and political protest activities have come to the attention of the SR. Language and cultural differences play their role in this pattern of discrimination, and they are not always sufficiently addressed by the state. Some countries have made progress in recognizing the specific needs of indigenous people in the field of justice and have adopted laws and institutions designed to protect their human rights. Indigenous customary law is being increasingly recognized by the courts and the lawmakers as well as by the public administration. Some countries are experimenting with alternative legal institutions and conflict resolution mechanisms, with encouraging results.

In his report, the Special Rapporteur recommends, among other things, that States carry out exhaustive reviews and, if necessary, reforms of their justice systems in order to better protect the rights of indigenous peoples. He invites the Commission on Human Rights to take up this issue with Member States. Such reforms should include respect for indigenous legal customs, language and culture in the courts and the administration of justice; the full participation of indigenous people in justice reform; and the establishment of alternative justice mechanisms.

Country visits in 2003

A crucial component of the Special Rapporteur's mandate is to visit countries in order to initiate constructive dialogue with the Government, indigenous communities and other relevant organizations, and report back to the Commission on Human Rights on the situation of the indigenous peoples. Country visits are an excellent way of analysing and understanding *in situ* the situation of indigenous peoples in the light of every possible circumstance and they also represent an important tool for awareness raising in the international community.

During the period under review, the Special Rapporteur carried out two official country missions, to Mexico in June, and to Chile in July.[2] The Special Rapporteur has continued to pay special attention to the situation of indigenous women and children when visiting countries, including specific gatherings to hear their concerns. Moreover, at the invitation of the First Nations of Canada, he visited that country in May 2003 and, at the invitation of the Sami Parliament, he visited northern Norway and Finland in October 2003 to observe the situation of indigenous peoples.

Mexico
The Special Rapporteur visited Mexico from 1 to 18 June 2003. The indigenous population of Mexico, which currently accounts for approximately 12 per cent of the total population, predominates in many rural municipalities, particularly in the south-east, and can also be

found in urban areas. The vulnerability of indigenous rights comprises a number of aspects. Human rights violations and political conflicts occur in many rural areas inhabited by indigenous peoples, mainly in the context of the system for prosecuting and administering justice.

Discrimination against indigenous people can be observed in low human and social development indices, extreme poverty, inadequate social services, the way in which investments and production projects are implemented and the huge inequality between indigenous and non-indigenous people in terms of wealth and income distribution. Where indigenous matters are concerned, the constitutional reform of 2001 does not meet the aspirations and demands of the organized indigenous movement. This means it provides less coverage in terms of protecting the human rights of indigenous peoples and makes renewal of the dialogue for peace in the state of Chiapas more difficult.

The SR recommends in his report, among other things, that the Government of Mexico should pay urgent attention to preventing and resolving social conflicts in indigenous regions; to reviewing the indigenous justice system in depth; to developing a consolidated economic and social policy for the indigenous regions with the active participation of the indigenous peoples, with special focus on migrants, displaced persons, women and children; and to reviewing the constitutional reform of 2001 so that peace can be achieved in Chiapas and the demands of the indigenous peoples for recognition and respect for their human rights met.

Chile

The Special Rapporteur visited Chile between 18 and 29 July 2003. The main indigenous peoples in Chile are the Mapuche, Aymara, Rapa Nui or Pascuense, Atacameño, Quechua, Colla, Kawashkar or Alacaluf and Yámana or Yagán. There are currently around 700,000 indigenous people in Chile, representing 4.6 per cent of the population.

Despite efforts made since the country's return to democracy, the indigenous population continues to be largely ignored and excluded from public life as a result of a long history of rejection, social and economic exclusion and discrimination on the part of the majority society, as the SR states in his report. Chile has still not undertaken any constitutional reform in this area and has not yet ratified the ILO Convention No. 169.

Human rights problems continue to affect all indigenous peoples in the country, although public attention has focused mainly on the situation of the Mapuche. Attention should be drawn above all to the high levels of poverty among indigenous peoples and their low standard of living which, according to various human development indicators, is below the national average. The Government's welfare policies are important but have so far not been sufficient to redress this situation.

One of the most serious long-standing problems affecting indigenous peoples in Chile, according to the SR, relates to land ownership and territorial rights, the result of a long process that has left them stripped of their lands and resources. The issue becomes more complicated when it concerns access to underground resources or other resources, such as water or products from the sea.

The SR also notes that the protection and promotion of indigenous peoples' rights have been affected by situations such as the construction of the Ralco hydro-electric power station in Alto Bío-Bío, the problems surrounding access to and use of water resources by the Aymara and Atacameño peoples in the arid northern region, and the restrictions imposed on many Lafkenche families along the coast of Araucanía, which hinder their access to their traditional fisheries and coastal products.

The Government has made significant efforts in the economic and social fields over the last 13 years but there is a pent-up demand for social services on the part of native communities. While many indigenous people have benefited, like others, from the sustained economic growth of recent years, their standard of living is still well below the national average and that of non-indigenous Chileans. Despite falling poverty levels, profound economic inequalities affect indigenous people more than other Chileans. In the field of health, for example, attention has been drawn to the systematic discrimination of indigenous people in accessing medical services and in the quality of these services. Their communities' traditional medicine has been devalued and ignored, if not banned altogether. The few attempts made to promote intercultural medicine in some hospitals in indigenous areas have produced promising results but the programme is still in its infancy.

Despite efforts made in the area of bilingual intercultural education, the majority of indigenous communities do not yet benefit from this programme, and the educational system has not yet fully met the demands from indigenous people to protect, preserve and promote their traditional culture. Calls for the preservation of their cultural identity were heard in all the regions visited. The Atacameño and Quechua peoples in the north, for example, complain about the loss of their language as a result of the "Chileanization" to which they were subjected after the War of the Pacific.[3] The Rapa Nui people sees its identity threatened by the rise in immigration to their island and their traditional authorities' inability to do anything about the implications of this inflow.

On the basis of these conclusions, the Special Rapporteur recommends to the Government of Chile, among other things, that the process of constitutional reform in relation to indigenous matters should be speeded up; that ILO Convention No. 169 should be ratified promptly; that any sectoral legislation in conflict with the Indigenous Peoples Act should be revised; that a programme to cut poverty in indigenous communities should be set up, with a realistic and clearly defined agenda; and that the necessary steps should be taken to establish a national human rights institution. He also recommends that urgent attention be paid to the prevention and resolution of conflicts over land tenure and use; that the Land Fund should be streamlined and expanded; that access on the part of indigenous communities to water and maritime resources should be guaranteed; that the necessary measures should be taken to avoid criminalizing legitimate protest activities or social demands; and that high-quality, bilingual legal assistance should be provided.

Communications

The Special Rapporteur receives a large number of communications providing him with information about allegations of violations of the human rights and fundamental freedoms of indigenous peoples. The main sources of these communications are non-governmental organizations, indigenous organizations, intergovernmental organizations and other United Nations procedures concerned with the protection of human rights. He analyses such information and decides whether or not to take action. The main type of communication sent by the SR is an "urgent appeal" when there is an imminent danger of the rights of an individual, or even an entire indigenous community, being violated. ❑

FACILITATING THE DIALOGUE

In 2003 IWGIA continued to give special priority to supporting indigenous initiatives aimed at facilitating the dialogue between indigenous peoples and the Special Rapporteur. In May, IWGIA funded a two-day workshop in Mexico City (May 30 and 31) in preparation for Dr. Stavenhagen's official visit to Mexico. In July, an IWGIA representative travelled as a resource person with the Special Rapporteur (SR) and his team to Chile, and in October the SR visited Copenhagen at the invitation of IWGIA.

The Mexico Workshop

The workshop was jointly organized by the Council of the Nahua Communities of the Alto Balsas (*Consejo de los Pueblos Nahuas de Alto Balsas*, CPNAB), ANIPA (*Asamblea Nacional Indígena Plural por la Autonomía*) and CIPO–RFM (*Consejo Indígena Popular de Oaxaca – Ricardo Flores Magón*).[4] Some 40 representatives – men and women - from all over the country were invited to participate in the workshop, but many more turned up for the event and more than 90 put their name on the list of participants. Sixteen of Mexico's 31 federated states were represented.

The purpose of the workshop was to compile the documentation that each delegation had prepared on the situation in their respective region and present it to the SR during his visit at the end of the workshop, as well as to discuss his travel schedule in order to ensure that he visited crucial areas.

This documentation, which was presented orally during the first day, and again, in an abbreviated form, to the SR, raised a great number of extremely diverse issues – ranging from cultural demands (e.g. unimpeded access to sacred sites, the establishment of an indigenous university, teaching of indigenous languages, etc.) to land conflicts (both as a result of illegal land appropriation but also due to overlapping land claims between two neighbouring communities) and human rights abuses. There were also several very moving personal testimonies on gross violations of human rights.

The workshop also discussed at length the draft agenda of the SR's visit, published a few days earlier. The workshop was quite critical of this agenda for not including a visit to some of the "hot spots" such as the state of Guerrero, and for not considering visits to the communities, where the SR would have been able to get a "feeling" of the situation of the indigenous peoples in Mexico.

The second part of the workshop – i.e. the afternoon of the last day – had been set aside for a three-hour meeting with the SR. First point on the agenda was reading a letter-document prepared by the workshop and handing it over. After that each state delegation was given 5-10 minutes to present the situation in their respective state, and finally there was an open discussion regarding the SR's travel itinerary.

Results of workshop

The workshop was in many ways a success. It was well organised, the participants represented a large spectrum of indigenous organisations from all over the country, and the meeting with the SR was characterized by mutual respect and understanding of the importance of the forthcoming official visit.

The results included the preparation of the letter-document, a 47-page long overview of some of the most crucial issues that indigenous peoples have to deal with in Mexico; the letter-document made some suggestions regarding the SR's agenda and the matters to be discussed during his visit. It also made proposals regarding concrete actions to be taken – among others, to intervene at government level to encourage compliance with the San Andrés Accords and the liberation of indigenous political prisoners.

The SR finally did go to Guerrero, albeit for a short two-hour visit to Tlapa, in the heart of the most conflict-ridden area of the state, the La Montaña region, where he met with several indigenous delegations.

Finally, several delegates stated that this was the first time they had participated in this kind of meeting and that it had made them aware that their own situation was not unique. Many, as a matter of fact, did not even know that there were states where the situation was far worse than theirs. Or, as one woman said: "Until recently I did not know that there were Indians in other states, I thought we were the only ones!"

The Special Rapporteur's visit to IWGIA

In October 2003, IWGIA invited Mr. Rodolfo Stavenhagen to visit Copenhagen on his way to a Conference organised by the Forum for Development Cooperation with Indigenous Peoples at the University of Tromsø, Norway.

During his stay in Copenhagen, Rodolfo Stavenhagen discussed with IWGIA developments related to the mandate of the Special Rapporteur, future challenges in the promotion and protection of the human rights of indigenous peoples and possible activities to support the work of the SR. Moreover, IWGIA arranged several meetings. One meeting was with the Prime Minister of Greenland, Mr. Hans Enoksen and several officials from the Home Rule Office in Copenhagen; another was with Ambassador Thyge Lehman, from the Human Rights Unit at the Ministry for Foreign Affairs, and his team, including members of DANIDA in charge of indigenous issues; and finally there was a meeting with Judge Per Wahlsoe, of Denmark's Supreme Court.

During the meeting with the representatives of Greenland's Home Rule the SR was briefed on Greenland's achievements with regard to the promotion and protection of the rights of the indigenous peoples. They also mentioned some remaining issues. The Special Rapporteur was also informed about the current situation of the "Thule case" regarding the displaced Inughuit's right to return.

The second main issue of discussion in the meetings that the SR had with both the Greenland Home Rule representatives and with Judge Per Wahlsoe was the legal system and the administration of justice in Greenland. Mr Whalsoe is one of the 15 members of the Commission on Greenland's Judicial System jointly appointed by the Government of Denmark and the Greenland Home Rule Office/Government in 1994. The Commission is mandated to review and reassess thoroughly the entire judicial system in Greenland, and is expected to release its final report soon.

Both the Greenland Home Rule Government and the Danish Ministry of Foreign Affairs extended a verbal invitation to the SR to visit Denmark and Greenland in the near future. ❑

Notes

1 E/CN.4/2004/80
2 The country mission reports are contained in documents E/CN.4/2004/80/Add.2 and Add.3 respectively.
3 The War of the Pacific was fought between Chile and the joint forces of Bolivia and Peru, from 1879 to 1884. Chile gained substantial mineral-rich territory in the conflict, leaving Bolivia a land-locked country. (Ed. Note)
4 Ricardo Flores Magón was a famous indigenous revolutionary from Oaxaca at the beginning of the 20th century.

THE UN PERMANENT FORUM ON INDIGENOUS ISSUES

The second meeting of the Permanent Forum on Indigenous Issues took place in New York from 12 to 23 May 2003 and was, by many standards, a success, with 1,800 registered participants, among them more than 600 indigenous representatives, and twice as many state representatives as last year. There was also an increase in the number of UN agencies and bodies attending the session, which shows a growing interest within the UN system on the work of the Forum.

The expert members of the Permanent Forum re-elected Mr Ole Henrik Magga (Norway) as their Chairperson. They also re-elected the four Vice-Chairpersons: Mr Antonio Jacanamijoy (Colombia), Ms Njuma Ekundanayo (Democratic Republic of the Congo), Mr Parshuram Tamang (Nepal), and Ms Mililani Trask (USA). Mr Willie Littlechild (Canada) was also re-elected as the Permanent Forum's Rapporteur.

Indigenous children and youth

The Forum focused this year on the theme "indigenous children and youth". A high level panel on this topic was organised on the first day of the second session. The panel included presentations by UNICEF, UNESCO, the World Health Organisation, the chairperson of the Committee on the Rights of the Child, the International Labour Organisation (ILO), the Foreign Minister of Ecuador, and a youth representative from the Cherokee Nation.

All participants stressed the particularly vulnerable position of indigenous children. Some of the risks that disproportionately affect indigenous children are child trafficking, child labour, lack of access to education and health care, and degradation of the environment. One of the results of this discussion was the commitment from the Committee on the Rights of the Child to devote a day of discussion to indigenous children and youth in September 2003.

The Permanent Forum draft recommendations on children and youth urged the World Bank, the International Labour Organisation (ILO), and UNICEF to carry out an in-depth comparative study of legal frameworks and social programmes for indigenous youth in selected countries, and urged all UN bodies whose work has an impact on indigenous children to report regularly to the Forum. Noting the large number of incarcerated indigenous children and youth, the Forum also recommended that governments ensure greater protection and humane treatment for those imprisoned individuals, and take steps for their rehabilitation.

The six mandated areas

This 2nd session also had on its agenda the discussion on the six mandated areas: Economic and Social Development, Environment, Health, Human Rights, Culture and Education.[1]

Under this discussion a large number of UN specialised agencies and associated bodies were invited to present their work and programmes regarding indigenous peoples to the Forum. There were interventions from the World Bank, UNDP, the ILO, UN-Habitat, UNEP and the Secretariat for the Convention on Biological Diversity, United Nations Population Fund, UNICEF, WHO, UNESCO, OHCHR and others.

In its 2nd session the Forum continued promoting and strengthening an interactive dialogue with indigenous representatives, governments and agencies speaking and responding to one another in order to emphasise participation and engagement.

Also scheduled during the session were several side events consisting of films and panel discussions, focusing on such topics as youth, women, the environment, human rights, genetic technologies, labour rights, and indigenous journalism. Every day during the official session's lunch break different panel discussions organised by NGOs, indigenous organisations or UN agencies took place.

After two weeks of deliberations the Forum outlined six draft decisions to be forwarded to ECOSOC for approval:

- Would authorise the UN Department of Economic and Social Affairs to convene a *three-day workshop on collecting data about indigenous peoples;*
- Would devote the *high-level segment of ECOSOC's 2006 substantive session to indigenous issues;*
- Would confirm *participation of members of the Forum* in meetings of ECOSOC's subsidiary bodies;
- Would confirm the practice of designating six members from the *Forum's bureau* as a method of work of the Forum;
- Would convene the *third session of the Forum* from 10-21 May 2004 at UN headquarters in New York;

- Would approve the *Forum's provisional agenda* and documentation for the third session, which will focus on *indigenous women, with an emphasis on their status and participation at the national and international levels.*

The Forum also adopted eight draft recommendations, which include the following proposals:

Economic and social development
- The Forum should create a three-year working group on free, prior and informed consent and participatory research guidelines, as they related to indigenous land and resources.

Environment
- The UN system should organise a workshop on resource extraction and indigenous peoples to further the dialogue on corporate accountability and the rehabilitation of mined-out areas, polluted water bodies, compensation to adversely affected communities, and sustainable development and land rights, with a view to developing a mechanism to address those issues;
- Establish an international ethical code on bio-prospecting to avoid bio-piracy and to ensure respect for indigenous culture and intellectual heritage.

Health
- Relevant UN bodies should incorporate indigenous healers and cultural perspectives on health and illness into their policies, and undertake regional consultations with indigenous peoples on those issues;
- Member states should expand their national health systems to provide holistic health programmes for indigenous children;
- Member states should address malnutrition in indigenous children by adopting special measures to protect the cultivation of traditional food crops.

Human Rights
- Country-specific Special Rapporteurs, experts and representatives of the Commission on Human Rights should pay attention to the situation of indigenous peoples;
- The UN Secretary-General should prepare an analytical study on ways indigenous issues had been addressed in UN bodies;

- Member states should adopt the draft UN Declaration on the Rights of Indigenous Peoples.

Culture
- The Forum recommended that governments introduce indigenous languages in public administration in indigenous territories wherever possible, and that governments and UN bodies support indigenous media and promote the engagement of indigenous youth in indigenous programmes.

Education
- An academic institution should be created to train indigenous leaders and public and private universities could help develop curricula.

Methods of work with the UN system
- The Inter-Agency Support Group should extend its membership to other UN bodies to promote wider participation in the Forum's work.

Future work
- Governments, foundations and others should give generously to the Voluntary Fund and additional resources should be made available for the Forum secretariat in 2004-05;
- A workshop should be convened to develop innovative working methods for future Forum sessions (a database has been created for recommendations).

Challenges ahead

There is no doubt that the Forum's future success will depend largely on its ability to have an impact on the UN system with regard to indigenous peoples issues and concerns. In this respect it is important to note that after only two sessions, the Forum has provided a new platform within the UN system for states, indigenous peoples, and UN agencies to engage in a constructive dialogue, which has already started to give some concrete results.

One of the key challenges of the Permanent Forum continues to be to reach out to indigenous communities in order to understand their concerns better and share with them information about the UN activities in the region and the work of the Forum. Rapporteur Willie Littlechild said that "one of the loud calls" from the Forum had been that "there has to be more meaningful, effective and direct participation by indigenous peoples" and that the views of indigenous peoples had to be taken into consideration when UN agencies were developing programmes and states were setting policies. The Forum will need to establish close cooperation with regional organisations and institutions to reach the most marginalised peoples, in order to have an effect at the grassroots level. Only by playing an active role will the Permanent Forum convince member states and indigenous peoples that it is not just another layer of bureaucracy.

Another challenge for future sessions is how to prioritise the Forum's recommendations so that they will be translated into action by the United Nations and other agencies. Several indigenous organisations urged the Forum to turn words and paper into real action for indigenous issues.

Although only a small percentage of the Permanent Forum's recommendations of the first session had been fully implemented, there are reasons to be optimistic about its future and it is important to take into account the work carried out during its first year of work.

- Its secretariat has been established in New York and it is up and running.
- The Permanent Forum's web page has gone on-line at www.un.org/esa/socdev/pfii.
- The UN General Assembly set up a Voluntary Fund in 2002, which will secure funding to carry out its own activities and several governments have already committed themselves to contribute to the fund.
- The PF members have been active throughout the year profiling the role of the Forum in different UN discussions.

The Permanent Forum will not function effectively without adequate financing. Its future success will be dependent on an appropriate budget allocation from the Economic and Social Council as well as voluntary contributions from member states. Every effort should be made to ensure that this financing is secured.

The ECOSOC and the Permanent Forum

During its 2003 substantive session held in Geneva in July 2003, the ECOSOC considered the report from the 2nd session of the Permanent

Forum including its decisions and recommendations. The Permanent Forum Chairperson Ole Henrik Magga presented the report. After consideration of the report the ECOSOC took the following decisions with regard to the Permanent Forum:

- To devote the high level segment of its substantive session of 2006 to indigenous issues and to invite the Chairperson of the Forum to participate.
- To hold a workshop on the collection of data concerning indigenous peoples.
- To request that all subsidiary bodies of the Council issue invitations to Forum members to attend all relevant meetings, conferences and seminars.
- Decided on the venue and dates for the third session of the Permanent Forum, its provisional agenda and documentation. (New York, 10th to 21st of May)
- To request that the General Assembly discuss the Forum's recommendation to consider a second International Decade of the World's Indigenous People.
- The ECOSOC postponed the discussion of the review of all existing mechanisms, procedures and programmes within the United Nations concerning indigenous issues with a view to rationalising activities, in order to avoid duplication and overlap and promoting effectiveness of UN bodies dealing with indigenous peoples' issues. This decision meant that the discussion on the future of the WGIP was postponed to next year.

❏

Note

1   The official report of the 2nd session is available at www.un.org/esa/socdev/pfii

THE UN DRAFT DECLARATION: 2003 DEVELOPMENTS

T he Working Group on the Draft Declaration on the Rights of Indigenous Peoples (WGDD) held its 9th session from 15 to 26 September 2003. The Working Group, set up by the UN Commission on Human Rights in 1995, was established with a mandate to complete the adoption of a Draft Declaration on the Rights of Indigenous Peoples within the timeframe of the International Decade of the World's Indigenous Peoples, due to end in 2004. Only one more session of the Working Group therefore remains before it must present its final report to the Commission on Human Rights.

For this reason, both the indigenous organisations that are actively participating in this process and a large number of governments arrived at this 9th Session of the Working Group firmly committed to achieving the adoption of a certain number of articles already discussed at previous sessions. It would thus be possible to demonstrate substantial progress in the Group's work to the UN Commission on Human Rights. Unfortunately, all expectations in this regard were frustrated, as this 9th and most probably penultimate session of the Working Group was unable to provisionally adopt any of the articles discussed.

During the first week's work great efforts were made by a majority of the indigenous representatives as well as by a large number of governments to reach a consensus on the text and content of the articles under discussion. Unfortunately, the situation changed considerably during the second week due to a lack of political will and commitment on the part of a small number of governments who managed to hinder any possibility of progress, frustrating all expectations created during the first week's work.[1]

This lack of progress, just one year before the Working Group's mandate comes to an end, means that there are now serious doubts over the future of this process, for there is a real risk that the Commission on Human Rights will decide not to renew the Working Group's mandate in 2005, meaning that it will have to terminate its work after the 10th Session, to be held in September 2004. For this reason, the future of the Working Group and - in short - of the Declaration now largely depends on intergovernmental negotiations to take place on this subject during the forthcoming sessions of the Commission on Human Rights.

Over the last few months, several indigenous organisations have expressed their concern at this state of affairs and have defended the urgent need for the Commission on Human Rights to renew the Working Group's mandate.

In this regard, we feel it is important to draw attention to the Joint Statement that a number of indigenous organisations with consultative status with ECOSOC such as the Grand Council of the Crees (Eeyou Istchee), Inuit Circumpolar Conference (ICC), International Organization of Indigenous Resource Development (IOIRD), Coordinadora de las Organizaciones Indígenas de la Cuenca Amazónica (COICA), National Aboriginal and Torres Strait Islander Legal Services Secretariat (NAILSS), Innu Council of Nitassinan, and the Foundation for Aboriginal and Islander Research Action (FAIRA) among others,[2] have sent to the Office of the High Commissioner for Human Rights regarding the urgent need to renew the mandate and to improve the processes for creating regulations governing the human rights of indigenous peoples.[3]

Given the significance and impact this declaration may have on discussions around the future of the Working Group and, indeed, the future of a Universal Declaration of Indigenous Rights, IWGIA has decided to reproduce the conclusions and recommendations of this important document in this article. ❏

ASSESSING THE INTERNATIONAL DECADE

URGENT NEED TO RENEW MANDATE AND IMPROVE THE U.N. STANDARD-SETTING PROCESS ON INDIGENOUS PEOPLES' HUMAN RIGHTS

CONCLUSIONS AND RECOMMENDATIONS

Major objective of International Decade – an impending failure

A   The International Decade of the World's Indigenous Peoples will be terminating on December 10, 2004. As declared by the U.N. General Assembly, "the adoption of a declaration on the rights of indigenous peoples [is] a major objective of the Decade". This key objective is highly unlikely to be realized prior to the end of the Decade.

B   From 1984-1993, a draft *U.N. Declaration on the Rights of Indigenous Peoples* had been carefully formulated and ultimately approved by the expert members of the Working Group on Indigenous Populations (WGIP). Indigenous peoples, States, specialized agencies and academics actively participated and exchanged views in this dynamic process. Then, in 1994, the Sub-Commission on the Prevention of Discrimination and Protection of Minorities approved the current text of the draft *Declaration*. Therefore, there is no legitimate reason for the impending failure of the U.N. to adopt such a Declaration within the International Decade.

C   Yet, during the past nine years, the UNCHR inter-sessional Working Group – that was created to consider and recommend a draft Declaration for adoption by the General Assembly – has only provisionally approved 2 of the 45 Articles of the draft *U.N. Declaration on the Rights of Indigenous Peoples*. This remarkable lack of progress is unacceptable.

D   The process in the UNCHR Working Group has been difficult in terms of achieving consensus or "making progress". In part, this could be attributed to the complexity of the issues and the unique nature of the status and rights of Indigenous peoples. However, to a significant degree, it is evidence of a long-standing problem. There is a lack of political will among a number of States to redress past and ongoing violations of our human rights and prevent such intolerable acts in the future.

E   The reluctance of some States participating in the inter-sessional Working Group to reach consensus on explicit human rights norms has far-reaching consequences for over 300 million Indigenous people in all parts of the world. This huge deficiency has tremendous implications for all States and peoples, as well as the United Nations system itself.

F   The present Joint Submission examines in some depth the U.N. standard-setting process, including the UNCHR inter-sessional Working Group, and the impediments to achieving substantial progress. We generally conclude that reform of the overall standard-setting process is urgently needed. In regard to the draft *U.N. Declaration*, the International Decade clearly should have had a more successful outcome.

G   We are especially concerned that the mandate of this inter-sessional Working Group may not be renewed after the end of the International Decade in December 2004. This would in effect terminate the principal and most far-ranging standard-setting process on the human rights of Indigenous peoples within the United Nations.

Successes related to draft *U.N. Declaration on the Rights of Indigenous Peoples*

H   In referring to the impending failure of the U.N. to adopt a Declaration on the rights of Indigenous peoples within the International Decade, it is important not to characterize the draft *U.N. Declaration on the Rights of Indigenous Peoples* as a failure.

I   Although the draft *U.N. Declaration* has not been adopted by the U.N. General Assembly, the human rights standards elaborated over many years and now included in the *Declaration* have assumed a normative value that has profoundly influenced organizations and forums at the international level.

J   The human rights norms in the draft *U.N. Declaration* are being cited by courts at the national level. In addition, the Inter-American Court of Human Rights has indicated that, in addressing Indigenous peoples' complaints of human rights violations, it is necessary to consider "developing norms and principles governing the human rights of indigenous peoples".

K   The draft *U.N. Declaration* and its human rights norms are fostering renewed relations between Indigenous peoples and States. The dynamic and ongoing dialogue concerning the draft *Declaration* at the international level is generating an increasingly important discourse at the domestic level with some States. Such constructive discussions promote mutual respect and understanding. They may also open the door to resolution of conflicts or disputes within States.

L   The United Nations and its Member States, specialized agencies and Indigenous peoples have invested considerable time, as well as human and financial resources, in contributing to the formulation of the draft *U.N. Declaration on the Rights of Indigenous Peoples*.

M   Therefore, it would be highly counter-productive for the United Nations to ignore the achievements to date and abandon its key objective of adopting a U.N. Declaration on the rights of Indigenous peoples.

Urgent need for adoption of *U.N. Declaration on the Rights of Indigenous Peoples*

N   It remains urgent and critical for the U.N. General Assembly to adopt a formal instrument that elaborates elevating human rights standards on the full range of basic issues concerning Indigenous peoples. This necessarily entails a comprehensive rights-based approach.

O   In all regions of the world, Indigenous peoples have been subjected to colonialism, widespread dispossession of lands and resources, discrimination, exclusion, marginalization, forced assimilation and other forms of cultural genocide, genocide and rampant violations of treaty rights. All of these elements are inseparably linked to violations of human rights.

P   This historical and ongoing contemporary situation underlines the urgency of adopting, as a first step, a strong and uplifting *U.N. Declaration on the Rights of Indigenous Peoples.* The legacy of colonialism, dispossession and repeated human rights violations has resulted in the debilitating impoverishment of Indigenous peoples. In turn, this acute poverty continues to largely inhibit, if not prevent, the enjoyment of our basic human rights. Severe poverty also undermines our participatory and other democratic rights. With renewed commitment and concrete assistance from the United Nations, we must bring to an end this destructive cycle.

Q   Severe violations and ongoing denial of Indigenous peoples' human rights, including our right of self-determination, have major adverse impacts. These debilitating actions severely undermine the integrity of Indigenous nations, communities and families and impair the mental and physical health and security of individuals. Indigenous children and youth are especially affected.

R   In regard to Indigenous peoples, the basic values and principles underlying international and domestic legal systems are not being applied fairly and in a non-discriminatory manner. This grave and recurring situation has far-reaching implications for all governments and peoples, as well as international institutions, that are concerned with such interrelated values and principles as democracy, equality, justice, peace, security, environmental protection, development, the rule of law and respect for human rights.

S   As applied to Indigenous peoples, these foundational principles and values of international and domestic legal systems are currently being undermined. Yet these same values and principles are the bases for solemn commitments and affirmed responsibilities by the U.N. and its Member States. These essential precepts provide additional reasons as to why the international community and States must take affirmative measures in relation to Indigenous peoples and vigorously safeguard our human rights.

T   In light of these foundational values and principles and related commitments and responsibilities, it would be contradictory for the U.N. and its Members to terminate the UNCHR standard-setting process concerning Indigenous peoples' human rights.

U   Failure of the United Nations to adopt a strong *Declaration on the Rights of Indigenous Peoples* results in the creation of a legal vacuum. This situation contributes to the perpetuation of grave and recurring problems and prejudices. Serious harms include the continuing impunity for human rights violations against Indigenous peoples in all regions of the world.

V   In addition, failure of the U.N. to adopt Indigenous human rights norms in a formal instrument serves to perpetuate impunity for human rights violations against Indigenous peoples in all regions of the world. Ongoing impunity for widespread and severe human rights violations in effect denies Indigenous peoples the human right to an effective remedy. Impunity weakens respect for human rights, the rule of law and democracy and must not be tolerated.

W   Further, the failure of the U.N. to adopt international human rights norms explicitly pertaining to Indigenous peoples serves to perpetuate an "ominous trend". Rather than take measures to ensure respect for the fundamental rights of Indigenous peoples, some States are criminalizing those Indigenous human rights defenders who protest or take other collective action to safeguard Indigenous lands, territories and resources.

X   This ongoing human rights crisis is a stark reminder that, in relation to Indigenous peoples, the international human rights system is woefully inadequate and incomplete.

Y   In particular, the universal human rights standard-setting process that was initiated internationally by the United Nations, with the adoption of the *Universal Declaration on Human Rights* and the two human rights Covenants, remains unfinished. However, the General Assembly has yet to adopt a U.N. instrument that explicitly, accurately and comprehensively elaborates upon our human rights.

Z   Adoption by the General Assembly of a *U.N. Declaration on the Rights of Indigenous Peoples* would not, alone, resolve the multitude of human rights violations suffered globally by Indigenous peoples. Undoubtedly, however, it would be a crucial and significant measure.

Human rights obligations of U.N. and Member States

AA   In regard to the human rights obligations of the United Nations and Member States, the Purposes and Principles in the *U.N. Charter* are explicit and clear.

BB   The Purposes and Principles require actions "promoting and encouraging respect" for human rights and not undermining them. According to the *U.N. Charter*, the duty to promote respect for human rights is to be based on "respect for the principle of equal rights and self-determination of peoples".

CC   In addition, the international obligation to respect human rights, including the right of self-determination, is of an *erga omnes* character. The same is true of the prohibition against racial discrimination. An *erga omnes* obligation signifies a duty that is binding upon all States. It is also a duty owed to to the international community as a whole.

DD   Yet, in the UNCHR Working Group, some of the participating States pay little attention to the Purposes and Principles of the *U.N. Charter*. They also show little respect for their *erga omnes* obligations relating to the right of self-determination and the prohibition against racial discrimination.

EE   This ongoing, illegitimate conduct has been a major contributor to the lack of progress on the draft *U.N. Declaration* within the UNCHR Working Group. Clearly concrete and effective measures are required by the United Nations, in terms of upholding the *U.N. Charter* and its most basic precepts and ensuring the proper functioning of the current standard-setting process.

"Impediments" to the adoption of a strong, uplifting *Declaration*

FF Major "impediments" to the adoption by the United Nations of a strong and uplifting Declaration on the rights of Indigenous peoples may be described under two broad categories. The first relates to approaches or techniques by some States that serve to lower human rights standards pertaining to Indigenous peoples. The second describes those specific issues that are of critical importance to Indigenous peoples, but continue to be opposed by some States.

GG In regard to illegitimate approaches or techniques, there is a tendency of some States not to approve any Article in the draft *U.N. Declaration* that differs with their own domestic policies or laws. This approach runs counter to a key purpose of the international human rights standard-setting process, namely, to elaborate the human rights of Indigenous peoples in a manner consistent with international law and its progressive development.

HH Some States are also (mis)interpreting international human rights treaties so as to conform to their domestic laws. This is not a valid approach and would lead to the creation of extremely low standards in regard to the human rights of Indigenous peoples. Nor is this a good faith application of the treaties concerned.

II Furthermore, some States participating in the UNCHR Working Group are invoking their constitutions or other domestic laws, in order to avoid including human rights norms in a U.N. Declaration consistent with their international obligations. However, under international law, States cannot invoke their internal laws or procedures as a justification for not complying with international rules.

JJ The United Kingdom and the United States have repeatedly proposed converting some of the basic rights in the draft *U.N. Declaration* to "freedoms". In light of the pervasive human rights violations suffered by Indigenous peoples worldwide, we find it wholly unacceptable that some States seek to weaken our fundamental rights in the draft *Declaration*.

KK There are a number of issues that are considered to be essential by Indigenous peoples, but are viewed as "impediments" to making progress on the draft *U.N. Declaration*. These key matters include: i) affirmation of the collective rights of Indigenous peoples; ii) use of the term "peoples" or "Indigenous peoples"; iii) affirmation of the right of Indigenous peoples to self-determination under international law; and iv) affirmation of Indigenous rights to lands, territories and resources.

LL   A further issue of contention is the insistence by some States to include in the draft *U.N. Declaration* the principle of territorial integrity. Indigenous representatives in the UNCHR Working Group agree that this principle already exists in international law. However, most Indigenous representatives in the Working Group are opposed to singling out "territorial integrity" in the draft *Declaration*, since this would entail a number of prejudicial effects.

MM   However, an examination of these issues reveals that the basic State arguments have little or no validity under international law. Rather the effect of such arguments would be to create unjust and discriminatory double standards that would be detrimental to Indigenous peoples under international law. In some instances, the conclusions of U.N. treaty bodies that do not in effect support State positions are also being ignored.

NN   The basic positions being taken by such States run directly counter to their international legal obligations, explicit commitments in numerous international instruments, and the fundamental values and principles underlying international and domestic legal systems.

OO   One of the most outrageous State strategies to limit Indigenous peoples status and human rights under international law continues to emanate from the United States. The National Security Council, which is headed by the President of the United States, has in effect targeted the world's 300 million Indigenous people as some kind of security risk.

PP   Without exception, the U.S. seeks to categorically deny the world's Indigenous peoples full and equal application of the right of self-determination under the international human rights Covenants. No other peoples in the world are singled out, as a class of people, for such wholesale discriminatory treatment. It is disturbing that not a single State participating in the UNCHR Working Group has challenged the U.S. as violating the Purposes and Principles of the *U.N. Charter*.

Need to renew mandate and improve U.N. standard-setting process

QQ   After careful examination, this Joint Submission concludes that there are diverse and compelling reasons for the United Nations and its Member States not to terminate or otherwise abandon the human rights standard-setting process concerning Indigenous peoples.

RR   Rather than penalizing over 300 Indigenous people worldwide by terminating the human rights standard-setting process, the U.N. should be examining ways to ensure that all participating States fulfil their responsibilities and fully respect their obligations under international law.

SS   *We strongly recommend that the U.N. and Member States renew the mandate of the inter-sessional Working Group.* Failure within the U.N. to continue this process could serve to undo the important work accomplished to date. In particular, most or all of the efforts of Indigenous peoples throughout the years in regard to the draft *U.N. Declaration* could be wiped out or severely diminished.

TT   We also strongly recommend that the U.N. significantly improve the operations and procedures of the UNCHR Working Group, in a manner consistent with the unique status and essential role of Indigenous peoples.

UU   Our recommendation to ameliorate the standard-setting process is consistent with current objectives to reform and strengthen the operations of the United Nations. Moreover, the need for an enhanced participatory role for Indigenous peoples is increasingly being emphasized by the U.N., its Member States and regional organizations.

VV   In regard to improving the performance of the UNCHR Working Group, there are a number of specific changes or innovations that would be worthy of serious and timely consideration. These include:

1. Introduction of specific criteria within the Working Group, so as to ensure strict adherence to the Purposes and Principles of the *U.N. Charter* when proposing new or modified human rights norms;
2. In particular, proposals to undermine the human rights of Indigenous peoples or create discriminatory double standards should not be permitted or tolerated within the Working Group;

3. Alteration of existing rules so as to allow the appointment of two co-chairs (one of whom would be an Indigenous person);
4. Fair and balanced consideration of Indigenous and State positions in preparing the Chair's yearly report;
5. Consensus within the Working Group should be explicitly confirmed as not requiring unanimity, but consensus must include both participating States and Indigenous representatives;
6. Improved translations procedures so that representatives of Indigenous peoples and States could have timely Spanish, French, Russian, etc. versions of proposed revisions to the draft *Declaration*;
7. Increased encouragement of *joint submissions* with a view to reaching consensus on specific Articles in the draft *Declaration*;
8. Use of U.N. web site to make available Indigenous and State positions on the various Articles of the draft Declaration;
9. Increased financial assistance to ensure equitable and democratic participation of Indigenous peoples from all regions of the globe;
10. Live transmission of UNCHR Working Group sessions;
11. Use of expert panels or committees to address specific human rights issues relating to Indigenous peoples;
12. Ensuring an effective role for the Permanent Forum and its members in advancing the goals of human rights standard-setting; and
13. Encouraging greater participation by the specialized agencies in the Working Group.

WW. With regard to the overall U.N. human rights standard-setting process concerning Indigenous peoples, the following additional changes or innovations should also be considered:

1. Increased attention and priority should be accorded by the U.N. General Assembly and Commission on Human Rights to the adoption of a strong and uplifting *U.N. Declaration on the Rights of Indigenous Peoples*;
2. At all stages of the standard-setting process, no Declaration should be provisionally approved or adopted by the U.N. unless it has the strong support of Indigenous representatives participating in such process;
3. New strategies should be developed to increase State commitment to the objectives of the human rights standard-setting process relating to Indigenous peoples;
4. There should be greater coordination between such standard-setting processes at the United Nations and those at a regional level (such as the Organization of American States); and

5. Public education and awareness of the importance of developing international human rights standards relating to Indigenous peoples should be increased.

XX. It is also timely and pressing that the U.N. carefully examine the question of the status and role of Indigenous peoples within this crucial international organization. In this regard, it is essential to ensure democratic and effective involvement by Indigenous representatives at all levels of the U.N. consistent with our unique legal status and rights. This vital examination should only be carried out with the full and effective participation of Indigenous peoples' representatives on an equitable global basis.

YY. Clearly, we must all seek to strengthen the United Nations and ensure that the international human rights system is fully inclusive of and just to all peoples and States worldwide. All actors in this most essential system must strictly adhere to and consistently apply the Purposes and Principles of the *U.N. Charter*, as well as democracy, equality, human dignity, justice, non-discrimination and other foundational principles and values of international law.

ZZ. Currently, Indigenous peoples globally are caught in legal systems, where a significant number of Member States discriminate against Indigenous peoples both within the United Nations and within their own States. In particular, States should not be permitted to block progress from being achieved in the UNCHR standard-setting process.

AAA. Consistent with the *Charter of the United Nations* and the progressive development of international law, we strongly and respectfully urge the United Nations to make the necessary and urgent changes. ❑

References

1   The official report from the 9th session of the WGDD is available at: http://www.unhchr.ch/Huridocda/Huridoca.nsf/(Symbol)/ E.CN.4.2004.81.En?Opendocument
2   The declaration has now been endorsed by many other indigenous and non-indigenous organisations. The full list of organisations is available at: www.gcc.ca y www.iwgia.org
3   The full version of this important document is available at the Web page of the Grand Council of the Cree: www.gcc.ca and at www.iwgia.org .

BREAKTHROUGH AT THE AFRICAN COMMISSION ON HUMAN AND PEOPLES RIGHTS

In November 2003, the African Commission on Human and Peoples Rights (ACHPR) adopted the comprehensive "*Report of the African Commission's Working Group on Indigenous Populations/Communities*". This means that a major African human rights body has now recognized the existence of indigenous peoples in Africa and acknowledged that they suffer from a range of human rights violations that must be addressed.

Mandated by the "*Resolution on the Rights of Indigenous Populations/ Communities in Africa*" adopted in Benin in October 2000, the report:

- Analyses the human rights situation of indigenous peoples and communities in Africa;
- Analyses the African Charter on Human and Peoples' Rights and its jurisprudence on the concept of "peoples", and
- Examines the concept of indigenous peoples and communities in Africa.

Regarding violations of the human rights of indigenous peoples, the report looks at: violation of the right to land and productive resources; discrimination; violation of the right to justice; violation of cultural rights; denial of rights to constitutional and legislative recognition and protection, and violation of rights to health and education.

The report concludes that land dispossession is a major problem threatening the survival of indigenous peoples and making them increasingly destitute and poverty stricken. It furthermore concludes that indigenous peoples and communities are, to a large extent, discriminated against by mainstream populations, that their cultural rights are violated, that they are poorly represented in key national structures and poorly protected by national legislation and constitutions, and that most of the areas still occupied by indigenous peoples and communities are under-developed, with poor infrastructure. The report further states that these conditions constitute violations of a number of different articles of the African Charter:

> *Indigenous peoples and communities in Africa experience a range of human rights violations that ultimately boil down to a threat towards their right to existence and to the social, economic and cultural development of*

their own choice. Articles 20 and 22 of the African Charter on Human and Peoples' Rights emphasize that all peoples shall have the right to existence and to the social, economic and cultural development of their own choice and in conformity with their own identity. Such fundamental collective rights are to a large extent denied to indigenous peoples. Land dispossession of indigenous peoples, widespread discrimination, denial of cultural rights, exclusion from political representation, lack of constitutional and legal recognition and protection etc. clearly bear witness to this fact.

The report concludes that the human rights situation of indigenous peoples and communities in Africa is a serious cause for concern, and that effective protection and promotion of their human rights is urgently required.

The report also analyses the African Charter on Human and Peoples' Rights and its jurisprudence relating to "peoples" and concludes that both the individual and collective rights provided for in the African Charter should be applicable to the promotion and protection of the human rights of indigenous peoples. The relevant articles include articles 2, 3, 5, 17, 19, 20, 21, 22 and 60.

The report takes the view that "as the African Charter recognises collective rights, formulated as rights of 'peoples', these rights should be available to sections of populations within nation states, including indigenous people and communities" and it points out that "the Commission has indeed started to interpret the term 'peoples' in a manner that should allow indigenous people to also claim protection under Articles 19 – 24 of the African Charter."

The overall conclusion is that indigenous peoples and communities in Africa suffer from a number of particular human rights violations that are often of a collective nature; that the African Charter is an important instrument for the promotion and protection of the rights of indigenous peoples and communities; and that the preceding jurisprudence of the African Commission opens a path for indigenous peoples and communities to seek protection of their human rights.

The report takes the view that, although contested, the term *indigenous peoples* is valid in an African context as it offers the victims of particular human rights abuses an important way forward to improve their situation. The report recognizes the concerns over the use of the term *indigenous peoples* in the African context. However, it concludes that

The overall present day international framework relating to indigenous peoples should be accepted as the point of departure. The principle of self-identification as expressed in the ILO Convention 169 and by the Working Group on Indigenous Populations is a key

principle, which should also be guiding in the further deliberations of the African Commission.

A window of opportunity

At its 34th Ordinary Session in the Gambia in November 2003, the African Commission adopted a resolution that provides for the adoption, publication and distribution of the report to all member states and for the establishment of a Working Group of Experts for an initial two–year term. The mandate of this Working Group is to gather information on violations of the human rights and fundamental freedoms of indigenous populations/communities in Africa, to undertake country visits, formulate recommendations on measures to remedy human rights violations and to submit an activity report at every ordinary session of the African Commission (every 6 months). While the establishment of the Working Group as a mechanism to promote and protect the rights of indigenous peoples is very commendable and unique in the context of the African Commission, a great deal of challenging and difficult work also lies ahead to secure the necessary resources and to effectively organize and carry out the mandate.

Hopefully, the Working Group and all the indigenous representatives and African human rights activists who are involved in this process will be able to put this window of opportunity to good use. With the adoption of the report and the resolution, indigenous peoples in Africa now have an important platform from which to shed light on the situation of indigenous peoples in Africa and to lobby African governments to recognize indigenous peoples, their human rights concerns and their particular needs.

African indigenous representatives have, over the past 3 years, participated actively in the sessions of the African Commission and the NGO Forum prior to the sessions. While the whole issue was initially received with scepticism and rejection by some members of the African Commission, the attitude is now both open and positive. The active participation of indigenous representatives and the contact and dialogue with commissioners, government and NGO representatives has been very important in creating interest and understanding. It is now up to all stakeholders to make sure that this promising process continues and that the momentum is used to improve the conditions, human rights and fundamental freedoms of the indigenous peoples of Africa. ❑

THE PROCESS OF THE WORLD SUMMIT
ON THE INFORMATION SOCIETY

The first phase of the World Summit on the Information Society (WSIS) took place in Geneva from 10 – 13 December 2003. The Summit was held under the patronage of the United Nations Secretary-General with its initial instigator, the International Telecommunication Union, taking the lead role in its preparations. The second phase will take place in Tunis from 16 – 18 November 2005.

The aim of the Summit was to develop a common vision and understanding of the Information Society and to draft a Declaration of Principles and a Plan of Action. The agenda was defined by an intergovernmental preparatory committee but the summit was hailed a "summit plus" because United Nations specialized agencies, the private sector and civil society were included in the preparatory process and in the summit itself. Indigenous participation in the preparatory phase was minimal but in response to demands made by indigenous representatives during the second session of the Permanent Forum on Indigenous Issues, a meeting devoted to indigenous peoples, the Global Forum on Indigenous Peoples and the Information Society (GFIPIS) was held in Geneva as an official part of the WSIS.

The Global Forum

The GFIPIS was a four-day event (8 – 11 December 2003) organized by the United Nations Permanent Forum on Indigenous Issues (PFII). The bureau of the Permanent Forum also acted as the bureau of the Global Forum. The Forum on the Information Society examined the potential of and the obstacles to the full and effective participation of indigenous peoples in the information society. It also drafted a separate Declaration of Principles and Plan of Action.

The Forum was attended by 286 people including representatives of member states, United Nations bodies, the private sector and indigenous and non-governmental organizations.

The work of the Global Forum was conducted during four topical workshops, with opening and closing plenary meetings. At the opening plenary, an open-ended Drafting Committee was established. The Drafting Committee prepared the Declaration and Plan of Action, which were discussed and adopted at the final plenary on 11 December 2003. During the workshops best practices from around the world were presented and discussed. Themes of the workshops included the information society and - economic and social development, environment, culture, education, health, human rights and crosscutting issues.

The indigenous declaration and plan of action were finalized on the last day of the indigenous meeting, leaving only half a day before the governments' declaration was formally accepted at the WSIS. This meant that there was almost no time left to lobby states and other stakeholders with a paper representing a unified position. This highlights the main organizational problem of this Forum, namely that it was set up in only 10 weeks time after the PFII had met with donors in September 2003. Despite these organizational problems participants agreed that the GFIPIS was an important meeting, which allowed first contacts and the establishment of a consistent indigenous position on the information society. But it was also recognized that more active and concerted activities by indigenous peoples and organizations need to be implemented at all levels during the preparatory phase to Tunis and thereafter.

Indigenous peoples and ICT

Some of the most critical aspects that appeared during discussions held at the GFIPIS included but were not limited to: a) the lack of recognition of the rights of indigenous peoples (particularly self-determination, land rights, intellectual property rights and the aspect of free, prior informed consent when states or private sectors take actions of importance for indigenous peoples); b) the lack of access to basic infrastructure and information. It was emphasized that bridging the "digital divide" was important but that basic needs (food, water, etc.) need to be addressed first and foremost. In this respect it is worthwhile noting that most workshop presentations were by indigenous participants from economically more developed countries; c) the lack of control over the introduction of information and communication technologies (ICT). This included questions on how to develop and use culturally appropriate, as well as age and gender appropriate technology, how to produce local content with a positive impact for indigenous cultures and how to protect traditional knowledge and territories.

As well as these critical aspects, positive impacts of ICT were also mentioned. These included the use of ICT to strengthen indigenous peoples' cultural, economic, political and ecological positions and rights. Although there were many criticisms, ICT was therefore seen as possibly making a positive contribution to the struggles of indigenous peoples. The crucial point emphasized by all participants was that it needed to be a tool that should be used and controlled by indigenous peoples for their own advancement.

The GFIPIS Declaration

The declaration and the plan of action[1] are both explicitly based on a human rights approach and together they present a fairly consistent indigenous position on the following themes: Human Rights, Education and Culture, Social and Economic Development, Health, Indigenous Cultural Property Rights and Environment.

The World Summit

The World Summit was a huge meeting with political leaders from more than 175 countries and approximately 13,000 representatives of civil society, international organizations and the private sector attending the three-day event.

Ultimately, this Summit was more an arena for various actors to mark their presence and make fruitful contacts than a space to take significant decisions.

The most controversial issues during this Summit were the governance of internet, the importance and recognition of alternative free software and access to ICT in less developed countries. These countries and various NGOs particularly pressed for the creation of a special fund to bridge the digital divide between poor and rich countries. Governments found agreement for all contentious issues by circumventing actual decision-making. For example they decided to establish a working group that should give advice by the end of 2004 on whether a fund to bridge the digital divide should be created. Despite the inclusive approach of the Summit both the NGO Caucus and the GFIPIS felt that the input from civil society and from indigenous peoples was not taken up adequately in the Summit's declaration and plan of action. During the second phase of the WSIS development themes will be key talking points again. The second WSIS in Tunis will assess progress made since the first meeting and adopt any further plan of action deemed necessary.

Indigenous issues in the WSIS declaration

Indigenous delegations at the WSIS were not satisfied with the final declaration of Principles and Plan of Action. The main contentious issues of concern to indigenous peoples were, once again, whether to refer to indigenous peoples (with an **s**) and how broadly traditional rights of indigenous peoples' should be interpreted. In the final declaration the term indigenous peoples has actually been used. Indigenous participants acknowledged this as a positive - but insufficient - sign. Indeed indigenous peoples are named only once in the declaration.

Further disappointments were the lack of reference to the protection of traditional indigenous knowledge in the declaration and the lack of any reference to indigenous peoples in Section B 8 "Cultural diversity and identity, linguistic diversity and local content" despite the fact that culture and language are a critical building block of indigenous identities.

Indigenous participants were also not satisfied with the Plan of Action in which there are five references to indigenous peoples or indigenous knowledge in the action lines. Although these recommendations address important issues the language is weak.[2]

Conclusion

The GFIPIS was an important meeting because it gathered indigenous people and organizations for the first time at a broad international level to discuss issues related to the information and communications technology and the new information society. These issues are likely to stay on the scene and have a great impact on the lives of indigenous peoples in the future. It further produced two useful working papers, the GFIPIS Declaration and the Plan of Action, which will serve as references in upcoming discussions. But this meeting took place at a very late stage in the WSIS process and indigenous peoples have, so far, had very little impact on this process. Indigenous participants rightly expressed disappointment about how few indigenous organizations had participated in the WSIS preparatory phase. This is partly due to the lack of adequate information about the summit and its preparations and to belated indigenous initiatives. This is regrettable because the most intense activity and negotiations occur during the preparatory phase. The declaration of the Global Forum recognizes this problem and explicitly recommends that (a) a broad based effort should be made to inform indigenous peoples about the dates, location and all relevant matters for the second phase, (b) travel and per diem grants should be funded by states and the private sector and that (c) indigenous members of the Permanent Forum in coordination with regional indigenous organizations should be included in the planning of the 2005 Tunis WSIS. Hopefully this will allow adequate indigenous representation in preparatory meetings since this is of paramount importance for a more satisfactory inclusion of indigenous positions in future plans and declarations. ❑

References

1   All official GFIPIS papers including the GFIPIS declaration and plan of action and report can be found on the homepage of the PFII: http://www.un.org/esa/socdev/pfii/wsis_gfipis.htm
    Further information about the GFIPIS including workshop presentations can be found on the Canadian Aboriginal Portal: http://www.aboriginalcanada.gc.ca/cac/international/discussion.nsf/international_nav.html
2   More information about the WSIS, its declaration and plan of action can be found on their homepage: www.itu.int/wsis/

INDIGENOUS PEOPLES AND THE CBD IN 2003

T he work of the Convention on Biological Diversity (CBD) in 2003[1] focused around the following meetings:

- Two meetings of the Subsidiary Body on Scientific, Technical and Technological Advice (SBSTTA8 and SBSTTA9);
- An ad hoc intersessional meeting on the Multi-Year Programme of Work (MYPOW);
- The third meeting of the Working Group on Article 8(j) and related provisions; and
- The second meeting of the Working Group on Access to Genetic Resources and Benefit Sharing.

The range of themes addressed by these various 2003 meetings, in which indigenous delegates participated, included: mountain biodiversity; protected areas; technology transfer; marine and coastal biodiversity; genetic use restriction technologies (GURTS); mechanisms for the participation of indigenous peoples and local communities in the work of the Convention; communications mechanisms for indigenous peoples under Article 8(j) and related provisions; guidelines on developments on sacred sites, lands and waters; a global "composite report" on status and trends concerning traditional knowledge; the development of *sui generis* (specially generated / of their own kind) systems for the protection of traditional knowledge; capacity-building for access to genetic resources and benefit sharing; mechanisms to ensure compliance with prior informed consent under the Bonn Guidelines on access to genetic resources and benefit-sharing; and, the opening stages of negotiation of an international regime on access to genetic resources and benefit sharing.

As this lengthy list reveals, tracking and influencing the range of issues relevant to the rights of indigenous peoples is an increasing challenge.

Meetings in SBSTTA

The Subsidiary Body on Scientific, Technical and Technological Advice (SBSTTA) held two meetings in 2003, both in Montreal - SBSTTA8, in March, and SBSTTA9, in November.

SBSTTA is the main scientific advisory body under the Convention and a key focus of its work is the development and revision of programmes of work on thematic issues. However, the ever-increasing number of work programmes is putting a growing strain on SBSTTA. In 2003, SBSTTA addressed issues including: the development of new programmes of work on mountain biodiversity and protected areas; revision of the programmes of work on inland waters, marine and biological diversity, dry and sub-humid lands; draft guidelines of biological diversity and tourism; technology transfer; the ecosystem approach; sustainable use; climate change, and monitoring and indicators. A total of two weeks was allocated for these tasks.

A small number of indigenous delegates participated in each SBSTTA meetings and this proved highly significant in advancing the recognition of indigenous peoples' rights across the spectrum of themes considered.

Protected areas

Another major theme under the Convention in 2003 was the development of a new programme of work on protected areas. This is an issue of vital concern to indigenous peoples and is reflected in high levels of indigenous peoples participation within the 5th World Congress on Parks in 2003. (See article on World Congress on Parks, this volume.)

The Working Group on Article 8(j)

The third meeting of the Working Group was held in Montreal between the 8th and the 12th of December 2003. This Working Group remains a key focus for many indigenous delegates seeking to participate in the work of the Convention on Biological Diversity.

The Working Group on Article 8(j) and related provisions has come to be regarded as holding a special place within the Convention for many reasons, but perhaps mainly because of the emphasis that the COP has placed on securing the full and effective participation of indigenous peoples in the work of the Convention. In this respect it is important to note that the Convention is unusual among United Nations Environment and Development agreements in its growing openness to indigenous peoples' participation. While there are many difficult battles to be fought, the Convention deserves to be congratulated for this openness to the participation of indigenous peoples.

The issues addressed during the meeting included the first phase of a global composite report on status and trends in the knowledge, innovations and practices of indigenous and local communities; the development of "guidelines for the conduct of cultural, environmental and social impact assessments regarding developments proposed to take place on, or which are likely to impact on, sacred sites and on lands and waters traditionally occupied or used by indigenous and local communities".

The Working Group also considered the key issues of participatory mechanisms for indigenous and local communities under the Convention and *sui generis* ("of their own kind" or specially generated) systems for the protection of traditional knowledge, innovations and practices. Other themes included consideration of the recommendations from the United Nations Permanent Forum on Indigenous Issues, technology transfer and cooperation, and Genetic Use Restriction Technologies.

Genetic resources and benefit sharing

The "fair and equitable sharing of the benefits arising from the utilisation of genetic resources" is the third objective of the Convention. This is perhaps the most contentious issue addressed under the Convention and is linked to the regulation of access to genetic resources and debates surrounding intellectual property rights, particularly the 1995 agreement on Trade Related Aspect of Intellectual Property Rights (TRIPS) under the World Trade Organisation.

These issues are of critical concern to indigenous peoples, because indigenous peoples possess detailed knowledge of their local environments and the uses and properties of plant, animal and other species, and indigenous peoples' lands and territories are located in areas with the highest biodiversity in the world or in other environments of outstanding importance. The practice of "bioprospecting" has become intimately linked with the phenomenon of "biopiracy" through which third Parties, who may be individuals, companies, or research organisations, appropriate indigenous peoples' knowledge and genetic resources and secure temporary monopolies over such knowledge and materials through the patent system. This constitutes a violation of the rights of indigenous peoples on multiple levels, notably: the right of indigenous peoples to permanent sovereignty over their natural resources; the provisions of the Universal Declaration on Human Rights; the International Covenant on Economic, Social and Cultural Rights, and ILO Convention No.169, among other existing and emerging international agreements relating to the rights of indigenous peoples.

Concerns surrounding the rights of indigenous peoples are also related to the recognition of state sovereignty over genetic resources under the Convention and the right of Parties to prior informed consent over such resources. This produces a tension between the permanent sovereignty of indigenous peoples over their natural resources and the rights of States.

Here Parties have sought to separate out the treatment of traditional knowledge from genetic resources and have given emphasis to regulating access and benefit-sharing over genetic resources. As a consequence, the rights of indigenous peoples over their knowledge are being separated from their rights over the natural resources within their lands and territories. Indigenous delegates are struggling hard to bring the two closer together on the grounds that the relationship between knowledge and resources is an *inalienable* one.

A third problem concerns the relationship between the Parties to the Convention. Developed countries are seeking to promote the emergence of a vibrant biotechnology sector and to maintain access to useful genetic materials to service their agribusiness and pharmaceuticals sectors. However, the majority of the world's biodiversity, and thus genetic materials, are located in developing countries. Developing countries have secured recognition of state sovereignty over biological and genetic materials under the Convention. Their aim is to regulate access and secure a share of any benefits, which arise from the exploitation of biological and genetic materials within their jurisdictions.[2]

The Working Group on Access to Genetic Resources and Benefit-Sharing

The third meeting of the Working Group on Access to Genetic Resources and Benefit-sharing 1 - 5 December 2003, was concerned with three principal issues: a) the development of an international regime; b) capacity building; c) mechanisms to ensure compliance with prior informed consent under the Bonn Guidelines. There was a strong presence of the International Indigenous Forum in discussions on these issues.

The main focus of the debate on the international regime was on whether the regime should be binding or non-binding and on the proposed elements of a regime. Here Parties focused on listing existing agreements. In contrast the Indigenous Forum focused on arguing for the need for the inclusion of the major international human rights instruments, including ILO Convention No.169, the development of models of prior informed consent, a code of ethics and a code of conduct, and the recognition of the role of customary law in connection with indigenous peoples' knowledge and resources.

The negotiation of an international regime on access to genetic resources and benefit-sharing presents important challenges and potential opportunities for indigenous peoples. This will require considerable reflection in a complex, and at times perilous, area. The significance of the proposed regime is that indigenous peoples will need to carefully consider the implications of a regime and establish their positions.

The International Indigenous Forum has adopted the position of seeking to secure the maximum protection of the rights of indigenous peoples in any proposal that emerges for an international regime. Securing the inclusion of human rights instruments, models of prior informed consent, codes of ethics and conduct, will be key areas of struggle for COP7 to be held in February 2004. The Forum has also placed a strong emphasis on capacity building among both indigenous peoples and Parties in relation to issues regarding access to genetic resources and benefit and the rights of indigenous peoples.

The third major area of debate within the Working Group focused on measures to ensure compliance with prior informed consent under the Bonn Guidelines. Two points stand out here. The first of these is that developed countries have argued that the negotiation of an international regime is premature until the Bonn Guidelines have been given time to work. However, at the same time the meeting revealed that developed countries have so far done relatively little to implement the guidelines. In order to control demand for a legally binding instrument, developed countries are now coming under increasing pressure to implement the guidelines. The second point is that while indigenous delegates have repeatedly stated that the Bonn Guidelines are unacceptably weak with regard to the rights of indigenous peoples, the recognition of prior informed consent of "indigenous and local communities" in two parts of the guidelines is proving to be very important.

During intense negotiations on prior informed consent, the Forum succeeded in inserting reference to the prior informed consent of indigenous and local communities in a carefully negotiated phrase that is unlikely to be renegotiated and which may feature prominently in future debates. The Forum also succeeded in inserting a paragraph for the development of national mechanisms for prior informed consent of indigenous and local communities with respect to both knowledge and genetic resources. In particular, indigenous delegates are increasingly combating efforts to restrict indigenous peoples' prior informed consent by including the phrase "consistent with international obligations" or "international law" in an effort to highlight human rights obligations in this area.

In concluding this discussion of access and benefit sharing, it is important to emphasise that this is an area about which indigenous peoples delegates have consistently expressed deep disquiet. This is perhaps the most complex and delicate area of the Convention: the road ahead will be difficult and the struggle will be bitter. It is important that indigenous peoples begin to prepare for this major emerging arena of struggle.

Concluding remarks

The year 2003 witnessed intense activity under the Convention on Biological Diversity with which Parties, indigenous peoples delegates and all participants have struggled to keep up. As the participants within the International Indigenous Forum have recognised, the scale of work under the Convention is such that no individual can seek to follow and participate in its work. This has revealed a need for increased specialisation in particular thematic areas by delegates, the dedication to continue following chosen themes and a willingness to trust fellow delegates from around the world to advance recognition and respect for the rights of indigenous peoples. It is a tribute to the dedication of all participants within the International Indigenous Forum that so much has been achieved in advancing recognition of the rights of indigenous peoples in so many different areas of the Convention in the year 2003. ❏

Notes

1   This report is a reduced version of the report prepared by Dr. Paul Oldham of the ESRC Centre for Economic and Social Aspects of Genomics (CESAGen) at Lancaster University in the UK. The author would like to acknowledge the valuable contribution of reports by members and support organisations working with the International Indigenous Forum on Biodiversity in preparing this review. The full report is available at www.iwgia.org.

2   In an effort to address these issues the Parties agreed during COP6 (2002), a set of voluntary guidelines on access to genetic resources and benefit sharing which are now known as the "Bonn Guidelines". The

International Indigenous Forum on Biodiversity regarded the guidelines as weak with respect to recognition of the rights of indigenous peoples. During the World Summit on Sustainable Development (WSSD), developing countries argued that the Bonn Guidelines were insufficient to address the problem and that a legally-binding international instrument should be negotiated under the Convention. This was transformed in the course of the WSSD into a proposal for an international regime on benefit sharing. This recommendation was then endorsed by the United Nations General Assembly in December 2002.

WORLD PARKS CONGRESS, DURBAN

Significant progress was made on the legal recognition of indigenous peoples' rights at the World Parks Congress in Durban, South Africa, which ended on 17 September 2003. The World Parks Congress, held every 10 years and comprising governments, conservation agencies and civil society organisations, is highly influential on conservation policy and practice. The theme of the recent Durban Congress was "Benefits Beyond Boundaries" and included the participation of a large number of indigenous representatives from all over the world.

The Accord and Recommendations agreed at Durban set important new standards for the rights of indigenous peoples living in and around protected areas. The Durban Action Plan contains a full section entitled "The Rights of Indigenous Peoples, Mobile Peoples and Local Communities Recognised and Guaranteed in Relation to Natural Resources and Biodiversity Conservation". It recommends specific targets and actions for governments and protected areas.[1] The Durban Recommendations and Action Plan call on countries to undertake reviews of existing conservation laws and policies that impact on indigenous peoples, and to adopt laws and policies giving indigenous peoples and local communities control over their sacred places. In many countries, conservation policy review will necessarily entail revision of old conservation laws that specifically preclude any subsistence activities within parks – even if parks overlap hunting and gathering peoples' traditional lands. Many believe that these laws are incompatible with international norms of indigenous peoples rights.[2]

The Durban Accord, Recommendations and Action Plan are not binding on States or conservation organisations, but will feed into consultations over the Convention on Biological Diversity (CBD), which is binding on signatory governments. During the COP7 of the CBD to be held in Kuala Lumpur, Malaysia in February 2004, representatives of indigenous peoples organisations and communities will contribute to the debates on the implementation of various CBD provisions, including Articles 8j and 10c. ❑

Notes

1   For the full texts see: www.iucn.org/themes/wcpa/wpc2003.
2   **MacKay, Fergus.** 2002. Addressing Past Wrongs. Indigenous Peoples and Protected Areas: the right to restitution of lands and resources. Occasional Paper, Forest Peoples Programme, Moreton-in-Marsh.

IWGIA welcomes new members. If you wish to apply for membership and become part of our network of concerned individuals, please consult our homepage at www.iwgia.org for details, including the benefits of being a member, and to download a membership form.

Membership fees for 2004 are:
US$ 60.00 / EUR 50.00 /DKK 375.00 for Europe, North America, Australia, New Zealand and Japan.
US$ 25.00 /EUR 20.00 /DKK 150,00 for the rest of the world.
US$ 35.00 /EUR 30.00 /DKK 225,00 for students and senior citizens.

Our membership is extremely important to us in terms of providing both political and economic support.

SUBSCRIPTION RATES 2004

INDIGENOUS AFFAIRS & THE INDIGENOUS WORLD

Individuals: US$ 60.00 / EUR 50.00 / DKK 375.00
Institutions: US$ 90.00 / EUR 80.00 / DKK 600.00

INDIGENOUS AFFAIRS, THE INDIGENOUS WORLD & BOOKS

Individuals: US$ 120.00 / EUR 100.00 / DKK 750.00
Institutions: US$ 160.00 / EUR 140.00 / DKK 1,050.00

ASUNTOS INDÍGENAS & EL MUNDO INDÍGENA

Individuals: US$ 60.00 / EUR 50.00 / DKK 375.00
Institutions: US$ 90.00 / EUR 80.00 / DKK 600.00

ASUNTOS INDÍGENAS, EL MUNDO INDÍGENA & LIBROS

Individuals: US$ 90.00 / EUR 80.00 / DKK 600.00
Institutions: US$ 140.00 / EUR 120.00 / DKK 900.00

IWGIA's publications are published on a non-profit basis. Your subscription is a direct contribution to the continuing production of IWGIA's documentation and analysis of the situation of indigenous peoples worldwide.

To subscribe – contact IWGIA by:
E-mail: iwgia@iwgia.org
Telephone: + 45 35 27 05 00
Web site: www.iwgia.org